P9-DXF-935

PRAISE FOR
THE LAW OF THE LAND

"Akhil Reed Amar writes in clear and entertaining English, with a journalist's eye for drama and detail and a patriot's eye for the sweep of the American experience. Smart general readers interested in constitutional law will be pleased and instructed."

> — **Richard Brookhiser, author of** *Founders' Son: A Life of Abraham Lincoln*

"Akhil Reed Amar has done it again! In his new book, *The Law of the Land*, Amar has woven a page-turning constitutional tapestry of our federal and state relationships that sings like a Woody Guthrie tune. In civics, politics, and biography, the genius of our geography—both historic and contemporary—comes alive as Amar guides us through the uniquely American landscape of law and its greatest constitutional prophets. Firmly grounded in the logic of place, this majestic narrative will enlighten and inspire lay and legal readers alike: it's a Magical Mystery Tour of a difficult subject made accessible by a masterful Sherpa."

> — **Laurence H. Tribe, Carl M. Loeb University Professor at Harvard University and Professor of Constitutional Law, Harvard Law School**

THE LAW OF THE LAND

THE LAW
OF THE LAND

A Grand Tour *of* Our
Constitutional Republic

AKHIL REED AMAR

BASIC BOOKS
A Member of the Perseus Books Group
New York

Published by Basic Books
A Member of the Perseus Books Group

Books published by Basic Books are available at special discounts for bulk
purchases in the United States by corporations, institutions, and other
organizations. For more information, please contact the Special Markets
Department at the Perseus Books Group, 2300 Chestnut Street, Suite 200,
Philadelphia, PA 19103, or call (800) 810-4145, ext. 5000, or e-mail
special.markets@perseusbooks.com.

Designed by Cynthia Young

Library of Congress Cataloging-in-Publication Data
Amar, Akhil Reed, author.
   The law of the land : a grand tour of our constitutional republic / Akhil Reed Amar.
      pages cm
   Includes bibliographical references and index.
   ISBN 978-0-465-06590-5 (hardback)—ISBN 978-0-465-06589-9 (ebook)
      1. Constitutional law—United States—States.   2. Constitutions—United
States—States.   3. Law—United States—States.   4. United States. Constitution.
2nd Amendment.   5. United States. Constitution. 4th Amendment.
   6. Constitutional law—United States.   I. Title.
KF4530.A43 2015
342.73—dc23

                                                              2014041017

10 9 8 7 6 5 4 3 2 1

For my parents, siblings, wife, and children,
with precious memories of our family road trips.

We got there.

CONTENTS

Preface   *xi*

PART I: CONSTITUTIONAL INTERPRETERS

1. ILLINOIS: Abraham Lincoln and the American Union   3

2. ALABAMA: Hugo Black and the Hall of Fame   29

3. NEW YORK: Robert Jackson and the Judicialization of the Judiciary 56

4. CALIFORNIA: Anthony Kennedy and the Ideal of Equality   78

PART II: CONSTITUTIONAL CASES

5. KANSAS: Living in the Shadow of *Brown v. Board*   109

6. IOWA: Rereading *Tinker v. Des Moines*   123

7. FLORIDA: Getting to the Bottom of *Bush v. Gore*   140

PART III: CONSTITUTIONAL PROVISIONS AND PRINCIPLES

8. OHIO: A Buckeye-State View of Presidents Without Mandates   165

9. TEXAS: A Lone-Star View of Presidential Selection and Succession   180

10. WYOMING: A Rocky-Mountain View of the Second Amendment 204

11. MASSACHUSETTS: A Bay-State View of the Fourth Amendment   229

12. NEW JERSEY: Lord Camden Meets Federalism   250

CONCLUSION   267

Acknowledgments   281
Appendix: The Constitution of the United States   285
Notes   307
Index   345

PREFACE

Fifty distinct states, spanning a vast continent, find shelter under a common federal Constitution. Some of these states would, as independent nations, rank high among the world's great powers. California now rivals France in economic output, though the French would say that they still hold the lead in wine.

This is a book about America's Constitution that aims to take states and regions seriously. Each chapter tells a national story about the American constitutional system, but does so through the window of an individual state, with particular attention to some person, case, idea, or event closely associated with that specific state or the broader region of which that state is a part.

My stories feature a dozen states and encompass every major region of the country—the Northeast (both New England and the Mid-Atlantic), the South (both deep and peripheral), the mid-American heartland (both the Old Northwest and the trans-Mississippi plains), and the West (both the Rocky Mountains and the Pacific Rim). Over the course of twelve chapters, I explore legal, political, and historical material from every era of our nation's history; discuss all three branches of the federal government and their interconnections with states and state law; and touch on many of our Constitution's largest themes, with particular emphasis on the presidency, the Supreme Court, and the Bill of Rights.

Constitutional interpreters, constitutional cases, constitutional provisions and principles—these are basic elements of America's constitutional saga, and all are showcased in the panoramic tour that follows. Specifically, Part I of this book profiles four of the most influential constitutional decision-makers in American history—Illinois's Abraham Lincoln, the mightiest constitutional figure of the past two hundred years; Alabama's Hugo Black, the dominant constitutional jurist of the twentieth century; New York's Robert Jackson, an especially graceful midcentury justice with many prominent admirers and disciples; and California's Anthony Kennedy, the powerful swing justice on the current Court. Part II probes a trio of special constitutional law cases: *Brown v. Board of Education* (1954), the most acclaimed judicial ruling since the Civil War; *Tinker v. Des Moines* (1969), an admittedly less famous opinion that holds a place in my heart for reasons I explain; and *Bush v. Gore* (2000), the most curious judicial decision of our still-young century. Part III ponders various structural principles involving presidential selection and succession and then parses a couple of constitutional provisions that usually get people's juices flowing—the Second and Fourth Amendments.

At the end of this transcontinental tour, I pull my individual stories together in a Conclusion that explains how the various chapters fit into a larger and distinctly American mosaic of federalism—a mosaic reflecting subtle constitutional variation from state to state and across broader geographic regions. Readers who just can't wait to see how the stories in individual chapters form parts of a more encompassing framework of federalism and regionalism are welcome to sneak a peek at this Conclusion at any time in their journey through this book. Especially impatient readers may even wish to scan or read the Conclusion before starting Chapter 1.

BOTH LITERALLY AND LEGALLY, this book covers a lot of ground. In my opening chapter, on Lincoln, I discuss the ground itself and describe how the distinct geographic landmass called America shaped the very idea of an American Constitution. The law of the land, indeed.

As you read this book in the quiet comfort of your home, or on a bus or at the beach, I hope you will occasionally imagine yourself actually setting foot and spending time in each of the featured locations, soaking up the local ambience and reflecting on how our common Constitution looks slightly different from state to state and across the various regions of this great land.

Akhil Reed Amar
New Haven, CT
Spring 2015

PART I

Constitutional Interpreters

ILLINOIS:

ABRAHAM LINCOLN AND

THE AMERICAN UNION

I llinois, the self-described "Land of Lincoln," claims a special kinship with America's sixteenth president, who in turn professed profound gratitude to his adopted home state. This is what President-elect Lincoln said about the state's capital city, Springfield, when he bade it farewell as he boarded an eastbound train in February 1861: "No one, not in my situation, can appreciate my feeling of sadness at this parting. To this place, and the kindness of these people, I owe every thing. Here I have lived a quarter of a century, and have passed from a young to an old man. Here my children have been born, and one is buried. I now leave, not knowing when, or whether ever, I may return, with a task before me greater than that which rested upon [General] Washington."[1]

Return he did to central Illinois, but not in life. To the heartland of his beloved Union the funeral train brought his corpse in 1865. In central Illinois the remains of Abraham Lincoln reached their final resting place.

In the fateful years between these two poignant train trips, Lincoln made a series of momentous constitutional decisions that establish him as the most significant constitutional interpreter and decision-maker of the past two centuries. No one else in American history, with the exception of George Washington, comes close: today's Americans live in the constitutional house that Lincoln and his allies remade, a house whose original half-slave / half-free foundation crumbled in the aftermath of Lincoln's election as America's first openly antislavery president.

Though Abraham Lincoln was not in Illinois when he made his epic constitutional decisions as president, Illinois was in him: throughout the course of his presidency, his views on the nature and meaning of the American union—its democratic essence, its constitutional structure, its geographic attributes, its racial characteristics—were shaped by the mid-western land from whence he sprang, and to which, in death, he returned.

A Democratic Union

As Lincoln left Springfield in early 1861, he described the task that lay before him as "greater than that which rested upon Washington." That task, of course, was nothing less than the preservation of the Union. After Lincoln won election in November 1860, and before he took office, seven state governments purported to declare their independence from the Union and to form the Confederate States of America. The lame-duck president, James Buchanan, proclaimed state secession unconstitutional, but did little to stop or reverse it. In his December 3, 1860, annual message to Congress, he declared himself constitutionally powerless to act unilaterally and also argued that Congress lacked the lawful power "to make war against a State" or to "preserve [the Union] by force." As emboldened secessionists stepped up their activities in the final days of the Buchanan administration, all eyes turned to Lincoln. Would he allow the Union to dissolve? What was his understanding of the Union, and of his role under it?

Lincoln's strong and clear answer came in his March 4, 1861, Inaugural Address: the unilateral attempt of various states to leave the Union was utterly unconstitutional, and as president he was duty-bound to resist this attempt and to maintain the Union.[2]

In his words:

> [N]o State, upon its own mere motion, can lawfully get out of the Union, [and] resolves and ordinances to that effect are legally void. . . . [I]n view of the Constitution and the laws, the Union is unbroken; and, to the extent of my ability, I shall take care, as the Constitution itself expressly enjoins upon me, that the laws of the Union be faithfully executed in all the States. Doing this I deem to be only a simple duty on my part; and I shall perform it, so far as practicable, unless my rightful masters, the American people, shall withhold the requisite means, or, in some authoritative manner, direct the contrary.

In short: "[T]he Union . . . *will* constitutionally defend and maintain itself." (The emphasis is Lincoln's.)

Elaborating on this vision of his own bounden duty, Lincoln added that "[t]he Chief Magistrate derives all his authority from the people, and they have conferred none upon him to fix the terms for the separation of the States. The people themselves can do this also if they choose; but the executive, as such, has nothing to do with it. His duty is to administer the present government, as it came to his hands, and to transmit it, unimpaired by him, to his successor."

IN SUPPORT OF HIS emphatic conclusion that no state may leave the Union unilaterally—"upon its own mere motion"—Lincoln mustered a host of arguments. First, he asserted that the Union must be perpetual as a matter of logic and first principles:

> I hold, that in contemplation of universal law, and of the Constitution, the Union of these States is perpetual. Perpetuity is implied, if not expressed, in the fundamental law of all national governments. It is safe to assert that no government proper, ever had a provision in its organic law for its own termination. Continue to execute all the express provisions of our national Constitution, and the Union will endure forever—it being impossible to destroy it, except by some action not provided for in the instrument itself.

This claim, if read broadly and in isolation, proves too much. Must the Union be perpetual even if, say, every single American voter in 1861 preferred a peaceful and fair dissolution of the Union into two or more smaller governments? More realistically, what if every state so agreed; or a regular constitutional amendment so provided; or a large, deliberate, and geographically dispersed national majority so desired? To insist that the Union must be perpetual regardless of what the states and the people wanted would threaten basic principles of federalism and democracy, principles that Lincoln himself eloquently affirmed in his Inaugural Address and on many other occasions. Indeed, in the very passages just quoted we have heard Lincoln say that: (1) although the president has been given no authority to let a state leave the Union unilaterally, "the people themselves can do this . . . if they choose"; and (2) although he as president would resist secession, his "rightful masters, the American people," might in some "authoritative manner" oblige him to change his course.

Fortunately, Lincoln made several other arguments that revealed his truest and best ideas about the Union. For starters, he put forth a clever response to the "compact theory" of the Union. According to most secessionists, the Union was a mere "compact" of preexisting and "sovereign" states. In 1776, each of the thirteen states had voluntarily chosen to enter the Union. Likewise, under Article VII of the Constitution no state was obliged to ratify the Constitution merely because its sister states had done so: "The Ratification of the Conventions of nine States, shall be sufficient for the Establishment of this Constitution *between the States so ratifying the same.*" Thus, the Constitution went into effect only among the states that chose to join. Why, then, wasn't each state similarly free at any time and for any reason to unilaterally withdraw from the Union? As one notable figure expressed the idea in 1860: "[A]s each [state] became [party] to the Union by the vote of its own people assembled in convention, so any one of them may retire from the Union in a similar manner by the vote of such a convention."[3]

Lincoln's Inaugural Address countered as follows: "[I]f the United States be not a government proper, but an association of States in the nature of a contract merely, can it, as a contract, be peaceably unmade, by less than all the parties who made it? One party to a contract may violate it—break it, so to speak; but does it not require all to lawfully rescind it?"

On this view, lawful secession would seem permissible only if every single state so agreed. Similarly, Article V, which explains how the Constitution itself may be amended by certain kinds of joint state-federal enactments, in effect provides that a state may secure an extra Senate seat only if every state agrees to this modification of the Philadelphia plan. This "unanimous state consent" theory of disunion neatly hoisted the compact theorists on their own petard.[4]

But did Lincoln really mean to affirm that a strong national majority might never peacefully dissolve the Union in some other way? Even if the state-compact theory of Union logically led to the conclusion that no state could leave without the consent of each and every other state, Lincoln's audience knew, and we should remember today, that Lincoln in fact *rejected* the compact theory as the proper account of the origins and nature of the federal Union. And the idea of unanimity among states gave each state, even the tiniest, an extreme minority veto—a result at odds with Lincoln's repeated insistence in his Inaugural Address on the bedrock principle of majority rule.[5]

At one point in this address, he pointed out that "if a minority" in a case of good-faith disagreement among members of a polity "will secede rather than acquiesce, they make a precedent which, in turn, will divide and ruin them; for a minority of their own will secede whenever a majority refuses to be controlled by such a minority." As Lincoln saw it,

> the central idea of secession is the essence of anarchy. A majority, held in restraint by constitutional checks, and limitations, and always changing easily, with deliberate changes of popular opinions and sentiments, is the only true sovereign of a free people. Whoever rejects it, does, of necessity, fly to anarchy or to despotism. Unanimity is impossible; the rule of the minority, as a permanent arrangement, is wholly inadmissible; so that, rejecting the majority principle, anarchy, or despotism in some form, is all that is left.

Time after time in his later public pronouncements, Lincoln would stress the ideas of majority rule and democracy. The issue of unilateral secession, Lincoln declared in his Special Session Address to Congress on July 4, 1861,

> presents to the whole family of man, the question, whether a constitutional republic, or democracy—a government of the people, by the same people—can, or cannot, maintain its territorial integrity, against its own domestic foes. It presents the question, whether discontented individuals, too few in numbers to control administration, according to organic law, in any case, can always . . . break up their Government, and thus practically put an end to free government upon the earth. . . . [Secessionists] are subtle, and profound, on the rights of minorities. They are not partial to that power which made the Constitution, and speaks from the preamble, calling itself "We, the People."

In response to these opponents of democracy and majority rule, Lincoln declared that

> it is now for [our people] to demonstrate to the world, that those who can fairly carry an election, can also suppress a rebellion—that ballots are the rightful, and peaceful, successors of bullets; and that when ballots have fairly, and constitutionally, decided, there can be no successful appeal, back to bullets; that there can be no successful appeal, except to ballots themselves, at succeeding elections. Such will be a great lesson of peace; teaching men that what they cannot take by an election, neither can they take it by a war.[6]

If a secessionist minority could simply disregard elections and unilaterally quit whenever it felt disgruntled, then democratic self-government would be at an end. The secessionists' claim to an extreme minority veto was nothing less than an assault on the idea of democracy itself—"government of the people, by the people, for the people."[7]

GIVEN THAT LINCOLN's rejection of unilateral secession ultimately rested on principles of popular self-government and national majority rule, how, exactly, might a *national* popular majority that *favored* secession effect its will? Lincoln did not address the question at length, but several possibilities are worth pondering. First, a formal constitutional amendment might have authorized secession and specified its terms—preserving northern rights of navigation down the Mississippi River, providing for an equitable apportionment of the preexisting national debt, specifying respective territorial rights in the American West, and so on.

Of course, to succeed in clearing the high numerical hurdles erected by Article V, such an amendment would as a practical matter have required support from the North as well as the South, thereby reflecting the deliberate judgment of the whole nation, and not merely the will or whim of a churlish part. This idea was central to Lincoln's First Inaugural, which urged secessionists to submit to "the judgment of this great tribunal, the American people" encompassing both "the North" and "the South."

A formal constitutional amendment would also harmonize with Lincoln's specific language to the effect that "the people themselves" could choose to "fix the terms for the separation of the States" but that "the executive, as such, has nothing to do with" any of this. Federal constitutional amendments are often described as actions of "the people themselves" as opposed to actions of ordinary government (even though such amendments typically are adopted by supermajorities of ordinary state and federal legislatures); and under the rules of Article V, the president plays no formal role in the amendment process. Rather, amendments are to be proposed by a special constitutional convention or by two-thirds of each house of Congress, and are then to be ratified by three-quarters of the states. Nowhere in this process is there any mention of the president.[8]

In light of Lincoln's overall political theory of popular self-government, he might also have envisioned a nonbinding national referendum. In the winter of 1861, Kentucky senator John J. Crittenden had proposed a set of constitutional amendments to preserve the Union and had called for a national referendum on his compromise package.[9]

Granted, Article V does not explicitly provide for any such national referendum. But even if such a vote were not legally binding, the results of such a national referendum in a regime based on the people's ultimate sovereignty would likely carry great moral weight with those government actors—Congress and state legislatures—ordinarily involved in the amendment process. Analogously, prior to the adoption of the Seventeenth Amendment, the electorate had no formal role to play in directly electing senators under the Constitution as written; but many states developed informal systems in which voters would express their views in "beauty contest" votes that state legislatures felt politically, even if not legally, obliged to honor. (The Lincoln-Douglas Senate race of 1858—in which the parties nominated US Senate candidates before the statewide election of state legislators, and the Senate candidates then brought their campaigns directly to the electorate via a series of personal debates—has been described as the first important step toward the Seventeenth Amendment.)[10]

Conceivably, both Article V amendments and national referenda might have aimed to pre-authorize a wholly lawful and peaceful secession. Other possibilities come into view when we recall that, by the time of Lincoln's Inauguration, powerful forces in one section of the country had already unilaterally attempted secession, gained control of the machinery of state government, and presented their fait accompli to the nation.

The proper constitutional response of the federal government should probably depend on how the Confederates managed to come to power. If they won control by toppling duly elected state governments merely by force of arms, the federal government would seem to be obliged to resist and if possible undo this antidemocratic coup d'état; that is one of the central meanings of the Article IV, section 4, clause under which the United States promises to guarantee to each state a "Republican Form of Government."

This was Lincoln's view. He explicitly invoked the Article IV guarantee clause in support of his unionism, and he condemned southern secession not merely as undemocratic at the *national* level (because it defied the sentiments of northern voters) but also as undemocratic at the *state* level (because it had been triggered by improper, unfair, and coercive votes, at best). As he explained to Congress on July 4, 1861, "it may well be questioned whether there is, to-day, a majority of legally qualified voters of any State, except, perhaps South Carolina, in favor of disunion. There is much reason to believe that the Union men are the majority of many, if not in every other one, of the so-called seceded States. The contrary has not been demonstrated in any one of them."[11]

But even in the case of a wildly undemocratic coup, practical imperatives might at some point require the national government, acting on behalf of the national people, to acquiesce; and the Constitution includes mechanisms for implementing this acquiescence. If foreign governments—Britain, France, Mexico—were to recognize the Confederacy as both the de facto and de jure government of the southern states, then couldn't the federal government properly make treaties with these foreign governments conceding that these states were no longer part of the Union? If the United States could, by treaty, acquire Louisiana from France, or cede disputed parts of Maine to British Canada, couldn't the United States likewise make treaties with France and Britain recognizing that it had lost control over, say, South Carolina? If America could win part of Texas by force of arms—and cement this victory with a treaty with Mexico—couldn't it likewise lose all of Texas by force of arms, and acknowledge this defeat with a comparable treaty with Mexico? Once these treaties with third-party nations were concluded, surely there would remain no constitutional obstacle to entering into treaties with the Confederacy itself, now fully recognized as a foreign government.[12]

Above and beyond secessionist coups that were unrepublican at the state level, what about other attempted state secessions? Suppose—counterfactually, according to Lincoln—that Confederate secessionists had won the support, in free and fair elections, of a strong and deliberate majority of the lawful voters of their respective states, as properly expressed in duly convened special state referenda and state conventions. On these assumptions, the republican guarantee clause would perhaps fade into the background. Its words would not oblige the federal government to intervene.

To be sure, Lincoln explained why the national government and the national people were not *required* to acquiesce in the South's unilateral action—but couldn't they *choose* to acquiesce? If a national majority preferred to let the South go, couldn't Congress pass a statute ceding the southern states, just as Congress in 1845 had passed a statute acquiring a southern state (namely, Texas)? Note that any objections based on the letter or spirit of Article IV's special guarantees of state territorial integrity would seem to be met if the peoples and governments of the Confederate states truly did support disunion.[13]

HAVING CONSIDERED SEVERAL possible mechanisms by which Lincoln's "rightful masters"—the American people as a whole, north and south, east and west—might have permitted disunion, via constitutional amendments, nonbinding national referenda, treaties, and congressional statutes, let us now ponder one more national mechanism that Lincoln apparently had in mind: if the American people truly wanted secession, they would be free to vote for an openly secessionist president in 1864.

This was a not-so-subtle refrain throughout Lincoln's First Inaugural Address. Early on, he pointedly referred to his "brief constitutional term of four years." One obvious way in which his "rightful masters, the American people," could in "an authoritative manner" "withhold" from him the "requisite means" of resisting disunion would be to oust him from the White House in 1864. Near the end of his address, he called upon fellow citizens to show "patient confidence in the ultimate justice of the people" and explained that the American people "have wisely given their public servants but little power for mischief; and have, with equal wisdom, provided for the return of that little to their own hands at very short intervals. While the people retain their virtue, and vigilance, no administration, by any extreme of wickedness or folly, can very seriously injure the government, in the short space of four years."

Lincoln returned to this theme in the closing paragraphs of his July 4, 1861, Special Session Address to Congress: "[W]hen ballots have fairly, and constitutionally, decided, . . . there can be no successful appeal, *except to ballots themselves, at succeeding elections.* . . . [N]o popular government can long survive a marked precedent, that those who carry an election, can only save the government from immediate destruction, by giving up the main point, upon which the people gave the election. *The people themselves, and not their servants, can safely reverse their own deliberate decisions.*"[14]

In this regard, it is supremely noteworthy (but rarely noticed by those who accuse Lincoln of acting like a dictator) that in 1864, in the middle of an all-out civil war, he allowed a regular presidential election to proceed, and pledged to abide by its outcome. And he did all this even though he thought it quite likely in the summer of 1864 that his opponent would prevail in November and would, once in office, negotiate terms of peace recognizing the Confederacy's independence and dissolving Lincoln's beloved Union.[15]

Like George Washington's decision in 1796–1797 to walk away from power after two terms, and John Adams's decision in 1800–1801 to accept the people's verdict and yield the presidency to his bitter political foe,

Thomas Jefferson, Lincoln's decision in 1864 to submit himself and his platform to the judgment of the supreme tribunal of the American people ranks as an epic exemplar of republican virtue. At the time, each of these three acts of executive restraint was virtually unprecedented in human history. Together, these three episodes have given the rest of the world a stunning illustration of the true meaning of constitutional democracy—government of, by, and for the people.[16]

THE IMPORTANCE OF the election of 1864 invites a closer look at the election of 1860 that brought Lincoln to power. Although Lincoln won the presidency with an absolute majority of electoral votes and a decisive plurality of popular votes, 60 percent of American voters in the unusual four-man race of 1860 had voted for someone else. Lincoln's legal right to the presidency was unassailable, but his "popular mandate," to use a modern phrase, was weak.[17]

Nevertheless, Lincoln's election was the result of a process far more national in scope and surely fairer than the unilateral state secession votes that followed. Moreover, it would have been democratically awkward to have awarded the presidency to anyone else, given that Lincoln had won many more popular votes than any of his three opponents. Even if all the non-Lincoln votes had gone to a single opposition candidate, Lincoln would still have won a clear electoral college majority.

Lincoln himself plainly understood and repeatedly mentioned that legal rules—such as the rules of the electoral college—helped define who could properly vote and how those votes should be properly aggregated. In his Inaugural Address, he carefully spoke of "a majority, held in restraint by constitutional checks," and in his July 4 Special Session Address he likewise took care to speak of "a majority of the legally qualified voters" and of "the numbers" of votes needed "to control administration, according to organic law." Democracy, Lincoln the lawyer understood, depended on law; in myriad ways legal rules and legal technicalities would determine who could claim democratic victory in any particular electoral contest.

Lincoln had learned all this the hard way, and he had learned it back in Illinois, the land whence he sprang politically. In the wake of the Lincoln-Douglas debates throughout Illinois in 1858, Lincoln's party in fact received more statewide votes than Douglas's party for the state legislature. Nevertheless, because of legally permissible gerrymandering, lawful malapportionment, other legal quirks, and the fact that not all state legislative seats were legally up for election in the 1858 election, Douglas won the "legal" vote for US Senate in the state legislature even though Lincoln in effect won the "popular" vote.[18]

OF COURSE, LINCOLN'S argument that as president he could make little mischief on his own did not in the end persuade southern secessionists. Why not? If Lincoln's election was arguably a fluke—the result of the failure of the Democratic Party to coalesce around a single candidate—why didn't the South simply show the patience Lincoln called for, wait four short years, regroup, and then send the man packing? After all, southern interests had largely dominated presidential politics since the Founding, thanks in part to the Constitution's three-fifths clause giving slave states extra clout in the electoral college. Virginia slaveholders had held the presidency for thirty-two of its first thirty-six years, and most recent presidents had either been southern apologists for slavery or "northern men of southern [proslavery] sympathies," such as Franklin Pierce and James Buchanan. Pro-South and proslavery antebellum presidents meant that the Supreme Court in 1861 was likewise firmly pro-South and proslavery; and southerners also had enough votes in the House and Senate to block many of the laws Lincoln might have backed. Why were proslavery southerners so threatened by Lincoln?[19]

One answer is that Lincoln, acting alone, could do something that the Slave Power viewed with dread. Wielding considerable patronage power over the post office, Lincoln could make local postal appointments across the length and breadth of the South. Once in place, this widely dispersed cadre of southern spoilsmen could help establish the Republican Party as a genuine and credible political force in that region.

Lincoln could also allow antislavery literature to circulate through the federal mails. Southern governments and Lincoln's proslavery predecessors in the White House had virtually closed off the mails to abolitionist pamphlets during the previous quarter century, but Lincoln could single-handedly pry the South open to free speech. In 1860, the Republican Party was virtually outlawed in many southern states; it was literally a crime to criticize slavery. Through the post office, Lincoln might begin to change all that.

The Slave Power viewed a truly free press and a genuinely open political process as an intolerable threat. Northerners who had tried to venture down south to speak against slavery had been viciously punished; and Lincoln was openly siding with the forces of free speech. On his view of Union, citizens of one state should be free to engage in political and religious discourse in sister states, and no state should be allowed to muzzle conversation about great national issues—such as whether slavery was moral and whether it should be expanded.[20]

Here, too, Lincoln brought to the national capital sensibilities that had taken shape in the rough and tumble of Illinois politics. Don E. Fehrenbacher, an acclaimed historian of Illinois's Lincoln and Lincoln's Illinois, has shown that fights for control of the Illinois post office were particularly intense among state politicians in the 1850s. With Lincoln's election in 1860, Fehrenbacher has explained, the political tables began to turn: Illinois's "Republicans were naturally the loudest complainers about Buchanan's use of the Post Office as a political instrument, but upon gaining power in 1861, they rivaled their enemies in the energy with which they wielded the patronage."[21]

A Constitutional Union

Lincoln argued that the essence of secession was anarchy. If South Carolina could lawfully choose to secede from the Union in 1860, he asked, why couldn't she lawfully choose to secede from the Confederacy in 1861? Why couldn't Charleston lawfully choose to secede from South Carolina in 1862, or a neighborhood lawfully choose to secede from Charleston in 1863?

The response of secessionists like Jefferson Davis was that Lincoln was right to emphasize majority rule, but wrong to emphasize a national majority rather than a state majority. Within a well-ordered democratic polity, the majority did properly bind the minority. Thus, on Davis's view, the minority of South Carolinians who preferred the Union were properly bound by the majority that preferred secession in a duly convened state election. Charleston had no lawful right to unilaterally secede from South Carolina, because the *state* was the proper juridical entity over which to tally votes. In other words, under the Constitution, the state was the relevant "sovereign"—and not Charleston on the one hand, or the Union on the other. Or so Confederates like Davis argued.[22]

In response, Lincoln countered that the Constitution privileged the Union over South Carolina, or any other state acting unilaterally. Lincoln was clearly right to hold this view, but perhaps wrong in some of his specific (and unnecessary) claims on behalf of it.

In his First Inaugural, Lincoln insisted that the Union preceded the states, logically and chronologically, and he elaborated these points at length in his July 4, 1861, Special Session Address to Congress. He began by labeling secessionism a "sophism" that derived "its currency from the assumption, that there is some omnipotent, and sacred supremacy, pertaining to a *State*—to each State of our Federal Union." Lincoln countered that "our States have neither more, nor less power, than that reserved to them, in the Union, by the Constitution—no one of them ever having been a State *out* of the Union. The original ones passed into the Union even *before* they cast off their British colonial dependence; and the new ones each came into the Union directly from a condition of dependence, excepting Texas. And even Texas, in its temporary independence, was never designated a State."

For Lincoln, these legal and historical facts doomed the secessionist position: "Having never been States, either in substance, or in name, *outside* of the Union, whence this magical omnipotence of 'State rights,' asserting a claim of power to lawfully destroy the Union itself? Much is said about the 'sovereignty' of the States, but the word, even, is not in the national Constitution."

Lincoln went on to insist that "no one of our States, except Texas, ever was a sovereignty. And even Texas gave up this character on coming into the Union; by which act, she acknowledged the Constitution of the United States, and the laws and treaties of the United States made in pursuance of the Constitution, to be, for her, the supreme law of the land." Thus, "[t]he States have their status *in* the Union, and they have no other legal status. If they break from this, they can only do so against law, and by revolution."

As Lincoln understood the American Revolution,

[t]he Union, and not [the states] themselves separately, procured their independence, and their liberty. By conquest, or purchase, the Union gave each of them, whatever of independence, and liberty, it has. The Union is older than any of the States; and, in fact, it created them as States. Originally, some dependent colonies made the Union, and, in turn, the Union threw off their old dependence, for them, and made them States, such as they are. Not one of them ever had a State constitution, independent of the Union.[23]

THIS IS A LOT TO TAKE IN, and some of it is hard to swallow. Men like Robert E. Lee found an alternative narrative of early American history compelling. Many today continue to find this alternative narrative compelling, and with good reason.

On this alternative view, British North America was founded and populated in the seventeenth century not as a single continental juridical entity—"America"—but as an assortment of distinct legal regimes, each with its own name, its own unique legal charter or authorizing instrument, and its own separate laws and legal institutions. In the 1760s, "Virginia" was, legally speaking, an obvious fait accompli—its House of Burgesses had been meeting continuously since the 1620s—but "the Union" as a legal entity was still waiting to be born. The British colonies were linked together by a common king, but not directly to each other. (A twentieth-century analogue might be the hub-and-spoke British Commonwealth circa 1935, encompassing India, New Zealand, Australia, Kenya, and so on.) No one in 1760 could know that in 1800, South Carolina would be "united" with Massachusetts, but not with, say, Jamaica or Newfoundland.

When thirteen specific colonies began to coordinate their resistance to British policies, they did so as separate legal regimes, bound together in a kind of international assembly—hence the name "Continental Congress" (like the later international "Congress" of Vienna in 1815) rather than "the American legislature." In 1776, these colonies declared themselves independent as "United States"—*united*, in a kind of league, but distinct and independent *states*, nonetheless. Each state designed for itself a new constitution or repurposed its old colonial charter, and these thirteen separate, distinct, and locally produced state constitutions were dramatic emblems of the independence and sovereignty of each state. The colonies' joint declaration of independence proclaimed themselves "free and independent states"—independent even of each other save as they chose, for sound military and prudential reasons, to concert their actions. They were allies, not an indivisible nation.[24]

Had 1776 been widely understood as a moment when Virginia somehow merged into some larger sovereign "Union," there would have been considerable conversation about this—especially given the conventional wisdom in 1776 that democracy could thrive only in a geographically small jurisdiction with a relatively homogeneous population shaped by a common climate and a common culture. Yet no deep and sustained conversations of this sort are evident in 1776 to warrant so dramatic a change in Virginia's deeply rooted identity. (Renaming her colonial "House of Burgesses" a state "House of Delegates" involved no great shift of identity or institutional practice; but saying that Virginians should henceforth be coercively governed by a newfangled "Union" dominated by non-Virginians would have been an altogether different thing.)

When the time came to legally specify the precise nature of the American alliance, the Articles of Confederation explicitly and emphatically proclaimed that each state was indeed "*sovereign*" and that the "Union" was simply a kind of treaty—a "firm *league* of friendship," a mere "*confederation*" of otherwise autonomous states. The 1783 treaty of peace with Great Britain was likewise best read as affirming the separate sovereignty of each state. And most dramatically of all, the Constitution itself emphatically recognized the separate sovereignty of each state circa September 1787: Article VII specified that each state was free to go its own way. No state would be bound by the Constitution unless that state chose to ratify it, regardless of what its allies in the "Union" chose to do. When George Washington was elected president in 1789, two of the original thirteen colonies were in fact acting as independent sovereign nations outside the Union: both North Carolina and Rhode Island declined to ratify the Constitution at first, and agreed to join the document only well after it had already gone into operation in the other states.[25]

Although this alternative narrative is not the only conceivable way to understand the pre-constitutional history of America, if I were forced to choose between this narrative and Lincoln's, I would choose this one.

DOES THIS MEAN that unilateral secession was, in the final analysis, constitutional, or that Lincoln was wrong to resist it? Not at all. For the real question is not "What was the status of states *before* they joined the Constitution?" but "What was the status of states *after* they joined?"

As Lincoln himself explained in passing, the fact that Texas was sovereign in 1841 does not mean that it remained sovereign in 1861. In the interim, Texas joined a Constitution whose Article VI supremacy clause, which Lincoln astutely invoked, clearly resolves the secession question, albeit without using the word "secession." Article VI says that whenever the federal Constitution conflicts with a state constitution, the federal Constitution always prevails: "*This Constitution . . . shall be the supreme Law of the Land . . . any thing in the Constitution or Laws of any State to the Contrary notwithstanding.*"

Thus, even if the people of Texas met in a state convention in 1861 and tried to redraft the basic ground rules in the constitution of Texas, they could not legally have done anything that violated the larger national Constitution—or at least they could not have done so unilaterally.

The two clauses sandwiching Article VI confirm this article's plain meaning. In dramatic contrast to Article VII—whose unanimity rule that no state can bind another confirms the sovereignty of each state *prior to ratifying* the Constitution—Article V does not permit a single state convention, *post-ratification*, to modify the federal Constitution for itself. Instead, Article V makes clear that a state is strictly bound by a federal constitutional amendment, even if that state votes against the amendment in a properly convened state convention, so long as enough other states (three-quarters of the whole), in conventions assembled, do vote to ratify the amendment. This sharp Article V break with the Article VII protocol of state unanimity in 1787–1788 is flatly inconsistent with the idea that states remain sovereign *after* joining the Constitution, even though they were sovereign *before* joining it.

Ratification of the Constitution itself marked the moment when previously sovereign states gave up their sovereignty and legal independence. During the ratification year of 1787–1788, Americans across the continent did in fact engage in a broad and deep debate about whether this dramatic change in each state's basic identity was warranted, and about whether this change could be harmonized with conventional political science as exemplified by the celebrated Montesquieu—an influential French writer who had seemed to insist that democracy could work only on a small geographic scale. Nor was the document opaque about the fundamental issue of future secession. Its Preamble proudly proclaimed its primary purpose to be the formation of a "more perfect union."

The phrase "perfect union" had a special resonance and a specific meaning in 1787. It was a pointed reference to the 1707 Act of Union between Scotland and England—an act to form, in the words of Queen Anne, an "entire and perfect union." This act was plainly understood to preclude unilateral Scottish secession, and was so explained by Blackstone's *Commentaries*, which were widely read in America. In *The Federalist* No. 5, John Jay (writing under the pen name "Publius") explicitly invoked the 1707 act and its "perfect union" backdrop as the template for the proposed Constitution; and in *The Federalist* No. 11, Alexander Hamilton (also writing under the pseudonym "Publius") went on to defend the idea that the "thirteen states" should be "bound together in a strict and *indissoluble* Union." Similarly, Federalist spokesman James Wilson insisted at the Pennsylvania ratifying convention that "the bonds of our union ought therefore to be *indissolubly* strong"; and fellow Federalist James Madison wrote to Alexander Hamilton that each state's ratification must be "*in toto* and *for ever*"—words that Hamilton in turn shared with the members of the New York ratifying convention at a particularly key moment, when the eyes of the entire world were fixed on the Empire State's convention proceedings.*[26]

In his First Inaugural Address, Lincoln himself invoked and stressed the "perfect Union" language: "[I]n 1787, one of the declared objects for ordaining and establishing the Constitution, was *'to form a more perfect union.'*" Clearly, Lincoln insisted, these words meant that a state could not ratify in 1788 and later unilaterally secede "upon its own mere motion."

And if we seek still more historical support for this view—if we yearn for some kind of smoking gun against the claimed right of unilateral secession—we will find it in a rather unlikely source. In his otherwise pusillanimous Address to Congress in December 1860, President James Buchanan in one brief passage hit the historical nail on the head: he noted that *never* in the great ratification debate of 1787–1788 had the Constitution's supporters endorsed a right of unilateral secession, even though such an endorsement would surely have eased the anxieties of those who opposed the Constitution in the name of states' rights:

> In that mighty struggle [between Federalists and Antifederalists] it never occurred to any individual, either among its opponents or advocates, to assert or even to intimate that their efforts were all vain labor, because the moment that any State felt herself aggrieved she might secede from the Union. *What a crushing argument would this have proved against those who dreaded that the rights of States would be endangered by the Constitution!* The truth is that it was not until . . . *after* the origin of the Federal Government that such a [pro-secession] proposition was first advanced.[27]

We shall soon encounter in more detail the 1787 Federalists' chief functional argument—a sweeping geostrategic argument—for their proposed "more perfect Union." This argument plainly presupposed the unavailability of unilateral secession. Once in the more perfect Union, no disgruntled state could unilaterally withdraw its unique landmass without

---

* Several of the quotations in this paragraph could be read to imply that even the national people should not be able to dissolve the Union, but the plain meaning in context is simply a rejection of the notion of unilateral state secession. All of the above-quoted Founders plainly understood that America's ultimate geographic contours would depend on future federal laws, treaties, and constitutional amendments. While emphatically rejecting the legality of future unilateral secession, they all accepted the possibility of genuinely national legal actions that might redraw the legal map.

winning the approval of fellow Unionists in adjoining states. Within the secure continental union, weapons and fortifications would point out at enemies, and could never be allowed to be unilaterally swiveled against fellow Americans.

THOUGH LINCOLN'S PRECISE historical narrative was problematic, we should try to understand why he said what he did. It turns out that his view of the Union was powerfully shaped by the land(s) whence he came.

Consider how the world looked to Robert E. Lee in 1861. Lee came from what was perhaps Virginia's first family, which could trace its roots back five generations to the arrival of Richard Lee from England in the first half of the seventeenth century. Both the general's father and his grandfather had served in Virginia's government, as had a great many extended relations. As a proud son of Virginia, whose forebears had played leading roles in Virginia politics for two centuries, General Lee was a Virginian first. For him, of course Virginia preceded America! Who could ever think otherwise?

Consider also how the world looked to a typical Texan in 1861. It was absurd to say that the Union came before the states; Texas proved otherwise! (Texans are usually quite good at seeing the importance of Texas; the problem is getting them to see the importance of anything else.)[28]

But now consider how the world looked to Lincoln in 1861. His forebears came from several states—Kentucky, Virginia, Pennsylvania, and possibly New England as well, though Lincoln was not quite sure. He himself had lived in three states, having been born in Kentucky and having moved to Indiana at age seven and then on to Illinois as a young man. He and his family were first and foremost not Virginians, or Pennsylvanians, or New Englanders, or Kentuckians or Hoosiers or even Illinoisans. They were Americans. And to him, it seemed natural that the Union did come first logically and chronologically. The lands that became the states of Indiana and Illinois were federal territories first, administered by the federal government prior to statehood. Indeed, Lincoln's family reached Indiana just at the point that the region was completing its transition from territory to state. Even more dramatic, the lands that would one day become Illinois and Indiana were part of the "Union" even before the Constitution was adopted—they were part of the Old Northwest Territory that was administered by the Congress under the Articles of Confederation.[29]

When we remember where Lincoln was quite literally coming from, it is easier to understand (whether or not we ultimately endorse) his repeated insistence that "[t]he Union is much older than the Constitution" and that "[t]he Union is older than any of the States; and, in fact, it created them as States." To a plainsman reared in the Old Northwest, this rang true, even as it grated on the ears of many Virginians and Texans.[30]

A GEOGRAPHIC UNION

This was not the only way that geography—and in particular, the geography of the Midwest—shaped Lincoln's view of Union. But before we confront Lincoln's view of geography and Union, let us consider the Founders' view of the matter.

Geography preoccupied the Founders. Classical political theory had suggested that democracies could not extend over large geographic areas; and the entire first section of *The Federalist* devoted itself to refuting this argument against a "more perfect union" aiming to span a continent. Today, we are most familiar with the argument made by James Madison (also writing as "Publius") in *The Federalist* No. 10 that a strong union would protect Americans from majority tyranny at the state level. But this particular unionist argument persuaded few skeptics in 1787–1788. A homegrown and electorally accountable Virginia legislature had been operating for more than 150 years, and most Virginians did not think they needed a new and untested continental Constitution merely to protect themselves from their fellow Virginians. Today, we celebrate this *Federalist* essay because its emphasis on the need for a strong federal presence to counter abusive state practices helps makes sense of our post-Lincoln, post–Civil War, post–Fourteenth Amendment, post–*Brown v. Board of Education* world; but before the twentieth century almost no one noticed the Tenth *Federalist*.[31]

Instead, Publius's key argument for union came well before No. 10, and stressed the need for a strong continental Constitution, not to protect Virginians from their own state, but to protect them from other states, and vice versa.

In essence, Publius argued that although rampant despotism reigned over almost all the European continent in 1787, England was a bright spot because of her unique *geography*. As an island, Britain was protected from the military depredations of her neighbors by the English Channel. So long as Britannia maintained a strong navy and ruled the waves (remember 1588!), she did not need to not overly concern herself with the horrible prospect of invasion. Navies, moreover, were relatively defensive creatures that could not easily be turned against Englishmen to impose tyranny on the home front.

Large standing armies, by contrast, posed obvious threats to domestic liberty. Yet Publius understood that regimes on the continent of Europe might well require such armies to defend land borders against invasion. Tragically, land borders often led to a race to the bottom in which a single ambitious regime arming itself for military adventurism forced each of its neighbors to build up its army to deter and (if necessary) repel invasion. Armies begot strong executives to lead them, and the combination begot domestic tyranny. Unlike navies, armies could easily be used not just to thwart invaders, but to crush domestic liberty.

The task for Americans, according to Publius, was thus to structure the New World in a manner that would avoid the general fate of the European Continent, as the English had done with a God-given moat (the Channel) and the Swiss with a God-given rampart (the Alps).

By 1787, the Articles of Confederation had proved utterly unworkable; the existing Confederation was at an end, practically speaking. Suppose, wrote Publius, that Americans were to replace the Confederation with thirteen separate nations, each with land borders with its neighbors, free to arm itself as it saw fit. Each nation-state might be inclined to raise an army, not just to defend itself against Indians or against British, French, or Spanish outposts, but also to impress or intimidate its neighbors. America would then replicate continental Europe and the near-universal tyranny that characterized that continent. To instead fashion a system of three or four smaller confederacies (perhaps a northern, a southern, and one or two mid-Atlantic leagues) would not be much better, especially given the many disputes that would predictably arise about control of western lands. If, however, a system of indissolubly united states could be fashioned, America could replicate the English recipe for freedom. The 3,000-mile-wide Atlantic Ocean would be America's moat, protecting her against repetition of, and subjugation by, the military tyrannies of continental Europe. Americans could defend themselves primarily with a modestly sized navy that would not imperil liberty.

Publius admitted that Americans might need a very small army to buttress the South and West against Indians, and the North against Canada. But under the proposed new Constitution, none of America's land-bordering neighbors could overawe the United States or provide the president an excuse to create a dangerously large standing army—unless

America's land neighbors received massive reinforcement from European monarchs, whom Americans must thus discourage from expanding their New World outposts. Here, too, truly *united* states would be more likely to parry European adventurism and prevent European strong men from pursuing New World divide-and-conquer strategies designed to pit republican American states against each other.[32]

This Publian vision helps explain many of the Constitution's specific words—its rules about state troops in Article I, section 10; its special skepticism of federal standing armies (but not navies) in Article I, section 8, and in the Second and Third Amendments; its specific language of the Constitution as the law of "the land" in Article VI—and much of its overall structure. It also helps explain much of the next seventy years of American history—what Washington meant in important parts of his Farewell Address, why Jefferson violated his own rules of construction to buy Louisiana from France, and how later presidents proclaimed the "Monroe Doctrine" and pursued America's "Manifest Destiny."[33]

WITH THIS BACKGROUND, let us now engage with fresh eyes the following passage from Lincoln's First Inaugural Address, a passage that he repeated verbatim in his Second Annual Message to Congress in December 1862:

> Physically speaking, we cannot separate. We cannot remove our respective sections from each other, nor build an impassable wall between them. A husband and wife may be divorced, and go out of the presence, and beyond the reach of each other; but the different parts of our country cannot do this. They cannot but remain face to face; and intercourse, either amicable or hostile, must continue between them. Is it possible then to make that intercourse more advantageous, or more satisfactory, *after* separation than *before*? Can aliens make treaties easier than friends can make laws? Can treaties be more faithfully enforced between aliens, than laws can among friends?

Lincoln's Second Annual Message also contained other notable and quite specific geographic arguments. The president began by pondering abstract philosophical ideas of nationhood and nationality, and then zeroed in on some basic commonsensical points about the American landmass:

A nation may be said to consist of its territory, its people, and its laws. The territory is the only part which is of certain durability. "One generation passeth away, and another generation cometh, but the earth abideth forever." It is of the first importance to duly consider, and estimate, this ever-enduring part. That portion of the earth's surface which is owned and inhabited by the people of the United States, is well adapted to be the home of one national family; and it is not well adapted for two, or more. . . . There is no line, straight or crooked, suitable for a national boundary, upon which to divide.

More concretely:

The great interior region, bounded east by the Alleghanies, north by the British dominions [i.e., Canada], west by the Rocky mountains, and south by the line along which the culture of corn and cotton meets, and which includes part of Virginia, part of Tennessee, all of Kentucky, Ohio, Indiana, Michigan, Wisconsin, Illinois, Missouri, Kansas, Iowa, Minnesota and the Territories of Dakota, Nebraska, and part of Colorado, already has above ten millions of people, and will have fifty millions within fifty years, if not prevented by any political folly or mistake. It contains more than one-third of the country owned by the United States—certainly more than one million of square miles. . . . In the production of provisions, grains, grasses, and all which proceed from them, this great interior region is naturally one of the most important in the world. . . . And yet this region has no sea-coast, touches no ocean anywhere. As part of one nation, its people now find, and may forever find, their way to Europe by New York, to South America and Africa by New Orleans, and to Asia by San Francisco. But separate our common country into two nations, as designed by the present rebellion, and every man of this great interior region is thereby cut off from some one or more of these outlets, not perhaps, by a physical barrier, but by embarrassing and onerous trade regulations.

On Lincoln's view, "These outlets, east, west, and south, are indispensable to the well-being of the people inhabiting, and to inhabit, this vast interior region. . . . [These outlets] of right, belong to [the American] people, and to their successors forever. True to themselves, they will not ask where a line of separation shall be, but will vow, rather, that there shall be no such line."

Strikingly, in Lincoln's vision the land becomes, metaphorically, a human actor, with its own needs and demands: "Our national strife springs not from . . . the land we inhabit: not from our national homestead. There is no possible severing of this [land] but would multiply and not mitigate evils among us. In all its adaptations and aptitudes it"—that is, the land itself!—"demands union and abhors separation. In fact, it would ere long force reunion, however much of blood and treasure the separation might have cost."

Like the Founders, Lincoln was concerned with militarily defensible borders, and the need to prevent the emergence of two powerful and hostile regimes side by side, generating an arms race or a trade war that might lead to the militarization or the impoverishment of the continent. From the Founding to 1860, the United States had flourished as a remarkable free-trade and demilitarized zone. Those who didn't like Union policies were free to leave, but they had no right to take the land with them, or to try to bind their pro-Union neighbors, whether many or few. All Americans had invested in Fort Sumter and had a stake in the Mississippi River, and no single state could unilaterally take its land or waters and go home. With these general geographic and geostrategic themes, Lincoln was following in a grand tradition of the Founders and his predecessor presidents.[34]

But if we listen closely, we can surely hear a midwestern twang in his particular version of the geostrategic story—a version that highlights the role of the Midwest, that emphasizes the lack of natural and defensible borders within the heartland, that envisions the enormous demographic and economic potential of this basin, that respects the huge significance of the mighty Mississippi, and that appreciates how wrong it would be to give New Orleans an economic stranglehold over the entire region from the Appalachians to the Rockies. Consider also Lincoln's comment after Ulysses S. Grant captured Vicksburg, thereby giving the Union control of the mighty Mississippi: "The Father of Waters again goes unvexed to the sea."[35]

So here, too, Lincoln gave us unionism with a midwestern accent.

A MULTIRACIAL UNION

There is in Lincoln's words a quasi-religious vision of the special bond between the American people and the American land. At Gettysburg, Lincoln conjured up a rich image of miraculous conception when he spoke of how "our fathers brought forth" upon "this continent" a newborn who would later experience a "new birth." These remarks were made, of course, at an event commemorating the placement of American bodies back into the land. What brave Americans did on this "great battle-field" made this "final resting place," in Lincoln's words, "hallow[ed] . . . ground."[36]

Lincoln at times also summoned up a strongly religious vision of slavery as America's original sin, for which she must suffer divine retribution and seek divine redemption. Lincoln's Second Inaugural Address is a haunting expression of this vision:

American Slavery is one of those offenses which . . . [God] now wills to remove, and . . . He gives to both North and South, this terrible war, as the woe due to those by whom the offense came. . . . Fondly do we hope— fervently do we pray—that this mighty scourge of war may speedily pass away. Yet [we cannot justly complain if] God wills that it continue, until all the wealth piled by the bond-man's two hundred and fifty years of unrequited toil shall be sunk, and until every drop of blood drawn with the lash, shall be paid by another drawn with the sword.

These two grand themes—the bond between America's people and America's land, and slavery as America's original sin—intermingled in Lincoln's Second Annual Message to Congress in December 1862. Specifically, Lincoln suggested that America's special patrimony of rich midwestern land could be offered up—tithed, in effect—to help atone for slavery's ills. Slaves should be emancipated by law, but masters would receive fair compensation, and the newly freed folk could then be sent, at government expense and with their consent, to some faraway foreign land. To pay for all this, the government would simply need to sell off, rent, or otherwise manage and monetize its bounteous real estate. "Our abundant room—our broad national homestead—is our ample resource." Lincoln was quite in earnest, piling up extensive statistics and projections to show how the plan was economically feasible.

Of course, he soon came to chart another path. As a war measure, he finalized his Emancipation Proclamation on New Year's Day 1863, declaring freedom for slaves held in rebellious areas. Blacks soon flocked to Union banners and formed a vital part of the Union Army. Ultimately, the Thirteenth Amendment—proudly signed by Lincoln, though his signature was legally unnecessary—provided for uncompensated emancipation, even in Union states. Gone was the public idea of compensation for slavemasters, and gone, too, was the professed dream of colonization of black folk beyond the Union. Lincoln came to realize at the end of his life what he had not seen earlier: blacks and whites could live together, and could win wars together, under conditions of civil and political equality.[37]

In a private letter probably penned in early 1864, Lincoln wrote:

> How to better the condition of the colored race has long been a study which has attracted my serious and careful attention; hence I think I am clear and decided as to what course I shall pursue in the premises, regarding it a religious duty, as the nation's guardian of these people, who have so heroically vindicated their manhood on the battle-field, where, in assisting to save the life of the Republic, they have demonstrated in blood their right to the ballot, which is but the humane protection of the flag they have so fearlessly defended.[38]

In his last major address, delivered four days before his death, Lincoln went public with his new, more inclusive vision: "It is unsatisfactory to some that the elective franchise is not given to the colored man. I would myself prefer that it were now conferred on the very intelligent, and on those who serve our cause as soldiers."[39]

This was an important transformation in Lincoln's view of the Union. For a "union" aims to unite not just territory, or states, but also persons—flesh-and-blood human beings. Lincoln's early vision was of an ultimate Union that would largely be of, by, and for whites. After getting their freedom, blacks would be encouraged to move elsewhere—say, Africa or Central America. But the experience of the Civil War itself, and the bravery exhibited by black soldiers, helped persuade Lincoln to embrace a more inclusive conception of Union, bringing together not merely different regions but also different races.

On this subject, too, Lincoln's upbringing and maturation in the lower Midwest influenced his early views. For some idealistic whites living in Maine or Massachusetts—or even Minnesota or Michigan, for that matter—the noble dream of a genuinely multiracial society with large numbers of blacks living amid whites may have seemed abstractly attractive and easy enough to accomplish. But for a political realist living in central Illinois, between the Ohio and the Mississippi, the issue was far from abstract. Black folk were all around. With St. Louis on one side and Louisville on the other, the inhabitants of downstate Illinois were not merely north of slavery, but also east and west of it, and even (in places like Cairo) south of it. Once slavery was abolished across the continent, the question of interracial relations between free blacks and whites would surface with obvious urgency in places like central Illinois. Lincoln's early thoughts on this issue reflected the racial bigotry and anxiety of his time and place.

Yet Lincoln was willing to rethink these views, to grow in office, and by the hour of his death to embrace a far more inclusive view of a multi-racial union of equal citizens, black and white, north and south, east and west. Even Lincoln's final vision had flaws and omissions, especially when judged by the standards of today. But it was a remarkable advance over an original Constitution that had powerfully protected slavery.

Thus Lincoln did more than preserve the Union. He also redefined it. In a deeper way than ever before, the nation after and because of Lincoln became "dedicated to the proposition that all men [and women] are created equal." In this largest sense, all Americans, whether or not they have ever set foot in Illinois, are living in the land of Lincoln.

CHAPTER 2

ALABAMA:
HUGO BLACK AND
THE HALL OF FAME

B aseball fans endlessly debate the comparative merits of hall-of-fam-
ers. Who is the greatest of all time—Babe Ruth or Willie Mays?
What about Hank Aaron, Lou Gehrig, and Ted Williams? We law
professors play a similar parlor game amongst ourselves, rating the various members of the Supreme Court. Who are the greatest chief justices
in history? Was Associate Justice Oliver Wendell Holmes, Jr., all he was
cracked up to be? Who is the most underrated justice in the modern era?
Who was the greatest player on Earl Warren's team—Warren himself, or
one of his teammates? Which, if any, justices were the judicial equivalents
of Presidents Washington and Lincoln?[1]

As we begin pondering such questions, let's recall the various constitutional rights that almost all Americans now take for granted. For example, Americans today cannot imagine that the Bill of Rights should
apply against only the federal government and not against state and local
officials. Ordinary citizens often express surprise when reminded that
the First Amendment explicitly speaks only of rights against "Congress."
Americans now assume that of course the rights of counsel and fair trial
mean that all indigent defendants facing serious criminal charges must
receive attorneys at public expense, in both state and federal trials. Nor
can most Americans today look back on Jim Crow policies with anything
but shame and incredulity. These grotesque attempts to entrench white
supremacy into law, we now think, were clearly unconstitutional. Likewise, Americans across the current political and juridical spectrum view
gross malapportionments of state legislatures or of congressional districts

as improper: one person, one vote is a bedrock constitutional ideal. Most thoughtful Americans also believe that government officials, state and federal, must not officially favor one religion over another. And from left to right, jurists and citizens embrace vigorous judicial protection of political expression. Obviously we cannot allow federal or state officials to suppress political critics.

Yet in 1936, the year before the appointment to the United States Supreme Court of Alabama senator Hugo La Fayette Black, none of these basic principles of our current constitutional order was cast in concrete, or at least in Court case law—even though the Constitution itself, when fairly read, strongly supports every one of them. More than any other twentieth-century justice, Hugo Black deserves credit for fixing these fundamental precepts in place. On my ballot, Justice Black ranks as one of the greatest constitutional jurists in American history.

The story of Justice Black should remind us that even as a man's geographic origins and early life experiences may profoundly shape his worldview, the manner in which a place exerts its pull over a person still leaves vast room for individual personality, free will, and intellectual evolution. Whereas Abraham Lincoln, a midwestern Unionist, stands as the mightiest constitutional figure since the Founding, the dominant Supreme Court justice of the twentieth century, and the man most responsible for judicially vindicating Lincoln's and his fellow Reconstruction Republicans' vision, was a white southern Democrat and onetime Klansman!

Because Black came from the Deep South, and because he spoke and wrote and thought in a distinctly southern way, and because he lacked highfalutin academic credentials prized in certain northern circles, his constitutional greatness has, I believe, eluded various influential Yankee mandarins who have failed to give the man his due.

Yet here, too, geography is not entirely destiny. Although I consider myself a California-Connecticut Yankee through and through, I do not share the disdain toward Black felt by several other leading northern academics. Is it possible that this difference between me and other Yankee scholars is itself influenced by geography of a certain sort? As we shall see, many who learned their law at Harvard have been particularly misguided about Black; but I learned my law elsewhere—specifically, at Yale, my academic home for the past three decades, and, interestingly enough, the alma mater of Justice Black's son and namesake, Hugo Black, Jr. And did I mention that the man who taught me in my very first semester at Yale

Law School, and who later hired me onto the faculty and has sustained me in every single step of my academic career, Guido Calabresi, himself clerked for Justice Black?

A POWER HITTER:
THE BILL OF RIGHTS AND THE STATES

Perhaps the most striking feature of twenty-first-century constitutional jurisprudence is the leading role that the Bill of Rights now plays both inside courtrooms and beyond. Things were very different before Hugo Black arrived on the scene.

A separate Bill of Rights was no part of James Madison's careful plan at the Philadelphia Convention of 1787, and the document that emerged from Philadelphia omitted an explicit Bill of Rights. The idea of adding a detailed catalog of rights was floated only near the convention's close, and the tired and homesick delegates simply failed to give the matter careful thought as they were rushing toward the finish line. When Anti-Federalist skeptics pounced on this omission during ratification debates, Federalists scrambled to defend the document with a jumble of counterarguments, most of them weak and contradictory. Madison himself promised to revisit the issue once the Constitution went into effect. Although he kept his promise, shepherding a set of amendments through the First Congress, many of his colleagues viewed the exercise as a "nauseous" distraction from more important and immediate tasks of nation-building.[2]

Once ratified, the Bill receded from view in the antebellum era, at least in court. No federal judge invalidated the Sedition Act of 1798, which in effect made it a federal crime to criticize President John Adams or his allies in Congress. Only once in the entire antebellum era did the Supreme Court use the Bill of Rights to strike down an act of the federal government, and that single episode was a curiosity, to say the least: in the 1857 case of *Dred Scott v. Sanford*, the Court made the outlandish claim that the Fifth Amendment's due-process clause invalidated free-soil laws like the Northwest Ordinance (which George Washington had signed into law in 1789) and the 1820 Missouri Compromise (which had earned the constitutional approval of James Monroe's entire cabinet, including the South Carolina slavocrat John C. Calhoun). In an extensive review of newspapers published in 1841, one scholarly study could not find a single fiftieth-anniversary celebration of the Bill of Rights.[3]

The Bill of Rights as conventionally viewed in the antebellum era looked profoundly different from the Bill of Rights as widely understood today. Born in the shadow of a Revolutionary War waged by local governments against an imperial center, the original Bill affirmed various rights against the central government but none against the states. Reiterating this point in the 1833 case of *Barron v. Baltimore*, involving the Fifth Amendment's promise of just compensation for public uses of private property, Chief Justice John Marshall observed that if the First Congress had intended to apply the Bill of Rights against the states, the amendments would have said so explicitly.

Moreover, the rights that the original Bill did affirm sounded more in localism than in libertarianism. (Madison, of course, had drafted the Bill in large part to ease the anxieties of Anti-Federalists.) Congress could not establish a national church, but neither could it disestablish any state churches that might exist or arise. The Second Amendment championed local militias—the heroes of Lexington and Concord; the Third Amendment's rules about the quartering of troops likewise reflected wariness of a central standing army. Much of the rest of the Bill reinforced the powers of local juries. The Fifth Amendment safeguarded criminal grand juries; the Sixth, criminal trial juries; and the Seventh, civil juries. Beyond these specific clauses, several other parts of the original Bill also envisioned a strong role for local and populist juries, who were expected to protect popular publishers against federal officials in First Amendment cases, hold abusive federal henchmen liable for unreasonable searches in Fourth Amendment cases, and help assess just compensation against the federal government in Fifth Amendment cases. The only amendment endorsed by every state convention demanding a Bill of Rights during the ratification debates was the Tenth Amendment, which emphatically affirmed states' rights.[4]

Madison himself wanted more—a Bill safeguarding individual rights and minority rights against both state and federal officials—but in the First Congress, he was swimming against the tide. His proposed amendment requiring states to respect speech, press, conscience, and juries passed the House (as the presciently numbered Fourteenth Amendment) but died in a Senate protective of states' rights.

ONLY AFTER THE Civil War dramatized the need to limit abusive states would a new Fourteenth Amendment and distinctly modern view of the Bill emerge, a view celebrating individual rights and preventing states from abridging fundamental freedoms. From the 1830s on, antislavery crusaders had begun to develop, contra *Barron v. Baltimore*, a "declaratory" interpretation of the Bill of Rights that viewed the Bill as affirming and declaring preexisting higher-law norms applicable to all governments, state as well as federal. On this declaratory view, although the First Amendment directly regulated "Congress," it also affirmed a more general and universal right to free expression. According to *Barron* contrarians, when the amendment referred to "*the* freedom of speech," it thereby implied a *preexisting* legal freedom. Perhaps this legal freedom of speech could not be enforced against states in federal court, some contrarians conceded. But the First Amendment reference to "the freedom of speech" was itself *evidence* that a true legal right against all governments existed, a right that states were honor-bound to obey even in the absence of a federal enforcement scheme.

And what was true of the freedom of speech was, for contrarians, also true of the other rights and freedoms explicitly declared in the remainder of the Bill of Rights—the First Amendment freedom of religious exercise, the Fourth Amendment right against unreasonable searches, the Fifth Amendment entitlement to just compensation, and so on.

This declaratory theory took shape in a world where many southern states (including the state of Alabama, the future birthplace of Hugo Black) had enacted extremely repressive laws to prop up slavery—censoring abolitionist speech and press, suppressing antislavery preachers, implementing dragnet searches of suspected fugitive slaves and slave-sympathizers, imposing savagely cruel punishments on runaway slaves and their allies, and, indeed, violating virtually every right mentioned in the federal Bill.

With the passage of the Fourteenth Amendment in the Reconstruction era, declaratory theorists in the Republican Party sought to write their views into the Constitution itself, and to overrule *Barron v. Baltimore* just as they sought to overrule *Dred Scott v. Sanford*. By proclaiming, in section 1 of the Fourteenth Amendment, that "[n]o state shall make or enforce any law which shall abridge the privileges or immunities of citizens of the United States," Reconstruction Republicans tried to make clear that, henceforth, states would be required by the federal Constitution, by federal courts, and by Congress, too, to obey fundamental rights and freedoms—"privileges" and "immunities" of American "citizens."[5]

Where would judges find these freedoms? Among other places, in the federal Bill of Rights itself. Inclusion in the Bill of Rights was strong evidence that a given right—free speech, free exercise, or just compensation, for example—was a fundamental privilege or immunity of all American citizens.* So explained the key congressional draftsmen of the Fourteenth Amendment's section 1, led by Republican representative John A. Bingham of Ohio.[6]

Of course, by seeking to enforce these rights against state governments, Bingham and his fellow Reconstruction Republicans were, in effect, turning the Founders' Bill of Rights on its head. The original Bill had reflected the localism of the American Revolution, whereas Bingham and company were animated by the nationalism of the Civil War. Images of British imperial misbehavior and local heroism had inspired the eighteenth-century Bill of Rights, whereas images of slave-state misconduct and national heroism hovered over the Thirty-ninth Congress that drafted the Fourteenth Amendment.

For example, the original First Amendment was worded to emphasize that Congress simply lacked enumerated power to regulate religion or censor political expression in the several states. Note how its language—"*Congress shall make no law . . .*"—echoed and inverted the language of the Article I, section 8, necessary-and-proper clause: "*Congress shall* have power . . . to *make all laws* [in certain domains.]" But Bingham's vision stripped away this original veneer of states' rights, stressing instead that, henceforth, *states* must not "abridge" the freedom of speech or of the press or of religion. What had initially been drafted, in part, as an amendment to protect state autonomy in religious matters became, in Bingham's revision, a basis for nationalistic restrictions on states.[7]

ALAS, IN AN 1873 lawsuit now known as the *Slaughterhouse Cases*, the Supreme Court strangled the Fourteenth Amendment's privileges-or-immunities clause in its crib, rendering it, in the language of Justice Stephen

---

* Given that the privileges-or-immunities clause was designed to prevent states from abridging fundamental freedoms and rights, such as those spelled out in the federal Bill, it might be asked why the Fourteenth Amendment went on to specifically ban states from depriving persons of due process of law. Wasn't due process (a right mentioned in the Fifth Amendment) a "privilege or immunity" already covered? For an answer to this puzzle, see Akhil Reed Amar, *The Bill of Rights: Creation and Reconstruction* (1998), 171–174 (explaining that the privileges-or-immunities clause speaks of the rights of "citizens," whereas the adjoining due-process clause sweeps more broadly, including aliens in its protections of all "persons").

Field's dissent, "a vain and idle enactment." In the wake of the *Slaughterhouse Cases*, *Barron*'s regime remained intact throughout the 1870s and 1880s, despite the Fourteenth Amendment's plain text and decisive legislative history.

The first step away from *Barron* came when Hugo Black was just a lad—in the 1897 *Chicago Burlington* case, which, like *Barron* itself, involved the norm of just compensation. The Court now held, contra *Barron* and thanks to the Fourteenth Amendment, that states were bound by the principle of just compensation proclaimed in the Fifth Amendment. Standing alone, *Chicago Burlington* could be dismissed as a sport, a ruling reflecting the special solicitude for property on the Gilded Age Court. But over the course of the early twentieth century, the justices began to use the Fourteenth Amendment to protect rights beyond the narrow domains of private property and just compensation. (Because *Slaughterhouse* had in effect neutered the Fourteenth Amendment's privileges-or-immunities clause, many of these twentieth-century jurists, reluctant to squarely overrule *Slaughterhouse*, turned to the Fourteenth Amendment's due-process clause, using it to accomplish many of the purposes originally intended for the now-neutered clause.)

The expansion process began, inauspiciously, in the 1907 case of *Patterson v. Colorado*, with Justice Oliver Wendell Holmes, Jr., writing for the Court. Holmes proclaimed that "even if we were to assume that freedom of speech and freedom of the press were protected from abridgment on the part not only of the United States but also of the states," the newspaper publisher in the case would still lose. On *Patterson*'s facts, this was a remarkably obtuse holding. The publisher had published material mocking the justices of the state supreme court. Unamused, the state court— sitting without a jury, proceeding without a specific statute authorizing punishment of non-litigants, and in effect acting as judges in their own case—held the publisher in contempt and levied a fine on him. All of which was just fine by Holmes.[8]

The elder Justice John Marshall Harlan (who had written the Court's majority opinion in *Chicago Burlington*) dissented in *Patterson*. Foreshadowing positions that Hugo Black would later elaborate, Harlan insisted that the privileges-or-immunities clause encompassed not merely the Fifth Amendment's just-compensation principle but also all the other rights set forth in Amendments One through Eight, and further insisted that the Constitution's free-expression freedoms meant far more than Holmes thought.

By 1925, Holmes's assumption for the sake of argument in *Patterson* had evolved into a stronger assertion, given voice by Justice Edward Sanford writing for the Court in *Gitlow v. New York*: "For present purposes we may and do assume that the freedom of speech and of the press—which are protected by the First Amendment from abridgment by Congress—are among the fundamental personal rights and 'liberties' protected by the due process clause of the Fourteenth Amendment from impairment by the States." Although criminal defendant Benjamin Gitlow, author of a leftist manifesto, ended up losing his case and going to prison, the Court in the 1930s began to build on *Gitlow*'s language confirming that the Fourteenth Amendment protected free expression. The result was a series of Fourteenth Amendment rulings invalidating state laws that impermissibly restricted speech, press, and assembly rights.[9]

During this same period, however, the Court also held that other provisions of the federal Bill did not fully apply against states. Writing for the Court in the 1937 case of *Palko v. Connecticut*, Justice Benjamin Cardozo upheld a state law permitting the prosecutor to appeal from an acquittal in a criminal case, if the acquittal had occurred simply because the trial judge had made a legal mistake in the defendant's favor. Assuming for the sake of argument that an appeal in a comparable federal case would be barred by the Fifth Amendment's double-jeopardy clause,[10] Cardozo distinguished between those aspects of the federal Bill that were, in his lofty but fuzzy phrase, "of the very essence of a scheme of ordered liberty" and those that were not. Unlike rights of free expression, the right in the case at hand fell into the latter category and should not be imposed on states, Cardozo argued. His majority opinion was joined in full by Justice Hugo Black, who had come onto the Court earlier that year.

Applying *Palko*'s lofty but loose "ordered liberty" framework over the next few years, the Court in *Cantwell v. Connecticut* (1940) and *Everson v. Board of Education* (1947) held that the Fourteenth Amendment made the First Amendment's free-exercise and nonestablishment principles, respectively, applicable against states.

THE STAGE WAS NOW SET for a great debate on the relationship between the Founders' Bill of Rights and the Reconstructionists' Fourteenth Amendment. In the 1947 case of *Adamson v. California*, Justice Black's dissent put forth his now-famous theory of "total incorporation." On this view, the Fourteenth Amendment encompassed—"incorporated"—all the rights and freedoms of the federal Bill and made them applicable against states in exactly the same way as against the federal government. Justice William O. Douglas joined Black's dissent, and two other dissenters—Justices Frank Murphy and Wiley Rutledge—also agreed with Black that the Fourteenth Amendment incorporated the Bill of Rights. Unlike Black, however, Murphy and Rutledge suggested that courts might also use the broad language of the Fourteenth Amendment to protect additional unenumerated rights beyond the Bill of Rights.

In a separate concurring opinion, Justice Felix Frankfurter vigorously disagreed. On his view, the Fourteenth Amendment required that states obey principles of fundamental fairness and ordered liberty, principles that sometimes might overlap with the Bill of Rights but that bore no logical or evidentiary relation to the Bill as such.[11]

Black may have lost the incorporation battle in *Adamson*, but he eventually won the war. With Frankfurter's retirement in 1962, the anti-incorporation logjam broke, and most of the previously unincorporated provisions of the Bill of Rights came to be applied against the states— though not via Black's theory. Rather, the Court pursued an approach advocated by Justice William Brennan, called "selective incorporation," by which the justices purported to play by Frankfurter's ground rules while reaching Black's results.

Under this third approach, the Court's analysis could proceed clause by clause, fully incorporating every provision of the Bill deemed "fundamental" without deciding in advance (as Black would have it) whether each and every clause would necessarily pass the test. On the surface, Brennan's approach seemed to avoid a radical break with existing case law, which had squarely rejected total incorporation. Brennan even purported to accept Frankfurter's insistence on fundamental fairness as the touchstone of the Fourteenth Amendment. But in actual operation, Brennan's approach held out the possibility of total incorporation through the back door. For him, once a clause in the Bill was deemed "fundamental," it had to be incorporated against the states in every aspect, just as Black insisted. And nothing in the logic of selective incorporation precluded the possibility that, when all was said and done, virtually every clause of the Bill would have been deemed fundamental. As things turned out, in applying this approach, the Warren Court almost always found that a given clause of the Bill did set forth a fundamental right, and post-Warren justices have followed suit. Today, virtually all of the Bill of Rights has come to apply with equal vigor against state and local governments.[12]

The Supreme Court's approach to incorporation has generated a vast amount of commentary. This is hardly surprising, given the enormity of the stakes: the process of incorporation has utterly transformed the meaning of the Bill of Rights, and has defined modern constitutional law.[13]

If anyone doubts this, here is a simple way to remove the doubt. Take a minute and think about the most notable Bill of Rights cases of all time. Odds are that most of the cases that spring to your mind are, strictly speaking, not cases where the Bill of Rights directly applies, but rather cases involving state and local governments, where the Bill applies only because of incorporation.

For example, in *Mapp v. Ohio*, the Court famously applied the exclusionary rule against *state* officials; in *Gideon v. Wainwright*, the Court mandated appointed counsel for indigent *state* criminal defendants; in *Miranda v. Arizona*, justices obliged *state and local* police officers to read custodial suspects their rights; in *New York Times v. Sullivan*, the Court struck down *Alabama's* repressive libel law; and in *Griswold v. Connecticut*, it was a *state* anti-contraception law that the Court invalidated in the name of marital bedroom privacy. Nowhere has the importance of incorporation in shaping American jurisprudence been more evident than in the field of constitutional criminal procedure. The overwhelming majority of criminal cases are prosecuted by state governments under state law; only after the incorporation of the Fourth, Fifth, Sixth, and Eighth Amendments did federal courts develop a robust and highly elaborate—if also highly controversial—jurisprudence of constitutional criminal procedure.

BEFORE TURNING FROM the general topic of incorporation to a few more specific examples of modern rights discourse, and of the impact of Hugo Black on that discourse, it's worth noting a few things about *Adamson* in particular and about Black's approach to constitutional interpretation in general.

First, although Black's *Adamson* dissent oversimplified, it was basically right: the framers and ratifiers of the Fourteenth Amendment did intend to prevent states from violating any of the fundamental rights spelled out in the first eight amendments. This was part of the core meaning of the amendment.[14]

Second, in insisting on this fundamental truth, Black stood against the received wisdom of his day. In 1947, no US Supreme Court case clearly supported total incorporation, and a great many Court cases seemed to repudiate Black's preferred approach. Before Black, no one on the Court, not even the elder Justice Harlan, had carefully assembled the impressive historical case for this position. It was the product of years of study on Black's part, reading and rereading primary and secondary sources—Reconstruction-era congressional speeches, journals, and committee reports; old oral arguments and half-forgotten judicial opinions; dusty academic books and articles—that his fellow justices had ignored or slighted. Thus Black was not simply carrying the insights of previous cases a small, incremental step further. He was challenging the basic judicial order and showing how the game should instead be played: judges should be bound not by wrongheaded Gilded Age precedent, but by the Constitution itself and its more admirable vision of liberty.

Third, and related, the dissent exuded a faith in ordinary Americans and expressed a certain skepticism of the judiciary. Black tried to move constitutional conversation away from the Court and toward the Constitution itself—a democratic document for a democratic culture.[15]

The text of the document came from the people and can easily be read by them. It is, after all, a short document. Although his argument in *Adamson* sounded more in history than in pure textual argument, note its obvious virtues for a card-carrying textualist: instead of fixating on the elaborate judicial gloss overlaid upon the relatively open-ended words of the Fourteenth Amendment (such as *Palko*'s ode to "ordered liberty"), Black proposed that judges simply attend to the more specific and more democratically accessible language of Amendments One through Eight. These words would give judges proper guidance and constraint and would resonate with the rights that ordinary citizens, with their pocket Constitutions in hand, would deem themselves entitled to.

This point brings us to a fourth and distinctly geographic insight (about insight). Perhaps it is not pure happenstance that it was a deep southerner who brought these themes of Reconstruction text and history so forcefully to the forefront. Black had an obvious and personal interest in the history of the Civil War and Reconstruction, an era that left a deep imprint on the Alabama of his youth. And perhaps his brand of constitutional fundamentalism played particularly well on Election Day in the South—a region known for a biblical fundamentalism that emphasized the Good Book's text as the literal word of God and paid close heed to what Jesus *really* meant when he said this or did that way back when.

To be sure, this suggested link between southern biblical fundamentalism and southern constitutional fundamentalism is speculative. But is it completely coincidental that the current justice most focused on constitutional fundamentals of text and original meaning, Clarence Thomas, also hails from the Bible Belt? (The man right behind Thomas in this regard is also the one who is right behind Thomas in having lived more of his pre-Court life in Dixie than any other current justice— Antonin Scalia, who spent his first four years as a law professor in Charlottesville, Virginia.)[16]

Of course, Thomas's vision in many ways sharply diverges from Black's. Geography and biography are not destiny; different individuals may respond differently to similar experiences. Hugo Black was a southern *liberal*, and Clarence Thomas, at present, is a southern *conservative*.

But among modern liberals and nationalists, Black was a distinctly *southern* liberal and a notably *southern* nationalist. Over the course of American history, each of the states has misbehaved at some point or other, but *southern* governmental misconduct was particularly egregious, pervasive, and sustained in the century prior to *Adamson*. Much of the post-*Adamson* work of the Warren Court can be understood as an effort to bring the southland in line with the best rights-respecting practices of northern and western states. Incorporation was one obvious way to accomplish this nationalizing and rights-protecting mission.[17]

Abraham Lincoln—who was born in the Upper South (Kentucky), married into a southern family, and was intimately familiar with many aspects of southern culture—sincerely believed that there were deep, if often silent and untapped, reservoirs of pro-Union and pro-constitutional sentiment in many parts of the South. Black's epic dissent in *Adamson* proved Lincoln right after the fact. In 1947—exactly four score and seven years after Lincoln's election—a highly visible pro-Lincoln southerner took center stage and declared his willingness to work heroically to redeem Lincoln and his fellow Reconstruction Republicans' vision in America's ongoing constitutional project.

A fifth point about Black's *Adamson* opinion concerns the deep logic of incorporation. Although Black's dissent tended to downplay the matter, it contained the seeds of large insight: in applying the Bill of Rights against the states, the Reconstruction generation actually redefined the Bill. The Framers' Bill of Rights, for example, included the first ten amendments, but Black's incorporated Bill included only Amendments One through Eight.

Finally, Black's towering contribution on incorporation exemplified an impressive mixture of humility, determination, and flexibility. As for humility, Black's dissent in effect required him to admit that he had erred early on in embracing Justice Cardozo's loose approach in *Palko*, which gave the Court too much discretion to under-protect rights in the first eight amendments that the justices subjectively deemed unimportant. As for determination, Black's incorporation argument did not prevail in *Adamson* itself, where it was subjected to harsh criticism by Justice Felix Frankfurter, a former Harvard Law School professor. Shortly thereafter, another Harvard product, Professor Charles Fairman, launched a savage attack on Black's masterpiece. But the Harvard men were wrong, and the lowly son of Clay County stood his ground.[18]

Eventually, the Court came around to Black's view of the matter, in effect, if not quite in theory, via the compromise of selective incorporation. And here we see Black's flexibility at work. Selective incorporation was not quite right in principle, he thought, but he would go along with the approach whenever it reached the right result, making applicable against states previously unincorporated rights. If Justice William Brennan—yet another Harvard man—could get five votes for the right result in a given case, Black would take the victory. Playing the game perfectly is very nice, but even more important is winning the big ones.[19]

A COMPLETE ATHLETE:
SOME MEMORABLE PERFORMANCES

Given the immense importance of the incorporation issue in modern American constitutional law, and Black's indispensable role in its ultimate resolution, *Adamson* alone would qualify Black for the Hall of Fame—as, say, the judicial equivalent of Reggie Jackson's towering performance in World Series play. But Black did more than help make the Bill of Rights applicable against states; he also played a leading role in broadly construing many of these rights in ways that previous cases had not, and he often did so in his early years on the bench, long before the heyday of the Warren Court.

For example, freedom of speech and freedom of the press are today construed generously, especially to protect critics of government policy and government policymakers; but this was not always so. It has become so in large part because of Hugo Black.

When Congress in 1798 made it a federal crime to criticize certain federal incumbents, US Supreme Court justices riding circuit cheerfully upheld this blatant constitutional violation. Years later, the antebellum South in effect criminalized all antislavery speech. In 1860, the

Republican Party was virtually outlawed in the Old South. (Lincoln did not receive even a single popular vote in Alabama or in any other state south of Virginia.) Yet the Supreme Court never stepped in to protect free expression against this repressive censorship.

We have already seen Justice Holmes and his brethren, in the 1907 *Patterson* case, blithely upholding punishment for a publisher whose only crime was criticizing judges; and in 1919, Holmes once again wrote for the Court, this time upholding a ten-year prison sentence for the political leader Eugene Debs, a man who had previously received close to 1 million votes for president and who would receive even more votes in 1920 from his prison cell. Debs's crime: giving a peaceful speech criticizing the federal government's war policy. Before 1925, the rights of free expression had never—not once—prevailed in the United States Supreme Court.

In 1930, Charles Evans Hughes became chief justice, and in 1937 Black became an associate justice. Now, at long last, freedom of expression had strong judicial champions able to win Court majorities and start to undo the damage done by earlier cases.

One of the most notable opinions repudiating the repressive logic of *Patterson* and *Debs* was handed down on December 8, 1941—the day after Pearl Harbor. The case, *Bridges v. California*, involved state judges who tried to punish publishers commenting on various state judicial proceedings. (Judges, as we saw in *Patterson*, can be very thin-skinned about those who criticize the judiciary itself.) Writing for a closely divided (5–4) Court, Black insisted that the First Amendment offered far more protection of expression than had prior English common law:

> [T]he substantive evil must be extremely serious and the degree of imminence extremely high before utterances can be punished. . . . For the First Amendment does not speak equivocally. It prohibits any law "abridging the freedom of speech, or of the press." It must be taken as a command of the broadest scope that explicit language, read in the context of a liberty-loving society, will allow. . . . No purpose in ratifying the Bill of Rights was clearer than that of securing for the people of the United States much greater freedom of religion, expression, assembly, and petition than the people of Great Britain had ever enjoyed.

Here, as in the later *Adamson* case, Black understood that freewheeling judges had not always been sufficiently sensitive to rights guaranteed in the Bill of Rights. As he would repeatedly emphasize, several of the provisions of the Bill of Rights were designed precisely to protect against judicial over-bearing. Thus, he was far less impressed by *Pattersonian* precedents, and far less willing to defer to the thin-skinned state judiciary in the case at hand, than were his four dissenting colleagues, led by Felix Frankfurter, who was himself, truth be told, an exceedingly thin-skinned judge.[20]

Today, *Bridges* is not remembered as the watershed that it was. Most observers instead point to *New York Times v. Sullivan* (1964)—a case involving black civil rights protesters in Alabama, the heart of Dixie—as emblematic of the modern Court's generous protection of those criticizing government officials. But *Sullivan's* spirit—that in America, "debate on public issues should be uninhibited, robust, and wide-open, and . . . it may well include vehement, caustic, and sometimes unpleasantly sharp attacks on government and public officials"—was there in *Bridges*, almost a quarter century earlier.[21]

In the prelude to this oft-cited passage in *Sullivan*, the Court's majority opinion, authored by Brennan, tipped its hat to Black's earlier opinion in *Bridges*, quoting it as follows: "[I]t is a prized American privilege to speak one's mind, although not always with perfect taste, on all public institutions." (Note Black's use of the telltale word "privilege"—an early statement of his later-elaborated view that free expression was one of the Fourteenth Amendment's privileges and immunities.) Right before announcing what it deemed "the central meaning of the First Amendment"—that Americans must be free to criticize officialdom, and thus, that the 1798 Sedition Act was obviously unconstitutional—the *Sullivan* Court once again signaled that it was standing on the shoulders of Justice Black in *Bridges*:

> Where judicial officers are involved, this Court has held that concern for the dignity and reputation of the courts does not justify the punishment as criminal contempt of criticism of the judge or his decision. [Citation to *Bridges*.] . . . If judges are to be treated as "men of fortitude, able to thrive in a hardy climate," surely the same must be true of other government officials, such as elected city commissioners. Criticism of their official conduct does not lose its constitutional protection merely because it is effective criticism and hence diminishes their official reputations.

Though many of the words here came from Brennan, some of the deep ideas had been elaborated years before by Black (who of course joined Brennan in siding with the civil rights protesters and against Alabama's oppressive libel laws).

There may be a larger lesson lurking here. Perhaps cases like *Sullivan* are now treated as more canonical and pathbreaking, and cases like *Bridges* are often overlooked, because some of what Black sought to build in *Bridges* was washed away by the Court's more repressive intervening free-expression case law in the early Cold War period. Black frequently found himself in dissent in these dark days—occasionally backed by Frankfurter, often opposed by him—and when the Court in *Sullivan* ultimately returned to the free-speech path that Black had helped mark out earlier, this return may have seemed more of a fresh start than it actually was.[22]

Also, in both the nineteenth and the twentieth centuries, speech suppression was particularly brutal and pervasive in the American South. The *Sullivan* case from Alabama, involving as it did the 1960s civil rights movement—in particular, friends and allies of Dr. Martin Luther King, Jr. —was a more emblematic case of state repression and federal judicial protection than the earlier *Bridges* case from California. (The regional and racial aspects of Warren Court free-expression case law as a whole were nicely captured in the very title of one of the best modern books on constitutional law: Professor Harry Kalven's 1965 classic *The Negro and the First Amendment*.) But it was an *Alabamian*, Hugo Black, as much as anyone, and far more than almost everyone, who saw the problem of press censorship and speech suppression early on—perhaps because of his intimacy with southern practices—and who laid the foundations upon which *Sullivan* and similar Warren Court cases built.

In some (but not all) academic circles, it is fashionable today to link Hugo Black with First Amendment absolutism—"'no law' means *no law*"—and then to mock that absolutism with clever hypotheticals.* But *Bridges* featured language that was not quite absolutist in tone: Black's statement that "the substantive evil must be extremely serious and the

---

* For a textbook example of precisely this criticism leveled at Black, see Cass R. Sunstein, "The Most Overrated Supreme Court Justice," *Bloomberg View*, Apr. 22, 2014. It is worth noting that Professor Sunstein, an eminent graduate of Harvard Law School, holds a distinguished chair at Harvard and indeed previously served as Harvard's Felix Frankfurter Professor of Law. Weeks before publishing his slashing critique of Hugo Black—whom he described as the "most overrated" justice of all time—Professor Sunstein unveiled his own list of the best Supreme Court justices. Cass R. Sunstein, "Home-Run Hitters of the Supreme Court," *Bloomberg View*, Apr. 1, 2014. Four of Professor Sunstein's eight nominees—Holmes, Brandeis, Frankfurter, and Brennan—were graduates of Harvard Law School.

degree of imminence extremely high before utterances can be punished" sounds rather like a balancing test, though one strongly weighted toward protecting expression. Thus, the main theme bridging *Bridges* and Black's later pronouncements was not absolutism as such, but rather the notion that political and religious expression deserves very strong judicial protection, especially when such expression condemns the established order. Professor Charles Reich (who clerked for Black and later lived in Black's home as a long-term houseguest) has argued that Black's rhetorical absolutism was a rather late development—a tactical response, perhaps, to the Court's dilution of other speech-protective judicial doctrines in the McCarthy era.[23]

Moreover, Black's later insistence on the grammatical absolutism of the First Amendment is far from the embarrassment that some scholars deem it to be. There are ways of understanding the words of the amendment to say what they mean and to mean what they say. As a matter of federalism, the words "Congress shall make no law" meant at the Founding that political censorship and religious regulation in the several states simply lay beyond the proper enumerated powers and purposes of Congress under Article I. And as a matter of rights, the First Amendment is indeed an absolute of sorts: within the realm political discourse, government generally may not ban anti-government opinion, or censor political expression in viewpoint-discriminatory ways. The amendment allows "speech" to be abridged, but not "the freedom of speech"—a system of discourse by which a democracy deliberates and governs itself, just as a legislature typically protects "freedom of speech and debate" on the legislative floor. In a well-functioning legislative assembly, "speech" in some sense may be abridged—say, by limiting each floor speaker to five minutes—but "the freedom of speech" should not be abridged. Thus, if speaker A is allowed to support administration policy X, speaker B must be allowed to condemn that same policy. Similarly, in cases like *Bridges* and *Sullivan*, if pro-government public speech was allowed, anti-government public speech should likewise be permitted.[24]

For redirecting us to the words of the amendment itself, and for encouraging Americans to think about how the words might be taken seriously and what principles might underlie them, Black deserves our thanks, not our sneers. In a classic article entitled "The First Amendment is an Absolute," the great First Amendment scholar Alexander Meiklejohn graciously bowed to Justice Black. (Meiklejohn had rather harsher things to say about Justice Holmes's decidedly mixed contributions to First

Amendment theory and practice.) Although Black and Meiklejohn may not have agreed in all particulars, their views substantially overlapped, both in method—taking the words of the document seriously—and in substance—understanding the primacy of political expression and political dissent in a self-governing democracy.[25]

IN STRESSING THE NEED to protect political expression, especially speech critical of government officialdom (including the judiciary itself), Black in *Bridges* was ahead of many of his brethren. A similar pattern is evident elsewhere. On a wide range of issues, Black was a prophet who often began in dissent or in relative obscurity only later to see his views prevail as ultimate and enduring Court orthodoxy.

For example, Black was one of the first on the modern Court to rediscover the Article I attainder clauses, and their possible use to protect political dissenters from legislative attack. The key case here was the Court's 1946 decision in *United States v. Lovett*, in which Black, writing for the Court over the objections of Frankfurter, wielded the Constitution's prohibition on federal bills of attainder to strike down a congressional act disqualifying three named suspected subversives from federal employment. *Lovett*'s vision laid the foundation for a later Warren Court classic, *United States v. Brown*, authored by Chief Justice Warren himself (with some help from his law clerk John Hart Ely), in which the Court prohibited Congress from heaping retrospective disabilities upon members of a named political party.

Once again, note the obvious advantages, for a card-carrying textualist, of breathing life back into dormant constitutional clauses, and showing ordinary citizens how these clauses connected to the larger themes of the document itself and the Framers' vision. The attainder clauses had yet another advantage for an incorporationist like Black: the Constitution clearly held both state and federal government to the same standard, with Article I, section 9, prohibiting all federal bills of attainder, and Article I, section 10, likewise prohibiting state bills of attainder.[26]

Another prominent Black theme, expressed in many cases over the years, was the importance of the jury in both criminal and civil cases. Early in his career, Black had been a hugely successful lawyer practicing before Alabama juries; and his extraordinary empathy with ordinary citizens also served him well as a populist senator. Black brought these sensibilities to the Court, where he brilliantly reminded his colleagues, in various contexts, of the central role juries were designed to play in the Bill of Rights.

Recall that the Fifth, Sixth, and Seventh Amendments all directly protect juries (criminal grand juries, criminal trial juries, and civil juries, respectively); and that several other amendments offer indirect protection. (The First Amendment rule against prior restraints was largely designed to privilege juries against judges, as was the Fourth Amendment's regime limiting warrants; and the Eighth Amendment imposed special restrictions on setting bail and sentencing criminals in part because in these contexts, judges would typically act on their own, unchecked by juries.) Black instinctively understood how the jury was itself a great engine of democratic self-government, in which ordinary citizens in the lower house of the judiciary might help counterbalance a more elitist and not always trustworthy upper house of permanent judges.

The contexts in which Black led the charge for the jury were multifarious: Should jury-trial rights apply against state governments? (The incorporation question.) Should there be a petty-crime exception to the right of jury trial? Should judicial contempt orders be upheld as a general exception to jury trial? Should a jury acquittal on a greater charge be presumed to be an implicit acquittal on lesser-included offenses? On these jury-law issues, Black regularly found himself contesting Frankfurter. Black often lost the early battles, only to win major victories later on, as the Warren Court gained steam. He did not so much come to the Warren Court; the Warren Court came to him.[27]

A FINAL EXAMPLE of this dynamic, and one with a distinctive regional twist, involves the now-sacred right of indigent criminal defendants to have court-appointed counsel. When Black took his seat on the High Court, the most obvious precedent on the topic was *Powell v. Alabama*, the 1932 Scottsboro case. In a kangaroo trial, Black's home state had tried to hurry innocent young black men into the electric chair. In response, the Supreme Court had stepped in to insist that capital defendants must be given lawyers—at government expense, if necessary.

But what about *noncapital* felony defendants? In its 1938 opinion in *Johnson v. Zerbst*, the Court, per Justice Black, found such a right for federal defendants in the Sixth Amendment right of counsel. How about *state* felony defendants? Four years after *Zerbst*, in *Betts v. Brady*—a case that arose in Maryland, just south of the Mason-Dixon line—Black crusaded to hold states to the same constitutional appointed-counsel rule that governed the feds, and foreshadowed his *Adamson* position that all provisions of the Bill of Rights should apply against states with equal force. Alas, Black was in dissent in *Betts*; Frankfurter and his allies had the votes.

Fortunately, Black had the last word in 1963, when the Warren Court expressly overruled *Betts* and anticipated the incorporation revolution in one of the most lauded cases in history, *Gideon v. Wainwright*. In *Gideon*, a case that arose in the Deep South (Florida, to be specific), the Court mandated that all states provide appointed counsel to all needy felony defendants. At the time of this ruling, only five states were flouting this basic principle of simple justice. All five were located in the Deep South: Alabama, Florida, Mississippi, North Carolina, and South Carolina. A century earlier, the four most southern of these five—South Carolina, Mississippi, Florida, and Alabama—had been the first four states to secede from the union after Lincoln's election.[28]

Black—the only midcentury justice who came from this region—spoke for the Court in this great case, forcefully repudiating the outlying practices of the Deep South. Once again, he had held true to his vision, and the Court eventually came around.

THE TEAM MVP?
HUGO BLACK AND THE WARREN COURT

Baseball features a nice blend of isolatable individual performance and cooperative team play. The same is true of the Supreme Court. Each of the nine members makes a distinct and often individually measurable contribution to an interactive group product. It is thus natural to ask the question: Who was the most valuable player on the Warren Court team?

An obvious answer is Warren himself. The great chief was undoubtedly the team captain, its formal leader. But was he truly the greatest athlete on the field? Another obvious answer is William Brennan, who in the mid-1960s rarely found himself in dissent, and often was tapped to write the key opinions and keep the majority coalition together. But how much of Brennan's contribution was genuine intellectual leadership, and how much mere tactical adroitness? True, Black was in dissent much more than Brennan during the high tide of the Warren Court—but, as we have seen, judicial leadership often begins in dissent. Though law fans can endlessly debate the issue (that's part of the fun), a forceful case can be made for Hugo Black as the true *intellectual* leader—the most valuable player—of the Warren Court.[29]

CONSIDER THE SIX most important achievements of the Warren Court. First was the incorporation revolution. Although Brennan devised the tactical technique of "selective" incorporation, the big idea here was Black's, as powerfully presented in his *Adamson* dissent, authored six years before Earl Warren's accession and almost a decade before Brennan joined the team.[30]

Second and related was the Warren Court's revolution in criminal procedure. (Many of the previously unincorporated rights were rights of criminal defendants.) At its worst, the Warren Court provided unduly strong protection for the guilty as such in cases exemplified by *Mapp v. Ohio* (1961) and *Massiah v. United States* (1964). *Mapp* extended the exclusionary rule to states, thus vastly increasing the suppression of entirely reliable evidence. (Innocent citizens generally have no need for an exclusionary rule; the rule operates only if the government finds evidence of actual guilt.) *Massiah* also tossed out reliable evidence—this time, in the name of the right of counsel, even though the defendant in the case had a lawyer and freely chose, post-indictment, to blab about his crimes to individuals who turned out to be government informants. Though the Warren Court's exclusionary-rule cases were the target of fierce academic criticism, most of these cases continue to stand, half a century later, as pillars of modern constitutional doctrine, and the record should reflect that Hugo Black helped erect these pillars. In fact, he provided the decisive fifth vote in *Mapp* and wrote a key concurrence putting forth a principled, though ultimately incorrect, theory about why it was constitutionally proper to exclude reliable physical evidence obtained via unreasonable searches and seizures.[31]

At its best, the Warren Court nobly sought to protect *innocent* defendants from unfair trials that might *wrongly* find them guilty. This was a powerful and consistent theme of Black's opinions long before the Warren Court even existed, in cases such as *Johnson v. Zerbst* in 1938 (declaring a right to government-appointed counsel in federal criminal trials), *Chambers v. Florida* in 1940 (invalidating highly doubtful confessions of southern black suspects rounded up in a dragnet sweep), *Betts v. Brady* in 1942 (with Black, in dissent, voting to require government-appointed counsel in an ordinary state felony trial), and *In re Oliver* in 1948 (invalidating secret punishment meted out by a self-interested judge). And there is no more admirable exemplar of the Warren Court's revision of criminal procedure than Black's very own *Gideon v. Wainwright*.

A third major achievement of the Warren Court was its assault on Jim Crow. Part of the Court's criminal-procedure restructuring was doubtless motivated by concerns about racial injustice; but of course the centerpiece of the Warren Court's commitment to racial equality was *Brown v. Board of Education*. The great chief spoke for the Court here and in *Brown*'s companion case, *Bolling v. Sharpe*. (Brennan was not yet on the Court.) Warren showed remarkable leadership in keeping the Court unanimous in these cases.[32]

But we should not overlook Black's role here. Here was a justice from the Deep South—the only justice on the Court from this region—standing with his northern, western, and border-state colleagues. Black suffered more criticism for *Brown* from his social circle—from old friends in his home state—than did any other justice. Yet he was among the Court's most stalwart crusaders for racial justice, confounding early critics, who feared that this former Klansman would never join an opinion like *Brown*. True, Black had been a Klansman early on—he joined many organizations as an ambitious young man seeking to further his political career—but he had never inhaled the toxic fumes of racial or religious hatred.*[33]

A fourth major accomplishment of the Warren Court was the reapportionment revolution, proclaiming an end to gross malapportionment. This campaign for electoral equality—each person's vote should count the same—both reinforced and went beyond the Court's crusade for simple racial equality. Some of the grossest malapportionments of the era privileged southern rural whites at the expense of urban blacks. But the one-person, one-vote principle swept beyond race and the South, affirming a broader equality ideal of national scope. The Court's two best-remembered decisions on the matter are *Baker v. Carr* in 1962 and *Reynolds v. Sims* in 1964. Justice Brennan spoke for the Court in *Baker*; Chief Justice Warren in *Reynolds*.

---

* My claims about Black's general freedom from bigotry, both before and during his time on the Court, are based on my extensive readings of things written by and about Black, and many interviews that I have conducted over the years with persons who knew Black intimately.

Here, too, Black played a decisive though now underappreciated role. In the early 1964 case of *Wesberry v. Sanders*, which invalidated Georgia's malapportioned *congressional* districts, Black spoke for the Court—after *Baker* had been handed down but before *Reynolds* had been decided. Construing the word "people" in strong populist fashion, Black insisted that when the Constitution provided in Article I, section 2, that members of the House of Representatives must be elected by "the People of the several States," the animating principle was that, "as nearly as practicable, one person's vote in a congressional election is to be worth as much as another's."

Black's specific textual and historical arguments may be questioned—especially his effort to smuggle Reconstruction sensibilities into the Founding text, without open acknowledgment, in yet another case arising in the Deep South (this time, Georgia). Nevertheless, Black's basic structural intuition seems sound: in a republic of equal citizens, votes should generally count equally, lest government be captured by an entrenched, self-perpetuating oligarchy within the electorate.[34]

Although often relegated to a footnote in modern casebooks showcasing *Baker* and *Reynolds*, *Wesberry* is the key conceptual case of the three. *Baker* merely ruled that the state legislative malapportionment claim before the Court was suitable for judicial resolution. To be sure, this was an important move, sidestepping an earlier 1946 plurality opinion by Frankfurter, *Colegrove v. Green*, which had held that judges had no business even hearing malapportionment cases. Black had dissented in *Colegrove*, proclaiming that the Constitution spoke of a right to vote, and thereby implied a right to have each vote counted equally—an early judicial endorsement of the one-person, one-vote rule: "[T]he Constitutionally guaranteed right to vote and the right to have one's vote counted clearly imply the policy that state election systems, no matter what their form, should be designed to give approximately equal weight to each vote cast." But Brennan's *Baker* pointedly declined to lay down a global one-person, one-vote rule—it deferred that question for another day, and some justices who joined the Brennan majority opinion in *Baker* explicitly disavowed one-person, one-vote as the constitutional benchmark.[35]

Thus, the first Court majority opinion to announce the voting equality rule in a legislative apportionment context of broad application—the first majority opinion to embrace Black's prophetic 1946 *Colegrove* dissent—was Black's own 1964 majority opinion in *Wesberry*, involving malapportioned congressional districts. *Wesberry* basically echoed the *Colegrove* dissent, and the still-later case of *Reynolds* in some ways merely echoed *Wesberry*—in effect, "incorporating" the rule for federal elections to state elections via the Fourteenth Amendment in keeping with Black's larger incorporationist framework. Warren's opinion for the Court in *Reynolds* itself framed the issue in just this way: "*Wesberry* clearly established that the fundamental principle of representative government in this country is one of equal representation for equal numbers of people, without regard to race, sex, economic status, or place of residence within a State. Our problem, then, is to ascertain, in the instant cases, whether there are any constitutionally cognizable principles which would justify departures from the basic standard of equality among voters in the apportionment of seats in state legislatures."[36]

Fifth, the Warren Court revolutionized the nature of public education by ousting government-led prayer from public schools. This line of decisions, too, exemplified a broader equality idea—government should not be in the business of naming some voters or some races or some religions as better than others, or of openly segregating public school students along religious lines. Here the lead Warren Court case is *Engel v. Vitale*, decided in 1962, and it was Justice Black who spoke for the Court. In doing so, he built on and refined his earlier 1947 opinion in *Everson v. Board of Education*, authored well before Earl Warren or William Brennan had appeared on the scene.[37]

The *Everson* case involved a government program that subsidized school buses for all private nonprofit schools—both parochial and secular. Formally, the program did not involve special treatment for any one religion or even for all religions. It gave religion equal treatment, not special treatment, and Black led his colleagues to uphold this practice in an opinion that powerfully stressed this neutrality theme. The buses, Black repeatedly observed, were part of a "general program" that aided all private nonprofit schools and children "regardless of their religion." The First Amendment required neutrality, not hostility, toward religion: "State power is no more to be used so as to handicap religions than it is to favor them." Black's *Everson* opinion did contain some loose language, but its basic logic was sound, as was its holding on its facts.

Likewise sound was *Engel*'s holding on its facts, striking down government-led prayer in public schools. Unlike the bus policy in *Everson*, *Engel*'s facts flunked the equality/neutrality test: the very idea of government-led *prayer* privileged religion *as such*, and openly took sides among religions in an explicitly religious context. In a notoriously marshy area of law, where so many fine justices have gotten lost, Black reached the right result in both cases and for the right reasons.* The laws at issue in these two cases were subtly but critically different, and Black saw the difference, leading the Court to properly affirm one law while properly condemning the other.[38]

Sixth and last, in cases such as *New York Times v. Sullivan*, the Warren Court revived a broad right of peaceful political expression—yet another right that Black had championed long before there was even such a thing as the Warren Court. Similarly, today's robust judicial protection of arguably incendiary speech—speech that advocates abstract violence or lawbreaking, but in situations where the threat of actual violence or lawbreaking is not imminent—approximates Black's dissenting opinion in the 1951 case of *Dennis v. United States*. (In *Dennis*, Frankfurter and Jackson, among others, had sided against Black and against the free-expression claim.) The key modern ruling is the 1969 case of *Brandenburg v. Ohio*, in which the Warren Court, joined by Black, effectively buried *Dennis*, which had allowed the punishment of leading Communists for their abstract advocacy of violent governmental overthrow.

BUT IF ALL THIS IS SO, why is Black's leadership not universally understood and applauded today? Part of the problem, as I have repeatedly hinted, is that one of America's largest and most influential law schools, located across the river from Fenway Park, has tended to root for its own—Holmes, Brandeis, Frankfurter, and Brennan, most prominently. Far from being a Harvard man, Black was the leading antagonist of Harvard's famous (and overrated) professor Felix Frankfurter. When Frankfurter's star began to fade, it was easier for many Harvard graduates to transfer their

---

* Felix Frankfurter and Robert Jackson must be counted among the lost in *Everson*: Along with two other lesser-known justices, both men dissented and voted to invalidate the formally neutral bus subsidy. Frankfurter is a particular puzzle. In the 1943 case of *West Virginia State Board of Education v. Barnette*, he had insisted (in sole dissent) that public school children could be expelled if they refused, as a matter of conscience, to engage in a stiff-armed classroom flag salute. Thus in Frankfurterland, government may punish children in public school for their opinions, but may not help children attend private school. Go figure.

admiration to their fellow Harvard graduate, William Brennan, than to admit that the unwashed Alabamian had been right all along.*[39]

More generally, Black's homespun southern style and scanty academic credentials (about which I shall say more in the next chapter) led many prominent Yankee mandarins to dismiss him, quite erroneously, as an embarrassing simpleton. A century earlier, Lincoln, too, was similarly misjudged and underestimated early on by several leading and highly educated northeasterners. Also, most accounts of the Warren Court tend to begin with Warren's accession to the Court, thereby excluding Black's pre-Warren opinions from the frame of analysis. And at the other end of his career, Black did not shine in the last few years before his death in 1971. Arteries harden, alas.[40]

Finally, some modern scholars might seek to expand my list of six Warren Court themes to include the right of sexual privacy. The big Warren Court case on this topic is *Griswold v. Connecticut*, decided in 1965, and it is hard to see Black as the Court's leader here. After all, he dissented. Although a robust vision of sexual privacy was the brainchild of the Burger Court more than the Warren Court, Black's hostility to the ground-laying *Griswold* decision must be weighed, and weighed negatively, as a part of his overall record.[41]

Black's dissent in *Griswold* forcefully expressed his long-standing objection to the idea that judges could properly use their own subjective intuitions to invalidate acts of democratically accountable legislatures. Fair enough. But the Constitution's text itself, in both the Ninth and the Fourteenth Amendments, does gesture toward unenumerated rights of some sort. Black slighted these words, overlooking plausible ways in which these texts can in fact be given proper judicial weight and meaning without sliding into pure judicial subjectivity in situations involving unenumerated

---

* Constitutional scholars who have celebrated Black or consciously followed in his footsteps include William Winslow Crosskey, John P. Frank, Charles Reich, John Hart Ely, Jim Simon, Michael Kent Curtis, Walter Dellinger, Philip Bobbitt, Richard Aynes, and Steve Calabresi. I am squarely in this tradition. Interestingly enough, all of us except Curtis and Aynes graduated from Yale Law School. By contrast, here is a list of famous scholars and judges who have either expressly disparaged Black or omitted him from their pantheons while lauding lesser justices: Charles Fairman, Morton Horwitz, Richard Posner, Cass Sunstein, Ruth Bader Ginsburg, John Roberts, and Elena Kagan. All these notables studied at Harvard Law.

rights. But even in dissenting in a case that today seems so obviously right on its facts, Black has something valuable to teach us—namely, the desirability of connecting judicial doctrine to the text, history, and structure of the document itself as distinct from the personal predilections of nine old judges.[42]

STATS, STYLE, AND THE HALL OF FAME

The Warren Court redefined modern constitutional law, and Hugo Black provided that Court's intellectual backbone. Above and beyond Black's many substantive contributions, we should not miss Black's general methodological insights. The Constitution is the people's document, not the judges'. It was ordained and established by "We the People" and amended over the years by the people, often at the behest of mass movements of ordinary citizens—abolitionists, woman suffragists, the Progressives, the 1960s civil rights activists. Black read this populist document in populist ways, celebrating the rights of the people and cautioning judges not to trust too much to their own wisdom. He believed in the Constitution— and he helped the rest of us believe in it, too. Like many of the great ones, he played the game with style.

Over the run of his extraordinary tenure on the Court, spanning an astonishing five decades—from the late 1930s to the early 1970s—Black had many bad days, of course.[43] So did all his colleagues. No justice bats a thousand or anything close to it. But very few have been as good as Alabama's Hugo Black.

CHAPTER 3

NEW YORK:
ROBERT JACKSON AND
THE JUDICIALIZATION OF THE JUDICIARY

R obert Jackson makes most short lists of the greatest Supreme
Court justices of all time—a remarkable achievement for a man
who never served as chief justice and who occupied the bench
for only a dozen years. Though Jackson's lifetime contributions do not
equal those of his sometime rival Hugo Black, whose long judicial service
bracketed Jackson's much shorter stint, Jackson offers a particularly nice
window onto the larger story of Supreme Court continuity and change
over the past century.[1]

In several ways, Jackson foreshadowed our current Court. He wrote
with style and flair—better than any of his peers or precursors, with the
possible exception of John Marshall—and in this respect he set a high
bar for all that followed. On today's Court, Antonin Scalia, Anthony
Kennedy, John Roberts, and Elena Kagan regularly use their pens to
slash or soar or sing, and do so, I suspect, with Jackson as their conscious
model.[2]

Moving from style to substance, we should note that two of the most
distinctive themes of the Court's jurisprudence over the past half-cen-
tury have been its strong interest in policing the separation of powers
and its special fondness for free-speech rights. The most notable cases
of our era surely include the separation-of-powers landmarks of *United
States v. Nixon* (the Nixon Tapes Case) and *INS v. Chadha* (the legisla-
tive-veto case); the corporate-free-speech case of *Citizens United v. FEC*;
and two separation-of-powers-meets-free-speech cases, *Buckley v. Valeo*
(a key campaign-finance case) and *New York Times Co. v. United States*

(the Pentagon Papers Case). On these topics, Robert Jackson got there first and set the model. In separation-of-powers law, no opinion has been more influential than Jackson's concurrence in the 1952 Youngstown Steel Seizure Case; and in free-speech law, something similar could be said of Jackson's opinion for the Court in the 1943 compulsory flag-salute case of *West Virginia State Board of Education v. Barnette*.[3]

And then there is geography. Jackson grew up, went to school, and established his law practice in New York—the home-state of Franklin Roosevelt, who appointed Jackson to both the cabinet and the Court, and the state where Jackson's remains now rest in peace. In his later years on the bench, Jackson was one of only two members of the Court who grew up in New York; today, that number is five. So in this way, too, Jackson presaged the modern Court.[4]

Jackson can also be seen as the judicial sire and grandsire, so to speak, of the two men who between them have occupied the key position of chief justice for the past quarter-century. William Rehnquist, who became chief justice in 1986, began his judicial career as one of Jackson's law clerks; and when Rehnquist died in 2005, the job of chief went to one of his own former law clerks, John Roberts, who, by the way, was born and spent his early school years in Jackson's home base—upstate New York.[5]

So in several respects it could be said that we are now living, judicially speaking, in the Age of Jackson.

And yet, by other measures, the current Court, by training and temperament, is miles away from Robert Jackson. Jackson had no judicial experience before joining the Court. He had never been a judge. He had never been a judicial law clerk. He had not gone to a fancy law school specializing in training would-be judges. He did, however, bring to the Court a wealth of high-level political experience, having served as FDR's attorney general, among other things. By contrast, all but one of the members of the current Supreme Court were federal appellate court judges before they became justices. Most began their legal careers as law clerks; and every one of them attended an elite law school specializing in training aspiring judges. None of them has ever served in the president's cabinet; none has ever been elected to the House or the Senate or to any important city or state office.

In short, we are witnessing an emerging new form of separation of powers featuring a far more pronounced separation of careers. The political career track and the judicial career track are being pulled apart, at least for would-be justices. Increasingly, those who aspire to sit where Jackson eventually sat—on the highest court in our land—must follow an entirely different path to power: a judge-centered legal education at a place such as Harvard or Yale or Columbia, one or two early judicial clerkships, a career of service as a lower-court judge, and no cabinet experience or comparably high-level political service. The current Supreme Court replenishment process seems far closer to a bureaucratic civil-service model than it was in Jackson's time. Whereas Jackson came to the Court horizontally—from outside the judiciary and late in life—today's justices all moved up vertically: within the judiciary, grabbing onto jobs lower down in the third branch at a much earlier stage of their careers, and then climbing up the judicial ladder. I call this emerging phenomenon "the judicialization of the judiciary."[6]

GETTING ON TRACK:
LAW SCHOOL AND CLERKSHIPS

Robert Jackson did not attend Harvard Law School or Yale Law School or Columbia Law School or anything of the sort. By modern standards, he had a remarkably short and distinctly humble formal legal education. After graduating from high school in upstate New York in 1909, Jackson did not go to college. He spent only a year in an academic legal setting, as a student at the Albany Law School in 1911–1912. He joined the bar the old-fashioned way, via an extended apprenticeship with a two-person law firm in his home district on the south shore of Chautauqua Lake.

Jackson's educational story was hardly unique among those who rose to meteoric constitutional heights in nineteenth- and early twentieth-century America. Abraham Lincoln had no more than a year's formal education—not higher education, mind you, but total official schooling—in his entire life, and never attended a day of college or law school. He, too, learned law the old-fashioned way—by reading law books, such as Blackstone's *Commentaries*, on his own; by carefully observing proceedings in local courthouses; and by working with more experienced local lawyers who taught him the ropes.

The man that Jackson sometimes saw as his leading rival on the Court—Hugo Black—had more in common with Jackson than either probably cared to admit. Each grew up far from the bright lights of a big city. Neither received a standard college education, and each spent much less than the now-universal three years as a student at a home-state law school—in Black's case, the University of Alabama at Tuscaloosa. Each man was largely self-taught and climbed up through the ranks as a successful local private lawyer, government attorney, and politico (though, as we shall see, the nature of their pre-Court political experience differed in key ways).[7]

Now flash forward to today's Court. Every single justice graduated from a four-year college and then spent three years in law school. (Two studied at Oxford in between college and law school, a third did his final year of college at the London School of Economics, and a fourth spent his junior year at the University of Fribourg.) Not only did every current justice go to college; every single one attended an extraordinarily selective and elite college. Three chose Princeton (or perhaps I should say Princeton chose them); two graduated from Stanford; one went to Harvard; one was schooled at Cornell; one studied at Holy Cross; and one took his degree from Georgetown. *Every one of the current justices started his or her formal legal training at either Harvard Law School or Yale Law School.* (For spousal reasons, Ruth Bader Ginsburg transferred to, and thus eventually graduated from, Columbia Law School.)[8]

To plot the same data on the map of America: *Fully two-thirds of the current Court spent their college years in New York or an adjoining state; and every single member of the Court went to law school in New York or a state bordering New York.*

What's more, four of the current justices became full-time law professors at some point between Harvard or Yale and the Court, and each of the four taught at one or more of America's fanciest law schools. One current justice (Ginsburg) taught at Columbia (among other places); another (Stephen Breyer) started and ended his professorial career at Harvard; yet another (Scalia) taught at the University of Virginia and the University of Chicago; and, not to be outdone, the most junior member of the Court (Kagan) taught at both the University of Chicago and Harvard over the course of her distinguished academic career, which included a highly successful stint as the dean of the Harvard Law School. To put it a different way, here are the schools that can with pride claim Elena Kagan as one of their own: Hunter College High School (one of New York City's most elite educational institutions), Princeton University, Oxford University, the University of Chicago Law School, and Harvard Law School.

IN SHORT, WE LIVE in a different academic, legal, and juridical world from the one that produced Abraham Lincoln, Hugo Black, and Robert Jackson. What should we make of this?

First, the constitutional greatness of Lincoln and Black and the near-greatness of Jackson should be constant reminders that constitutional law is a game that many can play and play well if they are smart and serious. A compact 4,500-word proposal came before "We the People" for their special approval at the Founding; ordinary Americans in 1787–1788 were expected to read the proposal for themselves and decide whether they were generally for or against it. The document's various amendments over the centuries have likewise been written in crisp, intelligible language designed to invite citizens into the process of serious evaluation and faithful interpretation. Some parts of the Constitution were especially designed for enforcement by juries acting alongside judges, thus driving home the idea that the document is not and should not be the exclusive province of mandarins. Although smart and serious interpreters will need to parse text carefully, read holistically, and pay close attention to history, one does not need decades of intense and single-minded advanced academic study to do constitutional law well. Constitutional law is not exactly rocket science or brain surgery.

A second point (in slight tension with the first) is that smart and serious constitutional interpretation does require a knowledge base— especially a deep familiarity with the history of the Constitution's framing, amendment, interpretation, and implementation—and a facility with various tools and techniques of constitutional interpretation. But this substantive knowledge can be acquired, and these techniques of constitutional interpretation and analysis can be learned and perfected, outside of formal and expensive academic institutions. Lincoln, Black, and Jackson were all self-taught to a great degree. They routinely attended debates, sermons, and public lectures. They read books voraciously.

Third, when Lincoln, Black, and Jackson were young men, fewer law schools existed, and the ones that did exist typically did not specialize in American constitutional jurisprudence. It is unclear how much of an advantage formal law-school training was—or, conversely, how much of a disadvantage the absence of such formal academic training was—for early American lawyers who aspired to become expert constitutional interpreters. Not until the mid-twentieth century, long after Black and Jackson began their legal careers, did Harvard, Yale, and other elite schools each start to feature an extensive menu of course offerings in constitutional law taught by a sizable group of serious constitutional researchers and writers.

Finally, the admissions and financial-aid practices of our most elite colleges and law schools have evolved considerably since World War II. True, places such as Harvard, Yale, Princeton, Columbia, and the University of Chicago can be frightfully expensive these days. But America's most selective colleges and universities are no longer merely finishing schools for the scions of rich, famous, and powerful families. Many of our most prestigious educational institutions now offer generous scholarships to low-born youngsters of exceptional promise. If Lincoln were a midwestern farm boy today, he would go to free public elementary and high schools, from which he could win a full ride to a place like the University of Chicago. Today's Yale Law graduates on the Supreme Court include Sonia Sotomayor and Clarence Thomas, both of whom experienced serious privations early in life.

To put it slightly differently, if Lincoln were alive today, perhaps his career path would resemble . . . Barack Obama's. Our current president came into this world with few financial resources and little paternal support, but his Lincoln-like smarts and drive got him into Columbia College (note: a New York school) and Harvard Law School; and from these elite educational platforms, he ultimately rose to a position from which he could name the likes of Sonia Sotomayor and Elena Kagan (both New Yorkers, interestingly) to the highest Court in our land.

So we should not worry overmuch that the narrowing career path to the Supreme Court will keep out future legal superstars merely because they were born undistinguished or impoverished. But we should worry about the dominance of a few great schools.

Not because they are great, and not because they are schools. Mediocrity does not deserve proportional representation on the Court. And it is plausible to think that all future jurists should indeed have extensive and special academic training in law—not merely constitutional law, but many more technical legal subjects that may in fact be closer to rocket science and brain surgery. In many European countries, all would-be judges take special judicial courses in law school and must pass special judicial exams before they are eligible to become members of the judiciary. This rationalistic, bureaucratic, Weberian civil-service model may well simply be the way things are, or must be, in a well-functioning, complex, modern legal system.

But a future in which all the justices come from just two or three law schools should give us pause.* How good is any process of Court replenishment that squeezes all aspirants through a narrow gate early in life? Even if we think that many future justices should have begun their legal studies at Harvard or Yale, must they all have studied at these two great schools? Isn't there something to be said for a broader and more diverse pattern of legal mentorship? What about someone who didn't get into these schools and then bloomed brilliantly later in her legal career? What about those college grads who dislike New Haven's weather and don't love the Red Sox?

As for judicial clerkships: recall that Robert Jackson came to the Supreme Court having never served as a judicial clerk. The same is true for Hugo Black and for all the other justices who sat on the Court during Jackson's tenure, for the simple reason that judicial clerkships did not exist on a broad scale until later in the twentieth century. But nowadays judicial clerkships are a pervasive feature of the American legal system. On today's Court, more than half the justices began their legal careers as judicial clerks. Three clerked for the Supreme Court itself, and the two youngest members of the Court did two clerkships each. (Both of these Court youngsters— John Roberts and Elena Kagan—were born in the Empire State; Roberts did his first clerkship with a federal circuit judge in New York City, and Kagan did her second clerkship with a justice from New York.)[9]

STAYING ON TRACK:
LOWER-COURT JUDGESHIPS

Robert Jackson not only never served as a law clerk; he never served as a judge of any sort before winning a seat on the Supreme Court. He did not climb a career ladder within the judiciary itself.

In this respect, too, he was emblematic of his era. Jackson's colleague and rival, Hugo Black, likewise came to the Supreme Court with no judicial experience, save for an early and short stint as a judge on a local police

---

* Don't get me wrong: I love Yale Law School, where I have taught for the past three decades, and I greatly admire both Harvard Law School and Columbia Law School, where I have repeatedly taught as a visiting professor. So it would probably be good for me personally if all would-be justices had to take my courses and learn constitutional law the way I think it should be taught. But would this be good for America?

court. Apart from the rather forgettable former senator Sherman Minton, who had sat on a federal appellate court for several years, none of the members of the Court that unanimously decided the iconic case of *Brown v. Board of Education* in 1954—not Robert Jackson, not Hugo Black, not Earl Warren, not Felix Frankfurter, not William Douglas—had *any* experience as a federal judge prior to joining the Court.

Before Jackson's judicial grand-clerk, John Roberts, became chief justice in late 2005, the Court had always had at least one member who had arrived without prior judicial experience.[10] The histories of America's chief justices are particularly arresting. From John Marshall, who was appointed in 1801 and served until 1835, through Melville Fuller, who served from 1888 until 1910, *every one* of the nation's chief justices came to the Court with zero prior judicial experience. The same is true of Earl Warren in the mid-twentieth century. Also, three other twentieth-century chiefs—Charles Evans Hughes, Harlan Fiske Stone, and William Rehnquist—had initially come to the Court as associate justices wholly lacking any prior experience as a judge.

Of course, none of this means these various pre-Roberts chiefs were unqualified. Rather, their pre-Court credentials derived from distinguished service *outside* the judiciary. But before we ponder the credentials that earlier Court members did bring, let's pause to reflect on how different—how un-Jacksonian—today's Supreme Court is. *On the day that Samuel Alito replaced Sandra Day O'Connor in early 2006, not only was every justice a former judge, but each had been a (1) sitting (2) federal (3) circuit-court judge at the time of his or her Supreme Court appointment.* Never before in history had the Court been so deeply judicialized.[11]

Since 2006, the basic pattern has remained in place. Like every one of her fellow justices, New Yorker Sonia Sotomayor came directly to the Court from a seat on a federal court of appeals. But she was even more judicialized than her colleagues, for she had begun her career in the judiciary as a federal district judge. Thus, she had started her climb up the internal judicial ladder at a lower rung. While all her colleagues had simply moved directly up one judicial rung—from a court of appeals to the US Supreme Court—Sotomayor had moved up two rungs over the course of an even longer continuous judicial career: from district court to appellate court to the Supremes.

Put differently, no justice in history came to the Court with more continuous and varied federal judicial experience—seventeen years on the bench, spread across two different types of court—than did Sotomayor.

Even *before she reached the Supreme Court*, a still young and vibrant Sonia Sotomayor had spent several more years on the federal bench than Robert Jackson would end up having spent *at the time of his death*. Notably, one of the few justices in history who comes close to Sotomayor in years of previous federal judicial service is the man who immediately preceded her on the Court, Samuel Alito—a fellow Princeton College and Yale Law School graduate (though not quite a New Yorker, even if his lower-court chambers in Newark were pretty close). Never before had two back-to-back appointees brought so much combined federal judicial experience to the Court. The associate justice immediately preceding Alito, Stephen Breyer, brought fourteen years of federal judicial experience to the Court. As a group, these three consecutive associate justices have nearly fifty years of prior judicial experience among them. All these facts and figures furnish dramatic evidence of the continuing and deepening judicialization of the judiciary.[12]

The more recent appointment of Sotomayor's fellow New Yorker, Elena Kagan, does not mark a significant departure from the general pattern. Granted, Kagan came to the Court without having previously served as a federal judge. But she had served as solicitor general (SG) of the United States, the one technically nonjudicial position in America that is closest to being a judge. The SG is tasked with representing the United States in courtrooms across America, and in the Supreme Court in particular. For good reason, this officer is often called "the Tenth Justice"; he or she has a formal office inside the Supreme Court building itself, symbolizing the post's historically unique relationship with the Court.[13]

This nuanced view of Kagan's credentials invites us to return to Robert Jackson and to revise our initial assessment. True, Jackson was never a judge before he was a justice. But he *was* solicitor general for two years shortly before joining the Court. In this respect he is perhaps best seen as a pivotal figure. In some ways he resembled John Marshall, Hugo Black, Earl Warren, and many other predecessors and peers who came to the Court without experience on the bench; in other ways he presaged a world in which many of his successors and disciples would move up within the judiciary from formally judicial positions *or from technically executive yet rather judicialized* entities, such as the Office of Solicitor General and the Office of Legal Counsel (OLC). Jackson's clerk, Rehnquist, came to the Court with experience as the head of the OLC, and so did Antonin Scalia; Samuel Alito also served as a young lawyer in the OLC, though not as its head; and John Roberts not only spent years in the SG's office, but also briefly served as acting solicitor general.[14]

After Jackson, the next former solicitor general to become a justice was none other than Thurgood Marshall—poetically enough, the man who argued and won the most famous case on which Jackson sat, *Brown v. Board*, and later the justice for whom Kagan herself clerked. (Marshall himself, in keeping with the larger pattern of judicialization, had been a federal appellate judge—in New York, interestingly enough—prior to his service as SG.)[15]

And speaking of Kagan's clerkship with Justice Marshall. . . . Recall that although Kagan was not a federal judge before she was a justice, she was a judicial law clerk—twice—at a very young age. If we count law clerkships as the first rung within the judiciary itself, Kagan should be seen as having started her formal judicial career in her twenties, even earlier than, say, Sotomayor. Whereas only one of the *Brown* Court justices (William Douglas, appointed directly to the Court at age forty) had *any* formal position within the federal judiciary before his forty-ninth birthday, eight of the current justices had held had a job inside the federal judiciary by the age of forty-one—and the ninth (Scalia) had by that tender age reached the head of the president's rather judicialized Office of Legal Counsel. Here, too, we see evidence of a separate and distinct judicial career track, one visible quite early (by historical standards) in the life of would-be justices.

SENATORS AND SECRETARIES NEED NOT APPLY

Although Robert Jackson was never a judge before he was a justice, he was a top cabinet officer—an attorney general who had worked intimately with, and reported directly to, the president of the United States. This key fact invites a close look at the other side of the career equation—the *nonjudicial* experience or lack thereof brought to the Court by its members, pre-Jackson and post-Jackson.

Among Jackson's colleagues, Hugo Black may not have been a sitting federal appellate judge when appointed to the Court, but he was a sitting US senator; two other members of the *Brown* Court—Sherman Minton and Harold Burton—had also come to the Court from the Senate (Burton directly and Minton via a post-Senate federal appellate judgeship).

Earl Warren had served as a three-term governor of California and in 1948 had come within a whisker of being elected vice president of the United States, as the running mate of New York governor Thomas Dewey. Tom Clark, another *Brown* Court justice, had, like Jackson, served as US attorney general, and William O. Douglas had headed up a major and politically salient federal agency, the Securities and Exchange Commission. Among Jackson's predecessors, even those who could claim prior federal judicial experience could often also claim equal or even more impressive nonjudicial experience. There is, of course, no better example than William Howard Taft, who had served as president of the United States (and also as a federal circuit-court judge and SG much earlier) prior to joining the Court as chief justice in 1921.

By contrast, *none* of the current justices has ever served in the cabinet or been elected to *any* notable legislative or executive position—city, state, or federal. This is a wholly new phenomenon—yet another aspect of the judicialization of the judiciary. In 2006, Sandra Day O'Connor—who had come to the bench having previously served as Arizona's state legislative majority leader—resigned from the Supreme Court and was replaced by Samuel Alito. *Before Alito's replacement of O'Connor, America always had at least one justice who had brought to the Court high-level elective or ultra-high-level appointive political service.*[16]

For most of American history, this nonjudicial expertise on the Court was embodied in no less a figure than the chief justice, though he was often not alone. In addition to Warren and Taft, John Marshall, Salmon P. Chase, and Harlan Fiske Stone had all held top cabinet posts—as secretary of state, secretary of the treasury, and attorney general, respectively—prior to joining the Court. Chase had also served as a US senator and as governor of Ohio; and had come close to becoming president. Marshall, too, had served in Congress and had dreamed presidential dreams.[17] Chief Justice Roger Taney had held two top cabinet posts, first as attorney general and then as a recess-appointed treasury secretary. Before he came to the Court, Charles Evans Hughes had served as a popular governor of New York; and later he served a full term as secretary of state in between his two stints on the Court (first as associate justice, and later as chief). Before he rejoined the Court as its chief, Hughes had come within a few thousand votes of winning the presidential election of 1916, bringing him much closer to the presidency than Marshall and Chase before him—though not quite as close, of course, as Taft.

WHAT FACTORS EXPLAIN the apparent antipathy to former politicians in the current Court replenishment process?

Let's begin by noting the mushrooming size of the federal judiciary. Nowadays, there are more sitting federal judges than ever before for presidents to pick from. In the 1790s there were six Supreme Court justices and only fifteen lower federal court judges. Today, while the size of the Supreme Court has inched up to nine, the number of lower federal court judges has skyrocketed to nearly one thousand. Around two hundred judges now sit on federal circuit courts. The main job of each of these judges is to write appellate opinions on a multi-member court—a job rather analogous to that of a Supreme Court justice in an increasingly specialized, bureaucratic legal world. So it is not surprising that presidents might look first to this wide and deep first-level federal appellate bench when deciding whom to put on the second-level federal appellate bench, a.k.a. the Supreme Court.

Also, appointment of a sitting federal judge gives a president a unique twofer opportunity, creating a lower-court vacancy that the president can fill with a second (and presumably grateful) appointee. If a sitting federal appellate judge placed on the Supreme Court is in turn replaced on the appellate bench by a sitting federal trial judge, a president can turn a single Supreme Court vacancy into an opportunity to make three(!) judicial appointments. And when a president opts to fill a vacant chief justiceship with a sitting associate justice who is in turn replaced with a sitting federal appellate judge who in further turn is replaced by a sitting federal district judge whose position is then filled by yet another candidate, a mind-boggling four presidential appointments can occur thanks to a single judicial departure at the very top of the judicial pyramid.

Now factor in the dynamics of today's televised Senate confirmation hearings. Long and highly publicized confirmation hearings did not exist in the era of Robert Jackson. Television back then was in its infancy, though the Army-McCarthy hearings were a sign of things to come. Today, an extended televised Supreme Court nomination hearing is the main event in the circus big top, with the crowd watching breathlessly to see if any of the acrobats—either the nominee being questioned or one of the senators doing the questioning—will fall off the trapeze. In the gotcha game of Senate hearings, nominees are publicly quizzed on fine points of current Supreme Court doctrine filled with elaborate jargon and intricate multipart tests. In this game, sitting federal judges, and also sitting SGs, whose daily jobs involve applying Court doctrine, have an advantage over thoughtful lawyers in other parts of the government who may be less fluent in Court-speak.

And let's not forget the value of vetting and pre-confirmation confirmation. Every sitting federal judge has already been confirmed once by the Senate for a judiciary-related job—as has the solicitor general—but a typical governor or state judge, for example, has not. Although prior Senate confirmation does not guarantee an additional confirmation—just ask Robert Bork, himself a former SG and sitting federal circuit judge at the time of his unsuccessful nomination to the Supreme Court in 1987— prior confirmation does mean that a sitting federal judge knows the confirmation drill and also knows the drillers. Because most state judges, governors, and various other plausible Supreme Court candidates have never been confirmed by the Senate for any position, their nominations to the Supreme Court might introduce more wild cards into the confirmation game.

Sitting federal judges thus have an edge over state judges and governors, and also over senators, who were regularly tapped to sit on our highest Court for much of our nation's history. At the Founding, senators were picked by state legislators, rather than by the voters directly. In that era, the job descriptions of the Senate and the Court overlapped more. Both bodies attracted cosmopolitan lawyer-statesmen, and the antebellum Senate was renowned for high constitutional debate, featuring the likes of Daniel Webster, Henry Clay, and John C. Calhoun.

Today, the Senate is a more populist body attracting a different legislative persona—a telegenic politician good at fundraising, glad-handing, advertising, credit-claiming, headline-grabbing, sound-biting, and democratic campaigning, but rusty (or worse) in the various techniques of close legal analysis necessary for sound judicial decision-making and exposition. Whereas no fewer than three of the men who decided *Brown* alongside Jackson (Black, Minton, and Burton) had previously sat in the Senate, no senator has been put on the Court since that era—thereby creating some of the vacuum now filled by circuit judges.

Moreover, a modern senator who aspires to bipartisanship may face considerable political resistance within his own party. Most senators today thus have partisan records that would make it difficult to present themselves, were they to be nominated to the Court, as neutral legal experts who transcend politics. Openly partisan appointments have become hard to pull off in recent decades, when the president's party has rarely, if ever, had filibuster-proof majorities in the Senate. Unlike senators, circuit judges are never obliged to wear their partisan affiliations on their sleeves. Their official garb is neither red nor blue, but black, and thus they may be more easily packaged as Court nominees who possess wholly judicial temperaments.

In one key respect, however, recent developments may make it easier for future presidents to name future senators to the Court. In November 2013, a bare majority of senators conclusively established the principle—popularly known as the "nuclear option," and also referred to as the "constitutional option"—that a simple Senate majority may on any day modify or even eliminate extended Senate filibusters. Although this epic Senate ruling at present does not formally apply to Supreme Court nominations, future Senates are free at any time to extend this reform to encompass such nominations—and thereby embolden a president to name a given senator to the Court, so long as the president's party controls a simple majority of the Senate.[18]

THE DEEP ROOTS OF the current polarization of American politics, which has prompted both unprecedented filibustering of late and unprecedented filibuster reform even more recently, can be traced to the last big case of Robert Jackson's life.

The Court's unanimous 1954 opinion in *Brown*, decided a few months before Jackson's death in October of that year, helped put race back atop the American agenda. Although the political branches were initially loath to leap into the fray, the Court's direct challenge to apartheid and segregationists' strong counter-mobilization against the *Brown* Court's constitutional vision made the issue impossible to ignore indefinitely. In the Civil Rights Act of 1964 and the Voting Rights Act of 1965, Congress finally took a stand and emphatically sided with *Brown* and its allies.

Almost immediately, the New Deal coalition between northeasterners, southerners, and westerners—a coalition that men such as Robert Jackson, Hugo Black, FDR, and Lyndon B. Johnson had epitomized—began to crumble. (Note that this quintessential group includes two northeastern democrats and two southern democrats, one of whom could also claim to be a westerner.) In the *Brown* era, there were a fair number of liberal and moderate Republicans, exemplified by California's Earl Warren and Ohio's Harold Burton, and a vast number of conservative southern Democrats. The parties were not yet completely opposed and polarized. After 1965, southern blacks overwhelmingly became Democrats, whereas conservative southern white Democrats became Republicans. This change, in turn, pulled the Democratic Party to the left while pushing the Republican Party hard to the right. Liberal midwestern and New England Republicans got shoved out of the GOP, in effect, and drawn into the Democratic fold.

Few national Republicans today closely resemble earlier Republicans, such as New York's Nelson Rockefeller and Jacob Javits, who began their careers in the Jackson era. Centrists, such as Jim Jeffords in Vermont, Lincoln Chafee in Rhode Island, and Arlen Specter in Pennsylvania, felt obliged to leave the Republican Party. On the Court, Minnesota's Harry Blackmun, Illinois's John Paul Stevens, and New Hampshire's David Souter are emblematic of this shift—each one joined the Court as a northern moderate Republican and left as a de facto Democrat. (Each was appointed by a Republican president but timed his resignation in a way that enabled a Democratic president to pick his successor.)

The result of all this shifting has been a massive party realignment in which there are hardly any remaining liberal Republicans or conservative Democrats. The most liberal Senate Republican is now to the right of the most conservative Senate Democrat on almost everything—from Obamacare to you-name-it. In this hyperpolarized, post-*Brown*, post-Voting-Rights-Act world, it is hard for senators of one party to support senators of the opposite party to sit on the Supreme Court. So if we want to see a nontrivial number of ex-senators on the Courts of the future, we should probably embrace additional filibuster reform.

THE ADVANTAGES OF NONJUDICIAL EXPERIENCE

But why, it might be asked, should we want any ex-senators—or ex-cabinet officers, or ex-governors, or other sorts of ex-pols, for that matter—on our highest Court?

Although a Court overloaded with ex-pols would be unfortunate, it would be good to have at least one or two justices who have experienced firsthand how Washington really works at the highest levels—who have seen up-close and over many years how presidents actually think, how senators truly spend their days, how bills in fact move through the Congress, and so on. In short, it would be sensible to have at least one or two justices whose resumes resemble those of John Marshall, Hugo Black, and Robert Jackson.

One idea here is simple portfolio diversification: A multi-member Court works best with justices who bring different perspectives to bear on difficult legal issues. Of course, we don't want diversity along every dimension: no stupid or lazy justices, please! But within the group of smart and serious lawyers, just as we should not confine Court membership to graduates of Harvard and Yale, we should aim for some geographic diversity. (Recall from Chapter 2 that Hugo Black's southern background may well have inclined him to notice certain important constitutional truths that his non-Dixie colleagues had overlooked.) For similar reasons, our current Court would be tempered and strengthened by the inclusion of at least a couple of justices whose career profiles were slightly less judicialized.

Constitutional law, done right, requires the deployment of various tools and techniques of constitutional argumentation and analysis. No one technique works best across all the constitutional questions that have ever arisen and that will eventually arise. Some constitutional problems will be best solved with the tools of close textual analysis of a particular clause and holistic analysis of the Constitution's overall structure. On other topics, the original intent behind a particular provision may be especially significant and pregnant with wisdom. Still other issues may be better approached through the prism of prior judicial case law. Sometimes, however, text, structure, original intent, and precedent may not cast much light on the legal issue at hand, and interpreters should instead focus on past institutional practices among the relevant nonjudicial actors—settlements and agreements reached by differently situated political branches that have glossed an ambiguous constitutional text in ways worthy of judicial respect. Ex-AGs such as Robert Jackson and ex-senators such as Hugo Black may enrich the Court by brilliantly deploying tools and techniques of constitutional interpretation that lifelong judges may too quickly neglect or misuse.[19]

One virtue of appointing sitting federal appellate judges to the Court is that such judicialized folk are already masters at applying Supreme Court doctrine—precedent. This is what circuit-court judges do on a daily basis: They study and apply what the Supreme Court has said about this or that legal issue. One problem is that sometimes the Supreme Court's constitutional precedent is dead wrong. Sometimes it is baloney—not at all what the Constitution, *rightly* read, *really* means.[20]

But lower-court judges who daily eat and slice this doctrinal baloney may be particularly ill equipped to see the problem. Specifically, they may be inclined to think that judges are more right than they really are; and that other branches more wrong than is truly the case. Lower-court judges may be particularly inept at analyzing constitutional text, history, and structure, because that is not what they do on a daily basis. They do doctrine. They don't have the time or the training or the inclination to seriously examine constitutional issues as a matter of first principles. If they read the Constitution seriously and carefully, it might only confuse them—at least it might if the Supreme Court case law in a given area is out of sync with the Constitution's text and history. The job of a lower court is to follow the Supreme Court's precedents, whether right or wrong.

But the job of the Court itself is in certain situations to correct its past mistakes—to overrule or depart from erroneous precedents. (*Brown* famously and gloriously did not follow *Plessy*'s malodorous "separate but equal doctrine.") Someone who has not spent his entire life reading Supreme Court cases—who has instead spent quality time thinking directly about the Constitution itself (its text, its original intent, its overall structure and purpose), and who has also spent quality time in a nonjudicial branch of government that has its own distinct constitutional perspectives and traditions—may be particularly good at knowing judicial baloney when he sees it.

To test this hypothesis, let's consider some key decisions made by Robert Jackson; his sometime rival, Hugo Black; and his grand-clerk, John Roberts.

PERHAPS JACKSON'S GREATEST opinion was his concurrence in the 1952 Youngstown Steel Seizure Case. In that case, the Court held that President Harry Truman had acted illegally in seizing private steel mills in order to prevent an industrial strike (which threatened to halt steel production at a time when steel was vitally needed for American troops on the battlefields of the Korean War). Although Hugo Black purported to speak for the majority of the Court, he actually staked out a position that did not truly command the assent of the Court's center, which was represented by Jackson. It is Jackson's concurring opinion, and not Black's faux majority opinion, that has come to be viewed over time as canonical in the field of separation of powers.

Black argued that, in general, a president could not seize private property far from a theater of active war to settle a labor dispute unless Congress affirmatively granted the president authority to do so. On Black's view, the text of the Constitution was clear: the president has only "executive" and not "legislative" power, and the power to take private property in the situation at hand fell exclusively to the legislature. The history of actual governmental practice in the years between 1789 and 1952 was largely irrelevant, said Black; he refused to credit the Truman administration's legal argument that various past presidents, with apparent congressional acquiescence, had in certain situations done things similar to what Truman was now doing. "It is said that other Presidents without congressional authority have taken possession of private business enterprises in order to settle labor disputes," Black wrote. "But even if this be true, Congress has not thereby lost its exclusive authority to make all laws necessary and proper to carry out the powers vested by the Constitution 'in the Government of the United States, or any Department or Officer thereof.'" (These last words are of course drawn directly from the Constitution's text—a classic textualist flourish that was Black's trademark.)

To create the impression of a unified Court, Jackson purported to join Black's opinion; but in fact Jackson sharply disagreed with both Black's interpretive method and Black's central substantive conclusion, as Jackson made clear in his own separate concurring opinion. On method, Jackson explicitly condemned "the rigidity dictated by a doctrinaire textualism"—an obvious swipe at Black. Relatedly, Jackson suggested that the history of actual presidential practice and congressional reaction between the Founding and the Korean conflict—the history that Black dismissed out of hand—contained important insights about how best to construe the respective powers of the president and the Congress.

On substance, Jackson argued that Black had gone too far. There was no need to say, as Black had said, that a president must always have an affirmative congressional statute on his side to do what Truman had done. It was enough to decide the case, Jackson argued, to note that a congressional statute had in effect prohibited the very thing that Truman had done. Congress had already clearly said no, and Truman could not act in contravention of Congress. If Congress had merely been silent, however, then Truman might have prevailed, depending on various practical factors and settled customs.

Though I share Hugo Black's reverence for constitutional text, I confess that some issues cannot be resolved simply by textual analysis. The precise scope of presidential power is one of those issues, as I have explained in detail in my book *America's Unwritten Constitution*. The ultra-terse constitutional text of Article II must be supplemented by analysis of actual presidential practice, beginning with the practices of George Washington himself. Particular attention must be paid to how Congresses and presidents over the years have worked things out between themselves, thereby glossing ambiguous patches of constitutional text with institutional settlements among the very branches of government to whom and about whom the texts speak, albeit imprecisely.

And this is exactly the analysis that Jackson's *Youngstown* concurrence provided. Jackson did not shine at textual analysis in this opinion. At one point, he botched a key clause—the opening sentence of Article II, vesting executive power in the president—and needlessly undercut his own conclusions. But Jackson's opinion did subtly analyze the practices of prior presidents and Congresses. This was just the sort of thing that one would wish for from an outstanding attorney general experienced at advising the president himself about the proper scope of presidential power, and just the sort of thing that might have exceeded the skill set and the knowledge base of a lifetime lower-court judicial functionary (or perhaps even a senator such as Black) who had never advised a president day after day and face to face about high matters of law and statecraft.[21]

Jackson's *Youngstown* concurrence repeatedly called attention to his own past professional life. His opening words reminded his audience that he had served "as legal adviser to a President in a time of transition and anxiety," an experience that, he candidly confessed, was probably "a more realistic influence" on his view of the case than anything else, including the Court's prior case law. From his unique vantage point, judicial precedent was not the be-all and end-all that some blinkered lifetime judicialized folk might imagine it to be. "Conventional materials of judicial decision . . . seem unduly to accentuate doctrine and legal fiction," he wrote. Later passages echoed this opening theme, with additional and obviously autobiographical references to "executive advisers" and "presidential advisers."

Jackson and Black, whose biographies were in some ways quite similar, had disagreed in ways that their biographies might have predicted. Black, a former member of Congress, read the Constitution as giving Congress more exclusive authority and the president less concurrent power than did Jackson, a former executive-branch official and presidential lieutenant. But both Jackson and his rival Black did agree in result, and did so in a way that proved that neither was a mere pol. Both Democrat-appointed justices held that the Democratic president had gone too far.

Jackson took pains to stress that he was not bound as a justice to endorse all the things he might have previously argued as the president's lawyer: "A judge cannot accept self-serving press statements of the attorney for one of the interested parties [i.e., the president] as authority in answering a constitutional question, even if the advocate was himself." Once he was a pol (or a pol's mouthpiece); but now he was a judge. Black robes and life tenure freed Jackson to act in a judicial fashion even though he had not been entirely free to do so in some of his earlier assignments. In all these openly autobiographical musings by Jackson, we see that one of the most canonical decisions of all time was greatly and self-consciously enriched by the nonjudicial experience that one of its notable members brought to the bench.

NOW TURN TO THE GREATEST constitutional contribution made by Hugo Black, which perhaps also ranks as the greatest constitutional contribution made by any jurist in the twentieth century. Before Black came along, the Supreme Court's basic doctrine on one of the biggest constitutional issues in history—the proper legal relationship between the Bill of Rights and the Fourteenth Amendment—was, in a word, baloney. In his heroic 1947 dissenting opinion *Adamson v. California*, Black, as we have seen, took aim at the baloney and offered up a compelling alternative.

Jackson, alas, did not join Black's magisterial dissent. He didn't much like Black in 1947, and in any event he and Black—perhaps because of their different pre-Court experiences—tended to favor different tools and techniques of constitutional analysis. Each had a healthy skepticism of judicial doctrine. Each had seen, from his own nonjudicial perch, how clueless judges at their worst could be. But Jackson was inclined to focus on actual institutional practice and institutional tradition, in keeping with his many years of lawyerly service within a large institution called the executive branch. Black, by contrast, stressed the Constitution's text and history.

Just as Jackson was openly autobiographical in his classic opinion in *Youngstown*, so was Black openly autobiographical in explaining his own grandest contribution to the Court. Here is what Black said in a post-*Adamson* case elaborating on his epic *Adamson* opinion:

> [M]y *legislative experience* has convinced me that it is . . . wise[st] to rely on what was said, and most importantly, said by the men who actually sponsored the Amendment in the Congress. *I know from my years in the United States Senate* that it is to men like Congressman Bingham, who steered the Amendment through the House, and Senator Howard, who introduced it in the Senate, that members of Congress look when they seek the real

meaning of what is being offered. And they vote for or against a bill based on what the sponsors of that bill and those who oppose it tell them it means. The historical appendix to my *Adamson* dissent leaves no doubt in my mind that both its sponsors and those who opposed it believed the Fourteenth Amendment made the first eight Amendments of the Constitution (the Bill of Rights) applicable to the States.[22]

So here, too, it is clear that nonjudicial experience has greatly enriched some of the Court's most important decisions—and has done so in a way that the justices themselves have candidly acknowledged.

IT REMAINS, FINALLY, to bring these lessons up to date, and to explain their relevance for the current Roberts Court.

Recall that in some ways, John Roberts is rather like his judicial grand-sire, Robert Jackson, and in other ways he is quite different. Like Jackson, Roberts served as solicitor general—albeit very briefly, and technically only as *acting* solicitor general in a situation where the formal SG, Kenneth Starr, had recused himself. Like Jackson, Roberts brought to the Court years of service as a lawyer within the executive branch. But unlike Jackson, Roberts never reached the highest rung of executive-branch service. He was never an attorney general who regularly interacted with and personally advised the president.

Now consider the biggest judicial decision of John Roberts's career—his decision to provide the decisive fifth vote to uphold Obamacare in the 2012 case of *NFIB v. Sebelius*. As I have explained in detail elsewhere—long before the issue ever reached the Supreme Court—the Obamacare law, whether or not it is good policy, is easily and obviously constitutional. But in our hyper-polarized political world, various interest groups and politicos ginned up newfangled constitutional attacks that, frankly, fooled some otherwise admirable justices appointed to the Court by Republican presidents.[23]

But Roberts was not entirely fooled. Though he did say some weird and troubling things in his swing opinion for the Court, he ultimately voted to uphold this law as a simple exercise of the sweeping congressional power to raise revenue. Obamacare is, among other things, a tax law, and the Constitution was emphatically adopted and later pointedly amended to give Congress sweeping tax power. None of the other conservative justices credited this basic point, but Roberts did.

One reason that John Roberts may have been more able to see this basic point is that he had spent more time than had any of the other conservatives in executive-branch positions in which the tax power was highly relevant. Anthony Kennedy, the current justice who exudes the most confidence in the judiciary itself in his voice and votes, never worked in the federal executive branch, or in Congress, for that matter. Before joining the Court, Clarence Thomas had executive-branch experience only in matters far removed from the federal fisc. Both Samuel Alito and Antonin Scalia did have wider experience within the executive branch. But neither of them had anything close to John Roberts's many years of experience operating at a moderately high (albeit subcabinet) level within the executive branch dealing with a very broad range of complex federal laws raising revenue and regulating the economy.[24]

I doubt that Robert Jackson would agree with everything that his grand-clerk wrote in the defining opinion of his still-young career as chief. But John Roberts did reach the right legal result in this key case. And he did so, I suspect, thanks in part to his own moderately high-level executive-branch experience; and he did so even though the party that had put him on the Court was none too pleased with this act of judicial integrity. Somewhere, Robert Jackson is smiling.*

---

* Roberts is likely smiling back. For evidence that Roberts himself ranks Jackson high in his personal pantheon of judicial role models, see Laurence H. Tribe and Joshua Maltz, *Uncertain Justice: The Roberts Court and the Constitution* (2014), 262, 367n.21 (noting that Roberts "is a devoted Robert Jackson fan—perhaps an admiration passed down from his mentor Chief Justice William Rehnquist who had clerked for Roberts," and quoting Roberts in his Senate confirmation hearings as follows: "I admire the judicial restraint of Holmes and Brandeis, the intellectual rigor of Frankfurter, the common sense and pragmatism of Jackson and the vision of John Marshall.").

With these remarks in his confirmation hearings, it is clear that Roberts, as a distinguished graduate of Harvard Law School, shares the typical Harvard view of the judicial Hall of Fame. For a critique of this view, see the preceding chapter. Recall also that Roberts did his first clerkship with the great judge Henry Friendly—who himself was born in upstate New York, and whose chambers were in New York City; who, like Roberts himself (and Holmes, too), graduated from Harvard College and Harvard Law School; who, while a student at Harvard Law, was a protégé of then-professor Felix Frankfurter; and who then went on, thanks to Frankfurter's support, to clerk for Justice Louis Brandeis, yet another HLS graduate.

CHAPTER 4

CALIFORNIA:
ANTHONY KENNEDY AND
THE IDEAL OF EQUALITY

B y instinct, I am a Northern Californian; by training, a constitutional scholar. At times, I have wondered whether there is a tension between these two identities. Massachusetts, it might be said, gave Americans the Revolution, while Pennsylvania gave lovers of liberty the Declaration of Independence and the Constitution (not to mention a hall and a bell). Illinois gave us Lincoln; Ohio gave us a slew of presidents and, via John Bingham, section 1 of the Fourteenth Amendment; and, more recently, the Deep South gave us both Hugo Black and Martin Luther King, Jr. What, it might be asked, has Northern California given to our constitutional tradition?

One answer—my answer in this chapter—is Justice Anthony Kennedy, who was born, grew up, went to high school, practiced law, first took the bench, and taught for many years in California's capital city of Sacramento, not far from where I myself was raised.

Analyzing Kennedy's constitutional contributions, however, poses a distinct expositional challenge for me. Abraham Lincoln, Hugo Black, and Robert Jackson belong to the ages. Anthony Kennedy still belongs to the present, and will, I hope, for many years to come remain a vigorous figure in the ongoing development of American constitutional law. For me, Lincoln, Black, and Jackson have been heroic words and images on paper and screens, and the stuff of inspiring stories recounted by others— but nothing more. Anthony Kennedy, by contrast, has over the years become a three-dimensional mentor and friend.

The discussion that follows comes in two parts. In the first part, I reprise remarks that I publicly delivered in Justice Kennedy's hometown of Sacramento in 1996, sketching out my sense of his early opinions on the Court at a time when I did not know him well. In the second half of this chapter, I bring my portrait of Anthony Kennedy up to date by measuring the justice's more recent opinions against his earlier ones, and with the benefit of having observed him over the intervening years in various informal settings. My aim here is to show how a constitutional thinker's vision can both persist and change over time—how a long career can take intriguing turns. The first part is, to borrow from novelist James Joyce, a portrait of the justice as a young man; and as we shall see in the second part, much has happened in recent years. We live in interesting times.

An Early Portrait, Circa 1996

In a wide range of cases raising rather distinct doctrinal issues, Justice Kennedy has summoned up an attractive and often inspiring vision—a vision of truly equal citizenship in a diverse, pluralistic, boisterous, participatory democracy. It is a vision remarkable in both substance and style.

Substantively, these early Kennedy opinions enable us to see many facets of the equality ideal. Indeed, each case can be usefully seen through the lens of a different constitutional clause. Sometimes this clause explicitly appears in Justice Kennedy's analysis; other times, his imagery and instincts summon it up more subtly, perhaps even subconsciously.

Stylistically, Justice Kennedy tries to teach us about the Constitution by example. The Constitution is a tolerant document enabling diverse folk to live together as democratic equals. And so Kennedy's tone is consistently tolerant and measured—he disagrees with his colleagues on the bench without being disagreeable. The Constitution proclaims itself in the name of ordinary citizens—We the People—and so Kennedy writes clean, straight prose, with as little legalese as possible. Tellingly, in none of the early opinions that I shall now proceed to examine does a footnote clutter the page. The gist of his argument reads well in the *New York Times* and the *Sacramento Bee*. The justice is a teacher here; all Americans are his students, and he tries to reach us by using words and images we can understand.[1]

CONSIDER FIRST THE 1989 case of *Texas v. Johnson*. During the 1984 Republican National Convention in Dallas, Gregory Lee Johnson participated in a political demonstration to protest the policies of the Reagan administration and of some Dallas-based corporations. At the end of the demonstration, Johnson unfurled the American flag, doused it with kerosene, and set it on fire as the protesters chanted, "America, the red, white, and blue, we spit on you." Texas criminally prosecuted Johnson for desecrating the flag. Johnson claimed that the First Amendment (made applicable against states via the Fourteenth Amendment) barred such prosecution. The case reached the Supreme Court in 1989—near the beginning of Kennedy's tenure on the Court. In fact, he was the most junior justice in the case.

He was also the swing justice in the case, for his eight senior colleagues split four-to-four on the issue. As Kennedy went, so would go the Court. In the end, he went with the First Amendment claim, and he explained his reasons in an elegant six-paragraph concurrence.

It is an extraordinarily respectful and deferential concurrence. He begins by praising "the words Justice Brennan chooses so well" in the majority opinion (which he joins); but he also goes out of his way to tip his hat to "our colleagues in dissent [who] advance powerful arguments." Both of these are generous gestures. Brennan's opinion makes some powerful logical points, but the "words [he] chooses so well" do not really soar or soothe. Conversely, Chief Justice Rehnquist's dissent bubbles over with emotion and rhetoric, but is rather short on hard logic; judged by conventional legal standards of text, structure, doctrine, and logic, "shoddy" might be a more accurate description of its arguments than "powerful." But it is also a less charitable description—and, as noted, Justice Kennedy chooses the path of charity.[2]

Justice Kennedy aims his remarks not so much at his colleagues as at his countrymen. He is aware that many ordinary citizens will be "dismayed by our holding"—especially, perhaps, veterans "who have had the singular honor of carrying the flag in battle."

Why, then, does Justice Kennedy in the end choose their "dismay"? Not because he respects what Gregory Lee Johnson said and did. On the contrary, he pointedly distances himself from Johnson. He refers to him only as "this respondent," and wonders aloud about whether the respondent even possessed "the ability to comprehend how repellent his statements must be to the Republic itself." Rather, Justice Kennedy holds for Gregory Lee Johnson because: (1) Justice Kennedy is a judge, and a judge must follow the law, even when—especially when—the law protects someone the judge may not like; and (2) the law in question—the Constitution—protected what Johnson did, however loathsome. Ordinary people need to understand both points, and so Justice Kennedy tries to explain both in clear prose.

On the first point: "The hard fact is that sometimes we must make decisions we do not like. We make them because they are right, right in the sense that the law and the Constitution, as we see them, compel the result." On the second point: "It is poignant but fundamental that the flag protects those who hold it in contempt. . . . The fact remains that [Johnson's] acts were speech, in both the technical and the fundamental meaning of the Constitution. So I agree with the Court that he must go free."

Justice Kennedy's second point merits careful analysis. First, Johnson's antics were "speech," in both a "technical" and a "fundamental" sense. The justice is right on both counts, synthesizing principled formalism and honest realism. Technically, and fundamentally, Johnson *spoke*: "America, the red, white, and blue, we spit on you." And had he spoken other words, his overall performance would not have been flag desecration, but flag respect. Patriots burn flags every day—when a flag becomes soiled, one is *supposed* to burn it. But patriots burn flags with respect, speaking words such as the Pledge of Allegiance. And even without the particular words spoken by Johnson and his fellow protesters, isn't it true, both technically and fundamentally, that Johnson was being punished for the message he communicated? Of course, burning is an act—but that doesn't make it non-speech. A sign-language gesture is an act; typing an essay is an act; vocalization of words is an act; laser printing is an act—but these are all speech, too, both technically and fundamentally. To deny this, as the *Johnson* dissenters tried to do, is gimmicky, even unworthy.[3]

But even if Johnson's antics were "speech," why must they be absolutely protected? This brings us to Justice Kennedy's claim that because Johnson's "acts were speech . . . he must go free." In formal doctrinal terms—terms that Justice Kennedy avoids, perhaps because they seem a bit too sterile for a lay audience in this highly charged case—the Constitution bars "viewpoint discrimination," especially viewpoint discrimination aimed at political critics of the government or the established order. In Kennedy's more poetic formulation, "the flag protects those who hold it in contempt."

"But where does the Constitution say that?" a critic might press. Surely "speech" is not an absolute. Surely a person may be criminally punished for uttering the words "Your money or your life," or "I'll pay you ten thousand dollars if you'll pardon me, governor." Surely a person may be sued for an intentionally false statement of fact that destroys another's reputation. Why are the words "America, we spit on you," any different?

Justice Kennedy does not directly engage this imagined critic in his short concurrence; but the Brennan opinion he joins makes clear that expressions of opinion are very different from threats or bribes or false statements of fact; and that the protection of political opinion, especially anti-governmental political opinion, lies at the core of the First Amendment. Hence, there is a strict ban on governmental discrimination based upon political viewpoint. If it is permissible to say, "I support government policy," it must be equally permissible to say, "I oppose government policy," or even, "I despise—I spit on—government policy." Implicit in this ban on viewpoint discrimination is a rather powerful ideal of equality of a certain sort—equality of political opinion. And so, because the flag protects those who adore it, and so profess, it must "protect those who hold it in contempt."[4]

JUSTICE KENNEDY POINTS to no specific constitutional clause in his six-paragraph concurrence. He speaks of "the Constitution" and "the law," and of "the flag" as a metaphor for both. He also speaks of "speech"—an obvious allusion to the First Amendment's freedom-of-speech clause, the centerpiece of Justice Brennan's opinion. But the simple word "speech" should also remind us of the other freedom-of-speech clause in the Constitution—the Article I, section 6, clause protecting freedom of "speech or debate" in Congress.[5]

If we think seriously about speech and debate in a well-governed legislative assembly—a town meeting or a parliament (literally, a "speaking body," from the French *parler*)—we see further confirmation of some of Justice Kennedy's insights and instincts. First, and most important, a well-running assembly should not discriminate on the basis of political viewpoint. If speaker A can take the floor to support the war, speaker B must be free to take the floor to oppose it. *Speech* may be limited: say, to ten minutes per person. But *the freedom of speech*—understood here as a protection against viewpoint discrimination—is an absolute. And the First Amendment can be understood as extending this absolute freedom beyond the legislative assembly hall itself to the people "out of doors"— the ultimate National Assembly. This, in a nutshell, is the insight of the great speech theorist Alexander Meiklejohn.

The image of freedom of speech in a well-run assembly also helps illuminate other aspects of our First Amendment tradition. Through it, we can see that political speech—the stuff of legislative speech and debate—is structurally and historically central, deserving priority of place over, say, commercial advertising. We can see that content-based discrimination—reserving Tuesday for a health-care debate and Wednesday for a tax-reform debate, for example—is in some contexts more permissible than viewpoint-based discrimination. We can see that a working democracy requires not merely negative protection against state censorship, but also affirmative government action to promote free speech—to create the town hall or assembly room or other public forum where the freedom of speech can occur. Finally, the assembly model reminds us of another equality principle: speech rights should not simply track property or wealth distributions. Even if Ross Perot and Steve Forbes own more than the rest of us put together, they are not entitled to speak at the town meeting longer than the rest of us put together. Speech time in our assembly hall should be distributed more equally—a working man should get his turn, too, as Norman Rockwell so beautifully reminds us. "Speech" is not merely property; it is also democracy, and thus it must be allocated with an eye toward equality.

THESE LAST POINTS WERE also at the heart of Justice Kennedy's message in his 1992 concurrence in *International Society for Krishna Consciousness v. Lee*. In that case, the major New York City airports had banned both the solicitation of funds and the distribution or sale of leaflets inside the terminals. Four justices voted to uphold both bans; three other justices voted to strike down both bans. In the middle sat Justices Sandra Day O'Connor and Anthony Kennedy, who thought that the ban on solicitation could stand, and that the ban on leafleting must fall. Although they reached this result by different paths, together these two justices cast the decisive votes, siding with the four to uphold the solicitation ban, and with the three to strike down the leafleting ban. Once again, we see Justice Kennedy in the center; as he (and in this case, Justice O'Connor) went, so went the Court.

Justice Kennedy's opinion contains several noteworthy moves. For starters, he insists that judges should not be stingy in recognizing special "public fora" where vigorous free speech receives special judicial protection. A couple of years before *Krishna Consciousness*, Justice Kennedy had put the point as follows: "As society becomes more insular in character, it becomes essential to protect public places where traditional modes of speech and forms of expression can take place."[6]

In *Krishna Consciousness*, he pleads with his colleagues not to adopt a rigid historical test that would deny "public forum" status to new venues (such as airports) simply because these places were not historically or traditionally viewed as such: "Our public forum doctrine ought not to be a jurisprudence of categories rather than ideas, or convert what was once an analysis protective of expression into one which grants the government authority to restrict speech by fiat. . . . Public spaces and thoroughfares that are suitable for discourse may be public forums, whatever their historical pedigree and without concern for a precise classification of property."

Once again, we see a beautiful synthesis of principled formalism and honest realism. Justice Kennedy is not making up new constitutional principles, but trying to apply old ones to new contexts. The deep principles of freedom of the press must apply not merely to printing presses, but to airwaves and cyberspace. The Fourth Amendment must protect our papers, but also our hard drives; it must limit physical government trespass upon our homes, but also high-tech wiretaps. Old public fora may be withering away, Justice Kennedy warns, and so judges must be vigilant to protect new fora, like airports: "Without this recognition our forum doctrine retains no relevance in times of fast-changing technology and increasing insularity. In a country where most citizens travel by automobile, and parks all too often become locales for crime rather than social intercourse, our failure to recognize the possibility that new types of government property may be appropriate forums for speech will lead to a serious curtailment of our expressive activity. One of the places left in our mobile society that is suitable for discourse is a metropolitan airport."[7]

In a trio of passages, Justice Kennedy distills his substantive vision of the freedom of speech. First:

The liberties protected by our doctrine derive from the Assembly, as well as the Speech and Press Clauses of the First Amendment, and are essential to a functioning democracy. See Kalven, The Concept of the Public Forum: Cox v. Louisiana, 1965 S. Ct. Rev. 1, 14, 19. Public places are of necessity the locus for discussion of public issues, as well as protest against arbitrary government action. At the heart of our jurisprudence lies the principle that in a free nation citizens must have the right to gather and speak with other persons in public places. The recognition that certain government-owned property is a public forum provides open notice to

citizens that their freedoms may be exercised there without fear of a cen-
sorial government, adding tangible reinforcement to the idea that we are
a free people.

Second:

The danger of allowing the government to suppress speech is shown in
the case now before us. A grant of plenary power allows the government
to tilt the dialogue heard by the public, to exclude many, more marginal
voices. . . . We have long recognized that the right to distribute flyers and
literature lies at the heart of the liberties guaranteed by the Speech and
Press Clauses of the First Amendment.

Finally:

"It should be remembered that the pamphlets of Thomas Paine were not
distributed free of charge." . . . The effect of a rule of law distinguishing
between sales and distribution would be to close the marketplace of ideas
to less affluent organizations and speakers, leaving speech as the preserve
of those who are able to fund themselves. One of the primary purposes of
the public forum is to provide persons who lack access to more sophisticated media the opportunity to speak. A prohibition on sales forecloses
that opportunity for the very persons who need it most.

In all this we see again an effort to harmonize formal legal theory with
flesh-and-blood, embodied reality. In *Johnson*, Justice Kennedy paid tribute
to ordinary citizens who "had the singular honor of carrying our flag in
battle," and here he again summons up a vision of ordinary citizens in action. These men and women need real freedom of speech, not merely formal
freedom of speech. This is what the justice means when he speaks of "*tangible* reinforcement to the idea that we are a free people." (My emphasis.)
He shows particular concern for poor folks' speech—for "marginal voices"
and "the very persons who need [speech protection] most." A strict formal-
ist might see a total ban on airport leaflets as viewpoint-neutral—formally
applying to liberals and conservatives, establishment and nonestablishment,
rich and poor alike. But Justice Kennedy sees that this formal neutrality
masks a real-life skew—the "*effect*" (again, my emphasis) of the rule is to
selectively "close the marketplace of ideas," to "tilt the dialogue."

If, in *Johnson*, Justice Kennedy's rhetoric wafted in the direction of First Amendment theorist Alexander Meiklejohn, in *Krishna Consciousness* he is much more explicit. He expressly invokes the assembly clause alongside the speech and press clauses, vividly bringing to mind the image of a democratic assembly. He reminds us that the First Amendment is "essential to a *functioning democracy*." (My emphasis, again.) He pointedly cites Meiklejohn's ally and co-theorist Professor Harry Kalven. He accentuates the *public* aspects of speech—in "public places" on "public issues." The entire structure of his analysis reminds us that government's role is not merely negative, but affirmative. Government must not censor, but it must do more than this. It must nurture the public forum. As Meiklejohn reminds us in his magnificent midcentury book *Political Freedom*, government may not abridge the freedom of speech, but it may and must promote it.[8]

If, in the spirit of constitutional holism, we seek a clause beyond the First Amendment to reinforce this vision, I nominate the Article IV, section 4, republican government clause: "The United States shall guarantee to every State in this Union a Republican Form of Government." In its essence this clause is about democratic equality and self-government—reminding us that, in Kennedy's grand phrase, "we are a free people." The clause goes beyond formal viewpoint neutrality to address the real need for robust political participation of all elements of the republic. The clause is not merely negative but affirmative: Congress must affirmatively guarantee the conditions of a free republic. And the clause, of course, highlights the centrality of the *res publica*—the public thing. This, in the end, is exactly what Meiklejohn, Kalven, and Kennedy mean to conjure up with images like town meetings, public spaces, and public fora—places where we the people do our public "thing" of republican self-government through the give-and-take of public discourse.[9]

ANOTHER PLACE WHERE the people do this thing is the jury box. And this is a public forum about which Justice Kennedy has had a lot to say.

Historically, each lawyer in a criminal case could typically strike a given number of would-be jurors from the jury box, and the lawyer could exercise these strikes and challenges in a peremptory fashion—without having to explain why some persons were struck and others were not. (These peremptory challenges are not to be confused with challenges "for cause"—for proven bias of a would-be juror or for some other good reason, as decided by an impartial judge.) But today's so-called peremptory challenges are not, in fact, entirely peremptory. Ever since the Warren Court, it has been clear that certain sorts of peremptory challenges are impermissible.

In the 1991 case of *Powers v. Ohio*, an Ohio prosecutor had used peremptory challenges to keep seven blacks off the jury in a murder trial. The defendant, a white man, objected, claiming that the prosecutor was excluding those would-be jurors because they were black. The courts below held that even so, it didn't matter; in a trial of a white defendant, a prosecutor could intentionally exclude black jurors. The Supreme Court reversed, in an opinion by Justice Kennedy. Here are his inspiring opening words: "Jury service is an exercise of responsible citizenship by all members of the community, including those who otherwise might not have the opportunity to contribute to our civic life."

Once again, we hear an ode to ordinary citizens in a participatory democracy. In *Johnson* we caught a glimpse of citizens who had "the singular honor of" serving their country in war; and here we envision ordinary citizens serving their country in peace through "an exercise of responsible citizenship"—what the justice refers to later in *Powers* as the "honor and privilege of jury duty." In *Krishna Consciousness* we saw a vision of face-to-face "discussion of public issues" by ordinary citizens who "lack access to more sophisticated media"; and here we see a similar effort to include "those who otherwise might not have the opportunity to contribute to our civic life."

For Justice Kennedy, the key to the case is that, whatever exclusion does to defendants, it violates the right to democratic participation of the excluded jurors:

> The opportunity for ordinary citizens to participate in the administration of justice has long been recognized as one of the principal justifications for retaining the jury system. . . . [As Tocqueville remarked:] "I do not know whether the jury is useful to those who are in litigation; but I am certain it is highly beneficial to those who decide the litigation; and I look upon it as one of the most efficacious means for the education of the people which society can employ." Jury service preserves the democratic element of the law, as it guards the rights of the parties and ensures continued acceptance of the laws by all of the people.[10]

Justice Kennedy then goes one step further, linking jury service with voting: "[W]ith the exception of voting, for most citizens the honor and privilege of jury duty is their most significant opportunity to participate in the democratic process. . . . 'Whether jury service be deemed a right, a privilege, or a duty, the State may no more extend it to some citizens and deny it to others on racial grounds than it may invidiously discriminate in the offering and withholding of the elective franchise.'"

Justice Kennedy's explicit textual basis in *Powers* is the equal-protection clause of the Fourteenth Amendment; but his instinct that jury service is closely allied with democracy, political participation, and voting rights should remind us of the obvious relevance of the Fifteenth Amendment. That amendment, of course, explicitly bars government from depriving a person of the vote because of his race: "The right of citizens of the United States to vote shall not be denied or abridged by the United States or by any State on account of race, color, or previous condition of servitude." Technically and fundamentally, this command is violated by race discrimination in jury selection. In the jury room, jurors *vote*—that is what they do—and typically, ordinary voters have been eligible to serve as jurors, as Justice Kennedy notes.[11]

This insight helps explain the result and reasoning in *Edmonson v. Leesville Concrete Co.*, also handed down by the Court in 1991, a couple of months after *Powers*. In *Edmonson*, a private litigant had used peremptory challenges to keep two blacks off a civil jury; and the Court, per Justice Kennedy, struck down this allegedly race-based denial of "the honor and privilege of participating in our system of justice." The dissenters in *Edmonson* claimed that the discrimination was mere private prejudice, rather than state action regulated by the Constitution. But Justice Kennedy understood that the jury is inherently a public body: "Though the motive of a peremptory challenge may be to protect a private interest, the objective of jury selection proceedings is to determine representation on a governmental body."

Surely the state could not empower some newfangled cadre of private "registrars" to deny blacks the right to vote in ordinary elections. And once we see that voting for legislatures and voting on juries are intimately linked, as Justice Kennedy teaches us in *Powers*, we can see that "private" race-based peremptories must also fall: choosing who should vote on Election Day and who should vote in a jury box are inherently *public* functions and cannot be delegated to purportedly private parties free from constitutional constraint. Justice Kennedy reinforced his framework in *Edmonson* by invoking the White Primary Cases—a series of lawsuits from the 1940s and 1950s in which the Court invalidated racial discrimination in primary elections, even though this discrimination had occurred in electoral contests conducted by purportedly "private" (that is, nongovernmental) political parties.[12]

If taken seriously, this democratic, participatory vision of jury service linked arm-in-arm with voting argues strongly for the abolition of peremptory challenges altogether, even when these challenges are not based on race. We do not allow "registrars" to refuse to let some eligible voters vote; why, then, should we allow litigants to exclude those voters from their other democratic "honor and privilege," during which they learn to become better citizens? Though Justice Kennedy has not yet gone this far, this is, I hope, where his vision might ultimately lead. No willing citizen should be peremptorily excluded from the jury box.[13]

Or from her high school graduation, as our next case makes clear.

THE PRINCIPAL OF A public school in Providence, Rhode Island, invited a rabbi to deliver prayers at the school's graduation ceremony. The principal gave the rabbi a pamphlet setting out suggested "guidelines" for the prayer, and advised the rabbi to offer a "nonsectarian" invocation and benediction. As delivered, the prayers made no explicit reference to "the Bible" or "the God of Israel"; but they did use some scriptural language—from Micah 6:8, for example. Graduating student Deborah Weisman and her father objected to the graduation prayers on establishment-clause grounds; and in 1992, the Supreme Court agreed with the Weismans by a narrow five-to-four vote.

Justice Kennedy wrote for the Court. Once again, we see the justice as a swing vote; as he went, so went the Court. To a remarkable extent, his opinion avoids sterile legalese. Thus, in his opening paragraph in *Lee v. Weisman*, he explains to lay folk that the Fourteenth Amendment makes the religion clauses of the First Amendment "applicable with full force to the States and their school districts." A justice less sensitive to the fact that many ordinary Americans are listening in to this debate would probably have used the more technical—but less inclusionary—legal shorthand of "incorporation."

In a similar vein, a less populist justice might have processed the facts at hand through the so-called *Lemon* test—a formulaic, three-pronged, analytic framework first set forth by the Burger Court in a 1971 establishment-clause ruling, *Lemon v. Kurtzman*, and subsequently deployed, sometimes rather mindlessly, in various other establishment-clause cases. But Justice Kennedy instead explains his result to ordinary citizens more

directly: "These dominant facts mark and control the confines of our decision: State officials direct the performance of a formal religious exercise at
promotional and graduation ceremonies for secondary schools. Even for
those students who object to the religious exercise, their attendance and
participation in the state-sponsored religious activity are in a fair and real
sense obligatory, though the school district does not require attendance as
a condition for receipt of the diploma."[14]

Justice Kennedy then proceeds to unpack these points in language
noteworthy for its candor, its common sense, and its grasp of principle.
To explain his first point—that "state officials direct the performance of
a formal religious exercise," Justice Kennedy notes the following facts: "A
school official, the principal, decided that an invocation and a benediction
should be given; this is attributable to the state, and from a constitutional
perspective it is as if a state statute decreed that prayers must occur. The
principal [also] chose the religious participant, here a rabbi. . . . [Third,
via his guidelines and advice,] the principal directed and controlled the
content of the prayer."

To explain his second point—that attendance and participation in this
state-run religious ceremony were "in a fair and real sense obligatory," Justice Kennedy reminds us of some basic social facts. Attendance at graduation is not formally required, but who would want to miss it? This is an
event to bring us all together, not to separate and divide us by creating
insiders and outsiders: "Graduation is a time for family and those closest
to the student to celebrate success and express mutual wishes of gratitude
and respect, all to the end of impressing upon the young person the role
that it is his or her right and duty to assume in the community and all of
its diverse parts."

And so, in response to the government's claim that the graduation
ceremony prayer was not coercive because Deborah and her father were
formally free to opt out, Justice Kennedy politely but firmly says, in effect,
"get real": "Law reaches past formalism. And to say a teenage student has
a real chance not to attend her high school graduation is formalistic in the
extreme. . . . Everyone knows that in our society and in our culture high
school graduation is one of life's most significant occasions."

But even if attendance is in a real sense obligatory, is participation in
the state-run religious event required? Why can't Deborah simply stand
aside during opening and closing prayers? Because of the whole chore-
ography and atmosphere of the event, Justice Kennedy reminds us. Graduation is a time for all to come together; and given the reality of peer

pressure in high school, it is not fair to force some to stand apart—and thus stand out—on a day when all should stand together: "The undeniable fact is that the school district's supervision and control of a high school graduation ceremony places public pressure, as well as peer pressure, on attending students. . . . This pressure, though subtle and indirect, can be as real as any overt compulsion. . . . Research in psychology supports the common assumption that adolescents are often susceptible to pressure from their peers towards conformity, and that the influence is strongest in matters of social convention."

Led by Justice Scalia, the dissenters mocked Justice Kennedy's analysis here; but for me at least, Justice Kennedy better describes the reality of high school and graduation ceremonies—and better grasps the true constitutional principle at the heart of the establishment and free-exercise clauses. That principle, it must be stressed, is deeply respectful of religion, not indifferent or hostile to it. Precisely because religion is so important, government must keep its hands off. As Kennedy puts the point in an effort to explain the Constitution to ordinary Americans (most of whom are religious), "[t]he First Amendment's Religion Clauses mean that religious beliefs and religious expression are too precious to be either proscribed or prescribed by the State." Do we really want government bureaucrats in the prayer-writing business? Won't this lead to watered-down civil religion—nonsectarian mush—that may in the end hurt true faith? Madison thought so, Kennedy reminds his readers. In the justice's own words, "while concern must be given to define the protection granted to an objector or a dissenting nonbeliever, these same Clauses exist to protect religion from government interference." Thus, he closes his *Weisman* opinion by making clear that "we express no hostility to [religion] nor would our oath permit us to do so. A relentless and all-pervasive attempt to exclude religion from every aspect of public life could itself be inconsistent with the Constitution."

This, in fact, was Justice Kennedy's message in the later *Rosenberger v. Rector* case, where, speaking for five justices, he invalidated a state university policy denying funding to student religious publications, a policy that he believed discriminated against religious speakers. Taken together, *Weisman* and *Rosenberger* again remind us of the middle course Justice Kennedy has steered. Only he and Justice O'Connor were in both majorities.[15]

Kennedy's vision of the establishment and free-exercise clauses— and of the speech clause, too, in *Rosenberger*—places powerful limits on the government's ability to create a favored religious caste, a hierarchical scheme of insiders and outsiders. In Justice Kennedy's vision, no citizen should be excluded from equal citizenship and respect simply because of who she is, or what she believes or feels. This was also Justice Kennedy's basic message in our next case, *Romer v. Evans*.

IN 1992, THE COLORADO electorate passed a statewide referendum known as Amendment 2. In relevant part, it proclaimed that no state (or city or county) agency should treat "homosexual, lesbian, or bisexual orientation" as a basis for heightened antidiscrimination protection. When the issue reached the Court in 1996, the justices struck down this referendum by a six-to-three vote. Justice Kennedy wrote for the majority.

Supporters of Amendment 2 portrayed it as affirming equal rights for all and simply denying special rights to gays. But Justice Kennedy saw that, both formally and realistically, the amendment targeted gays for specially disfavored treatment and heaped unique disabilities on them. Heterosexuals could get laws protecting themselves from being discriminated against on the basis of their sexual orientation; but gays and bisexuals could not seek symmetric laws. Under Amendment 2, Aspen could pass an ordinance preventing a gay apartment-complex owner from posting a "For Rent—No Straights" sign; but Aspen could not likewise prevent a straight apartment-complex owner from posting a "For Rent—No Queers" sign. In its larger social meaning Amendment 2 itself was a kind of "No Queers" sign writ large—a targeting of gays, lesbians, and bisexuals, singling them and them alone out for disfavored treatment.

Once again, Justice Kennedy writes an opinion that keeps formulaic jargon about tiers of scrutiny and so forth down to a minimum. Instead, in everyday words that are at once plain and poetic, he explains to decent, fair-minded, ordinary citizens what was wrong with Colorado's referendum. In a nutshell, Amendment 2 created outcasts and outsiders—a group of second-class citizens subject to special disfavor and humiliation simply because of their status. Sexual orientation—as distinct from sexual conduct—implicates fantasies, desires, thoughts, and the like that should not be made the basis of legal penalty. Amendment 2 wrongly singled some persons out and made them pariahs because of who they were rather than because of anything they did. In this respect, Amendment 2's efforts to treat gays as unclean and untouchable resembled Jim Crow—a legal regime classifying and degrading a class of persons because of their status.

Here are Justice Kennedy's opening words, quoting the legendary dissent from *Plessy v. Ferguson*: "One century ago, the first Justice Harlan admonished this Court that the Constitution 'neither knows nor tolerates classes among citizens.'" And here are his closing words: "Laws singling out a certain class of citizens for disfavored legal status or general hardships are rare. . . . [Amendment 2] is a status-based enactment[,] a classification of persons undertaken for its own sake. . . . 'Class legislation . . . [is] obnoxious to the prohibitions of the Fourteenth Amendment.' We must conclude that Amendment 2 classifies homosexuals not to further a proper legislative end but to make them unequal to everyone else. This Colorado cannot do. A State cannot so deem a class of persons a stranger to its laws."

As with the other Kennedy opinions we have discussed, *Romer* exemplifies an elegant blending of legal formalism and legal realism at their best: the justice sees both the technical and the real-life inequality in Amendment 2. Everyone else in the world, from heterosexuals to hot-dog vendors to fat people, can seek special antidiscrimination laws, but gays and bisexuals—who, the justice realistically notes, may need these laws most—cannot. Exclusionary laws singling out persons because of who they are are in tension with our constitutional tradition and should be strongly disfavored.[16]

But what about a law singling out persons for inclusion rather than exclusion—a law, that is, extending specially targeted *benefits* or *protections* to a small and discrete group? This seems rather different, perhaps. Justice Kennedy's opinion in *Romer* provides some clues as to why we might view these targeted-inclusion laws differently.

While Justice Kennedy's *Romer* opinion places primary emphasis on the equal-protection clause, he also waves in the direction of another provision: the Article I, section 10, clause prohibiting states from enacting "any Bill of Attainder."[17] Strictly speaking, a bill of attainder is a law singling out a person by name and pronouncing him guilty of a capital offense. But for centuries, American lawyers and judges have understood the spirit of this clause to sweep far more broadly, condemning all sorts of statutes singling out named persons for all manner of legal disadvantage. Under this clause, a law singling out, say, Jagdish Chadha by name for deportation would be unconstitutional (as Justice Lewis Powell noted in the famous 1983 *Chadha* case). But a law singling out Jagdish Chadha by name for special advantage—a private immigration bill—would not be unconstitutional. At some point, if special favors created a truly privileged upper caste, the deep equality principles of the Constitution's rules prohibiting state and federal governments from creating "titles of nobility" might be violated; but not every specially targeted benefit creates such an upper caste.[18]

CONSIDER, IN THIS REGARD, the vexed question of whether public universities should ever give a special and limited "plus" to underrepresented racial minorities in a competitive admissions process. Should this use of race to include those who have been historically excluded or underrepresented be constitutionally permissible? If the attainder and nobility clauses were the only texts at stake, it would be hard to see university diversity programs as unconstitutional. Surely, blacks in America are not an aristocracy even if they do benefit from affirmative action.

But what about the equal-protection clause itself? Under this clause, is all diversity-based affirmative action in public universities unconstitutional?

In the past, Justice Kennedy has been a strong believer in the principle of colorblindness: government should not judge a person by his race, or take race into account in allocating benefits and burdens. In *Romer*, as we saw, the justice began by invoking Justice Harlan's celebrated dissent in *Plessy*, which proclaimed that "[o]ur constitution is color-blind, and neither knows nor tolerates classes among citizens." In *Powers*, Justice Kennedy championed colorblindness in two ways: by preventing prosecutors from taking into account a juror's race; and by making clear that, when blacks are excluded from juries, a white defendant has just as much of a right to object as would a black defendant. So, too, in *Edmonson*, the justice spoke of "the racial insult inherent in judging a citizen by the color of his or her skin."

But a powerful case can be made that not all uses of race are or should be unconstitutional. The equal-protection clause nowhere prohibits all color consciousness. Leading scholars have argued that the Congresses that passed the Reconstruction Amendments also passed race-conscious laws to help the newly freed slaves. Judges can use race in remedial contexts—for example, to integrate high schools. Why should public universities be barred from using race to bring us together? On this view, using race in order to separate, or stigmatize, or degrade, or divide is quite different from using race in order to integrate, to unite.[19]

Justice Kennedy's jury and public-forum cases envision places where diverse people come together to democratically discuss and deliberate. And this is the democratic mission of the public university—to bring

Americans together to a place where they will talk to and learn from each other face-to-face as democratic equals. No special affirmative action may be necessary to generate diverse jury panels; the lottery wheel, combined with *Powers*'s limits on peremptories, will guarantee diversity within the jury. But without some affirmative action, some historically excluded racial groups may be all but absent in public universities. As in *Krishna Consciousness*, here, too, the "dialogue" may be "tilted" in "effect," and perhaps government may need to go beyond formal equality to ensure that Americans, at a formative point in their lives, are exposed to those who have lived in different neighborhoods, and have had very different lived racial and cultural experiences. Even if affirmative action in other contexts (like set-asides reserving a certain percentage of government contracts for minority-owned companies) is unconstitutional, might education be different, as a special public forum in which special sensitivity to "marginal voices," to use Justice Kennedy's own phrase, might be permitted?

Justice Powell thought so in the 1978 case of *Regents of the University of California v. Bakke*, which arose at the University of California at Davis Medical School, just a few miles from Justice Kennedy's hometown of Sacramento.[20] In that case, Powell cast the decisive fifth vote, opining that educational administrators could constitutionally take minority-race status into consideration as a limited "plus" factor in competitive admissions programs, in order to achieve a more diverse student body bringing together students of different backgrounds, perspectives, and lived experiences.

Must *Bakke* be overruled? What will Justice Kennedy—who now sits in Powell's seat—say about *Bakke*, if the Court is forced to decide the matter in some future case? Here, too, Justice Kennedy may well be a swing voter. Will he adhere to the formal principle of colorblindness? Or will he decide that the law may "reach[] past formalism"? What will the great justice from Northern California say, in the end, about the great case from Northern California, *Regents v. Bakke*?

An Updated Portrait, Circa 2015

Time and again, my 1996 Sacramento remarks emphasized Justice Kennedy's centrality to the modern Court. As he went, I repeatedly said, so went the Court. If anything, this central point about his centrality is even truer in 2015. In Sacramento I mentioned in passing that on certain issues, Justice O'Connor stood alongside Justice Kennedy at the center of the Court.

Justice O'Connor, of course, no longer sits. Justice Kennedy not only continues to sit, but continues to tip the balance. In most important areas of constitutional law, he decides: as he goes, so goes the Court.

To give just one example from a quadrant of constitutional law unmentioned in Sacramento, in two significant separation-of-powers cases decided in 2010 and 2014, the Court split 5–4 each time. In the 2010 case of *Free Enterprise Fund v. Public Company Accounting Oversight Board*, the Court stressed the importance of presidential oversight and control in the staffing and operation of the modern administrative state; but in the 2014 case of *National Labor Relations Board v. Noel Canning*, the Court ruled against the president in a case involving the filling of important administrative positions via recess appointments. Only Anthony Kennedy joined both Court majorities.[21]

The most notable—and to my mind, happy—exception to the general rule that Kennedy typically tips the balance on the current Court occurred in the 2012 Obamacare case, where Justice Kennedy's views did not prevail. As mentioned at the end of the preceding chapter, Chief Justice Roberts joined the four Democrat-appointed justices (Ginsburg, Breyer, Sotomayor, and Kagan) to uphold the basic structure of the Affordable Care Act over the dissent of Justice Kennedy and three others (Scalia, Thomas, and Alito), who would have struck down the law in its entirety.

One highly notable—and to my mind unhappy—case where Justice Kennedy's views were decisive is *Bush v. Gore*. Although Justice Kennedy did not write under his own name in this December 2000 case, he and Justice O'Connor quite obviously collaborated on the main opinion for the Court. As I will explain in Chapter 7, which is devoted to untangling all the big knots in this intricate case, I do not find this unsigned opinion particularly persuasive, although I reserve my harshest criticism for the concurrence authored by Chief Justice Rehnquist.

The Obamacare dissent and *Bush v. Gore* are powerful reminders that good justices have bad days. I suspect the same is even true of constitutional law professors. The question is thus not whether a given justice—or professor or president for that matter—had any bad days. The questions are, rather, how many good and truly great days did he have, and what was his net contribution?

UNLIKE JUSTICE O'CONNOR, who often split the difference between left and right, Justice Kennedy has sometimes enthusiastically joined liberals and other times just as enthusiastically joined conservatives. For example, in the aforementioned 1990s cases concerning racial equality in jury rooms, Justice Kennedy condemned race-based peremptories in both criminal prosecutions (*Powers v. Ohio*) and civil cases (*Edmonson v. Leesville Concrete Co.*). By contrast, Justice O'Connor split the difference: she voted (with Kennedy) to condemn race-based peremptories in criminal cases, but also voted (against Kennedy, and in dissent) to uphold race-based peremptories in civil cases. Thus, O'Connor split whereas Kennedy swung—and in this quadrant of law, he swung left.*

Now consider a pair of race cases handed down after my Sacramento talk, *Grutter v. Bollinger* and *Gratz v. Bollinger*, involving affirmative action in higher education—specifically, the University of Michigan's race-based admissions policies in its law school and its flagship undergraduate college, respectively. In these two high-profile 2003 cases, O'Connor once again split and Kennedy once again swung, but this time, Kennedy swung right. Writing for the Court, O'Connor upheld the law school's use of a racial "plus" system for underrepresented minorities aimed at achieving a suitably diverse student body, while striking down the undergraduate college's more mechanical and quota-like racial admissions system. Justice Kennedy, by contrast, condemned the admissions policies of both the law school and the college. Thus, he joined Justice O'Connor in voting to strike down the quotified college-admissions system, and he dissented

---

* In 1996, I expressed the hope that Justice Kennedy's critique of race-based peremptory challenges might eventually lead to the abolition of all peremptories, across the board. That day has not yet arrived. But building on *Powers* and *Edmonson*, the Court, with Justice Kennedy specially concurring to express his "full agreement," has held that sex-based peremptory challenges are every bit as unconstitutional as race-based ones. See *JEB v. Alabama* (1994). In 2014, the Ninth Circuit, expressly relying on Justice Kennedy's own recent judicial pronouncements about gay rights, held that peremptory challenges based on sexual orientation are likewise unconstitutional. *SmithKline Beecham Corp. v. Abbott Labs*, 740 F.3d 471 (9th Cir. Cal. 2014). When the issue reaches the Supreme Court, I would expect and hope that the Court, led by Justice Kennedy, would agree; and would likewise agree that religious-based peremptory challenges are impermissible. After that, class-based and occupation-based peremptories would seem ripe for attack. At that point, wouldn't it make the most sense—and be in keeping with Justice Kennedy's big idea that jury service is akin to voting—to eliminate all peremptories and merely allow challenges for actual bias of a given prospective juror? In the justice's own words in *JEB*: "The injury [of a peremptory challenge] is to personal dignity and to the individual's right to participate in the political process."

from O'Connor's and the Court's willingness to uphold the more subtle, but still overtly race-based, affirmative-action policies of the law school.

Now that Justice O'Connor has left the bench, and has been succeeded by Justice Samuel Alito, who is far more hostile to race-based affirmative action, Justice Kennedy is the median voter on the Court on this issue. It was in anticipation of just such a scenario that I ended my 1996 remarks, noting that the fate of affirmative action in higher education might well be decided by Justice Kennedy.

In a high-profile 2007 case involving race-based assignments to selective public high schools, *Parents Involved v. Seattle School District*, Kennedy was quite obviously the swing justice. Four justices on one side voted to strike down virtually all race-based affirmative-action plans and four justices on the other side adopted a stance much friendlier to explicitly race-based policies designed to achieve educational integration and diversity. Alone in the middle stood Justice Kennedy. While voting to invalidate what he viewed as the overly crude and blunt uses of racial classifications in the case at hand, Justice Kennedy also pointedly suggested that in some educational contexts, government could properly take race into account in order to promote the legitimate and important goal of racial integration.[22]

Justice Kennedy's swing opinion appears in a particularly interesting light when seen through the prism of his opinion in the 1991 race-based-peremptory-challenge case of *Powers v. Ohio*. In *Parents Involved*, Justice Kennedy appeared to give his blessing to certain kinds of pro-integration, pro-diversity educational decisions that he admitted were race-conscious—such as a decision to locate a neighborhood school in a given spot because that spot would make it particularly likely that students of different races would attend that school. These sorts of race-conscious decisions, however, would not involve highly visible, potentially polarizing, and constitutionally troubling race labeling and race classification at an individual level. No government actor would need to say that Smith but not Jones could attend School X, because Jones's skin color was two shades lighter or darker than Smith's, or because Smith had one more or one less nonwhite great-grandparent than Jones.

Recall that this sort of individual race-labeling was one of the very things that Justice Kennedy condemned in *Powers*. If race-based peremptories were used in the jury selection process, the defendant had a right to object, whether or not his own skin color was identical with or even close to that of the excluded jurors. Recall also Justice Kennedy's words in *Edmonson* regarding "the racial insult inherent in judging a citizen by the color of his or her skin." Justice Kennedy's words in *Parents Involved* reprise and refine these earlier themes: "[S]trategic site selection of new schools; drawing attendance zones with general recognition of the demographics of neighborhoods; allocating resources for special programs; recruiting students and faculty in a targeted fashion; and tracking enrollments, performance, and other statistics by race . . . are race conscious [policies] but do not lead to different treatment based on a classification that tells each student he or she is to be defined by race."

But certain forms of *Bakke*-style affirmative action do operate on a more individual, race-labeling, race-defining level. In both *Grutter* and *Gratz*, Justice Kennedy voted against the University of Michigan's affirmative action programs, but in *Parents Involved* he signaled his understanding of the importance of precedent—in particular, the precedent of *Grutter* itself, which built on *Bakke*. Though Kennedy is more conservative than O'Connor on this issue, he has not—at least not yet—completely rejected *Bakke*.

In the closely watched 2013 *Fisher v. University of Texas* case involving affirmative action in university admissions, Justice Kennedy, writing for the Court, notably declined to repudiate Powell's opinion in *Bakke* or O'Connor's similar opinion for the Court in *Grutter*. However, the *Fisher* plaintiffs had not squarely challenged *Bakke* and *Grutter*, and so the issue remains open for possible reconsideration by Kennedy. My conclusion in 1996 thus continues to ring true: the story of affirmative action in education is ongoing, and Justice Kennedy remains the key to how this story will unfold in the years to come.

WHAT I SAID IN 1996 about Justice Kennedy's concurrence in the 1989 flag-burning case, *Texas v. Johnson*, also continues to ring true. Back then, I praised Justice Kennedy's bottom line and condemned the dissenters' arguments as "shoddy." Today, none of the four *Johnson* dissenters (one of whom was Justice O'Connor) still sits, and I would guess that none of the dissenters' replacements shares these shoddy views on this issue. In 1996, I said that Justice Kennedy was clearly right; and today, I would bet that all nine current justices would agree, as would the vast majority of today's constitutional scholars—left, right, and center.

The justices in *Texas v. Johnson* did not break down along conventional ideological or partisan lines. The five-justice majority consisted of William Brennan (a Democrat appointed by a Republican president); Thurgood Marshall (a Democrat appointed by a Democratic president); and Harry

Blackmun, Antonin Scalia, and Anthony Kennedy (all three Republicans appointed by Republican presidents). The four dissenters were William Rehnquist, Sandra Day O'Connor, John Paul Stevens (all Republicans appointed by Republicans) and Byron White (a Democrat appointed by a Democrat). Viewed from this angle, no obvious pattern appears.

But now let's slice the 1989 Court not ideologically but geographically. None of the four dissenters was born or raised anywhere near the Atlantic or Pacific Ocean. Rehnquist and Stevens came from the Midwest, White hailed from Colorado, and O'Connor came from Arizona. By contrast, four of the Court's majority were north-coastal kids—Kennedy from the Northwest; Brennan, Marshall, and Scalia from the Northeast. Is it possible that coasts in general (and especially America's northern coasts) are more cosmopolitan places than noncoastal areas, featuring greater diversity of peoples and ideas, and more atmospheric tolerance for eccentric and even outrageous speakers and speech? On an issue, like flag-burning, that hits at least some people in a particularly primal way, is it further possible that deep instincts formed in childhood affect primal perception?[23]

If any of these speculations holds any water, then the current unanimity of the Court on flag-burning might be especially easy to understand: Eight of the current nine justices (all except John Roberts) grew up as coastal kids, and seven of the eight (all except Clarence Thomas) grew up as northern coastal kids.[24]

ON THE RELATIONSHIP between free expression and equality, recent developments are more complicated. In 1996 I tried to link Justice Kennedy's free-expression ideas to a certain vision of equality; but many readers today might point to Justice Kennedy's controversial 2010 opinion for the Court in *Citizens United v. FEC* as an anti-egalitarian monster. In that case, the Court, by a narrow 5–4 majority—with Justice Kennedy, once again, playing a pivotal role and indeed writing for the Court majority—invalidated certain statutory spending caps on independent expenditures aimed at persuading voters to support candidate A or oppose candidate B in an upcoming election.

Where truly independent expenditures are at issue—an ad in the McClatchy newspapers, or an editorial endorsement in those papers, for that matter—our law generally sides with the press right of those who own or can rent presses to say what they want, with virtually no permissible limits on the amount they are free to spend on these independent publications.* If this private press–private property approach makes sense, it does so because in the end, equality has its day—Election Day, to be specific—when each voter gets to decide for himself whether to heed the McClatchy ads or editorial endorsements. On that day, all the votes are counted up equally. One person, one vote. And corporations do not get to vote on Election Day. Not yet, at least.

Where the issue is instead one of campaign contributions, there is far less reason to see the matter as one of pure property rights. A person or a corporation has no absolute right to give property to a government official in exchange for the official's favor. We call that "bribery," and it is in fact an impeachable offense in the Constitution itself. True, when the property is given not directly to a candidate for his personal use, but rather to his campaign fund, the matter is slightly different. But this campaign fund can be used to pay for campaign pizza, campaign gasoline, and hefty campaign-staff salaries to the candidate's friends and family—spouse, in-laws, nieces and nephews, and so on. Pizza, gasoline, and hefty salaries for cronies are not themselves intrinsically and entirely expressive; they are not themselves pure speech protected by the First Amendment as such.

In other words, sensible campaign finance reforms going forward should focus on (among other things) limiting campaign contributions to the candidates' campaign funds, and should not aim to stifle truly independent expenditures for pure expression. And Justice Kennedy's opinion for the Court in *Citizens United* was, to repeat, an opinion affirming a broad right of independent expenditures financing books, magazines, newspapers, television and radio ads, and the like.

On this view, the far more troubling Court decision, from a proper egalitarian point of view, is the more recent 2014 ruling in *McCutcheon v. Federal Election Commission*, in which the Court struck down aggregate limits on individual donors' campaign contributions to candidate-controlled campaign war chests. Although Justice Kennedy did not write

---

* It bears repeating that we are dealing with situations where, by hypothesis, the speech at issue is not being controlled by the candidate; and where the money that is being independently spent goes into intrinsically expressive activities, such as printing and broadcasting, as opposed to, say, salaries or perks for the candidate's cronies.

in this case, he did join Chief Justice Roberts's troubling plurality opinion. Were I to speak directly to Justice Kennedy about this vote, here is what I would say:

Mr. Justice, voting rights are intrinsically egalitarian, as a rule: one person, one vote. By contrast, property rights may end up resulting in widespread and indeed republic-destroying inequality. Some folks have only a little property, while others have lots of property (meaning, of course, not just land but other assets, including printing presses, stocks and bonds, jewels, Rolex watches, fancy cars, and cold hard cash); and those that have lots may well try to use their vast wealth to undermine democratic equality by, in effect, buying up lawmakers and laws.

Of the six main rights in the First Amendment, five are strongly egalitarian—intrinsically so, in that equality of a certain sort is built into the very logical structure of the right, properly conceived. Religious free exercise is a right of each and every natural person, who has a conscience and a soul and a body and a mind. This right is not about wealth or property as such. It is not about oil-industry PACs. The right against religious establishments (if we choose to interpret the nonestablishment principle in this way—an interpretation that makes special sense if we read the First Amendment through the prism of the later Fourteenth Amendment experience) is a right against government-supported religious monopolies of a certain sort. This, too, has a distinctly egalitarian feel.

Now turn to the right of the people to assemble. This is a right of people—of natural persons. Yes, yes, for some legal purposes, as the man said, "corporations are people, my friend." But at its core, the First Amendment right of assembly is about natural persons gathering in political and religious conclaves—one person, one body. No one can assemble in multiple places at once; the right by its very nature features a highly egalitarian distribution. The First Amendment right to petition is also distinctly egalitarian—one person, one signature, as a rule. Yes, of course you can scribble a petition and personally sign it fifty-three times if you like, but what sense would it make to count your signature more than once in tallying the number of signatures on the petition?

Mr. Justice, let us recall that the First Amendment's freedom of speech is also based upon an intrinsically egalitarian ideal—namely, parliamentary freedom of speech and debate. Parliament is a speech spot, a parley place. But it is a place for a special kind of speech, speech about political affairs—as distinct from, say, speech about why someone should buy and smoke Marlboro cigarettes. In eighteenth-century England, only Parliament had absolute freedom of political opinion—broad "freedom of speech and debate," in the language of the 1689 English Bill of Rights. But when America proposed the words "freedom of speech" exactly one century later in its 1789 Bill of Rights, it extended this textual right to the ordinary citizenry. Here, we, the people, are the ultimate Parliament. We, the people, are sovereign, and we must therefore enjoy a sweeping right to express political opinions among ourselves free from any government interference or abridgment.

The sixth right in the First Amendment—the freedom of the press— is less intrinsically democratic. It focuses not on a sociological group—the "media," the institutional press corps—but on a physical item, a printing press. It focuses on a thing—on a piece of property. And in 1791, not everyone had a printing press. The press, in essence, was free to those fortunate enough to own a press. But "the freedom of the press" at the Founding was a rather limited freedom, a freedom merely from licensing laws and systems of prior restraint. The broader freedom of expression that America properly claims today is thus much more directly and firmly rooted in the freedom of speech, and not the freedom of the press. And the freedom of speech, as I have just noted (and explained in more detail in my 1996 Sacramento lecture in your honor, Your Honor), is in fact rooted in images and ideas that are deeply and intrinsically democratic and egalitarian.

The question of campaign finance thus becomes, How should we resolve the tension between equality and property—between freedom of speech and freedom of the press? Though of course we should not subordinate the right of the owners and renters of printing presses and the like to make their arguments and in the process to engage in truly independent expenditures, we should not conflate this with a right to give unlimited sums to the candidates themselves or directly to their campaigns in a way that might undermine the deepest and oldest—and highly egalitarian!—meaning of freedom of speech.[25]

Of course, I cannot be sure that Justice Kennedy would agree with the foregoing analysis; but hope springs eternal.

TWO FINAL THOUGHTS. First, no one who heard me in 1996 analyzing Justice Kennedy's opinion for the Court in the 1992 school prayer case, *Lee v. Weisman*, should have been shocked that Justice Kennedy—and thus the

Court, which often pivots on his vote in this corner of case law—might have a contrasting view of invocation prayers at town council meetings. In May 2014, Justice Kennedy, writing as the swing justice for a Court plurality in the case of *Town of Greece v. Galloway*, upheld the government-facilitated prayer at issue and distinguished *Lee v. Weisman* on several grounds—almost all of which were foreshadowed by my 1996 remarks. On Justice Kennedy's view, the invocation prayers at town council meetings in the bedroom community of Greece, New York, did not involve the same level of functional coercion as was evident in *Lee*. As Kennedy saw it, the town meeting did not involve youngsters or the public school setting; and those citizens who needed or wanted to attend the town meetings and who did not wish to be part of the prayer event could easily enter the room after the opening prayer, or could easily stand aside or stand apart during the prayer itself. In addition, Justice Kennedy noted that officials in the town of Greece (unlike the officials in *Lee*) did not attempt to tightly regulate the content of the prayers delivered by the various invited clergy members. Justice Kennedy further noted that the opening prayers at issue did not, in general, demean other religions or add up to a pattern of proselytizing on behalf of any one faith.

Last and emphatically not least, let us remember the issue of gay rights, an issue that may well end up as Justice Kennedy's most enduring legacy. Justice Kennedy's majority opinion in the 1996 *Romer v. Evans* case, an opinion that showed admirable sensitivity to the sheer meanness of Colorado's anti-gay Amendment 2, was the first big victory for gay rights in Supreme Court history. Since then, the Court has delivered two additional landmark rulings in strong support of the liberty, dignity, and equality of gay Americans. In 2003, the Court held in *Lawrence v. Texas* that laws purporting to prohibit various common forms of sexual intimacy—such as oral and anal sex—violate the Constitution, whether these purported prohibitions seek to limit the freedom and dignity of heterosexual couples, same-sex couples, or both. In 2013, the Court held in *United States v. Windsor* that the federal government is constitutionally required to give full effect, credit, and dignity to same-sex marriages that are valid under relevant state law.[26]

In both cases, the Court was sharply divided; and in both cases, it was the swing justice, Anthony Kennedy, who spoke for the Court majority. As he went, so went the Court; and in both cases this justice from Northern California—a corner of the country renowned for its respect for alternative lifestyles—went for gay liberty, equality, and dignity. If and when the Court decides, sometime soon, that the Constitution requires each and every state to accord full marriage equality rights to same-sex couples, we should not be surprised if this landmark ruling is announced, perhaps on behalf of a closely divided Court, by Justice Anthony Kennedy.*

And when that historic day arrives, I expect I will want to give yet another public lecture—in Northern California, of course—in honor of this good and great California constitutionalist.

---

* On the divisions within the current Court: In a long string of culture-war cases, Justice Kennedy, a 1988 Reagan appointee, has spoken for the Court, and Justice Scalia, a 1986 Reagan appointee, has penned the main dissent, which has often featured harsh language aimed at Justice Kennedy. Justice Kennedy has not responded in kind: as a rule he disagrees with Justice Scalia without sounding disagreeable. (This is easier to do when one is almost always on the winning side.) Cases fitting this general culture-war pattern include *Lee v. Weisman* (1992, commencement prayer); *Planned Parenthood v. Casey* (1992, abortion) (opinion of the Court per curiam); *Romer v. Evans* (1996, gay rights); *Lawrence v. Texas* (2003, gay sex); *Roper v. Simmons* (2005, death penalty); and *United States v. Windsor* (2013, gay marriage).

PART II

Constitutional Cases

CHAPTER 5

KANSAS:
LIVING IN THE SHADOW OF
BROWN V. BOARD

T he system of American apartheid—Jim Crow—that prevailed
across the South in the first half of the twentieth century also in-
fected many cities and states north of Dixie. In the century's most
legendary judicial ruling, the Supreme Court underscored the fact that
legal segregation was not entirely a southern sickness, but rather was a
more widespread American disease. The Court did so by designating a
lawsuit from Topeka, Kansas, as the lead case in what was in fact a consolidated set of suits arising from several different jurisdictions, mostly
southern. The other cases that were consolidated with the Topeka case
arose in South Carolina, Virginia, and Delaware. Alongside these consolidated state cases, the Court also heard and decided *Bolling v. Sharpe*,
a case involving school segregation in Washington, DC—a jurisdiction
governed directly by the federal government. By giving the Topeka litigation top billing, the Court aimed to take some of the sectional sting out of
the case—to soften the sense among many belligerent white southerners
that their region was once again being singled out by officious outsiders
who simply failed to understand the southern way of life.

The caption choice had the effect of making Topeka synonymous,
at least among modern constitutional lawyers, with the broader issue of
Jim Crow. Much as "Yorktown," "Gettysburg," and "Pearl Harbor" immediately conjure up images of the Revolutionary War, the Civil War,
and World War II, respectively, so "Topeka" provokes a highly predictable
response. Go up to a constitutional lawyer and simply say the word, "Topeka," and her brain will likely flash to *Brown v. Board of Education*.

But when this iconic 1954 case pops into her head, what else should come to mind? In particular, what should this case prompt her to think about constitutional law in general? And how should non-lawyers—in Topeka itself, in Kansas, and elsewhere—live their lives in the light of, and in the shadow of, *Brown v. Board*?

BROWN AND THE LEGAL ACADEMY

There are probably as many different legal academic perspectives on *Brown v. Board of Education* as there are legal academics: if you laid all the law professors in America end to end, they would not reach a conclusion. Each emphasizes a different facet of *Brown*, often a facet reflecting his or her general jurisprudential framework.

Consider just a few examples. Alexander Bickel, who openly rejected "original intent" as the ultimate interpretive touchstone, argued that the Fourteenth Amendment's framers did not specifically intend to outlaw racial segregation. On the contrary, they probably meant to allow it, but (said Bickel) this fact should not have been binding on the *Brown* judges, who properly felt themselves free to evolve open-ended constitutional language to do justice. Conversely, the originalist Michael McConnell has argued that *Brown* can be supported by a careful look at the legislative history of the Reconstruction Congress. Bruce Ackerman thinks that *Brown* is really all about the New Deal—isn't everything? By contrast, John Hart Ely insisted that the case exemplifies his broader theory that judges should protect certain discrete and insular minority groups against whom there exists widespread prejudice. Early in his career, Michael Klarman had a similar but narrower view of the proper judicial role—so he justified the biggest case of the twentieth century by stressing the key fact that American blacks in 1954 were largely disfranchised and thus could not adequately protect their own interests in the legislative process.[1]

David Strauss has argued generally for constitutional gradualism, and so has Cass Sunstein of late. They both accent yet a different aspect of *Brown*: the fact that it was the culmination of a long series of cases reflecting an evolution of social attitudes. Here was no bolt from the blue, they emphasize. Similarly, Edward Lazarus has argued that anti–death penalty crusaders in the 1960s and 1970s, led by Anthony Amsterdam, saw in *Brown* the lesson that clever and committed public-interest lawyers could change the world by carefully orchestrating an extended litigation campaign and bringing a series of lawsuits in just the right order. Lazarus himself is skeptical that this is the true lesson of *Brown*. In general, Lazarus calls for broad consensus among justices in deciding controversial issues of social policy; for him, the critical fact to be kept in mind is the unanimity of the *Brown* Court. Gerald Rosenberg thinks that courts are less able to transform social policy than is commonly recognized; thus, his account of *Brown* highlights how little judicially ordered desegregation actually occurred before Congress and the president strongly weighed in with civil rights laws and policies in the mid-1960s. Derrick Bell believed that whites rarely give blacks anything unless the gift somehow serves whites' own interests; more recently, Mary Dudziak has similarly noted that *Brown*'s verdict served the propaganda needs of a Cold War America trying to win the hearts and minds of colored folk in Africa and Asia.[2]

BROWN AND THE CONSTITUTION

So what, you may ask, is *my* account of *Brown*? In general, I have argued in a wide range of contexts that the Constitution itself is a rich source of guidance if read with care. So let's start by looking carefully at the document.

Begin at the beginning. "We the People . . . do ordain and establish this Constitution." With these bold words, the document seems to commit itself to the project of democratic self-rule. Monarchy and aristocracy are rejected. Here, the people rule. Democracy is not simply what the Preamble says. It is also what the Preamble does. The Preamble announces an act, a doing, an ordainment and establishment. And this act of constituting—of *constitution*—was at that time the most democratic act in the history of planet earth. Hundreds of thousands of ordinary folk got to vote, via elections for special ratification conventions, on the basic ground rules for themselves and their posterity. This kind of broad and explicit popular consent was unheard of in most parts of the world, ruled as most of it was by strongman fiat or edicts derived from immemorial custom. None of the ancient Greek democracies had allowed the citizenry to actually vote on the constitution itself.[3]

Likewise, most state constitutions during the Revolution had not been put to a popular vote; nor had the Declaration of Independence or the Articles of Confederation for that matter. Thus, the Preamble's bold text and deed should not be passed over lightly. In this Constitution, the Preamble makes clear, We the People rule—not kings or princes or dukes or earls or mere custom and tradition.

Popular sovereignty—rule by the people—is also the big idea of the Article IV clause that "the United States shall guarantee to every State in this Union a Republican Form of Government." No monarchies or aristocracies will be allowed to take root in the several states—only republics based on self-government among free and equal citizens.[4]

If we simply read these two clauses at face value, I think we could generate an admittedly broad yet straightforward argument that neither the federal government nor the state governments may properly pursue apartheid policies in public schools. (Remember, the *Brown* case raised the issue of racial segregation by state officials; and its companion case, *Bolling v. Sharpe*, required the justices to rule on the constitutionality of federal segregation—in particular, the racially segregated public schools in the District of Columbia.) The straightforward constitutional argument against American apartheid goes like this: The purpose and effect and social meaning of racial segregation in America in 1954 is to create two hereditary classes of citizens—first-class (white) citizens, and second-class (black) citizens. This hereditary class system is an obvious echo of aristocracy, assigning citizens unequal and intergenerationally entrenched places on the basis of birth status. This is a violation of the deep democratic structure of our Constitution, as exemplified by the Preamble and the republican-government clause.

A critic of this broad argument might wonder whether the Preamble binds the state government as well as the federal government; and might also wonder whether the republican-government clause, which speaks of states, obliges the federal government to honor basic principles of republicanism. The critic might also wonder whether we are over-reading these two small patches of constitutional text. Is the deep structure of the document really so dead set against hereditary aristocracy?

I think it is, and as further evidence I would point to two other clauses of the Constitution that are rarely noticed. Article I, section 9, forbids Congress from granting "titles of nobility"; and Article I, section 10, imposes a similar ban on states. Here are clauses clearly designed to work in tandem—we are not over-reading when we consider these clauses as a paired set. And these clauses are written to condemn the idea of *lordship* in America: these words proclaim that ours is a democratic republic, not a hereditary aristocracy based on birth and blood. If read in a broad but straightforward way, these clauses reinforce the simple argument against government-sponsored segregation in public schools as follows: No government in America can, consistent with these clauses and the broader constitutional ethos they embody, name some Americans "lords" and others "commoners." But if no government may properly name some (light-skinned) Americans "lords" and other (dark-skinned) Americans "commoners," surely no government may do the same thing through racially segregated schools whose combined purpose and effect and social meaning is to create a blood-based and hereditary overclass and underclass.[5]

Yet another reinforcing argument against Jim Crow derives from the paired set of clauses in Article I, sections 9 and 10, prohibiting the federal and state governments, respectively, from enacting "bills of attainder." These anti-attainder clauses ramify broadly, but one of the deepest ideas they embody is that no legislature may properly single out a person by name and subject him to special penalty or ridicule or disadvantage. Legislatures may pass general and prospective laws—"all who henceforth commit deed X shall suffer penalty Y"—but the legislature may not target human beings for disfavored treatment because of who they are as opposed to what they do. And there is a special historical link between attainders and "corruption of blood" in which legislatures try to taint or stain a person's bloodline—a link visible in yet another clause of the Constitution that provides that "no Attainder of Treason shall work Corruption of Blood." If we take these deep ideas seriously, they bar state and federal lawmakers from passing laws designed to humiliate or demean all persons descended from slaves, or all persons with black (corrupt) blood.[6]

HERE THEN IS A SET of rather straightforward textual and structural arguments against American apartheid. When the words of the Founders' Constitution are read at face value, they seem to condemn a system that creates a hereditary aristocracy fixed at birth, and that seems aimed at humiliating the disfavored race. The fundamental problem with these arguments, however, is that the Founders' Constitution cannot be taken at face value—at least where slaves are concerned.

Make no mistake: the Founders' Constitution made its peace with, and even propped up, a regime of chattel slavery. The Framers were ashamed to use the words "slaves" and "slavery," so the document is rife with euphemism here. Thus, Article I, section 2, elliptically speaks of "free persons" and "all other persons"—that is, *unfree* persons. Under the rules of this section, the more unfree persons—slaves—a state imported or bred, the more seats it got in the House of Representatives. Under Article II, that state also got more clout in the electoral college.

The electoral college was largely designed to help slave states such as Virginia. In a system of direct national election, Virginia would have derived no clout from her slaves, since slaves, of course, could not vote. The electoral college, by contrast, enabled Virginia and other slave states to count for more than their fair share of total national voters. Perversely, if Virginia were to free some of its slaves, who then moved elsewhere (say, Pennsylvania or Ohio), Virginia would actually lose seats in the Congress and in the electoral college. Consider also the odious rule laid down by the Article IV fugitive-slave clause. This clause actually obliged free states to play the role of slave catchers, and return human beings to bondage when their "rightful owners"—the scare quotes are mine to signal the obscenity of the phrase within them—came to recapture them.

These and other constitutional protections of slavery suggest that we cannot simply read the Preamble or the republican-government clause, or the nobility and attainder clauses, at face value. Slavery was surely a relic of the ancièn regime, rooted in hereditary and intergenerational inequality based on blood and birth status. In the antebellum South, there were indeed "lords" and "serfs" notwithstanding the nobility clauses. Slave children were attainted at birth because of their own and their ancestors' allegedly corrupt blood, despite the spirit of the attainder clauses. The point is hardly unique to these clauses. Slavery contradicted a huge part of the Constitution if naïvely read at face value. How could persons born on American soil be deprived of their right to speak and to worship as they pleased? How could persons be sentenced to life imprisonment at birth without any due process, without any individualized adjudication of personal wrongdoing?

Perhaps we could solve these contradictions by saying that slaves were simply not part of "We the People." Rather, they were more like aliens among us, not entitled to be part of collective self-governance or the regime of constitutional rights. On this reading, however, free blacks were quite different and had to be treated in accordance with the Preamble and the other clauses we have canvassed.

But prior to the Civil War, proslavery and racist interpreters of the Constitution, typified by Chief Justice Roger Taney in the 1857 *Dred Scott* case, read the proslavery clauses broadly and read the Preamble and other anti-subordination clauses narrowly, even in cases involving free blacks. *Dred Scott* said many outlandish things—Lincoln once called it "an astonisher in legal history"—but for present purposes it suffices to note that *Dred Scott* claimed that, in general, even free blacks could never be citizens, and that only citizens had constitutional rights. And so for decisive constitutional support for the result in *Brown* and *Bolling*, we must turn to the amendments adopted after the Civil War by the Reconstruction

Republicans, who emphatically repudiated Taney's proslavery, pro-subordination, racist reading of our Constitution.[7]

The Thirteenth Amendment abolishes slavery everywhere and forever; and with this new birth of freedom our contradiction evaporates. No longer are we forced to read the Preamble or the other clauses we have canvassed at less than face value.

The Fourteenth and Fifteenth Amendments provide even clearer and more emphatic support for the idea that our Reconstructed Constitution is refounded on principles of free and equal citizenship. The first sentence of the Fourteenth Amendment confers birthright citizenship on all who are born in America—black and white, male and female, rich and poor alike. Contra *Dred Scott*, all are citizens, and the clear idea here is that all are *equal* citizens. A variant of this first sentence had appeared in the earlier Civil Rights Act of 1866, which had made explicit that citizenship itself entailed a right to "full and equal" civil rights. As the elder Justice John Marshall Harlan later put the point in the 1896 case of *Gibson v. Mississippi*, "all citizens are equal before the law." (Note that this citizenship clause proclaims a perfectly general rule that applies to all governments, federal as well as state; note also that in *Gibson*, Justice Harlan spoke for a Court majority, unlike the contemporaneous case of *Plessy v. Ferguson*, in which Harlan famously dissented.)[8]

In the Fourteenth Amendment's next sentence, the word "equal" explicitly appears, promising that all persons—black as well as white—will receive "equal protection." (Although the words of this clause speak explicitly of states, these words were also understood as declaring an entailment of "due process of law" and thus bound federal officials as well.)* Finally, the Fifteenth Amendment, barring race-based suffrage laws, makes clear

---

*Both the Fifth and the Fourteenth Amendments promised "due process of law"—the Fifth vis-à-vis the federal government and the Fourteenth vis-à-vis states. As understood by Reconstruction Republicans, who in effect rewrote the Fifth Amendment by adopting a later amendment echoing it, "law" in its nature was general, equal, and impartial. Thus, the "due process" that generated "law" had to respect law's nature by ensuring that lawmaking would be general and prospective, while law execution and law adjudication would be impartial. Implicit in due process, as understood by the Reconstruction Republicans, was a profound equality idea: proper "law" had to be equal and pursuant to fair process. To punish or stigmatize a person on the basis of his birth status violated this vision, which the Reconstruction Congress understood as a first-principles limit that derived from the nature of law and thus bound all levels of government.

that blacks cannot be excluded from their equal right to participate in the grand project of American democratic self-rule. Although the Fifteenth, by its express terms, applies only to race discrimination in regard to "the right to vote," its drafters and ratifiers had reason to understand that it should be read to encompass a broad right against racial discrimination in the general domain of political rights, including the rights of jury service and office-holding. (To recast this point into a more literalistic textual argument, "the right to vote" encompassed *voting* on juries and *voting* within legislatures.)[9]

With all these clauses in view, the basic argument for *Brown* and *Bolling* is clear and clean: Jim Crow in 1954 was not truly equal. American apartheid was an effort to create a kind of subordinated caste in violation of the vision of the Thirteenth Amendment; to perpetuate two classes of unequal citizenship in violation of the logic of the first sentence of the Fourteenth Amendment; to deprive blacks of genuinely equal laws in violation of the command of the next sentence of the Fourteenth Amendment (and of the companion Fifth Amendment); and to keep blacks and whites apart in ways that undercut the promise of the Fifteenth Amendment that Americans of different races must come together as equals—at the polls, in the legislature, in the jury box—to govern ourselves.[10]

LET US NOW CONSIDER some obvious objections to this account. Some argue that the framers of the Fourteenth Amendment stated that their amendment would not prohibit segregation. How then can we read their amendment to do exactly what they denied it would do? I submit that this criticism under-reads the text of the amendment, and over-reads the legislative history. The text mandates equal citizenship and equal protection, pure and simple. The text does not say that there is some exception for segregation; there is no clause providing that "segregation is permissible even if unequal." Nor did the sponsors think that there was such a categorical exception. They merely argued that segregation was not ipso facto unequal and unconstitutional.

As a matter of strict mathematical logic, they were right. Logically, it is possible to imagine some kinds of segregation that are not unequal. Consider, for example, separate bathrooms for men and women. Today, these sex-segregated bathrooms are not generally viewed—by either men or women—as invidious or stigmatizing or subordinating. Not yet, at least. But it is possible to imagine a different world (or perhaps a future world) in which it is generally understood—either by most men or most women, or both—that separate bathrooms are a way of keeping women down. By 1954, I submit, it was clear that racially separate schools—and racially separate bathrooms, for that matter—were not equal in purpose or effect or social meaning. They were a way of keeping blacks down. Blacks knew this, as any secret-ballot vote among them would have revealed. And whites knew this, too, in their hearts, though many denied it with their lips.

Admittedly, Jim Crow had a different legal form than a series of state laws on the books in the mid-1860s generally known as "Black Codes"—a series of laws that the Fourteenth Amendment's framers avowedly sought to prohibit as paradigmatic examples of improper government action. The 1860s Black Codes were formally asymmetric: they imposed disabilities on blacks but not whites. Jim Crow, segregationists argued, was different from the Black Codes because American apartheid was formally symmetric—blacks could not go to the "white" school, but whites were symmetrically barred from attending the "black" schools. (Similarly, men today cannot use women's restrooms and women symmetrically cannot use men's restrooms.)[11]

But Jim Crow had the same purpose and effect and social meaning as the 1860s Black Codes: both Jim Crow and the Black Codes aimed at keeping blacks down and depriving them of equal status. Formal symmetry does not mean the law is necessarily valid; it just means the law is not *automatically* invalid (as the Black Codes were). Thus, we must look to a Jim Crow law in its entirety, and ask whether it really was equal in purpose and effect and social meaning. It is possible to imagine some alternative world where strong majorities of both blacks and whites genuinely preferred a system of mutually respectful racial segregation, a world where no stigma in fact attached to pervasive racial segregation, a world where racial apartheid was not simply a way by which whites kept blacks down. But that was not the world of 1954, to any honest observer.

Note also that on my account, certain forms of affirmative action need not, perhaps, be seen as the legal and moral equivalent of Jim Crow. Consider, for example, the kind of educational affirmative action that Justice Lewis Powell was willing to endorse in the famed 1978 *Bakke* case. Does this kind of affirmative action in effect make racial minorities a favored aristocracy? Is its purpose and effect and social meaning to demean or humiliate or attaint whites, or keep whites down? Is its ultimate aim a two-class society of unequal castes? Is it truly the legal and moral equivalent of the 1860s Black Codes? These are some (though they are not the only) questions that my approach would invite us to ask.

Now consider another possible objection to my account. Some have argued that the Fourteenth Amendment prohibited only violations of "civil rights" as opposed to "social rights" and "political rights." Even if we accept this view, it cannot justify a system of government-mandated apartheid in public education. To see why, let's take a closer look at the categories of "political rights" and "social rights."

"Political rights"—voting, militia service, jury service, and office-holding—were repeatedly and emphatically claimed by the supporters of the Fourteenth Amendment to lie beyond the reach of section 1.[12] A textualist, of course, is entitled to ask where the words of the amendment signal this limitation of scope. The textual answer is as follows: The Fourteenth Amendment language of "privileges" and "immunities" of "citizens" is adapted from Article IV, which in general demands that State A not discriminate against visiting citizens of State B. If State A allows its citizens to own real property, it must allow visitors from State B to do the same. Likewise for a vast range of "civil" rights such as the rights to contract, sue and be sued, testify in court, worship, speak, move about, and own a business. But a visitor from State B is not entitled to serve in State A's militia or jury or legislature, or to vote in State A's elections, on equal terms with the citizens of State A. These "political rights" lie beyond the scope of Article IV—and so, too, they lie beyond the scope of the similar language of the Fourteenth Amendment, as the Court ruled in an 1875 case, *Minor v. Happersett*. Nor is the language of "equal protection" designed to apply to voting and other political rights. This language applies not merely to "citizens," but to all "persons"—paradigmatically, aliens who do not have a constitutional right to vote.

What does this all mean for *Brown*? If we read the Fourteenth Amendment to exempt "political rights," *Brown* still seems plainly right, because *Brown* was not, strictly speaking, a voting-rights case or a jury-service case or a militia-service case or a legislative-office-holding case. *Brown* was a public-education case, and public education is not strictly limited to voters, or as tightly linked to voting as, say, jury service or militia service or elective service. Alternatively, if public education were so tightly linked, the rules of the *Fifteenth* Amendment—forbidding race discrimination in voting and all kindred political-rights scenarios—would pick up exactly wherever the Fourteenth Amendment left off. Other clauses governing political rights would also come into play. So whether government-mandated apartheid in public education is deemed a violation of "civil rights" or of "political rights" or of both, it is unconstitutional.

Put differently, when we read the Fourteenth Amendment not in isolation, but in tandem with the later Fifteenth Amendment, we see that today's governments must include blacks as full equals in all "civil" and "political" domains, regardless of where we draw the exact line between these two domains.[13]

So much for "political rights." What about "social rights"? Here, the basic idea is that the Fourteenth Amendment does not compel "social equality" between the races. This is what many supporters of the amendment said in the 1860s; and once again, we are entitled to ask where the text says anything of the sort. And the answer I think is as follows: As a private citizen, you remain free to be, bluntly, a racist. You can view your race as superior, and you are free, for example, to refuse to invite members of other races to your private dinner parties. The textual basis for this continued freedom is what we today call the "state-action" doctrine. Under this doctrine, the Fourteenth Amendment limits the actions of government (the "state"), but does not impose all the same restrictions on private citizens. A government may not enact a Black Code, but a private citizen is free to have a kind of Black Code for his dinner guests: no blacks allowed at the Smith house.

But *Brown*, of course, was not about private dinner parties. The government was *mandating* segregation—it forbade even students of different races who *wanted* to socialize together in school from doing so in the public system.

The issue might have been trickier had the government set up three schools—one for blacks, one for whites, and one open to both—with perfect freedom of choice among the schools. Such a scheme might seem to allow genuine "private choice" and "social" freedom not to associate, but even here there is ground for skepticism. Would the choice genuinely be free, and untainted by past governmental discrimination or current pressure?[14] Why only three schools, and not, say, four? For example, what about Asian Americans? Would they be obliged to go to the mixed school, whereas blacks and whites had choices? And what if a "black" decided that she was really "white" and insisted on attending the school for whites? Wouldn't the government need to enforce its scheme with an odious set of Nuremberg-style laws specifying the exact percentage of blood that made a person "black" or "white"? (This issue is somewhat less problematic, as a practical matter, for sex-segregated bathrooms, given the conventional view that sex is binary—male/female—with rather few in-between cases.)

BROWN AND THE MEANING OF LIFE

There is, of course, much more that could be said about *Brown*, but I hope I have said enough to illuminate the basic constitutional issues. I conclude by drawing a few lessons of the case, both for those of us who have chosen to live our professional lives in the law and for Americans and human beings more generally.

The first lesson is holism. In both life and law we must try to see the big picture. I have suggested that a complete account of *Brown* requires us to confront several parts of our Constitution, and to synthesize the meaning of both the Creation era (which gave us the Founders' Constitution) and the Reconstruction experience (which gave us a new birth of freedom in Amendments Thirteen through Fifteen).

As with many other vocations, the practice of law can sometimes be narrowing. One becomes an expert in subparagraph 4(A)(ii) of section 1723 of some code or other, and one spends much of one's professional life immersed in that subparagraph. So, too, the practice of constitutional interpretation can sometimes be narrowing—"clause-bound," in John Ely's fine phrase.[15]

I suggest that we resist the narrowing impulse. Good constitutional interpretation is marked by a view of the whole as well as the part. Peripheral vision is important; we must attend to how various words, principles, and policies intersect and interact in kaleidoscopic ways.[16]

The second lesson is humility. American constitutional lawyers and judges have at times done great good, but at other times have betrayed the Constitution's grand promise and explicit promises. *Dred Scott* read the Constitution in a mean and perverse way. The Supreme Court in the 1954 *Brown* case was part of the solution, but let us not forget that the Supreme Court in the 1896 *Plessy v. Ferguson* case was part of the problem. The Court itself had blessed Jim Crow in *Plessy*, calling racial separation "equal" when it was not. This explicit blessing helped entrench American apartheid, leading to huge injustice for many years in many places. The Court in 1954 had blood on its hands.

The *Brown* Court did not apologize for *Plessy*. The Court did not even squarely overrule *Plessy*. The justices merely said that *Plessy* did not apply to public education. Although there were perhaps good reasons for this rhetorical caginess and reticence on the part of the Court in 1954, a candid confession of error is often better than a stubborn refusal to admit one's past mistakes. This is particularly true for lawyers and judges, but it is also true more universally.[17]

The final lesson is humanity. American apartheid was an oppressive, soul-deadening, and degrading system of subordination, yet many persons at the time supported it or acquiesced in it. The same thing could be said of antebellum slavery. But we are hardly at the end of history today. Are there similar injustices, inhumanities, and systems of subordination today that we are ignoring or even supporting? Is the distribution of wealth in our society—or in the world—a just and humane one? Does our law continue to demean and degrade some persons because of morally irrelevant traits fixed at birth—sexual orientation, perhaps?

RECALL THAT IN 1954, Jim Crow was hardly unique to the state of Kansas or to its capital city of Topeka. Legal apartheid existed in many other American cities and states. But in 1954 de jure segregation was emphatically not a blot upon every state and region. America in 1954 was geographically divided, and Kansas was not entirely on the right side of this divide.

Now flash back from 1954 to 1854. Then, too, America was geographically divided. Then, too, the division involved race—not racial segregation, but a racialized slave system. And then, too, Kansas was not altogether on the right side of justice and history. In the aftermath of the 1854 Kansas-Nebraska Act, the Kansas Territory was itself deeply divided—bleeding, both literally and figuratively. It was, in fact, the amoral enactment and the immoral implementation of the odious 1854 law, opening up Kansas's previously free soil to possible control by proslavery forces, that propelled Illinois's Abraham Lincoln back into national politics.

The events of 1854 and of 1954 are powerfully memorialized in modern-day Topeka. The Brown v. Board of Education National Historic Site—the only unit of the National Park System named for a Court case—features a particularly poetic exhibit, "From Brown to *Brown*," tracing a uniquely complex Kansas story that highlights John Brown and Bleeding Kansas in the 1850s and the Brown family plaintiffs in the 1950s.

But remembering the past is not enough. We must also redeem the past.[18] We must be worthy of the sacrifices and promises made by our constitutional fathers—and mothers. And so I ask the good people of Topeka, and the good people of Kansas: on the issue of gay equality, are you, *today*, on the right side of history and justice?

America is once again geographically divided. Many a state has affirmed the full marriage equality of same-sex couples. Kansas has not—not yet, at least. Why not?

As I write these words in 2015, Kansas is one of approximately thirty states whose extant and operative state laws purport to ban all same-sex marriage. Strikingly, ten of the eleven states that joined the Confederacy in the 1860s are members of this modern-day hall of shame; only Virginia, the northernmost ex-gray state, has cheerfully transitioned toward recognition of same-sex marriage, thanks to recent choices made by the state's governor and attorney general. In the years before *Brown*, all eleven former Confederate states were also particularly egregious nests of Jim Crow. I wonder what Abraham Lincoln and Hugo Black would think.*

Of course, there are important differences between race discrimination and sexual-orientation discrimination. But there are also important similarities (and also important similarities to religious discrimination). History never repeats itself exactly. But it often rhymes.

Three score years after *Brown*, the Court's condemnation of Jim Crow seems clearly right. History has not judged the diehard segregationists of the 1950s kindly. Three score years from now, how will history judge Kansas's current hostility to marriage equality? How will history judge the policies of other anti-gay-marriage states, which at present have likewise failed to redeem the inspiring and still unfolding inclusive and egalitarian logic of America's Constitution and of the great case captioned *Brown v. Board*?

_____

*As for what Anthony Kennedy might think, see the previous chapter, pp. 92–93, 104–105. There are nice questions of categorization involved in determining which state laws formally on the books remain truly operative, as state executive authorities ponder their enforcement and litigation options at a time of extraordinary legal and political flux. My tally here distinguishes between those forward-leaning states (such as California and, more recently, Virginia) whose chief executives now cheerfully recognize the lawfulness of gay marriage even if state laws on the books say otherwise, and those foot-dragging states in which gay marriage either remains unlawful or is lawful only because of a federal court order whose constitutional correctness continues to be contested or questioned by the state's governor or attorney general. In this latter cluster of states, which includes Kansas, future gay marriages might be prohibited in the event that the federal court order were to be lifted. Stay tuned; this story is fast-breaking. For more on Virginia as a modern-day bellwether state, see this book's Conclusion, p. 272.

CHAPTER 6

IOWA:

REREADING

TINKER V. DES MOINES

W hen I was a high school sophomore in Walnut Creek, California, something happened that changed my life, putting me
on a path that led directly to law school and, indeed, to my
current job. In 1973–1974, as a staff member of my school newspaper, I
wrote a biweekly political humor column that tried to mimic the style of
my favorite journalist, Art Hoppe, a brilliant satirist for the *San Francisco
Chronicle*. Several of my pieces mocked then-president Nixon. Apparently,
my high school principal didn't share my sense of humor. Unamused, he
prohibited the publication of one of my columns.

My journalism adviser, Ms. Ruth Ann White, stood by me. So did
another one of my teachers, Mr. James Hand. They pointed me to various
articles and books discussing the constitutional rights of public school
students, and told me about a 1969 Supreme Court decision, *Tinker v. Des
Moines Independent Community School District*. The case had involved high
school students claiming free-expression rights against thin-skinned and
overbearing school administrators. The justices, I was amazed to learn, had
sided with the high school students and against the high school principal!
On the way to this remarkable result, the Court had resoundingly proclaimed that students do not "shed their constitutional rights to freedom
of speech or expression at the schoolhouse gate."

What I read about the *Tinker* case stiffened my resolve to stand up and
speak out. My friends and I organized a respectable student protest. (In
general, protesting oppression is more fun than doing homework.) Eventually, we won the principal over and the censorship stopped. It probably

didn't hurt that, while the censorship debate was unfolding, our school newspaper began to win various interscholastic journalism awards that increased the credibility of the student newspaper staff and of our faithful faculty adviser, Ms. White.

As a result of all this, I began to think in a serious way about constitutional rights. The following year, I wrote a detailed investigative article about sex discrimination in our school's sports program. The principal did not love my story; but he did let it run. In retrospect, I see a straight line between all these events and my present job as a teacher and scholar of constitutional law, with a special interest in the Bill of Rights and related issues of sex and race equality.

In this chapter, I revisit the *Tinker* case. To put this case into a broader constitutional context, I shall try to weave together three stories—stories of the constitutional lessons that emerged from three bloody wars in American history.

The first story involves the Revolutionary War, which led to the creation of the nation, the establishment of the Constitution, and the birth of the Bill of Rights, which includes, of course, the First Amendment. Next comes the story of the Civil War, which prompted the Reconstruction of the nation and the rebirth of the Bill of Rights and the First Amendment through the Fourteenth Amendment. Finally, there is the story of the Vietnam War and the *Tinker* case itself, a case powerfully illuminated by the lessons of the first two stories.

THE REVOLUTIONARY WAR AND THE FIRST AMENDMENT

Recall that British North America was founded over the course of the seventeenth and eighteenth centuries as a series of distinct British colonies, established at different times and operating under different charters and via different legal institutions. As late as 1763, as the Seven Years' War between England and France was drawing to a close, New Yorkers had no idea that they would soon become part of a single continental entity connected to North Carolina but not to Nova Scotia, to British New Jersey but not to the British West Indies. Georgia was by overland travel weeks away from Massachusetts. South Carolinians were more likely to follow events in London than in Boston.[1]

The American Revolution was waged against an imperial center. In the 1760s and 1770s, the British unwittingly forced the American colonies to band together by treating these very different entities alike and by imposing similar burdens and taxes on all of them. As America began to develop a continental consciousness, provincial governments led the charge against Parliament. When Parliament went too far, colonial governments mobilized opposition by forming committees of correspondence and reinvigorating militias. It was the several states, in an international assembly—a transnational "Congress" of ambassadors akin to the later Congress of Vienna in 1815—that declared independence. The Articles of Confederation likewise embodied a confederacy of sovereign states.

The political ethos of the Founding strongly associated liberty with localism. The rallying cry of the American Revolution—"No taxation without representation!"—was not pure and simple anti-taxation, as some would have us believe. The Revolution was not so much anti-taxation as pro–provincial rights. Taxation was acceptable so long as the taxing entity was the provincial government, in which the interests of the taxed were faithfully represented. In contrast, the colonists had no representation in Parliament.

Americans were living in a world where vast geographic empires— Spanish, Russian, Ottoman, and so on—were associated with unfreedom. Liberty was local. The history of the world up to that point was one in which no continent-spanning regime had ever been democratic. Genuine democracies and self-governing republics—various ancient Greek city-states, Venice, and pre-imperial Rome—had extended only over small geographic areas. Once Rome became an empire, it needed an emperor, and an emperor rules with a standing army and heavy taxes. Ancient empires were neither representative nor democratic.

Thus, it was in the best tradition of liberty, as then understood, that the Articles of Confederation gave most of the power to state and local governments. But that loose system of confederation was not strong enough to hold the new union together, and so thirteen years after independence, a new Constitution came onto the scene. This new Constitution created a much stronger central government, and because of that, its Federalist supporters had a lot of persuading to do. Anti-Federalist skeptics wondered whether it was possible to have a truly trustworthy and freedom-loving continental government. These skeptics insisted that, if the Constitution was going to create such a powerful central government, it must also include some special safeguards beyond what had been proposed by the Philadelphia Convention. These safeguards became our Bill of Rights.[2]

It is important to remember how the original Bill of Rights was associated with localism and, in some important ways, with majority rule rather than minority rights. Recall the First Amendment's first words: "Congress shall make no law . . . " From the outset, this was an amendment that applied against the "Congress"—against the federal government, but not against state and local governments. Likewise, the rest of the original Bill of Rights applied only against the federal government—a point confirmed by the 1833 Marshall Court case of *Barron v. Baltimore*.[3]

Congress at the Founding was seen by Anti-Federalist skeptics as unrepresentative, much as the colonists had viewed its predecessor, Parliament. Of course, colonists had not been allowed to vote for Parliament at all, whereas citizens of the new nation would get to vote for Congress; but many Anti-Federalists still wondered whether a tiny elite in Congress could truly be representative of the vast diversity of the nation. How much power should be granted to twenty-six senators, of whom a quorum would be fourteen, eight of whom would constitute a majority? How much of the business of this wide continent could be entrusted to eight people? Compared to a typical state legislature with a hundred or more lawmakers, the Senate seemed dangerously small and unrepresentative. Even the national House of Representatives was smaller than most state legislatures.

Anti-Federalists worried that only great men—grandees with extensive reputations—would be elected to Congress from large geographic districts. (The wider the district, the more money and fame would typically be needed to win on Election Day.) The fear was that these lordly men would go off to an Imperial American Capital City where they would take up permanent residence, hobnob with haughty European diplomats and ambassadors, rule with a federal standing army, and impose unpopular taxes on the folks back home. Virginians—at least white, male, propertied Virginians—thought that they could trust the Virginia House Delegates (originally the House of Burgesses) because it had been up and running for more than a century and a half, since 1619. It was already older for the Founding generation than the Fourteenth Amendment is for us today. What Anti-Federalists feared was not the old, established state legislature, but this newfangled "Congress," the likes of which had never before been seen in human history, a purportedly democratic legislature empowered to govern a continent.[4]

To check the new central government, the original Bill of Rights was designed not simply to protect individual rights or minority rights, but also to protect states' rights against the federal government. The Tenth Amendment is a clear statement of states' rights, but this same principle can also be found in the First Amendment. Recall from Chapter 2 that the wording "*Congress shall make no law*" is actually a gloss on the wording of the Article I, section 8, necessary-and-proper clause, which reads: "*Congress shall* have Power . . . To *make all Laws* which shall be necessary and proper for carrying into Execution the foregoing Powers." (My emphasis.)

The original First Amendment is thus saying that there is no federal power over certain domains—no power not just as a matter of individual rights, but simply as a matter of Article I, section 8, enumerated authority to legislate. There is no enumerated federal power to censor the press; there is no enumerated federal power on the topic of church-state policy in the several states. Certain things are left to state policy. So, when the First Amendment says "Congress shall make no law respecting an establishment of religion," these words prevent a nationally established church; they do not prevent a state-established church. State-established churches were perfectly permissible under the original First Amendment.

The picture at the Founding was even more dramatic than that: the Founders' First Amendment actually protected a state's right to have an established church. Depending on how one counts, six of the thirteen states had government-sponsored churches at the time the Constitution was adopted. Even the "nonestablishment" states generally had laws that were pro-Protestant or, more generally, pro-Christian.[5] The First Amendment said not only that Congress could not create a nationally established church, but also that Congress could not disestablish any existing or future state churches. A federal disestablishment law would be a congressional law "respecting"—that is, on the topic of—"an establishment of religion."

Why did the Anti-Federalists trust states to legislate in these areas while distrusting the federal government? Partly because states were seen as closer to the people. Also, a uniform, one-size-fits-all continental policy on religion would have been inappropriate because America was so religiously uneven, with different religions spread across different regions. There were Anglicans down South, Quakers in Pennsylvania, Baptists in Rhode Island, Catholics in Maryland, and Congregationalists in New England. Two and a quarter centuries ago, that was tremendous religious diversity, and it translated into wide variation in church-state policy across the several states. The only thing that all could agree on at the Founding was that the federal government should keep its hands off.

The original First Amendment was, in effect, modeled on the European Peace of Augsburg of 1555 and the Treaty of Westphalia of 1648, in which the basic idea was that the Holy Roman Empire would have no uniform imperial policy on religion. Instead, the matter would be left to local choice. Analogously, the Americans basically said: "We cannot agree on the national level about the proper relationship between government and religion, so we are going to leave that up to each state to decide for itself."

Beyond the First Amendment's rules limiting Congress in the domain of religion, the amendment also emphatically prohibited Congress from abridging freedom of speech. Historically, the phrase "the freedom of speech" was at its core a guarantee of political speech and expression. The phrase appears prominently in the English Bill of Rights of 1689, which says there shall be free speech and debate in Parliament. "Parliament" is of course a place where people parley—that is, speak—and a place, in particular, where they speak about politics.[6]

One of the big ideas of the American Constitution is that, on this side of the water, Parliament is not sovereign; "We the People" are. Therefore, "We" should have the same freedom of speech—the same freedom of political discourse—that in England was reserved specifically for the legislature. Thus the First Amendment aims to protect political expression, especially the expression of opposition to a possibly unrepresentative national government.

As it turned out, some Anti-Federalist fears were justified. Within a decade of the adoption of the Constitution and Bill of Rights, Congress passed the infamous Sedition Act of 1798. This law, signed by President John Adams, made it a federal crime to criticize the president of the United States or a member of Congress. Tellingly, it did not make it a federal crime to criticize the vice president, who at the time happened to be Thomas Jefferson, the leader of the opposition party. The law did not make it a crime for members of Congress to criticize their challengers—only for the challengers to criticize the incumbents—and it expired after the next election. The Sedition Act was a textbook example of governmental self-dealing, and people began to organize and speak out against it.[7]

Where did they do so? Not so much in newspapers, because attacking the Sedition Act in newspapers opened the attacker to prosecution under the Sedition Act itself. So opposition took shape in the state legislatures, where speakers were assumed to have immunity for their legislative speech and debate. With the help of James Madison and Thomas Jefferson behind the scenes, the Virginia and Kentucky legislatures enacted resolutions publicly condemning the Sedition Act in an effort to mobilize constituents against Congress, much as earlier colonial legislatures had mobilized opposition to Parliament.

The Kentucky and Virginia Resolutions of the late 1790s highlight an important point about freedom of speech at the time of the Founding: the right was in some ways majoritarian. It was centrally about protecting a majority of the citizens against a possibly unrepresentative Congress trying to suppress popular speech, like the speech of the Jeffersonians in 1798–1800. Jefferson won the election of 1800–1801, and once in office he allowed the ill-conceived Sedition Act to expire and pardoned all who had previously been convicted under it. Thus, his victory was a victory for the rights of dissenting speakers and dissenting speech.[8]

But "dissenting speech" here means "somewhat popular speech against an unpopular central government," and it was protected largely by empowering state and local governments and local juries. Decades earlier, the hero of the 1730s case of John Peter Zenger, who published a newspaper in colonial New York and was prosecuted for seditious libel, was the local jury that let Zenger go free because he was printing popular things against an unpopular, royally appointed governor.[9]

Building on the Zenger experience, the general rule against "prior restraint," a rule that is part of our original First Amendment tradition, is also pro-jury. If the goal is to directly protect free expression, a rule saying that government cannot prohibit speech in advance, but can chop the speaker's hand or head off afterward, is not so obviously protective. (The knowledge that speakers who go too far tend to lose their hands or heads exerts, to borrow a phrase, a certain "chilling effect.") How, then, does a rule against prior restraint actually protect free expression if the speaker can still be punished after the fact?

Here's how: Prior restraints, on the one hand, were enforced by judges issuing injunctions and by administrators and licensors—professional organs of the state. After-the-fact punishment, on the other hand, would require conviction by a jury of ordinary citizens. If the speaker was saying relatively popular things that the people in his locality liked, the jury could acquit—essentially, nullify the law—just as Zenger's jury had famously acquitted/nullified. So the prior-restraint rule of the First Amendment was very much about empowering local juries, making sure that they, too—and not merely federal judges, who were, after all, appointed by presidents, who in turn might be thin-skinned types like John Adams—served as the co-protectors of free expression.[10]

Now this first story paints a very different picture of the First Amendment than the standard picture of the amendment that dominates our modern imagination. In the story I have just told, the amendment is largely localist and majoritarian, celebrating local juries and states' rights, safeguarding the authority of states to have established churches, and protecting a certain kind of political dissent, but only against Congress.

This first story captures only part of what a case like *Tinker* is about. To fully understand *Tinker* and the modern vision of free-expression law that it epitomizes, we also need to examine the second big war in American history, the Civil War—a war not about the oppressiveness of an imperial central government, but rather about the tyranny practiced in certain state governments.

THE CIVIL WAR AND
THE FOURTEENTH AMENDMENT

In our first story, the trans-Mississippi West, which today comprises Iowa and its neighboring states, was only a gleam in the eye of the most far-sighted Founders. But after America acquired the Louisiana Territory from France in the early 1800s, the North and the South had to start thinking seriously about the far West. The most momentous questions about the West concerned the deepest divide between North and South: slavery.

In the aftermath of the Missouri Compromise of 1820 and Nat Turner's slave rebellion in 1831, a new wave of American abolitionists swept onto the scene, waging a religious crusade against slavery. To these crusaders, slavery was first and foremost a sin, and they tried to persuade slaveholders one at a time to renounce sin, to free their slaves, and thus to free themselves from their own bondage to slavery. In many circles, religious abolitionists in the 1830s were dismissed as kooks and cranks, zealots and fanatics. They were a small minority, shunned by respectable people. But they happened to be right, morally and, ultimately, legally.

The religious crusade against slavery in the 1830s later ripened into a political crusade to limit slavery's expansion and thereby put slavery on a path of ultimate extinction. Thus, in 1860 the party of Lincoln's first goal was to stop the western expansion of this Evil Empire called the Slave Power; then, once that was accomplished, the goal would be to push slavery back. The idea was very similar to the domino theory of communist containment a hundred years later: first stop communist expansion at the world level, then try to roll back the advances it had already made.

The Civil War was precipitated by extremely aggressive slavocratic attempts to stifle liberty, both by expanding slavery into the West and by restricting freedom in the South itself. First, of course, the liberty of slaves was snatched away, via a system requiring brutal repression, slave by slave. Then, it became necessary to oppress free blacks down south, because these men and women, by their very example of being free and walking around, were an incitement to slaves. Next, it became imperative to suppress antislavery southern whites—and there were more than a few such people. (Most white southerners were not, in fact, slave owners.) Finally, the Slave Power had to suppress northerners who tried to come down south and preach against slavery—and in some of the most notorious cases, these antislavery speakers were literally "preaching" against slavery in pulpits and other religious venues. Thus, in order to prop up slavery, the Slave Power had to embark upon an ever-widening spiral of oppression—and, especially relevant for our purposes, speech suppression.

The Republican Party in 1860 was an outlawed party in the Deep South. It was, in effect, a crime in some southern states to be a Republican; it was sedition. The First Amendment did not yet protect citizens against state oppression of this sort. There were no remedies to be found in federal court. Let's recall that Abraham Lincoln's name did not appear on the ballot in any deep southern state and that he received not a single popular vote south of Virginia. But he was elected nonetheless; the southern states then seceded, and the Civil War ensued.

At the war's end, the Republican Party needed to reconstruct southern states before they could be allowed back into normal relations with the rest of the Union. The Republicans needed to establish fundamental preconditions for a healthy democracy. In order to do that, they adopted what was, in essence, a second Bill of Rights, the Fourteenth Amendment.

The Founding era had witnessed broad concern that far-off, aloof, unrepresentative governments could violate liberty—first Parliament, in which the colonists had no vote at all, and then Congress, which was feared as possibly unrepresentative and prone to self-dealing. These Founding-era realizations established the need for a Bill of Rights against the imperial center. In light of lessons learned from the Slave Power and the Civil War, it became clear that even supposedly democratic states and local governments could also threaten liberty. This type of oppression called out for a new Bill of Rights, one against the periphery, and one that would complement the initial Bill of Rights against the center.

A NEW BILL OF RIGHTS against states made especially good sense in light of the antebellum experience of geographic expansion into places such as Ohio, Illinois, Indiana, and Iowa. The story of the Fourteenth Amendment is thus not simply a north-south saga, but also a tale of east-west relations.

Whereas states in the Founding era had banded together to form the federal government, the later experience of territorial expansion had reversed this polarity: in the early nineteenth century, the federal government was creating new states at a prodigious rate. (Recall from Chapter 1 that midwesterners such as Lincoln understood this point instinctively.) These new midwestern states typically began their lives as territories.

When Congress legislated for these territories, it was obviously bound by the federal Bill of Rights. The same was true when Congress delegated its regulatory powers over a given territory to a home-grown territorial legislature elected by the people of the territory. If Congress, thanks to the Bill of Rights, could not abridge free press or fair trial in, say, the Iowa Territory, then neither could the territorial legislature of Iowa abridge these rights. Surely, this local legislature could not exercise any more power than Congress itself could exercise. (As lawyers might put the point, surely a mere "agent" acting on behalf of a "principal" has no more power than the "principal" himself has.)

But when the Iowa Territory became the State of Iowa, and when its territorial legislature thus became a state legislature, it seemed odd that this new legislative body should be allowed to invade rights that the old legislative body had been obliged to respect. Shouldn't the good old Bill of Rights continue to apply against the local legislature, just as before? And, if not, shouldn't the Constitution be amended to correct this oddity, via a new Bill of Rights against state abuses?[11]

THE CANONICAL EXPRESSION of this new Bill of Rights is the second sentence of the Fourteenth Amendment: "No State shall make or enforce any law which shall abridge the privileges or immunities of citizens of the United States . . . " What was meant by "privileges [and] immunities"? Things like freedom of speech and of the press, freedom of religion, freedom against unreasonable search and seizure, as well as the right of habeas corpus. As we have seen in previous chapters—the point is absolutely central to the history of American constitutional law—the Fourteenth Amendment's privileges and immunities encompassed at a minimum the rights in the original Bill of Rights, plus rights found elsewhere in the Constitution. These rights are privileges and immunities of American citizens that no state may abridge. Note, in particular, how the Fourteenth Amendment borrows from the language of the First: "Congress *shall make no law . . . abridging*" in the First, and "*No* State *shall make* or enforce any *law* which shall *abridge*" in the Fourteenth. (My emphasis.) But the Fourteenth says that we need a Bill of Rights against the *states*, a new Bill of Rights to be protected and enforced by federal courts and by the federal government against the periphery.[12]

After the Civil War, juries were no longer viewed as quite so trustworthy, because they might reflect the same forces of social intolerance that the rights were meant to protect against. The Revolutionary Founders loved juries: in 1760, colonists did not get to vote for Parliament (and they certainly did not have any say in who was to be king), so one of the few places where they could actually make their voices heard was a local jury room. In most colonies, imperial officials appointed colonial judges, so judges were not always heroes to the colonists. The colonial jury thus naturally evolved into a political institution—one of the most truly representative institutions in the colonies—so it is unsurprising that the jury emerged as the main bulwark of the original Bill of Rights. We can see the Founders' emphasis on the jury explicitly in the Fifth Amendment's grand jury provision, in the Sixth Amendment's criminal jury provision, and in the Seventh Amendment's civil jury provision. We can also see it implicitly in things like the First Amendment's prior-restraint rule and the Second Amendment's celebration of local militias, which were close cousins of local juries.

The Civil War experience, however, tempered American enthusiasm for juries. A new model of dissent emerged, involving a commitment to protect not only those who opposed government policy (although that continued to be very important), but also those who challenged the majority viewpoint. Of course, the paramount virtue of the jury to the Framers was its fundamentally populist makeup, but a majoritarian jury provides a less than complete safeguard for this new kind of dissent.

Part of the reason it is important to protect the lonely dissenter is that, given enough time to make her case, she might be able to persuade a majority. Abolitionists were a case in point: dismissed as utter extremists in 1830, these crusaders had become the heart and soul, the dominant force, of the Republican Party by 1866. Even a strict believer in majority rule has to protect the current minority in order to give it a chance to ripen into an ultimate majority if allowed to make its case.

The reconstructed Bill of Rights protects not merely political expression but also religious speech. At the Founding, religion was in the First Amendment along with freedom of speech, but was included largely for reasons of states' rights and enumerated federal power: Congress had no Article I authority to regulate religion or repress free expression. No previous state constitution had linked religion and speech, or religion and press. Only the federal Bill of Rights linked them, and it did so on the theory of enumerated power.[13]

By the time of the Fourteenth Amendment, there was a different vision aborning, one that favored the absolute protection of religious speech, and not simply the relegation of the matter to local governments. This new vision came about in part because Americans now understood that religious and political speech were intimately connected, as exemplified by the abolitionists. This vision also came about in part because of a resurgent respect for individual conscience, a respect evident in the writings of Ralph Waldo Emerson, Henry David Thoreau, and John Stuart Mill.[14]

These men were all mid-nineteenth-century thinkers and writers. They postdate the Founding, and it is anachronistic to simply read their nineteenth-century views back into an eighteenth-century First Amendment text. But these post-Founding thinkers and writers did of course predate the Fourteenth Amendment, and that amendment was in fact adopted with these thinkers and writers centrally in mind. Ideas about protecting religious and artistic and female speakers, such as Harriet Beecher Stowe; ideas about protecting the lonely northern carpetbagger down south; ideas about protecting a black man like Frederick Douglass in a white country—these are Fourteenth Amendment ideas more than First Amendment ideas. This new birth of freedom in the Fourteenth Amendment helps redefine the entire American ethos to include more emphasis on the individual, and the need to protect him or her against majoritarian oppression and social intolerance, not just against unrepresentative government.[15]

All of which brings us to *Tinker*.

The Vietnam War and
the *Tinker* Case

In 1969, the Supreme Court decided *Tinker v. Des Moines Independent Community School District*. Here are the facts of the case, as described by the Court itself:

> Petitioner John F. Tinker, 15 years old, and petitioner Christopher Eckhardt, 16 years old, attended high schools in Des Moines, Iowa. Petitioner Mary Beth Tinker, John's sister, was a 13-year-old student in junior high school.
>
> In December 1965, a group of adults and students in Des Moines held a meeting at the Eckhardt home. The group determined to publicize their objections to the hostilities in Vietnam and their support for a truce by wearing black armbands during the holiday season and by fasting on December 16 and New Year's Eve. Petitioners and their parents had previously engaged in similar activities, and they decided to participate in the program.
>
> The principals of the Des Moines schools became aware of the plan to wear armbands. On December 14, 1965, they met and adopted a policy that any student wearing an armband to school would be asked to remove it, and if he refused he would be suspended until he returned without the armband. Petitioners were aware of the regulation that the school authorities adopted.
>
> On December 16, Mary Beth and Christopher wore black armbands to their schools. John Tinker wore his armband the next day. They were all sent home and suspended from school until they would come back without their armbands. They did not return to school until after the planned period for wearing armbands had expired—that is, until after New Year's Day.

In a watershed ruling on the free-speech rights of students, the Court sided with the Tinkers and Eckhardt, and against the Des Moines school principals. According to the Court's majority opinion, penned by Justice Abe Fortas, students do not "shed their constitutional rights to freedom of speech or expression at the schoolhouse gate," and these constitutional rights surely encompassed the right to engage in "a silent, passive expression of opinion, unaccompanied by any disorder or disturbance on the part of petitioners."*

IN LIGHT OF THE FOUNDING and Reconstruction stories that I have recounted, what are we to make of the *Tinker* case?

Tinker surely reflects some abiding lessons of the Founding story. Consider, for example, the *Tinker* Court's vigorous protection of political expression—in particular, expression that criticized government policies, namely, the Johnson administration's policies in prosecuting the Vietnam War. The Court exhibited special vigilance in *Tinker* because the challenged school rule seemed specifically aimed against this kind of oppositional speech. In the Court's words: "It is . . . relevant that the school authorities did not purport to prohibit the wearing of all symbols of all political or controversial significance. The record shows that students at some of the schools wore buttons relating to national political campaigns, and some even wore the iron cross, traditionally a symbol of Nazism. The order prohibiting the wearing of armbands did not extend to these. Instead, a particular symbol—black armbands worn to exhibit opposition to this Nation's involvement in Vietnam—was singled out for prohibition."

The school's apparent targeting of those speaking out against government policy violates a core Founding idea. Governments are especially

---

* Two justices dissented—Justice John Marshall Harlan the younger and Justice Hugo Black. The latter, three days shy of his eighty-third birthday, was the oldest justice on the Court, and he died less than three years later. Recall my earlier reminder, supra p. 54, that arteries harden, and that Justice Black's opinions near the end of his life were not, as a whole, as impressive as his earlier opinions. Black's later opinions were best when he was simply revisiting fact patterns and constitutional issues identical or closely related to facts and issues that he had pondered early on—incorporation, counsel rights for indigent defendants, malapportionment, and so on. When confronted with new issues and facts late in life, he did not always shine. In 1943, for example, Black understood that schoolchildren could not be obliged to participate in a compulsory flag-salute in school. He thus joined and strongly supported Justice Jackson's landmark opinion for the Court that year in *West Virginia State Board of Education v. Barnette*, which overturned an earlier 1940 Court decision authored by Frankfurter, *Minersville School District v. Gobitis*, that Black had joined but had now come to see as mistaken. The *Tinker* majority opinion repeatedly invoked *Barnette*, but Justice Black failed to see the strong connection between the issues raised in *Barnette* and the admittedly different but nonetheless analogous questions posed in *Tinker*.

apt to try to clamp down on dissent in times of war, and America's free-speech tradition warns us to be especially skeptical in these episodes. Much as the Sedition Act of 1798—which James Madison condemned as utterly antithetical to the First Amendment that he had helped draft a decade earlier—was born in an attempt to stifle criticism of government during a quasi-war against France, so the school policy in *Tinker* arose in an apparent attempt to stifle antiwar (and thus anti-government) criticism during the Vietnam era.

But here is where we must move beyond the Founding and its emphasis on local juries and states' rights. The school's anti-speech rule that was challenged in *Tinker* did not come from Congress or the Johnson administration or any other part of the federal government. Rather, the speech-suppression policy at issue in *Tinker* came from local government, presumably supported at the time by the majority of the local community. In 1965, the Vietnam War was not yet hugely unpopular. On the contrary, both the war and the Johnson administration were riding high in popular opinion in 1965. Had this case been tried by a jury in Des Moines, the Tinkers and Eckhardt might have lost. According to the record, only 7 students out of 18,000 wore armbands in defiance of the schools' policy. The *Tinker* Court was sensitive to that fact, and specifically spoke of the need to protect this minority against majority intolerance: "Any departure from absolute regimentation may cause trouble. Any variation from the *majority*'s opinion may inspire fear. Any word spoken, in class, in the lunchroom, or on the campus, that deviates from the views of another person may start an argument or cause a disturbance. But our Constitution says we must take this risk. . . . [The state] must be able to show that its action was caused by something more than a mere desire to avoid the discomfort and unpleasantness that always accompany an *unpopular* viewpoint."[16]

These are the themes of the Fourteenth Amendment more so than of the Founding. Federal judges, rather than somewhat suspect juries, have become the heroes, protecting liberty against localities. At the Founding, by contrast, local juries were often the heroes, and federal judges were the ones who cheerfully incarcerated those who violated the Sedition Act, brushing aside the defendants' First Amendment challenges to the law.

In pondering how free-expression principles interact with issues regarding the respective powers of different institutions—judges versus juries, for example—we should also note that *Tinker*'s facts did not directly involve a legislature as such. The case involved a censorship regime devised by a group of school administrators—mainly, school principals. Yet free-expression, anti-censorship principles obviously applied.[17]

Here, too, we see the significance of the Fourteenth Amendment to the facts of the case. Strictly speaking, the First Amendment's words concern only legislative action: "*Congress* shall *make* no *law*" abridging free speech. But the Fourteenth Amendment textually widens this narrow institutional focus by targeting not just legislatures making law but all other governmental institutions adjudicating, applying, and fashioning laws and policies and regulations in various nonlegislative contexts: "No state shall make *or enforce* any law" abridging the rights of free expression.* (My emphasis.)

Another central Fourteenth Amendment theme on display in *Tinker* is that of the outsider. Women were highly visible and important speakers at the time of the Fourteenth Amendment. Because of their exclusion from political participation, women became very involved in church organizations, and consequently in religious crusades, which ultimately became political crusades. Anticruelty, temperance, antislavery, antigambling, and women's suffrage movements were all born or widened in the mid-nineteenth century, and all heavily involved women. Women were plainly protected speakers under the Fourteenth Amendment, even though they were not voters. Blacks, too, who were not voters in some of the states, were likewise plainly protected speakers under the amendment. *Tinker* was a natural extension of an amendment designed to protect those kinds of social outsiders. Children in the 1960s, like women and minorities in the 1860s, were social outsiders of sorts.

Also, the Court showed a deep understanding of our Fourteenth Amendment experience when it wrote: "In our system, state-operated schools may not be enclaves of totalitarianism." That image of *totalitarianism* very much captures the essence of the southern states before the Civil War. Another quote from *Tinker*: "School officials do not possess absolute authority over their students. Students in school as well as out of school are 'persons' under our Constitution." The word "persons" appears

---

* In saying that "[n]o state" shall do certain things, the Fourteenth Amendment, like the rest of the Constitution when limiting a "state," of course means that "[n]o state or any subdivision thereof" may do these prohibited things. Cities within states, school districts within cities, principals within school districts, and so on, are, from the viewpoint of the federal Constitution, all arms of states.

in quotation marks because the Court is invoking the first sentence of the Fourteenth Amendment. "All persons born or naturalized in the United States" are citizens thereof, whether they are males or females, born slave or born free, children or adults. All of these are persons, and all are indeed citizens under the Fourteenth Amendment, and therefore entitled to various privileges and immunities of citizenship.

These are core Fourteenth Amendment themes, and they deal with inclusion of formerly marginalized groups and protection of these groups against majority oppression and intolerance. Part of the logic here is that those who might seem like nuts and cranks today, if allowed to make their case, might tomorrow convince the majority of us that they were right after all. This was the story of the antislavery movement in the mid-nineteenth century, and it is also, I suggest, part of the story of the antiwar movement in the mid-twentieth century. So in thinking about *Tinker*, we must ponder not just the First Amendment and the Founders' Bill of Rights, but also the new birth of freedom—the new Bill of Rights—reflected in the Fourteenth Amendment.

HOW MUCH DID I TRULY understand about the deep logic of *Tinker* and the wide background of the Founding and Reconstruction eras when I was a high school sophomore in the early 1970s? Not much, truth be told. But the case did inspire me to believe that even high schoolers have rights, and that rights are important.

Ultimately, rights survive only if the society as a whole—and not just a handful of lawyers and judges—understands these rights, their history, their purpose, and their appropriate limits. For me, that understanding began in high school. While I am now sure I did not fully understand *Tinker*'s deep logic when I first encountered it, I am also sure that the case inspired me to engage the Constitution—to care passionately about this document, to study it, and to share the fruits of that study with my fellow citizens.

Hence this chapter and this book, neither of which might exist but for the courage of a few hardy souls in Des Moines, Iowa, who, many years ago, profoundly inspired a youngster from Walnut Creek, California.

CHAPTER 7

FLORIDA:

GETTING TO THE BOTTOM OF

BUSH V. GORE

T he Bush-Gore Florida extravaganza at the end of the 2000 presidential election gripped the nation and the world, dominating
the headlines and the airwaves day after day. In the battle for the
most powerful position the planet has ever known, more than 100 million
Americans had gone to the polls on Election Day (or in early voting), and
Democrat Al Gore had an undeniable edge in the national popular vote
over Republican George W. Bush. But legally, Gore's half-million-vote
advantage in this national vote counted for naught. Without Florida's 25
electoral votes, Gore had only 266 of these golden tickets—four shy of
the 270 needed to win. If Bush could prevail in Florida, he, and not Gore,
would take the oath of office in January.

So everything came down to vote counting and recounting (and re-re-
counting . . .) in a single electorally dysfunctional state. Within that state,
Bush and Gore were locked in a statistical dead heat, with the contest so
close that a mere feather on either side of the scale—a few hundred votes
here or there—would actually tip the balance. If only a feather could be
found or fabricated! The heat was on and tempers flared.

For weeks, complex and fast-paced litigation ping-ponged between
multiple courthouses as various Florida counts and recounts occurred.
And then, in mid-December, the United States Supreme Court abruptly
stepped in to announce that the recounting must stop. Now! Five justices
purported to join a per curiam opinion proclaiming that the state recount
process was an irreparable violation of voting-equality principles; and
three of these five wrote a separate opinion claiming, in addition, that the

state judiciary overseeing the recount had usurped the constitutional authority of the Florida legislature. Game over, said the Court. Bush won.*

Fifteen years later, now that all the shouting has subsided and the case has receded from the public eye, what is left to say about this Florida fiasco? Let's start by noticing that a wide range of scholars seem to agree with the following proposition: "The Supreme Court twisted the law in the Bush-Gore affair." But here's the rub: *Which* Supreme Court did the twisting? Some scholars (mostly liberals) say that the United States Supreme Court played fast and loose with the law, while other scholars (mostly conservatives) insist that it was the Florida Supreme Court that acted in a lawless, partisan fashion.

In this chapter I explain who was right and who was wrong in *Bush v. Gore*, and why it still matters.

THE COURT(S) AND THE CONSTITUTION(S)

Before I offer my own take on this topic, here is a taste of the highly charged commentary thus far. On January 13, 2001, a month after the United States Supreme Court definitively ended the Florida recount, more than five hundred law professors from over one hundred schools published a joint statement in the *New York Times*. Signatories included Stanford's

---

* Ever since the days of Chief Justice John Marshall, the Court has tried when possible to speak with one voice, by designating one opinion as an opinion of the Court joined by at least a majority of the Court's members. Usually, the justice who takes the lead drafting this opinion puts his name on it, even as others also join it and thereby affirm that they accept its reasoning and result. (Recall from Chapter 2 that opinion-writing resembles baseball in featuring identifiable individual performance within the context of a team effort.) However, in a "per curiam" opinion—Latin for "by the Court"—no single justice claims credit as the lead author. The opinion is presented as a pure team product of every member who signs onto it. In *Bush v. Gore*, four justices—John Paul Stevens, David Souter, Ruth Bader Ginsburg, and Stephen Breyer—dissented from the Court's decision that the recount must end. Three other members of the Court—Chief Justice William Rehnquist and Justices Clarence Thomas and Antonin Scalia—purported to join the Court's per curiam opinion, but wrote a separate concurrence that, as we shall see, suggests that they did not really buy into the per curiam opinion's approach. By a process of elimination, we may deduce that the Court's "per curiam" opinion was in reality the joint product of Justices Anthony Kennedy and Sandra Day O'Connor.

Margaret Jean Radin, Mark Kelman, and William Cohen; Columbia's George Fletcher; Yale's Robert Gordon; New York University's Derrick Bell; the University of Michigan's Terrance Sandalow; and the University of Texas's Sanford Levinson, to mention just a few. In brief, their joint statement charged that "by stopping the vote count in Florida, the U.S. Supreme Court used its power to act as political partisans, not judges of a court of law. . . . [T]he conservative justices moved to avoid the 'threat' that Americans might learn that in the recount Gore got more votes than Bush. . . . But it is not the job of the courts to polish the image of legitimacy of the Bush presidency by preventing disturbing facts from being confirmed. Suppressing the facts to make the Bush government seem more legitimate is the job of propagandists, not judges."[1]

Elaborating on her views in *Bush v. Gore: The Question of Legitimacy*, which collected the commentary of many prominent legal scholars, Professor Radin pulled no punches: "[I]nstead of deciding the case in accordance with preexisting legal principles, . . . five Republican members of the Court decided the case in a way that is recognizably nothing more than a naked expression of these justices' preference for the Republican Party. . . . [T]he Republican justices' 'analysis' doesn't pass the laugh test, particularly their decisions to stop the vote count and forbid the Florida Supreme Court from addressing the constitutional problems the federal Supreme Court purported to find." Radin went on to ask, "How many readers can say with a straight face that if the case had been *Gore v. Bush* —that is, if all facts were the same except that Florida was controlled by Democratic officials, Gore were a few hundred votes ahead in the count, and Gore brought a federal case to stop a recount Bush had sought under state law—it would have come out the same?" Her bottom line was that "we cannot now afford . . . to pretend that we see the rule of law when we know that we are seeing the opposite."[2]

Several other distinguished contributors to the *Question of Legitimacy* volume leveled similar accusations of lawlessness against the US Supreme Court. Professor Jed Rubenfeld proclaimed that *Bush v. Gore* was, "as a legal matter, utterly indefensible. . . . There was no December 12 deadline [for completing recounts]. The majority made it up. On this pretense, the presidential election was determined." On Rubenfeld's view, the "illegality," "breathtaking indefensibility," and "wrongness" of the justices' action reflected a complete lack of judicial principle, thereby making *Bush v. Gore* "worse even than the notorious *Plessy*." Professor Jack Balkin opened his essay as follows: "On December 12, 2000, the Supreme Court of the

United States *illegally* stopped the presidential election and handed the presidency to George W. Bush."[3]

Professor Bruce Ackerman offered a similarly harsh assessment: "I . . . protest[] in the name of the rule of law. . . . *To demand equal protection but to prevent Florida from satisfying this demand*—this is not bad legal judgment; this is sheer willfulness. The Court's defense—that no time remained for Florida to meet the state's own December 12 deadline—is simply preposterous. Florida law contains no such 'deadline.' Every lawyer knows that the Supreme Court should have sent the case back to the Florida courts. . . . And the court gave no legally valid reason for this act of usurpation."[4]

So much for the scholars on one side of the debate. Now hear the voices of scholars who saw the Florida Supreme Court as the lawless villain in the drama. In a 2001 essay collection, *The Vote: Bush, Gore and the Supreme Court*, Professor Richard Epstein condemned the Florida Supreme Court for its "manifest errors" and its "abuse of discretion for partisan political ends." Professor Michael McConnell was even blunter: "In the Florida Supreme Court, which [was] composed entirely of Democratic appointees, Gore's lawyers found a . . . sympathetic ear. On grounds that seemed dubious at best and disingenuous at worst, the Florida court ruled each time in favor of Gore. . . . [The Florida Supreme Court] disregarded the plain language of the [Florida election] statute and substituted a new deadline entirely of its own making. This was obviously not 'interpretation.' From its denunciation of 'hypertechnical reliance upon statutory provisions' to its fabrication of new deadlines out of whole cloth, the court demonstrated that it would not be bound by the legislature's handiwork."[5]

Professor Charles Fried—himself a former member of the Massachusetts Supreme Judicial Court and former US solicitor general—was more pointed still. He began his essay by quoting an "expla[nation of] Florida politics" offered by the fictional gangster Johnny Rocco in the 1948 movie *Key Largo*: "I take a nobody [and] get his name in the papers and pay for his campaign expenses. . . . Get my boys to bring the voters out. *And then count the votes over and over again till they added up right and he was elected.*"[6]

Having set the stage with this unsubtle suggestion of fraud and chicane in the Sunshine State, Fried proceeded to flay the Florida Supreme Court for its "clear act of insubordination" to the US Supreme Court's *Bush v. Palm Beach County Canvassing Board* (*Bush* I) decision, the Court's first foray into the Florida 2000 litigation. According to Fried, the US Supreme Court in *Bush* I "had unanimously vacated [a prior] judgment of the Florida Supreme Court and asked the Florida court to clarify the basis for it. The Florida court . . . had disregarded the Supreme Court's mandate, and without even adverting to it, had [by continuing and extending the recount] given important effect to its own previous, now vacated, decision. . . . [Thus, the] Florida court, in a dispute that touched the whole nation, acted in a strangely irregular way [that] gave rise to a reasonable concern that this was partisan manipulation. (As the Bush people put it: Keep on counting until Gore wins.)"[7]

And if readers somehow missed the connection between this "keep on counting" barb and his opening punch line from the *Key Largo* gangster, Fried ended with a bang, intimating in his closing paragraph that *Bush v. Gore* was a case in which "a state court had been caught trying to steal the election."[8]

WITH THE LINES OF SCHOLARLY debate now in plain view, let us take a step back. If, correctly or incorrectly, the Rehnquist Court believed that the Florida Supreme Court was acting in bad faith, then perhaps this belief could explain why the US Supremes felt they had to stop the recount altogether, rather than remand once again to judges whom they had come to view as judicial cheats. Perhaps the US justices might even have felt themselves justified in bending the law—if only to equitably straighten out the twists that they believed had been improperly introduced by the Florida justices. As Professor David Strauss has shown in a splendid essay, many things both large and small that the Rehnquist Court did in the *Bush v. Gore* litigation make the most sense if the US justices had in fact believed that they were dealing with a lawless, partisan state bench trying to steal the presidency for its preferred candidate.[9]

Suspicion arose in part because in overseeing the recount, the Florida Supreme Court seemed to have gone well beyond the words of the Florida election statute. Suspicion also arose because the Florida justices were presiding over a recount with uneven standards for counting disputed ballots.

We will come soon enough to the issue of unevenness and inequality. For now, let's concentrate on the claim that the Florida justices were clearly wrong, or perhaps even lawlessly partisan, because they did not hew strictly to the letter of the Florida election code.

In his concurring opinion in *Bush v. Gore*, Chief Justice William Rehnquist, joined by Justices Antonin Scalia and Clarence Thomas, declared that by straying from the text of the election law adopted by the Florida legislature, the Florida Supreme Court had violated the federal Constitution's Article II, section 1, clause 2, which provides that "[e]ach state shall appoint, in such Manner as the Legislature thereof my direct," presidential electors. For these three justices—and for many subsequent scholarly defenders of the US Supreme Court's ultimate decision in *Bush v. Gore*, such as Professors Epstein, McConnell, and Fried—the key word here is *legislature*. The US Constitution says that the state *legislature* gets to make the rules for choosing presidential electors. And, the argument runs, if the state judiciary disregards those rules, the federal Constitution itself authorizes federal judges to step in to protect the state legislature's federally guaranteed role. Although this argument did not command a majority in the Supreme Court, we must consider it with great care, because the most prominent conservative legal academics who have tried to defend the result in *Bush v. Gore* have hung their hat on this peg—a peg that turns out to be embarrassingly unsturdy.

The Article II issue first arose in the *Palm Beach* case, an earlier round of the recount litigation. In a unanimous decision handed down in late November 2000, the Florida Supreme Court openly referred to its decades-long tradition of construing the Florida election statute in light of the Florida Constitution. In particular, the Florida justices stressed the right to vote as expressed in the Florida Constitution's Declaration of Rights: "Because election laws are intended to facilitate the right of suffrage, such laws must be liberally construed in favor of the citizens' right to vote. . . . Courts must not lose sight of the fundamental purpose of election laws: The laws are intended to facilitate and safeguard the right of each voter to express his or her will in the context of our representative democracy. Technical statutory requirements must not be exalted over the substance of this right." For this reason, the Florida Supreme Court declared that the Florida election code for presidential elections was valid only if the code provisions "impose no 'unreasonable or unnecessary restraints' on the right of suffrage" guaranteed by the state constitution.[10]

On December 4, 2000, in *Bush v. Palm Beach County Canvassing Board* (*Bush* I), the Rehnquist Court unanimously vacated the Florida Supreme Court's *Palm Beach* ruling and sent the case back to the state court system for clarification. The *Bush* I Court's short per curiam opinion hinted that the Florida justices may well have violated the federal Constitution's Article II by using the Florida state constitution to limit the Florida state legislature.

On remand, the Florida Supreme Court failed to explain clearly why, notwithstanding Article II's broad grant of power to the Florida legislature, the Florida judiciary nevertheless had understood itself to be authorized to use the state constitution to cabin, modify, disregard, and supplement various parts of the election code adopted by the state legislature.[11] Whereas the initial *Palm Beach* ruling had been unanimous, the Florida Supreme Court on December 8 split 4–3, and its chief justice, Charles Wells, dissented in an opinion that worried aloud about the Article II issue.[12] Although the Florida court supplemented its splintered decision three days later with yet another opinion—this one commanding the votes of six out of seven justices[13]—it was too little too late: the US Supreme Court had already granted review of the earlier decision and had stayed the recount pending its review.[14]

As we have seen, Professor Fried pointed an accusatory finger at the Florida justices for their failure to address the US Supreme Court's concerns in *Bush* I about whether and how the Florida Constitution could limit the Florida legislature in the face of Article II's seemingly plenary empowerment of the state legislature. For Fried, the Florida justices' actions were insubordinate to the US Supreme Court, to Article II, and to the Florida legislature. Professors Epstein and McConnell likewise highlighted the Florida Supreme Court's seeming violation of Article II and usurpation of the Florida legislature's role under that federal constitutional provision.[15]

It was a momentous mistake for the Florida Supreme Court, after the *Bush* I remand, to have issued a decision that neglected to address the Article II issue in detail. But this neglect was not necessarily the product of intentional insubordination to the US Supreme Court. The clock was ticking down fast, and the Florida justices had a head-spinning number of intricate legal issues to deal with all at once.[16]

And here is the key point: despite their failure to address the issue squarely, the Florida justices acted in perfect harmony with Article II, rightly understood, when they relied on Florida's Constitution to go behind and beyond the words of the Florida legislature's election code. The very structure of that code deputized the Florida judiciary to construe and implement the code's myriad provisions in a manner that would strictly conform to the grand voting-rights principles of Florida's Constitution.

Had the Florida Supreme Court been clearer on this pivotal issue, either in the initial *Palm Beach* case or on remand, the basic error of the Article II assault on the Florida judiciary would have been clear for all to see. Once we understand the proper role of the Florida Constitution in the *Bush* litigation, the arguments of Chief Justice Rehnquist and Justices Scalia and Thomas, and of Professors Epstein, McConnell, and Fried, do not just dissolve. They boomerang.

HERE IS WHAT THE Florida Supreme Court should have said in response to the Rehnquist Court's per curiam opinion in *Bush* I:

> Just as Article II of the US Constitution empowers the Florida legislature to direct the process of selecting presidential electors, Article II of course also allows the Florida legislature, if it chooses, to cabin its own power in light of our state constitution, and to delegate the last word to resolve and manage disputed presidential elections in Florida to the Florida judiciary. We hereby hold that the Florida legislature has done just that by once again deputizing us, the Florida judiciary, to construe the Florida statutes and regulations regarding presidential elections against the backdrop of the Florida Constitution—just as the legislature has deputized us in previous elections going back many decades. Indeed, the Florida legislature has empowered us, the Florida judiciary, to equitably adjust and modify the sometimes hypertechnical and confusing maze of election regulations and code provisions so as to bring the letter of election law into harmony with the spirit and grand principles of the state constitution.
>
> As our long-standing case law makes clear, the Florida Constitution emphatically affirms the people's right to vote and right to have every lawful vote reflecting a clearly discernable voter intent counted equally. We need not decide today whether, in a presidential election, the Florida Constitution applies of its own force; rather, we hold that the Florida Constitution applies simply because the Florida legislature has made it applicable and has deputized us to vindicate its spirit in presidential elections here in Florida.
>
> This legislative power is not merely consistent with Article II; it in fact derives from Article II. In general, no federal court (not even the US Supreme Court!) may lawfully intervene to protect the Florida legislature from the Florida courts in the name of Article II, for any such federal court intervention would in logic boomerang: such attempted federal judicial intervention would itself violate the very principle of Article II

being asserted. To repeat: pursuant to Article II, the Florida legislature has designated the Florida judiciary as its chosen deputy in this matter.

Surely Article II would have been satisfied had the Florida election statute explicitly stated that "every provision of this presidential election code should be judicially construed or judicially revised to conform to the letter and spirit of the Florida state constitutional Declaration of Rights, as that Declaration has been and will continue to be definitively construed by the Florida judiciary." We believe that the Florida statute has done just that in substance, albeit in different words.

Here is why: The Florida election code's rules for presidential elections are the same as the Florida election code's rules for other elections, including state elections for state positions. It is absolutely clear that the Florida Constitution does apply to these other elections. It is equally clear that this court—the Florida Supreme Court—is broadly empowered to protect the fundamental state constitutional right to vote in these state elections, even if protecting that right may require this court to go beyond and behind the strict and at times hypertechnical words of the statutes and regulations. Unless the state legislature clearly indicates otherwise—and it has never done so—the same interpretive principles concerning the importance of the right to vote and the authority of Florida judges to construe all rules and regulations against the backdrop of that right sensibly apply to presidential elections as well.

For example, if a voter were to use an ink pen rather than a lead pencil to fill in the oval bubble that appeared next to a candidate's name on a printed ballot, long-standing Florida case law makes it clear that this pen mark would ordinarily constitute a valid vote, even if the regulations instructed voters to use number-two pencils when marking their ballots. Given that pen marks on a particular ballot should be counted in an election for state representative, or for any other state, local, or federal official, surely the presidential-election section of the ballot should be handled the same way. It would be exceedingly odd—absent a very clear legislative indication to the contrary—to count pen marks everywhere else on this ballot and yet refuse to count virtually identical pen marks in the presidential-election section of the very same ballot.

ALAS! THE FLORIDA justices never offered up such a crisp and cogent Article II explanation of their conduct in the 2000 election—although they did come very close to doing so in a too-little-too-late decision handed down days after the Rehnquist Court had dramatically stayed the recount, and just hours before that Court's final ruling in *Bush v. Gore*.[17]

Despite their failure to hammer home the Article II propriety of their earlier reliance on the Florida Constitution, the Florida justices' actions in general were thus legally defensible, and often quite admirable. Though the Florida Supreme Court did not explain itself perfectly in the rush of the moment, it largely did the right legal things and for the right legal reasons. What is more, its rulings in November and December 2000 were quite consistent with its rulings on similar election issues that had arisen long before George W. Bush squared off against Al Gore. (The same cannot generally be said of the Rehnquist Court.)[18]

Early on in the Bush-Gore litigation, the Florida justices intuitively saw the presidential election in light of similar issues that had come before them (and before other state supreme courts with similar state constitutional guarantees) in previous nonpresidential elections. In these earlier cases, the Florida courts and other, similarly situated state supreme courts had at times gone beyond—and even against—the strict letter of election laws in order to vindicate the larger spirit behind those laws, a spirit aimed at assuring that all votes would in fact be counted if voter intent could be deduced.[19]

According to this long-standing and admirable set of cases, in Florida and elsewhere, even if a code or a regulation instructed a given voter to use a pencil to check a box or fill in a bubble on a printed ballot, a ballot that used a pen (a technical "undervote") should still be counted. Even if a code or a regulation instructed a voter not to write in the name of any candidate whose name already appeared printed on the ballot, a ballot that both checked the box alongside the candidate name and also wrote in the same name (a technical "overvote") should be counted. Even more obviously, a voter should not have his vote go uncounted because some bureaucrat goofed or some machine failed to give effect to the voter's manifest intent. The Florida legislature was fully aware of judicial rulings championing voter intent, and the state legislature blessed this well-established case law when it continued to enact election statutes against the backdrop of, and in extended dialogue with, the various election-law rulings of the Florida courts.

One final, parenthetical point on this topic. Nothing in the Florida election code said that Florida courts owed super-strong, unwavering deference to all rulings of Florida's secretary of state or county election boards, regardless of the context of the election issue involved or the reasonableness of the initial rulings made by these nonjudicial officials. General principles of state constitutional law and state administrative law properly counseled judicial skepticism of such nonjudicial decision-makers where basic elements of the fundamental right to vote were at stake and where these nonjudicial officials appeared to be acting in a highly partisan or highly inexpert manner.[20]

Nothing in Florida's laws or traditions required Florida's secretary of state in 2000 to be law-trained, and in fact, Florida's secretary of state, Katherine Harris, was not law-trained. She showed dubious legal judgment in deciding before the 2000 election to serve as a campaign official for candidate George W. Bush. Professor Steven Calabresi—the cofounder of the Federalist Society, an organization with strong ties to America's leading conservative thinkers and doers—has publicly labeled her decision "foolish."[21]

Early rulings made by Harris raised a vivid specter of severe partisanship, and also suggested that she simply failed to fully appreciate the deep constitutional principle that every legal vote with a truly discernable voter intent should be counted, regardless of bureaucratic mumbo jumbo or statutory legalese. (One particularly important Harris ruling early on was sharply and persuasively contested by the Florida Attorney General's office, an office with a long tradition of legal and state constitutional expertise.) The law-trained Florida justices were sensitive stewards of deep and long-standing constitutional principles when they declined to give blind deference to dubious decision-makers such as Harris.[22]

THE ROLE(S) OF THE LEGISLATURE(S)

Let us now focus even more directly on the entity explicitly empowered by Article II, namely, the Florida legislature.

In the umpteen-ring circus that was Florida 2000—with riveting dramas and curious comedies simultaneously playing out in various county canvassing boards, in multiple state and federal judicial proceedings, in the Florida Secretary of State's office, in the Florida Attorney General's office, and elsewhere—the Republican-controlled Florida legislature also craved a piece of the action and a part of the limelight. Meeting in Tallahassee, lawmakers in late November and early December began to make noises about their alleged right to take matters into their own hands by naming their own set of electors (who would be pledged to George W. Bush) if the recount did not end quickly and with the pro-Bush result that these legislators demanded.

At first blush, such a legislative assertion might seem wholly justifiable. After all, Article II explicitly empowers the state legislature to direct how presidential electors shall be chosen. But on sober second thought, the rumblings of the Florida legislators should strike us as deeply troubling. For the Florida legislature had *already* spoken—had already laid down the rules in its initial election laws. These rules provided that the Florida judiciary—and not the Florida legislature—would ultimately oversee and adjudicate electoral disputes for all elections (other than, perhaps, elections for state legislative positions, for which each legislative house might indeed claim state constitutional authority to be the final election judge).[23]

To be clear: Prior to the November election, the Florida legislature was not obliged to have structured the presidential election rules as it did. Had it so chosen, the Florida legislature in, say, January 2000 might have enacted a law naming itself as the arbitration board of all presidential election disputes that might arise in November. Going against the grain of the unbroken and universal state practice of the past century and a half, perhaps the Florida legislature might even have chosen to dispense with a presidential election altogether in Florida. In this weird alternative universe, perhaps the Florida legislators might have simply provided that the legislature itself would name its own set of presidential electors come November—the voters be damned!

But, of course, the Florida legislature did none of these outlandish things prior to Election Day. Instead, it kept in place the state's traditional election and adjudication process, which contemplated no ongoing legislative role after the people of Florida had spoken on Election Day and the courts had adjudged any legal issues that might have arisen. Had the legislature in December 2000 actually tried to insinuate itself into the process, it would have been changing the rules in the middle of—actually, after—the game, in violation of basic rule-of-law ideals.

To recast the point in the more technical language of Article II, the "legislature" that was constitutionally empowered was the Florida legislature before Election Day, not the Florida legislature after Election Day. Any effort by that later legislature to change, supplement, or "clarify" the rules would have come at the expense of the pre–Election Day legislature—the legislature empowered by Article II—and would thus have violated Article II itself, much as the Rehnquist concurrence that we considered earlier did violence to the very Article II provision it claimed to be championing. Again, in both Tallahassee and Washington, DC, the pro-Bush argument based on Article II did not merely dissolve; it boomeranged.

Other constitutional and federal statutory language completes and confirms this rule-of-law point. True, Article II, section 1, clause 2, does empower the state legislature; but one paragraph later, Article II, section 1, clause 4, clarifies the temporal boundaries of that empowerment: "The Congress may determine the time of chusing the Electors." Acting pursuant to that clause, Congress long ago enacted a federal statute, 3 USC section 1, which clearly says that presidential electors shall be appointed in each state on America's traditional Election Day—the first Tuesday after the first Monday in November. With this statute, Congress made plain which state legislature is empowered under Article II—namely, the legislature acting before Election Day.

But what should happen if the Election Day selection process misfires? Here, too, Congress laid down a clear rule long ago, pursuant to its explicit authorization under clause 4. According to 3 USC section 2, "[w]henever any State has held an election for the purpose of choosing electors, and has failed to make a choice on the day prescribed by law, the electors may be appointed on a subsequent day in such a manner as the legislature of such a State may direct." This section does empower a post–Election Day legislature to jump back into the game and to oust the voters—but only if the election "*failed* to make a choice." Imagine, for example, that Florida election law provided that a candidate would win electors on Election Day only if the candidate received an absolute majority of the statewide popular vote; and that in a three-way race, no candidate emerged with such an absolute majority on Election Day. Under those circumstances, the Florida legislature could step in post-election.

But nothing of the sort happened in 2000. The voters *had* made a choice on Election Day. True, uncertainty existed about which candidate the voters had in fact chosen. But this was not a *failed* election; it was simply a *very close* election, one that called for an extremely careful final count. Nothing in the language of the congressional statute suggests any right of the state legislature to overturn the voters' verdict under these circumstances, and the clear negative implication of the congressional statute is that the state legislature has no such right, outside the context of a truly failed election—that is, an election that had not yet *and that never would or could* generate a legally sufficient outcome after careful tabulation.[24]

It would be silly to read the congressional law as allowing a state legislature to oust the voters if no definitive victor had been declared before midnight on Election Night. And if the legislature may not oust the voters on the Wednesday morning after Election Day simply because careful counting is still taking place, then surely the legislature may likewise not oust the voters on any subsequent day simply because the counting continues. Nothing in the language of the federal statute suggests that the rule that obviously applies on the Wednesday morning after the election somehow lapses on Thursday or Friday or any later day.

Nor would a broad reading of the word "failure" vindicate Congress's purpose in enacting a uniform Election Day. As Professor Bruce Ackerman astutely observed in the *New York Times* as the Florida fireworks were exploding, "Congress established a level playing field among the states by requiring them to hold elections on the same day. . . . Before [Congress enacted this statute] states competed with one another for influence by setting their election dates as late as possible, thereby swinging close elections by voting last." A loose reading of the word "failure" would encourage states to game the system in the very ways the statute was plainly designed to prohibit.[25]

Here, too, it would seem that the harsh critics of the Florida judiciary have gotten the issue wrong. The real problem in Florida 2000 was not that the state courts were inappropriately threatening to usurp the proper constitutional authority of the state legislature, but the reverse: the state legislature was inappropriately threatening to usurp the proper constitutional authority of the state courts. Or, more precisely still, the post-election state legislature was threatening to usurp the proper authority of the pre-election state legislature, which had deputized the state courts to resolve any disputes that might arise—and in the process, to do what judges typically do with any statutory scheme, namely, clarify its ambiguities and iron out its wrinkles.

IN LATE 2000, there *was* in fact one court that inappropriately inserted itself at the expense of the legislature. But that court was the Rehnquist Court, which took upon itself to resolve various issues that were properly Congress's to decide as the body tasked by the US Constitution with the counting of electoral votes and the resolution of electoral-vote disputes. The federal Constitution thus envisioned a certain adjudicatory role for

Congress in presidential elections, but state legislatures and the Supreme Court were not given an analogous role.

In its rush to judgment, then, the Rehnquist Court not only did an injustice to the Florida judiciary—and to the pre-election Florida legislature that had deputized the Florida judiciary—but also to Congress, and to the constitutional structure that made the federal legislature, and not the federal judiciary, the ultimate judge of close presidential elections.[26]

EQUAL PROTECTION

What about the claim in the Supreme Court's per curiam opinion that the recount being overseen by the Florida judiciary was proceeding with unacceptably uneven standards? Here, too, upon close inspection, many of the criticisms hurled at the Florida Supreme Court do not merely dissolve; they boomerang. The unevenness occurring in the judicially monitored recount was in general far less severe than the unevenness that had occurred in the initial, less-monitored counts on Election Day and shortly thereafter. Harvard professor Laurence Tribe has pointed out that "[m]inority voters were roughly *ten times* as likely not to have their votes correctly counted in this election as were non-minority voters." The recount process being supervised by the Florida Supreme Court represented the last best chance to reduce and judicially remedy some of the inequalities and inaccuracies and disfranchisements that had tainted the initial counting process.[27]

Some of the problems that seemed to surface in the initial and intermediate stages of the recount might well have been cured by later corrective action from state judges, had these judges been allowed to proceed without interference from the Rehnquist Court, and with Congress waiting in the wings as the ultimate monitor and constitutionally appropriate final judge. Alternatively, the US Supremes might have identified their specific concerns about the unfolding recount and remanded the matter to state courts with guidelines for a still-better recount process. Instead, by abruptly demanding an end to the recount process, the Rehnquist Court simply froze in place inequalities of the same sort, and of greater magnitude, than the inequalities the Court claimed to care about.

What were the inequalities that captured the Court's imagination? During the recount process being overseen by the Florida judiciary, some dimpled chads* were being treated as valid votes, others not. According to the Rehnquist Court per curiam opinion in *Bush v. Gore*, "the standards for accepting or rejecting contested ballots might vary not only from county to county but within a single county from one recount team to another. . . . A monitor in Miami-Dade County testified at trial that he observed that three members of the county canvassing board applied different standards in defining a legal vote. And testimony also revealed that at least one county changed its evaluative standards in the counting process. . . . This is not a process with sufficient guarantees of equal treatment."

This passage raises many questions. If the Florida recount was constitutionally flawed, why wasn't the initial Florida count—which the Court's judgment in effect reinstated—even more flawed? The initial count, we must remember, featured highly uneven standards from county to county. Different counties used different ballots (including the infamous butterfly ballot)† and even counties using the same ballot used different interpretive standards in counting them. This happened not just in Florida, but across the country. Were all these elections unconstitutional?

The idea that the Constitution requires absolute perfection and uniformity of standards in counting and recounting ballots is novel, to put it gently. For decades, if not centuries, American voters have been asked to

---

* Though many political junkies in 2000 learned the lexicon, it's worth reminding general readers fifteen years later what a "dimpled chad" was (and is). Some parts of Florida relied on a system in which the voter used a stylus to punch a tiny rectangular hole in a thin cardboard punch card opposite each preferred candidate's name for each contest on the ballot. An IBM-style punch-card reader would then process and tabulate the hole-filled punch cards. But if the stylus did not push all the way through the card, the tiny paper rectangle (the chad) that was supposed to fall away cleanly, and thereby create the hole, would not do so, and the punch card might be merely indented—dimpled—rather than properly holed. Also, if this system was not properly maintained, chads created by previous voters could accumulate and make punching-through and tabulating more difficult. This was known in the business as "chad buildup."

† The so-called butterfly ballot configured candidate names in a confusing way. Literally thousands of Florida voters ended up having their votes counted for a third-party candidate they likely loathed—Pat Buchanan—instead of the man they thought they were voting for, Al Gore. These several thousand lost votes for Gore easily surpassed Bush's official 537-vote margin of victory.

put their "X" marks in boxes next to candidate names, and human umpires have had to judge if the "X" is close enough to the box to count. On Election Day, different umpires officiating in different precincts have always called slightly different strike zones. If these judgments are made in good faith and within a small zone of close calls, why are they unconstitutional? If they are unconstitutional, then virtually every election America has ever had has been unconstitutional.

Regardless of what the US Supremes may themselves have thought at the time, it was a mistake to believe that the Florida recount process was proceeding in some especially bad-faith manner that should have caused that process to be viewed with more suspicion than the initial counting process (which occurred without judicial oversight). The Rehnquist Court claimed that its new-minted equality principles applied only to judicially supervised state recounts, and not necessarily to other aspects of the electoral system. But the Court gave no principled reason for this absurdly ad hoc limitation.[28]

The fact that the *Bush* case involved recounts monitored by a judge with statewide supervisory power cuts against the Court's per curiam opinion: less cheating in tabulation is likely when judges and special masters—and the eyes of the world—are watching; and a court with a statewide mandate could help mitigate inequalities across different parts of the state. True, in a recount it might at times be foreseeable that a particular ruling might tend to favor a given candidate, but this was also true of various rulings made during or even before the initial counting.

Critics of the recount, both on and off the Rehnquist Court, were also far too quick to think they had somehow established smoking-gun evidence of foul play—"*Aha!*"—whenever they pointed to certain changes in counting protocols over time or certain variations across space. True, various Florida counties in prior elections had not counted dimpled chads. But the Florida Supreme Court had not blessed this past practice; and no uniform anti-dimple rule applied in the many sister states that, like Florida, affirmed the primacy of voter intent.[29]

Facts matter. If, for example, certain precincts in 2000 had particularly high rates of dimples or other mechanical undercounts, this statistic might well be evidence of chad buildup or machine deterioration over the years. A strict anti-dimple rule that made sense in 1990 might not have been sensible a decade later, given much older machines, more buildup, and a higher incidence of machine undercounts.

So, too, the chad rule in precincts with short lines might not sensibly apply to precincts with much longer lines, where some voters may have felt a special need to vote fast so that others could take their turns. If the rates of dimpled chads or other undercounts were especially high in precincts where lines were longest, and where voters were most hurried—or were especially elderly and frail, or especially unlikely to understand English-language instructions about the proper use of punch-card styluses—it might well make sense to treat dimples in those precincts as particularly likely to reflect genuine attempted votes rather than intentional non-votes.[30]

These sorts of issues could not have been easily addressed in each precinct on Election Day itself; but they were just the sort of problems that a statewide court might have been able to sensibly address with an adequate factual background developed in the very process of recounting, a process in which fine-grained data about the precinct-by-precinct (and even machine-by-machine) distribution of each sort of voting problem would become available. But the US Supremes short-circuited the whole recount and remedy process, privileging the less accurate, less inclusive, and more discriminatory initial counting process—and privileging that highly unequal process in the name of equality, no less.

The Rehnquist Court per curiam opinion failed to cite a single case that, on its facts, came close to supporting the majority's analysis and result. To be sure, we can find lots of forceful voting-equality language in the Supreme Court's pre-*Bush* case law—but on their facts these were mainly cases about citizens simply being denied the right to vote (typically on race or class lines); or being assigned formally unequal voting power, with some (typically white) districts being overrepresented at the expense of other (typically black) districts.[31]

The Fourteenth Amendment's equal-protection clause, adopted in the wake of the Civil War, was first and foremost designed to remedy the inequalities heaped upon blacks in America. The Fifteenth Amendment extended this idea by prohibiting race discrimination with respect to the vote. For most of the twentieth century, various state governments—and especially state governments in the Old South, most emphatically including governments in Florida—mocked these rules. For decades, large numbers of blacks in many southern jurisdictions were simply not allowed to vote.

When Congress finally acted to protect the rights of black voters in the 1960s, the situation dramatically improved overall, but subtle inequality persisted in various places. In Florida, for example, black precincts in 2000 typically had much glitchier voting machines, which generated undercounts many times the undercount rates of wealthier (white) precincts with sleek voting technology. In raw numbers, this sizable inequality dwarfed the picayune discrepancies magnified by the Rehnquist Court. Under-maintenance of voting machines, chad buildup, long voting lines in poor precincts—these were some of the real ballot inequalities in Florida 2000.[32]

In Florida, those who were the most serious about real equality, as envisioned by the architects of Reconstruction, persuasively argued that the government should not ignore the very large and racially nonrandom voting-machine skew. Rather, the government should do its best to minimize and remedy that skew, albeit imperfectly, via manual recounts. Even if such recounts were not required by equality, surely they were not prohibited by equality.[33]

In fixating on the small glitches of the recount rather than on the large and systemic glitches of the machines, the Rehnquist Court majority turned a blind eye to the real inequalities staring them in the face, piously attributing the problems to "voter error" (as opposed to outdated and seriously flawed machines) and inviting "legislative bodies" to fix the mess for future elections.

VOTER INTENT IN BUSH VERSUS GORE AND *BUSH V. GORE*

Before we conclude our analysis of the Florida fiasco of 2000 and turn our eyes to the future, one more aspect of Bush versus Gore, the election, and *Bush v. Gore*, the case, deserves attention: the issue of voter intent.

Think first about the election. Sometimes, a voter might sensibly cast a vote for someone who is not in fact the voter's true first choice. Via a *strategic* vote, a voter might well vote for candidate A, even though she truly prefers candidate C, because a sincere vote for C may increase the odds that her least favorite candidate, B, might win. Thus, in Florida 2000, many voters strategically voted for Al Gore, even if they sincerely preferred Ralph Nader, because they understood that a sincere vote for Nader would in effect be a wasted vote that (compared to a vote for Gore) would make it more likely that George W. Bush would in fact prevail. (And to those who actually did cast their votes for Nader, I ask: What were you thinking? Did you intend to throw your vote away? Did you truly have no preference whatsoever between Bush and Gore, who were the only two candidates who had a realistic chance of winning?)

Other voters in Florida failed to vote for their true first choice not because they were *strategic* but because they were *confused*. The notorious butterfly ballot effectively disfranchised thousands who fully intended to and in fact tried to vote for Gore, but who ended up casting mistaken ballots that had to be counted in favor of Patrick Buchanan.

Consider, finally, overvotes and undervotes. In an overvote, a voter might, in confusion, vote for two different candidates for the same single position—say, both Bush and Gore. In an undervote, a confused voter might simply fail to indicate which candidate he or she truly preferred.

Now turn from Bush versus Gore, the election, to *Bush v. Gore*, the case. Here, too, we can see strategic voting in action, and also possibly confused voting—both overvotes and undervotes.

First, strategic voting. There are good reasons to suspect that Chief Justice Rehnquist and Justices Scalia and Thomas did not, deep down, sincerely agree with the exuberant and unprecedented equal-protection analysis at the heart of the per curiam opinion that these three justices formally joined. The equal-protection approach ran counter to the general approach that these three justices had typically followed in prior equal-protection and voting-rights cases. The per curiam opinion also raised some special problems for principled originalists.*

---

* In brief: There is strong evidence that the equal-protection clause of the Fourteenth Amendment was not intended to apply or written to apply to voting discrimination. This is, indeed, why a wholly separate amendment—the Fifteenth Amendment—was understood by the Reconstruction generation to be needed to end race-based suffrage laws. Ordinarily, the inapplicability of the equal-protection clause might be thought to be a moot point for dedicated originalists, because most of the voting cases that have relied on the equal-protection clause could be reconceptualized and defended as Article IV republican government cases. But without some fancy footwork of the sort that Rehnquist, Scalia, and Thomas typically disavow, Article IV would not seem to apply to a presidential election; nor have these justices ever endorsed any other textualist or originalist theory trying to link the Constitution's words to a general right to vote equally. For background on the inapplicability of the equal-protection clause, as originally understood, to voting, and discussion of alternative textual theories of voting-equality rights, see, generally, Akhil Reed Amar, *The Bill of Rights: Creation and Reconstruction* (1998), 216–217, and n.*; Akhil Reed Amar, *America's Constitution: A Biography* (2005), 391–392; Akhil Reed Amar, *America's Unwritten Constitution* (2012), 183–194, 223–230. See also supra Chapter 2, p. 51, and p. 318n.34; and Chapter 5, p. 118.

Moreover, the Court's equal-protection argument was in considerable tension with the Article II analysis favored by these three concurring justices. The more one insists on the plenary power of state legislatures under Article II to make the rules for presidential elections, the more awkward it is to also insist that the state must satisfy a super-strict system of voting equality, down to the third decimal point of uniform micro-standards for evaluating chads, regardless of the counting and recounting system established by the legislature itself.

Why, then, did the three believers in the Article II argument join what they probably saw as a highly problematic and implausible equal-protection opinion? In other words, why did they opt to join the per curiam opinion—thereby purporting to accept its reasoning—rather than simply concur in the judgment based solely on their Article II theory?

Most likely, because they were voting strategically (much as the Naderites who voted for Gore in Florida). Without their three votes for the per curiam opinion, *Bush v. Gore* would have been a case in which there were five votes to end the recount and decide the election, but no single majority opinion or majority theory to justify this outcome. Imagine how the *New York Times* headline the next day might have read: *Court Backs Bush But Cannot Agree Why*. Or imagine the lead paragraph of such a news story: "Last night, for the first time in American history, the US Supreme Court decided a presidential election. By a 5–4 vote, the Court conclusively stopped votes from being recounted in Florida, even though a majority of justices in fact rejected each of the only two theories put forth by the Bush campaign to end the recount. The only things the five justices could agree on were that George W. Bush must win, Al Gore must lose, and the counting must stop."[34]

Strategic voting, it would seem, may thus well have occurred both in Florida and in Washington, DC.

So, too, at least one justice in the case appears to have overvoted and undervoted, as some confused Floridians had the previous month. Although both Justices John Paul Stevens and David Souter dissented in *Bush v. Gore*, they dissented in separate opinions, and for good reason: these two justices took diametrically opposite positions on the plausibility of the per curiam opinion's equal-protection analysis. Justice Stevens thought the argument was a clear loser, whereas Justice Souter bought this turkey. And Justice Stephen Breyer—who is, I can personally attest as his former law clerk, one of the world's most agreeable humans—agreed entirely with *both* Justices Stevens and Souter. Which brings to mind one of my favorite punch lines from *Fiddler on the Roof:* "But, Rabbi, they can't both be right!"[35]

Nor is the matter completely clarified in Justice Breyer's own dissenting opinion, in which he acknowledged that there were equality problems with the Florida recount, but did not quite say that these problems rose to the level of a constitutional violation. I would call this an undervote, with no clear voter intent on Breyer's part. On this issue, my old boss was as enigmatic as some of the dimpled Florida punch cards at the center of the storm.[36]

THE FUTURE

Although I have been quite critical of the Rehnquist Court's per curiam opinion in *Bush v. Gore,* I do strongly agree with that part of the opinion that spoke of the need for "legislative bodies nationwide [to] examine ways to improve the mechanisms and machinery for voting." Nor is this the only sort of reform that is desperately needed. In the 2000 election in Florida, thousands of lawful voters—disproportionately black—were incorrectly, and in many cases illegally, purged from state voting rolls on Katherine Harris's watch.[37]

Both in Florida and beyond, government officials have often made it too difficult to register to vote and too difficult to actually cast a vote on Election Day. Under the banner of combating fraud, many jurisdictions are imposing inappropriate burdens on those who are fully eligible to vote, burdens that often disproportionately disadvantage young, old, nonwhite, and non-wealthy voters.

The integrity of voting rights in each state would be enormously important even if only state and local offices were at stake. Recall that every leading man considered in Part I of this book—Lincoln, Black, Jackson, and Kennedy—championed a vigorous federal role in guaranteeing rights of individual Americans against their own home states; and recall further that in both of the other cases featured in Part II of this book, *Brown* and *Tinker,* the federal judiciary nobly protected citizens from state and local officials who were violating core constitutional rights of liberty and equality.

But the issue of electoral integrity in Florida involves far more than the rights of Floridians. Thanks to the electoral college and the winner-take-all system in place in virtually all states, a shabby state-run election for president adversely affects all Americans, and does so especially in a big swing state such as Florida.

To be sure, Florida is not the only important state in the continental presidential sweepstakes. Thus, our next two chapters explore issues of presidential selection and succession with a special emphasis on two other states that have played outsized roles in modern presidential selection, Ohio and Texas.*

---

*Both of these states played particularly notable roles in the 2000 election. The Florida fiasco would have been irrelevant to the ultimate presidential outcome in 2000 had Gore managed to carry Ohio. But George W. Bush—then the sitting governor of Texas and the son of a former president from Texas—won Ohio by a comfortable margin, 3.5 percentage points. Four years later, incumbent President Bush would have lost his bid for reelection had he lost Ohio, even though he still would have had a considerable national popular-vote edge over his opponent, John Kerry. But once again, the Texan carried Ohio, this time by a nail-biting 2.1 percentage points.

PART III

Constitutional Provisions and Principles

OHIO:

A BUCKEYE-STATE VIEW OF

PRESIDENTS WITHOUT MANDATES

O hio is, or at least for much of our history has been, the home of presidents. The Buckeye State invites us to analyze not merely what various persons have done as presidents, but also how they became presidents. To bend a phrase, we might say that some men were born to be president (John Quincy Adams comes to mind); others achieved the presidency—against the odds of their birth, and through sheer force of will (think of Abe Lincoln); while still others had the presidency thrust upon them (for example, Millard Fillmore).

In this chapter, I focus on some of the presidents in the last category—on several men who became and remained president without ever being voted president by the American people. As it turns out, Ohio looms large in my tale.

VICE PRESIDENTIAL ASCENSION AND
THE PROBLEM OF TICKET BALANCING

Our story begins with William Henry Harrison, the ninth president of the United States, and the first president from Ohio. Much of the history of the first century and a half of our national existence can be seen in the shift from the early Virginia presidents to the later Ohio presidents, a shift that reflected westward expansion and ultimate northern ascendancy. George Washington, Thomas Jefferson, James Madison, and James Monroe—Virginians all—collectively held the presidency for thirty-two of its first thirty-six years, but from the ascension of Ulysses S. Grant in 1869 to Warren G. Harding's death in 1923, Ohioans occupied the White House for more days than all non-Ohioans put together, so long as we embrace a suitably expansive definition of "Ohioans."

Harrison himself personifies this great transition and this caveat. Born in Virginia (under the British flag), and the son of a man who signed the Declaration of Independence, Harrison later moved to the Northwest Territory, eventually settling in North Bend, Ohio. With his inauguration in 1841, Ohio had its first president.

But not for long. Harrison was also the first president to die in office, succumbing to pneumonia after only a month in the White House. The reins of power fell into the hands of Vice President John Tyler, a man who hailed from—of course—Virginia.

At this point, a nice constitutional question arose. Was Tyler, strictly speaking, merely the vice president acting as president, or did he instead actually become president upon the death of Harrison? Tyler ultimately settled on the latter position and his contemporaries came to accept his claim. The relevant words of Article II, section 1, seem fiendishly ambiguous: "In Case of the Removal of the President from Office, or of his Death, Resignation, or Inability to discharge the Powers and Duties of the said Office, *the Same* [my emphasis] shall devolve on the Vice President." Did the words "the Same" in this devolution clause mean the "said Office" itself, or merely "the Powers and Duties" of the office?

At first we might wonder what would turn on such a legal technicality. Surely not Tyler's formal authority to veto laws, for even under a narrow reading, such authority seems obviously included as among the "Powers and Duties" of the presidency. Nevertheless, Tyler's exuberant use of the veto during his presidency provoked torrents of criticism and even serious calls for his impeachment. Whereas his predecessors had typically used the veto pen rather sparingly, confining most of their vetoes to bills they deemed unconstitutional or invasions of executive turf, Tyler felt freer to veto bills that he thought were merely bad policy. Perhaps a president with a strong and personal mandate from the American people could have expanded the office in this way with more credibility, but John Tyler was no Andrew Jackson. No one had voted for Tyler as president, and he was derisively referred to by his many critics as "His Accidency" (a pun on "His Excellency"). Tyler's policy views were in general sharply at odds with those of the man the people had chosen, namely, Harrison. In 1840, the Whig Party had opted for a balanced ticket, hoping that Tyler would appeal to a different slice of voters than would Harrison, but not seriously thinking about what would happen were Tyler to be vaulted from obscurity to authority.

If Tyler's formal powers did not turn on whether he was actually the president, or merely the vice president acting as president, what else was at stake? Perhaps his tenure in office? Probably not. Here is the relevant constitutional language in its entirety: "In Case of the Removal of the President from Office, or of his Death, Resignation, or Inability to discharge the Powers and Duties of the said Office, the Same shall devolve on the Vice President, and the Congress may by Law provide for the Case of Removal, Death, Resignation or Inability, both of the President and Vice President, declaring what Officer shall then act as President, and such Officer shall act accordingly, until the Disability be removed, or a President shall be elected."

True, this passage does contain language that certain transfers of power would end when "the Disability shall be removed, *or a President shall be elected*." (My emphasis.) These words did contemplate the possibility of a special off-year election cutting short the ordinary four-year presidential term, but only in the following situation: if *both* the president *and* the vice president were to die or leave office, Congress could by statute designate an officer to be a successor, and this statutory successor would, if Congress so provided, act as a caretaker only until a special off-year presidential election was held. Grammatically, the "shall be elected" language applies only to *double*-vacancy scenarios—involving death or resignation of both the president and vice president—as would have been crystal clear had the document placed a period rather than a comma before the words "and the Congress . . ."[1]

When Congress implemented this clause by adopting the Presidential Succession Act of 1792, it indeed provided for a special off-year election to pick a new president who would have a clear mandate, but this law applied only in the event of statutory succession triggered by double vacancy. Thus, it seems that Tyler—who was not a mere statutory successor but an ascending vice president—was entitled to wield all presidential powers for three years and eleven months, regardless of whether, strictly speaking, he had become president.[2]

However, at least two things *were* at stake. First was the issue of salary. A presidential salary was not quite part of the "Powers and Duties" of the presidency, but it surely was part of the "Office" itself, which Tyler claimed as his own. Calling himself "president," Tyler thereby claimed the higher presidential salary (which under the Constitution was fixed for the entire term, and thus immune from any congressional carrot-and-stick reprisals for his maddening vetoes). Second was the issue of the formal title itself. We are apt to miss the import of such a seemingly small formality in our highly informal world of "Jimmys" and "Bills" rather than "Mister Presidents," but the formal issue of title loomed larger in an earlier era, when America was surrounded by regimes rife with dukes and earls and barons and counts and kings. Two separate clauses of the federal Constitution condemned "titles of nobility," and a third anti-title provision cleared Congress as a proposed constitutional amendment in 1810, only to fail at the state ratification stage. (This amendment would have stripped US citizenship from any American accepting a foreign title of nobility.) From a modern perspective, an unfathomable amount of wrangling occurred at the Founding over the issue of the president's title. Some of Washington's admirers suggested that he be formally addressed as "His High Mightiness, the President of the United States and Protector of their Liberties," but the First Congress ultimately opted for the more republican-sounding "Mister President."[3]

With Tyler having fixed in place a practical precedent resolving the open textual question, later vice presidents also proclaimed themselves presidents upon the deaths of their running mates. After Harrison, the next presidential death occurred in 1850 when yet another Virginia-born president, Zachary Taylor, passed away in office, whereupon Vice President Millard Fillmore became President Millard Fillmore.

Then came Lincoln's assassination in 1865, with presidential power falling into the hands of Andrew Johnson. Like Tyler before him, Johnson insisted on wielding the powers of the presidency, especially the veto pen, with exuberance, even though he had no personal mandate, and came to stand for things quite at odds with what Lincoln would likely have stood for. Although Johnson had run on Lincoln's Republican-Union ticket in 1864, Johnson was in his bones an old-school Democrat. Lincoln, by contrast, had always been in the mainstream of the fledgling Republican Party that he himself had helped found in the 1850s.

Johnson's opponents were outraged. Who did this fellow think he was, this self-proclaimed president wielding such awesome power by dint of one man's bullet rather than all men's ballots? For the first time in history, Congress, dominated by true Republicans aghast at the faux Republican now in the White House, overrode a major presidential veto and eventually impeached Johnson, with a strong Senate majority (but not the necessary two-thirds) voting to convict. As with the power shift from Harrison to Tyler, the lurch from Lincoln to Johnson exemplified a general problem raised by ticket balancing, with Americans voting for presidential policy X and ending up with presidential policy Y.

BEFORE WE PONDER that problem more generally, let us trace to its end the other thread of the Tyler precedent—the question of whether a vice president actually becomes president. When the elected president actually dies, and dies quickly—as did Harrison, Taylor, and Lincoln—we have seen that very little turns on that question. Salary and title are more than trivial but less than momentous. But the next presidential assassination showed that a great deal more might be at stake.

In 1880, the nation elected James Garfield—of Ohio, of course. Four months after assuming office, Garfield was shot in a train station by a dissatisfied office-seeker, Charles Guiteau. Garfield did not die immediately, but lingered for months, waxing and waning in bed. Meanwhile, the nation listed, rudderless, without a leader at the helm.

Given that the president was obviously disabled, why didn't Vice President Chester A. Arthur step in temporarily? Partly because of the Tyler precedent. Suppose that Arthur had stepped forward and started acting as president. Under the Tyler precedent, wouldn't Arthur thereby become president? But then what would happen if Garfield later recovered (as initially expected)? If Arthur had already become president, would Garfield be ineligible to resume his old post? If so, Arthur would have in effect staged a palace coup, permanently ousting Garfield.[4]

True, this rather troubling reading of the Constitution's succession language was hardly self-evident. A more sensible reading would have held that only when a president died (as had happened in the Harrison-Tyler, Taylor-Fillmore, and Lincoln-Johnson episodes) did his vice president officially become president under the relevant precedents. In the case of mere presidential "Inability," the argument might run, whatever it was that "devolved" upon the vice president—whether the presidential "Office" itself, or merely its "Powers and Duties"—devolved back when the real president recovered, and his previous "Inability" ceased. But even if this interpretation was in fact the soundest reading, it was not utterly incontrovertible, and it existed in some tension with the notion that in a situation of presidential death, the office itself irrevocably devolved upon the vice president. If this devolution was irrevocable, why was disability any different? The obvious answer—that death is different, and itself irrevocable—was sensible enough; but, to repeat, the issue was not beyond all doubt and contestation, especially in light of the Tyler, Fillmore, and Johnson precedents.

Two further complicating factors were at work. First, it was far from clear exactly who should decide whether Garfield was suffering from a devolution-triggering "Inability" within the meaning of the Constitution. Garfield alone? Arthur alone? The cabinet? The Congress? The Supreme Court?

Second, Garfield and Arthur came from opposite wings of the Republican Party, representing different sets of policies. Garfield seemed to smile upon a professional civil service, while Arthur believed that government jobs should reward the party faithful. In the political jargon of the era, Republicans ticket-balanced a "Half-Breed" and a "Stalwart." Garfield paid dearly for his views. Upon arrest, the gunman Guiteau told police, "I did it and will go to jail for it. I am a Stalwart, and Arthur will be president!" In Guiteau's pocket, police found a letter addressed "To the White House" proclaiming Garfield's death a "sad . . . political necessity" to "unite the Republican Party," and a letter addressed to Arthur making various recommendations for cabinet restructuring.[5]

Arthur of course had had nothing to do with this madman, but for the vice president to move in too soon would look like a coup of sorts. So Arthur did nothing, and months went by with the country effectively without a president. Garfield eventually died, and under the Tyler precedent, Arthur thereupon became president.

A similar situation arose in 1919. In 1913, Woodrow Wilson became the first Virginia-born president since Zachary Taylor, having defeated an incumbent Ohio president, William Howard Taft, in a three-way race that also included Teddy Roosevelt. Late in Wilson's second term, he suffered a serious stroke that spelled the practical end of his presidency. Once again, the vice president—in this case, Thomas Marshall—did nothing, in part because of the uncertainty created by the Tyler precedent. Recall that, read narrowly, the precedent might merely mean that when a president died, his vice president became president; but that in the event of disability, a vice president could act as president only until the disability subsided. But read broadly, perhaps the precedent might mean that the moment a vice president started wielding presidential powers, he irreversibly became president. With so much at stake, and little definitive legal guidance, vice presidents acted with extreme caution.

Today, of course, definitive guidance does exist, in the form of the Twenty-fifth Amendment, proposed and ratified after the assassination of John Kennedy and the ascension of Lyndon Johnson. This amendment, which we shall analyze in much greater detail in the next chapter, makes clear that when the president dies or resigns or is removed from office—and only then—the vice president does in fact "become President." Otherwise, if the president is merely disabled (perhaps only temporarily) from exercising the powers and duties of his office, then the vice president may step in and "assume the powers and duties of the office as Acting President," without impairing the president's ability to resume his post when he has recovered from his disability. The amendment also provides a detailed framework for determining whether the president is in fact disabled. Its biggest flaws are that it provides no satisfactory mechanism for determining *vice presidential* disability, and that in the event of a vacant or disabled vice presidency, its rules for determining presidential disability will not work, pivoting as they do on key decisions that can be made only by a fully functional vice president.[6]

The Twenty-fifth Amendment does one more noteworthy thing: in the event of a vice presidential vacancy (created either by vice presidential death, removal, or resignation, on the one hand, or by vice presidential ascension to a vacant presidency, on the other), the president may nominate a candidate to fill the vacancy, who must then be approved by majority vote of each house of Congress before becoming vice president. This is of course the mechanism by which Gerald Ford became vice president (and later president) in the mid-1970s, and by which President Ford in turn paved the way for Nelson Rockefeller to become vice president. Although the American people do not directly vote in this process, their representatives in Congress do vote, and thereby confer a personal mandate upon the vice president.

IT IS PRECISELY THIS STRONG personal mandate that is to some extent lacking in ordinary elections of a vice president. Generally, American voters are not allowed to vote for president and vice president separately in a process that would give each one a direct and personal mandate to govern (though the mandate of the vice president would obviously be a contingent one, triggered only by mishap). Rather, voters are confronted with a single ticket, and they must take the package as a whole. There is nothing in the Constitution that requires this way of voting; it is purely a matter of state law. (Recall from our previous chapter the broad authority over presidential elections each state legislature enjoys, thanks to Article II.) And there is good reason to question the current and well-established way of voting for tickets. Here we return to the other thread of the Harrison-Tyler succession problem: the problem of ticket balancing.

The problem, simply put, is that Americans vote for a president at the top of a ticket, without much attention to the vice president at the bottom of the ticket. So long as nothing happens to the president, all this may be harmless enough, but what if something does happen to the president? Having voted for A, the American people end up with B. B lacks a strong personal mandate to govern, yet has the legal right to wield all the awesome power of the office. The situation is even worse when parties balance tickets with candidates from opposite party wings, so that the electorate votes for one set of policies and ends up with a very different set.

Let's now consider four examples from American history of troubling ticket balancing. Each of the four examples, interestingly, has an Ohio connection. First, as we have seen, democracy and constitutional structure were not well served when the people voted for President Harrison and ended up with President Tyler, who nearly provoked an impeachment. Lest we simply personalize all this, and heap the blame on Tyler, let us note that virtually the same thing happened when the people voted for President Lincoln and ended up with President Johnson, who actually did precipitate an impeachment. (In a few moments, I shall highlight the role of Ohio in this episode, in the person of Ohio senator Ben Wade, who would have become president had Johnson been convicted by the Senate in his impeachment trial.) The situation with Presidents Garfield (of Ohio) and Arthur seems even worse. Here, the ticket balancing actually induced an assassination. After the bullets struck and disabled Garfield, Arthur was in a poor position to confidently lead the country, had strong leadership been necessary. Thus, Arthur understandably did nothing until Garfield died, and thereafter, Arthur's occupancy of an office meant for Garfield was, at best, awkward. In 1900–1901, the country once again voted for one kind of Republican—Ohio's William McKinley—only to get, after the intervention of yet another deranged presidential assassin, a somewhat different kind of Republican as president. True, vice-president-turned-president Theodore Roosevelt turned out to be a man of great ability, and in fact he made a point of trying to carry out McKinley's policies early on. But how much of this continuity and competence was a result of the Constitution's structural genius, and how much was simply good luck? Because Americans never vote directly and squarely for a vice president, parties have unduly weak incentives to fill this bottom slot with a truly worthy figure, and, especially in earlier eras, many talented politicians have shunned the assignment.

One possible solution would be for state legislatures to let Americans vote directly for the vice president, separately from the presidential ballot—something that the Constitution would clearly permit. In the event of the president's death or disability, the vice president would then be able to lead more effectively, because he would have already received a personal vote of confidence from the nation he must lead. Parties would be more likely to field one of their most worthy candidates for the job, because the separate election would compel voters to focus more carefully on the bottom of the ticket. Talented and ambitious politicians would be more willing to accept the number-two spot if it came with a personal mandate from the entire nation—which no other politician in America (aside from the president) enjoys. Even if the president stayed healthy in office, the vice president would be in a stronger position to run for president on his own later on.[7]

True, separate election of the vice president would raise the specter of a divided White House, with a president and vice president of opposite parties. But this possibility also exists under the current system. (Imagine a three-way race with no party winning an electoral college majority. In such a scenario, the House would pick the president and the Senate would pick the vice president, according to the Twelfth Amendment; and of course the House and the Senate might be controlled by different parties.) In a world where states allowed voters to split their ticket between presidents and vice presidents, the most likely result would be single-party control of the White House, but with a stronger and more capable vice president, and one more likely to come from the same wing of the party as the president. In general, the White House would probably be less divided, not more, with less blatant ticket-balancing within each party, and less temptation to fill a party's VP slot with an unqualified or only marginally qualified candidate.

For example, imagine what might have happened had state legislatures provided for separate vice presidential election in 2008. In that year, Republican presidential candidate John McCain chose Sarah Palin as his running mate, and even some voters who preferred McCain to Democratic nominee Barack Obama had concerns about Palin's basic presidential competence. At first, we might think that if separate election had been allowed, a split ticket—McCain for president and Democrat Joe Biden for vice president—would have been a real possibility. But the very fact of separate election would likely have induced McCain to pick a more credible running mate, better able to stand on his or her own—say, Elizabeth Dole or Mitt Romney or Rob Portman. (Dole was then a sitting senator and the spouse of Robert Dole, who had himself won both the Republican vice presidential and presidential nominations in years past; Romney was runner-up in the 2008 Republican primary race and would himself win the party's presidential nomination the next time around; and Portman was an up-and-coming Ohioan with far more experience on a national stage than Palin, and someone who might himself seek the presidency one day. In midsummer 2008, all three of these names were in fact prominently mentioned in the press as possible McCain running mates.)

STATUTORY SUCCESSION

Having pondered some of the implications of our constitutional scheme of succession, let us now note some of the features of our statutory scheme of succession, which would swing into operation in the event of double death or double disability. Double trouble has never yet happened—and after the Twenty-fifth Amendment, it is less likely to happen, because we now have a mechanism for filling a vacant vice presidency. But if it were to happen, the stakes would be more serious than any succession America has previously faced, since the nation would have lost (at least temporarily) its two highest leaders.

Return once again to the words of the Constitution: "Congress may by Law provide for the Case of Removal, Death, Resignation or Inability, both of the President and Vice President, declaring what Officer shall then act as President, and such Officer shall act accordingly, until the Disability be removed, or a President shall be elected." There are two fundamental questions we must answer in the event of double death. First, who should take over? Second, for how long? Over the centuries, Congress has enacted three different succession statutes, each of which offered different answers to these two questions. None of these statutes has answered both questions correctly, and the current statute is a disaster—a true constitutional catastrophe waiting to happen.

Recall that under the Presidential Succession Act of 1792, in a double-vacancy scenario a statutory successor simply would act as a caretaker, holding the office only until a special off-year presidential election was held, at which point the special-election winner would immediately take office. This act got the "how long" question right. Because a statutory successor will lack a strong mandate from the American people, the successor should simply hold the fort for the minimum amount of time necessary to run a smooth election that will generate a leader who does have such a mandate.

But the 1792 act got the "who" question wrong. It designated the Senate president pro tempore as the caretaker officer. As James Madison pointed out at the time, this designation is unconstitutional. Members of the House and Senate are not, strictly speaking, "Officers of the United States" as the Constitution uses that phrase or its cognates in a wide variety of clauses. For example, House members and senators cannot be impeached, because only federal "officers" are impeachable, and members of Congress are plainly not covered by this language—a point made clear by constitutional text and structure and confirmed by long-standing Senate precedent. Under a proper reading of the succession clause, only "Officers" of the United States may be designated as statutory successors; the clause contemplates that a cabinet officer (or a judicial officer, perhaps) picked by the president, and not a legislator, should hold the fort.[8]

It is worth highlighting a few of the most vicious features of legislative (as opposed to cabinet) succession, because these features directly involve the Buckeye State, and these features helped lead to the repeal of the act of 1792. When Andrew Johnson was impeached by the House, and tried by the Senate, in 1868, the vice presidency was vacant. (It had been vacated by Johnson himself, and prior to the Twenty-fifth Amendment, no means existed to fill the vacancy.) Thus, had the senators who sat in solemn judgment over Johnson found him guilty of high crimes and misdemeanors and removed him from office, the 1792 act would have swung into operation. Who, then, would have moved into the White House to replace Johnson? The Senate president pro tempore, who happened to be the leader of the Senate's opposition to Johnson—Senator Ben Wade of Ohio. Rumor had it that while sitting in solemn judgment over Johnson, in a judicial trial under oath and presided over by America's highest jurist, Chief Justice Salmon P. Chase, Wade had already been picking his cabinet. Thus the act of 1792 had the obvious potential for corrupting judicial judgment, effectively making Wade a judge in his own case and creating an obvious conflict of interest.[9]

Such an arrangement could hardly be expected to inspire confidence and reduce cynicism among ordinary Americans. Had Wade actually succeeded in succeeding, what kind of mandate would he have had, coming into power in such a smelly way? Legislative succession also smacked of creeping parliamentarianism, threatening to transform the Founders' highly judicialized model of impeachment into a pure political vote of no-confidence, and thereby unraveling the fixed presidential term prescribed by the Constitution and allowing the legislature to usurp the power that the Framers so carefully sought to deny them—the unilateral power to pick their own leader as president.

Repulsed by the sordidness of the Wade affair, and persuaded that Madison may well have been right on the constitutional question, Congress in 1886 repealed the 1792 act and replaced it with a new Presidential Succession Act providing for cabinet officer succession. This new statute got the "who" question right—a fallen president's fort should be held by the person whom the president selected to carry his flag. But the 1886 act got the "how long" question wrong by failing to specify that a cabinet officer should simply act as a caretaker until a proper special election could be held. Given that cabinet officers are not directly elected, they lack a strong personal mandate, and should act as president for as short a time as possible. (Under a sound statute that properly provided for a special election, a caretaker officer could choose to run in that election, and thereby win a personal mandate to stay in office until the end of the deceased president's term.)[10]

In 1947, Congress changed the statute once again, giving us the worst of both worlds—truly a lose-lose result. The 1947 Presidential Succession Act restored legislative succession (this time putting the Speaker of the House ahead of the Senate president pro tempore). And it utterly abandoned the idea of a special election.[11]

The supporters of the 1947 act denounced cabinet succession on the grounds that unelected cabinet officers have an insufficient democratic mandate. There is some truth here; this is why a statutory successor simply should serve as a caretaker until a new election can be held that will give someone a democratic mandate. But the alternative solution proposed by the 1947 law fails to solve the problem. True, the House and Senate leaders who sit atop the current statutory line of succession are directly elected by home-state voters. But these congressional barons are not directly elected by the voters of the nation as a whole. A president should have not only a democratic mandate but a national one. And that mandate cannot simply come from fellow legislators unless we are to revert to the very system of unilateral legislative selection of chief executive, à la Parliament, that our entire system of separation of powers was painstakingly crafted to repudiate.

What does all this mean today? Under the 1947 succession statute currently in place, the foreman of the constitutional grand jury that is charged with overseeing the president and the vice president has a blatant conflict of interest. If that grand jury (that is, the House of Representatives) indicts (that is, impeaches), then the foreman (that is, the Speaker of the House) moves one huge step closer to the Oval Office. Would public confidence be enhanced, and public cynicism put to rest, if a congressional leader of one party were to move into the Oval Office after an impeachment (or two) of the leader(s) of the opposite party whom the American people had chosen on presidential Election Day? Would such a statutory successor have the requisite legitimacy to govern when there are such strong arguments that the very statute that swept this non-officer into the White House is patently unconstitutional? Why do we bother holding national presidential elections if our law treats them with such evident disrespect?

ELECTORAL COLLEGE GLITCHES

Here is another little-known pocket of law that is a constitutional accident waiting to happen. Suppose that in some future election, the ticket of Alice Ace and Kevin King easily defeats opponents Carla Queen and Joseph Jack. Hours before the scheduled meeting of the electoral college in December, Ace dies. Many states have laws on the books that purport to bind electors to vote for the ticket to which they pledged themselves on Election Day. Even if those laws are unconstitutional or unenforceable—arguably, the Constitution itself makes presidential electors complete free agents who cannot be legally bound—imagine that most electors, reeling from the news and without much time to consult legal experts, simply cast their electoral votes for Ace (as pledged) under the assumption that on Inauguration Day, Ace's running mate, King, will move into the Oval Office. In this event, who would actually become president in January? Quite possibly, not King but Queen—the very candidate Americans had just voted down.

How could this be? Once again, our story takes us back to Ohio. In November 1872, Ohio-born President Ulysses Grant, running for reelection, defeated Horace Greeley of New York. Shortly after the election but before the meeting of the electoral college, a brokenhearted Greeley died. Some electors nevertheless cast their votes for Greeley, as pledged. But when Congress met to tally these votes, as provided for in the Constitution, Congress refused to count the votes for Greeley. Little turned on the issue then—after all, Greeley lost no matter what—but the situation is very different in our hypothetical, where the decedent had won on Election Day. Were members of Congress to blindly follow the Greeley precedent in our hypothetical, they would refuse to count the votes for Ace; and the person with the most (perhaps the only) "valid" electoral college votes for president might well be Queen.

But the obviously sensible result in this situation is that King, and not Queen, should be sworn in as president. And there is a simple way to get to this result. Though it may sound counterintuitive at first, Congress should simply count the votes of the dead candidate as if she were alive. The Greeley precedent was ill-considered and should not be followed. On this approach, Ace's votes count; she wins when the electoral votes are tallied; and as she is unable to discharge the office on Inauguration Day— she is, after all, dead—her vice presidential running mate, Kevin King, becomes president.[12]

There is another accident waiting to happen that also requires a legal fix. Suppose that Ace had died one day before the popular election. What should happen? The best solution in this tragic situation, and one that can be prescribed by a simple statute (passed in advance of the election) is to postpone the election so that the national parties and the candidates and the people can calmly assess the situation. If substitute candidates must be fielded, let this be done before the people vote rather than after, so that the people will know which precise persons they are voting for, and will accept as fully legitimate whichever candidates ultimately win the election.

FROM EVERYTHING THAT we have seen thus far, it seems clear that serious problems can arise—and indeed have arisen—when the people vote for A and end up with B. These problems have occurred even when A and B were running mates—though I have suggested that these problems could be lessened if voters were allowed to vote for A and B individually rather than as a ticket. With a separate vote on the vice presidency, if the people get B upon A's death, then they are getting what they voted for, and voted for personally and unambiguously.

But when voters vote for *party* A and get *party* B instead, the mandate problems are compounded. Consider two late nineteenth-century elections—both involving Ohioans—in which more Americans voted for presidential party A than for presidential party B, but ended up with party B in the White House.

In 1877, Ohio's Rutherford B. Hayes was proclaimed the electoral college winner even though his opponent, Samuel J. Tilden, was credited with having won more popular votes nationwide. Although electoral college irregularities and chicanery further clouded Hayes's election, the simple fact that his rival apparently received more popular votes was one factor among many that contributed to a widespread sense that his occupancy of the White House was less than fully legitimate—a sense reflected in cruel nicknames, such as "His Fraudulency," "the Usurper," and "Rutherfraud B. Hayes."

In the election of 1888, Benjamin Harrison—the grandson of William Henry Harrison, born on the family homestead in North Bend, Ohio—ousted Grover Cleveland from the White House even though Cleveland won more popular votes nationwide. The very next time the people were consulted, they promptly put Cleveland back in power, in the rematch election of 1892.

THE GENERAL WEAKNESS of the presidency in the late nineteenth century—an era that roughly corresponds with the dominance of presidents from Ohio—is a fact well known to scholars of this period. We can now see that much of this weakness was the result of a string of presidents without popular mandates because of death and the quirks of the electoral college.[13]

Today, America's role in the world is much more central than it was then, and the powers of the presidency are far greater. Can we afford to run the risk of a string of future presidents who similarly lack democratic mandates? If not, twenty-first-century reformers may need to revisit not merely rules governing presidential balloting, presidential succession, and election timing, but also rules governing the basic structure of the electoral college.[14]

The current rules undoubtedly tend to benefit large swing states, such as Ohio. Notably, no one since JFK has managed to win the presidency without carrying the Buckeye State. Put differently, Ohio has been on the winning side in every single presidential election since JFK. No other state can say the same, and every other sizable state except Florida has been on the losing side at least twice in this era.[15]

But is everything that is good for Ohio good for America and the wider world? And speaking of JFK . . .

CHAPTER 9

TEXAS:
A LONE-STAR VIEW OF
PRESIDENTIAL SELECTION AND SUCCESSION

M y first television memory is from November 22, 1963, and even
now I flinch whenever a news bulletin flashes across the screen.
This chapter examines the constitutional significance of that
dark day in Dallas, which prompted the proposal and ratification of the
Twenty-fifth Amendment to our Constitution. This amendment, a seemingly small tweak to our system of presidential succession, actually has some
large implications and potential applications, several of which have not yet
been appreciated by scholars, politicians, and the American electorate.

A thin Texas triangle stretching from Dallas to Stonewall to Craw-
ford offers a special spot from which to survey the relevant constitutional
issues. This triangle encompasses not just the poignant place where JFK
fell, but also the Texas ranch of the man who caught and carried forward
Kennedy's flag, Lyndon B. Johnson, and, in addition, the Texas ranch of
George W. Bush, the first president to formally invoke section 3 of the
Twenty-fifth Amendment to temporarily transfer power to his vice president. This thin triangle sits "deep in the heart of Texas," and in precisely
that part of Texas where the South meets the West. The story of modern
presidential selection and succession appears in a particularly interesting
way when seen from a Texan, southwestern angle.

THE LONE STAR STATE

It is conventional to divide America into four regions—the Northeast, the
Midwest, the Deep South, the Far West. The Lone Star State is particularly

intriguing in this schema. Texas sometimes presents itself as part of the South, but at other times identifies with the West—and parts of the Texas Panhandle might even claim to be midwestern. The famous motto of Dallas's sister city, Fort Worth, is "Where the West Begins."

With all this in mind, let us recall the previous chapter's story of the geography of presidential selection, but now let us update that story by bringing the Lone Star State into the picture. Thus, let us plot the broad shift in presidential home bases over the centuries from Virginia to Ohio . . . *to Texas.*

America's early presidency tilted south, with some help from the three-fifths clause, which gave slave states extra seats not just in the House of Representatives but also in the electoral college. Eight of the nation's first nine presidential elections placed a Virginian in the nation's highest seat. We may profitably think of Virginia as the Texas of the Founding—an enormous state by population and landmass, and also a state where the North met the South, on terms favorable to the South, and where both met the West. In 1789, Virginia stretched far from the Atlantic coastline to encompass what are now Kentucky and West Virginia, and its northern panhandle—yes, it had one, too—rose north and west of Pittsburgh to within 150 miles of Canada.[1]

Lincoln's election in 1860 and the ensuing Civil War shattered the Founders' system, and with it the domination of the presidency by the Old South. On reflection, it is understandable why Ohio emerged as the big winner in the presidential sweepstakes from Reconstruction to the Great Depression. The Buckeye State was north enough to be distinctly Unionist ground. Thanks to the Northwest Ordinance, Ohio's soil had always been free; and in the Civil War, Ohio's men had formed the steely backbone of the Union Army and the Republican Party—Generals Ulysses S. Grant and William Tecumseh Sherman, Treasury Secretary Salmon P. Chase, Representative John A. Bingham, and so on. But Ohio also bordered Kentucky, and southern parts of the Buckeye State shared some of the culture and character of its bluegrass neighbor across the river. Thus, post–Civil War Ohio was the crossroads of America, where the East met the West and the North met the South—but met on solidly Unionist ground. I stress "Unionist ground" because the memory of southern secession and the Civil War powerfully shaped the generations that followed. Although Dixie had absolutely dominated the presidency until Lincoln, no self-described southerner was elected president for the entire century after the bombardment of Fort Sumter.[2]

Then came that day in Dallas, followed by a dramatic demonstration that Texas—as embodied by Lyndon Baines Johnson, the driving inside-the-beltway force behind the landmark 1964 Civil Rights Act—was ready to rejoin the Union in spirit as well as letter. In retrospect, we can now see that in 1963–1964 the presidential torch passed to a new region: after a century of Union-state presidents, five of the next seven men elected to the presidency came to office from the former Confederacy. In 1992, both major-party candidates came from Dixie, as did third-party candidate Ross Perot. Thus, virtually everyone voted for a southerner that year.

Now let's rotate from the North-South axis to an East-West perspective. Before LBJ's election in 1964, only one president in history (Herbert Hoover) had come from what we today would count as the West—that is, from somewhere west of Dallas–Fort Worth. But beginning with LBJ—and counting Texas, as it often likes to be counted, as southwestern—five of the next seven elected presidents (three Texans and two southern Californians) came from the American Southwest.[3]

Putting it all together: *Whereas no elected president for more than a century had come from the South, and only one had come from the modern-day West, all seven men elected president from 1964 through 2004 came from the South and/or the West.* I say "and/or" here to capture the fact that Texas swings both ways. And Texas alone can claim three of these seven elected presidents in this period.

Now bring both presidential and vice presidential candidates into the picture. From 1960 through 2004, a Texan was on the ballot in a staggering nine of twelve presidential elections. And, except for 1992—when two Texans (Bush 41 and Ross Perot) between them garnered a sizable popular-vote majority, but a non-Texan progressive southern Democrat running in the tradition of LBJ (Bill Clinton) managed to win in the electoral college—every time a major party ran a Texan, it won.[4]

All of which makes Illinois senator Barack Obama's electoral achievement in 2008 remarkable. He became not just America's first black president, but also the first real northerner to be elected president since JFK. And Obama did this without a southerner or a westerner as his running mate—a JFK without an LBJ, so to speak. Notably, Obama prevailed only by besting a southwesterner in the general election: Arizona's John McCain, who had teamed up with the far-western Sarah Palin.*

Later in our story, we shall return to President Obama, and to the presidential election to succeed him that will take place in 2016. But before we get there, we need to examine with care the constitutional amendment that came into existence as a result of the shocking events in Dallas a half century ago.

The JFK–LBJ Amendment

Cold-hearted as it sounds, America dodged a bullet on November 22, 1963. Our beloved president was slain, but our constitutional system and our vital national interests survived without catastrophic damage. Imagine, instead, what might have happened—in a nuclear world, and in the shadow of the Cuban missile crisis—had Lee Harvey Oswald's bullets merely damaged rather than completely destroyed President Kennedy's brain. What if Kennedy had lingered in medical limbo for weeks or months while crises erupted at home and abroad? Or suppose JFK made a surface recovery masking the fact that he was actually cognitively unable to function properly in office? What if he was incapable of comprehending his own unfitness and thus unwilling to yield power—an unwillingness that was actually itself a symptom of his mental unfitness?

As America's leaders pondered such deeply unpleasant questions in the days after Dallas, a consensus emerged that the Constitution should be amended to address with suitable specificity some of the imaginable scenarios. The upshot was the Twenty-fifth Amendment, proposed by bipartisan congressional supermajorities in the summer of 1965 and ratified by the last of the requisite thirty-eight states in early 1967.

---

* Obama himself might also technically be classified as a far-westerner, having been born and raised in Hawaii; but by 2008 his political base was emphatically the state of Illinois, which of course lies east of Dallas–Fort Worth. Were we to count Obama as both eastern and western, both northern and southern, then our story of the modern rise of southwestern presidents becomes even more stark: strictly speaking, Hawaii is America's most southwestern state, though its history and culture are quite distinct from those of other states that are typically understood as constituting America's Southwest.

Recall from our previous chapter that section 1 of the amendment codified the century-old understanding that when a president dies or leaves office, his vice president immediately becomes not merely an acting president, but a president full-stop, indistinguishable from any other duly chosen president, and thus entitled, among other things, to a full presidential salary, undiminishable by Congress.

Section 2 introduced a seemingly small but actually substantial and (as we shall see later) potentially transformative innovation: whenever the vice presidency becomes vacant—either because of a vice presidential death, resignation, or removal, or because a former vice president has now become president under section 1—the president can fill the vacancy by nominating a new vice president, who must win approval by a majority vote of each house of Congress before taking office. This section constitutionalized several important and interrelated principles—principles that, though not explicitly mentioned in the text of section 2, combine to form this section's animating vision.[5]

Let's begin with the No Vacancy Principle and the Competence Principle. Section 2 reflects the ideas that gaps in the line of succession should be filled as soon as possible—that, ideally, no vice presidential vacancies should exist for any extended period—and that America should at virtually every instant have a sitting and highly competent vice president ready and able to take over immediately.

Prior to this amendment, there was simply no way of filling a vacant vice presidency. For nearly 40 of the first 175 years under the Constitution, the nation had managed to make do without a vice president.[6] Had something happened to the president during these windows of vulnerability—fortunately, nothing ever did—a federal statute would have kicked in, shifting presidential power to some official named by law. (Recall the previous chapter's detailed analysis of America's three successive succession statutes, enacted in 1792, 1886, and 1947.)

Section 2 of the JFK-LBJ Amendment reflects the idea, made shockingly vivid by Dallas, that when disaster strikes, primary reliance should not be placed on this rickety backup scheme of statutory succession, a scheme that could give presidential power to someone wholly unprepared for it. In a nuclear world, a full-time executive understudy who receives regular executive briefings should always be at the ready—namely, a vice president who is prepared to take the helm at a moment's notice.

Section 2 of the JFK-LBJ Amendment also reflected the principles of Handpicked Succession, Party Continuity, and Anti-Assassination. A president himself should name the protégé within his party who will succeed him—who will carry forward his flag, in the event he cannot—for the entire four-year term for which he was elected. In obvious ways, the Handpicked Succession Principle reinforces the Competence Principle. A president is generally well positioned to know his job and to know who can complete this job in the event of his own death or disability. A president will also have good incentives to keep his vice president fully briefed on all critical matters if the president has handpicked this protégé instead of having an understudy foisted upon him by some other person or institution. Would-be political assassins would never be rewarded with the mind-boggling power of completely reversing the outcome of the previous presidential election; bullets would never be able to transfer the White House to the party that the voters had rejected on presidential Election Day. Instead, a fallen president's policies would be vindicated by his handpicked successor, much as LBJ went on to brilliantly champion JFK's unfinished agenda.

As a check on potential presidential corruption or gross misjudgment, Congress under section 2 would need to approve the president's handpicked choice—further buttressing the Competence Principle. Congressional approval would also embody the related principle of National Democracy. By saying yes to a president's nominee, a majority of each house of the national legislature would give the new vice president a resounding democratic stamp of approval.

In ordinary circumstances, quadrennial presidential elections vindicate all six of our principles. A party's presidential nominee *handpicks his chosen successor*, who serves as his vice presidential running mate. A national electorate approves both candidates on Election Day, thereby vouching for their *presidential competence*, conferring upon them a *national democratic mandate*, and *avoiding vacancy* by filling the Number 2 slot in advance of any possible mishap. In the event something bad happens to Number 1, *party continuity* is preserved when Number 2 takes over. Would-be political *assassins are never rewarded* with the power to wrest the presidency away from the party that won it on Election Day and transfer it to the party that lost this presidential contest. Whenever the people vote for Party X for the presidency, America gets four full years of Party X's policies in the Oval Office, as implemented either by the person who himself won the voters' support, or by his handpicked, full-time, and democratically approved partner and protégé.*

Sections 3 and 4 of the JFK-LBJ Amendment added additional elements and refinements. Section 3 established procedures under which a president may declare himself "unable to discharge the powers and duties of his office" and thereby temporarily transfer presidential power to the vice president until the president acts to recover his powers, under a complementary set of procedures also provided in section 3. Section 4 outlines rules by which the vice president may assume the powers of an "Acting President" in situations where the president is "unable to discharge the powers and duties of his office" but has not himself transferred power under section 3.

Together these sections introduced two more implicit concepts, the Smooth Handoff Principle and the Cabinet Monitoring and Mediating Principle, into America's post-Dallas Constitution. Section 3 makes it easy for a president who anticipates a merely temporary disability—say, a planned routine surgery—to hand off power seamlessly to his handpicked vice president, and to do so in a manner that makes it easy for

---

* Recall from the previous chapter that although the current system confers a personal mandate of sorts on the winning vice presidential candidate, this personal mandate is not as clean and emphatic as it could be, and that our system might be improved were states to allow citizens to vote separately for president and vice president and thereby bestow a more direct and more personal mandate upon the latter. To put the point a different way: the JFK-LBJ Amendment envisions that the Congress will generally approve a president's handpicked successor, so long as the successor is truly competent and of proper character. In presidential elections, a separate ballot line for the vice president should likewise be designed to induce voters to focus squarely on the competence and character of the vice presidential candidate. Both Congress and the voters on Election Day are apt to give the president and the presidential candidate, respectively, wide deference in picking his (or her) junior partner; but having an independent check on what would otherwise be unlimited discretion to handpick incompetent cronies will give each president and presidential candidate good incentives to handpick a genuinely worthy wingman (or wingwoman).

In the rare case that the voters on Election Day elect a split ticket (either under the current system or in some future reformed system of separate election), an assassination of the president might indeed shift policy—but in a way that the voters themselves in some sense preapproved. The resulting policy shift, though still troubling, would be less democratically disastrous than would be the case if an assassination handed the presidency to a party that undeniably lost the *entire* presidential election.

him to resume presidential power when the disability has passed. These smooth section 3 handoffs back and forth can occur in an instant and might last only a few days or perhaps even a few hours. But as Americans had come to realize after Dallas—and with memories of the Cuban missile crisis still quite vivid—days and even hours matter in the atomic age. Section 3, with its contemplated handoffs back and forth, works best when a president and vice president understand themselves as a team—as they are wont to do when the president handpicks his teammate, either at his party convention in an election year, or under section 2 of the JFK-LBJ Amendment.

Section 4 envisions scenarios when a president is himself disabled but does not know it or cannot admit it. It enables the vice president to take over—but only when backed by the president's cabinet. (Section 4 also allows Congress, by law, to designate some entity other than the cabinet—for example, a team of medical experts—to make this decision, but Congress has never made such a legal designation.) This procedural gear nicely intermeshes with the other carefully crafted gears put in place by the amendment's other sections. A vice president may be trusted not to use section 4 to attempt a palace coup precisely because he is the president's own handpicked partner and protégé. He is not, for example, the leader of the opposition party. Moreover, a vice president who invokes section 4 to grasp the reins of power must typically act with the backing of the president's handpicked cabinet—a body that presumably has worked intimately with both the president and the vice president and is in a good position to monitor the situation and mediate various complications.

THE JFK-LBJ AMENDMENT
PASSES ITS FIRST TESTS

Having examined the main provisions and principles of the JFK-LBJ Amendment, let us now see how the amendment has operated, post-LBJ.

President Johnson himself had no occasion to invoke the amendment, but his successor, Richard Nixon, did. On October 10, 1973, Nixon's handpicked running mate, Spiro T. Agnew, resigned his position as vice president and pled guilty to felony tax-evasion charges arising from Agnew's shady financial dealings and bribe-taking prior to his federal service. A short two days after Agnew's resignation—a brisk timeline in perfect keeping with the No Vacancy Principle—President Nixon nominated Gerald Ford to fill the now-empty vice presidential slot under section 2 of the JFK-LBJ Amendment. On December 6, Ford received the necessary congressional backing and took office as the first vice president ever to hold office under the JFK-LBJ Amendment.

On August 9 of the following year, Nixon himself had to resign in disgrace in the Watergate scandal. Gerald Ford immediately became president under the express provisions of section 1 of the JFK-LBJ Amendment.

By becoming president, Ford had created a vacancy in the vice presidency. Though he came into office facing a proverbial sea of troubles requiring immediate attention, Ford properly gave priority to the No Vacancy Principle. Thus, only eleven days after moving into the Oval Office—on August 20, 1974—President Ford nominated Nelson Rockefeller to fill the vacancy Ford had himself created by moving up. This time, it took Congress a full four months to say yes; and Rockefeller took office on December 19, 1974. The JFK-LBJ Amendment was less than eight years old, and already its new No Vacancy Principle had twice been put into operation.

But on both occasions, had Congress needlessly slow-walked the section 2 confirmation process? Presidents had acted promptly, and then Congress had dawdled, acting with considerable deliberation but not much speed. A cynic might wonder whether the Presidential Succession Act of 1947 was creating bad incentives, contrary to the deep principles of the JFK-LBJ Amendment. Had something terrible happened to President Nixon (a Republican) after Agnew's resignation but before Ford's confirmation, or, in turn, had some disaster befallen President Ford (a fellow Republican, of course) before Rockefeller was sworn in, who would have moved into the Oval Office as acting president of the United States until January 20, 1977? A *Democratic* Speaker of the House, pursuant to this 1947 law. So perhaps some congressional Democrats were dragging their feet and crossing their fingers. But if a Democratic Speaker of the House had moved into the White House as a result of presidential mishap and vice presidential vacancy, this statutory succession would have undermined the basic principles of Party Continuity and Handpicked Succession at the core of the JFK-LBJ Amendment.

Thus, one key implication of the foregoing analysis of the Twenty-fifth Amendment of 1967 is that the earlier Presidential Succession Act of 1947 needed and still needs to be revamped to ensure that the deep principles underlying the more recent and more sensible amendment are given their due.*

The Democratic House Speaker during the Nixon-Ford years was Oklahoma's Carl Albert—not a Texan, but close. Had Albert in fact become acting president under the 1947 statute during a period of congressional slow-walking of a vice presidential nominee, the most honorable course of action for him would have been to resign the presidency immediately after the nominee was eventually confirmed. The American people had voted for Republicans in the presidential election of 1972; and thus, Republicans were democratically entitled to hold the White House until the next regularly scheduled presidential election in 1976.

How might a supremely honorable Albert have blunted the unfortunate rules of the 1947 statutes? By creatively using the JFK-LBJ Amendment, of course. Had Nixon been hit by lightning and killed during the Agnew vacancy, Acting President Albert himself could have renominated Gerald Ford, and upon Ford's congressional confirmation, Albert could have stepped down in favor of Ford (who would then be free to pick Rockefeller as his understudy). Or had Ford become president without incident, Albert could have done a similar thing to help Ford out during the Rockefeller nomination process: in the event that lightning struck and killed Ford,† Acting President Albert could have used the JFK-LBJ

---

* Some might wonder how a presidential succession amendment and a presidential succession statute can formally coexist. Why doesn't the amendment simply repeal any existing statute and eliminate the need for any new statute? The answer is that the JFK-LBJ Amendment addresses single-vacancy issues, whereas the statute concerns itself with double-vacancy scenarios, in which both president and vice president are unavailable for service. So the problem is not the very existence of a succession statute—we need one now and always will—but rather the specific content of the 1947 succession statute still on the books, whose rules and incentives are in serious tension with the spirit of the more recently adopted amendment.

† A personal aside: In 1975, after Rockefeller had been confirmed, two would-be assassins in separate and unrelated incidents did take deadly aim at President Ford. Both assassination attempts failed. One of these attempted assassins, Sara Jane Moore, had several years earlier attended my family's annual Christmas party. At that time, she was the wife of a Bay Area physician who worked with my parents. I have no strong recollection of the day this woman came to my house, but my parents do, and this may be one more reason why, decades later, I continue to be obsessed with the constitutional issues surrounding assassination attempts.

Amendment itself to renominate Rockefeller and then step aside upon Rockefeller's congressional confirmation.

True, Albert wouldn't have been required to make these moves, and therein lies the problem with the Presidential Succession Act of 1947. But these are certainly the kinds of moves that any good-faith interpreter of the Twenty-fifth Amendment's deep structural principles ought to contemplate.

TEXAS AGAIN—AND BUSH 41

In 1976, Gerald Ford ran for election in his own right and lost to Jimmy Carter. Both in the popular vote and in the electoral college, the count was extremely close. Interestingly enough, Texas was a key swing state in this election. Ford won every western state—every single state in whole or in part west of Dallas–Fort Worth—in the continental United States, except Texas, which he lost by a narrow margin. Had Ford won Texas plus any one of the other states he barely lost, he would have triumphed in the electoral college.

Four years later, the Republicans, having learned the lesson of 1976, put Texan George H. W. Bush on the bottom of the ticket, alongside Ronald Reagan from Southern California. The two men swept Texas by double digits and won the White House handily. In retrospect, this thumping Republican victory in Texas in 1980 symbolizes a momentous shift in the geography of the modern presidential selection game. In the eleven presidential elections that have taken place since Texas Democrat Lyndon Johnson left office, 1976 is the only time the Democrats managed to carry Texas. An electoral cornerstone of the Democrats' New Deal–Great Society coalition is no more.

Although Republicans emphatically won the presidential race both in Texas and in the nation as a whole in 1980, it was only luck—and not sound legal design—that enabled the GOP to keep the fruits of its electoral triumph. In 1981, another gunman took deadly aim at a popular and charismatic president. This time, thankfully, the president survived and recovered. Imagine, however, that John Hinckley's bullet had in fact killed Reagan. And imagine further that upon assuming the presidency under section 1 of the JFK-LBJ Amendment, George H. W. Bush had made a proper nomination to fill the now-vacant vice presidency, pursuant to section 2 of the amendment. Suppose, finally, that a Democrat-controlled House one again slow-walked this nomination, and that something catastrophic happened to Bush 41 in this interval. (These are not outlandish hypotheticals: ours is a dangerous world, especially for presidents.)

In such a scenario, who would have moved into the White House for the next three and a half years? Democratic Speaker of the House Tip O'Neill—Reagan's main domestic nemesis, representing the party that voters had thumpingly rejected in the presidential election of 1980. So says the outdated Presidential Succession Act of 1947, in violation of virtually all the basic principles of the JFK-LBJ Amendment.

Plainly, an O'Neill presidency would have stood the Anti-Assassination Principle on its head, enabling one man's bullets to reverse all voters' ballots. (Lincoln's words with respect to *secession* ring true with respect to *succession*, too: "[B]allots are the rightful, and peaceful, successors of bullets; and . . . when ballots have fairly, and constitutionally, decided, there can be no successful appeal, back to bullets.") Far from being Reagan's handpicked helper—or at least a handpicked helper of the man Reagan had handpicked, Bush 41—a President O'Neill would have been one of the last persons in town that Reagan or Bush 41 would have chosen to carry their flag. Party continuity would have been flouted; and congressional slow-walking would have been rewarded, contrary to the No Vacancy Principle.[7]

Had Bush 41 merely been temporarily disabled in our hypothetical rather than killed, and had Bush eventually recovered, the handoffs back and forth between Bush and O'Neill would have likely been anything but smooth. In fact, O'Neill would have been obliged by the clear command of the clunky 1947 succession statute (and by the Constitution, properly construed) to leave the House in order to act as president, making it virtually impossible for him to smoothly return to his old post whenever Bush 41 recovered.[8]

What about the Competence, National Democracy, and Cabinet Monitoring Principles? It turns out that serving as Speaker of the modern House is not a particularly good way of preparing for the presidency. Most Speakers are amateurs on the world stage and hyper-partisans to boot. Speakers become Speakers nowadays by winning repeatedly in reliably safe districts that are either far more conservative or far more liberal than the nation as a whole, and then by winning the votes of a majority of their party colleagues, who are also either far more liberal or conservative than the median American voter. A president must win votes of the middle of America; a Speaker of the House must win the votes of the middle of the party. Speakers are unlikely to possess significant foreign policy expertise; nor do they typically have daily interactions with cabinet officers, who, under section 4 of the JFK-LBJ Amendment, might be called upon to make key decisions about whether the president is truly disabled at the outset of a succession crisis and whether he remains disabled thereafter.

In short, if we tweak the actual facts of the 1981 attempted assassination—the closest we have come as a nation to a repeat of Dallas—and if we then measure our hypothetical O'Neill presidency against the underlying principles of the JFK-LBJ Amendment, it becomes evident that the 1947 Presidential Succession Act is a constitutional disaster waiting to happen. Nor is there anything unique about the year 1981 or about O'Neill in particular. Presidents and vice presidents are always in some danger; most modern presidents—indeed, all presidents since LBJ except Jimmy Carter—have had to face an opposition-party Speaker of the House at some point; and Tip O'Neill was hardly unique among modern-day Speakers in being entirely unsuited for the presidency.

And therein lies hope. Because Speakers of both parties have typically been unfit for the presidency, and because both parties in recent years have won the presidency fair and square on various Election Days, both parties should favor reform going forward. By now, both sides should agree that whenever a party wins the presidential vote, that party should hold the presidency for four years, because that is what Americans voted for, and because even good opposition-party Speakers would be bad successor presidents.

The most sensible reform would replace the outmoded Presidential Succession Act of 1947 with new rules more in sync with the deep principles of the JFK-LBJ Amendment—ideally, new rules putting the secretary of state or some other presidentially handpicked cabinet officer first in the line of succession after the vice president, in a return to the more sensible succession system that was in place before 1947, under the Presidential Succession Act of 1886.*

---

* For more on the 1886 act, recall the discussion in the previous chapter at p. 176. In June 2009, the Continuity of Government Commission, a joint project of the American Enterprise Institute and the Brookings Institution, issued a report endorsing my proposal to scrap the 1947 act—a report all the more notable because commission members included former Republican House Speaker Newt Gingrich and former Democratic House Speaker Tom Foley. See *Preserving Our Institutions: The Continuity of the Presidency. The Second Report of the Continuity of Government Commission* (June 2009, AEI-Brookings). Two native Texans who have worked with me to vindicate the deep principles of the JFK-LBJ Amendment via a revamped presidential succession statute deserve special thanks: Professor Philip Bobbitt from Austin, Texas (whose maternal uncle was none other than LBJ himself), and Senator John Cornyn. We haven't succeeded yet, but I remain hopeful.

TEXAS AGAIN—AND BUSH 43

It is now time to bring three more Texans into the conversation. In the summer of 2000, the sitting governor of Texas, George W. Bush, having already locked up the Republican Party nomination for the presidency, handpicked Dick Cheney as his vice presidential running mate. Cheney, who had been living in Dallas, promptly announced his intention to relocate his residence to Wyoming—a state that he had previously represented in the House of Representatives and where he still maintained a home.

The reason for this relocation was obvious to constitutional experts. The Twelfth Amendment explicitly provides that when presidential electors cast ballots for president and vice president, at least one of these two candidates "shall not be an inhabitant" of the electors' own state. In other words, Texas's electors in December 2000 could not lawfully cast their electoral votes for two Texans, no matter how popular this ticket was among Lone Star State voters on Election Day. And without Texas's big prize of 32 electoral votes, it was doubtful in the summer of 2000 that Cheney, as the bottom half of the Bush-Cheney ticket, could reach the magic national number of 270 total electoral votes on Election Day. So the simple solution was for Cheney to announce in July 2000 that he would leave Texas and return to his old stomping ground of Wyoming. If Paris was worth a mass, surely the vice presidency was worth a move.

Enter University of Texas law professor Sanford Levinson, who cried foul in a *New York Times* op-ed on August 4, 2000. Entitled "2 Texans, Not 1," Levinson's op-ed argued that constitutionally conscientious Texas electoral college members might not be able to cast their votes in December for both Bush and Cheney, and that this inability might open the door for the Democratic vice presidential nominee to sneak into the vice presidency even if Bush ended up winning the November presidential sweepstakes. Though Bush could get to 270, thanks to Texas, Cheney might be left out in the cold.

Professor Levinson is a brilliant man, but how could he speak with any confidence in *August* about where Dick Cheney might lawfully reside in *December*? Surely a person can make a legitimate change of residence over a course of months. Let's assume that Cheney's motives were entirely political. So what? A person is entitled to move states for job-related reasons and to realize his dreams. Put more precisely, the right to travel and to relocate one's state residence has long been recognized as an essential part of the Constitution's basic structure; as an implicit component of the freedom of interstate commerce; as one of the interstate privileges and immunities of American citizenship under Article IV; and as an explicit guarantee of the opening sentence of the Fourteenth Amendment. As great as the Lone Star State is—and as hard as this might be for some Texans to fathom—today's Texans have an absolute right to leave Texas, should they so desire. Misguided though they might be, Texans even have a right to become Wyomingites.

The matter might be different if Cheney were seeking to wriggle out of Texas taxes or Texas child-support payments or some other basic civic obligation. (I am reminded here of the great country music classic, "All my exes live in Texas.") But instead, Dick Cheney in 2000 was offering himself up to the nation for public service, and he was doing so as the hand-picked choice of a major-party presidential candidate. In other words, the deep principles of the JFK-LBJ Amendment were highly relevant to the constitutional question Professor Levinson raised. Alas, nowhere in his August op-ed, or in a forty-nine-page law review article on Cheney's move that Levinson later coauthored, did the JFK-LBJ Amendment even make an appearance. Yet surely this amendment—which of course post-dates the Twelfth Amendment and which reflects modern America's considered judgment about the proper relationship between presidents and vice presidents in an era of political assassins and ICBMs—should exert a strong gravitational pull as sound interpreters ponder whether to read the Twelfth Amendment's inhabitant clause very expansively à la Levinson or more modestly à la Cheney.[9]

In short, the JFK-LBJ Amendment should remind us that presidents need to be exquisitely comfortable with their vice presidents in order to ensure that vice presidents will remain in the loop, and will be able to receive and return smooth handoffs of power during routine presidential surgeries and the like. Thus, we should strongly disfavor a contestable reading of some other clause of the Constitution (such as Levinson's overly broad reading of the Twelfth Amendment inhabitant clause) that undermines the Handpicked Succession Principle, which should be understood to entitle a president or would-be president to his *first choice* among legally permissible wingmen, so long as that first choice is upright and competent to fill the big chair should disaster strike.

Likewise, the JFK-LBJ Amendment teaches that vice presidents should ordinarily be members of the president's party, should be able to work closely with cabinet members, and should enjoy a national democratic mandate. All these Twenty-fifth Amendment principles would be violated by Levinson's approach, which would have made it harder for Bush-Cheney to win election even if a clear majority of Texas voters and a clear majority of the national electoral college wanted that team.

Had Texas electors somehow been forced to throw away their second-choice ballots, and had Democrat Joe Lieberman, Al Gore's running mate, somehow become George Bush's vice president, the sizable policy space between these two men would have created correspondingly sizable assassination incentives. The ever-real possibility of presidential assassination is something that Texans, in particular, should never forget, given what happened in their own state in 1963. Thus, so long as there is any room for good-faith debate over the boundaries of the Twelfth Amendment inhabitant clause, sound interpreters should disfavor any approach that makes it hard for would-be vice presidents to relocate their places of inhabitance, even for brazenly political reasons.

It might be objected that my proposed approach over-reads the Twenty-fifth Amendment, which addresses the issue of presidential succession and says nothing explicit about presidential elections. This objection misses how the two topics are connected. The amendment, sometimes called the Presidential *Succession* Amendment, is designed to preserve the fruits of the previous presidential *election*. Remember: All of the amendment's *succession* principles—Handpicked Succession, Party Continuity, Anti-Assassination, and so on—were designed to mimic the generally operative principles of modern presidential *elections*. The central idea of handpicked succession codified in section 1 of the Succession Amendment was based on the modern practice—a practice that emerged long after the Twelfth Amendment—of the party nominee personally picking his first-choice running mate rather than having this running mate imposed on him by his party convention.[10]

Or, if we reverse the camera angle: The whole point of a proper presidential and vice presidential election is to pick a pair of persons who will be able to work together smoothly as a team under the letter and spirit of the Twenty-fifth Amendment. We should construe any ambiguities in the presidential and vice presidential election rules by always keeping in mind the basic job descriptions of the modern presidency and vice presidency and the proper working relationship between these two offices, as outlined by the JFK-LBJ Amendment.

To put the point a different way, we must understand that the Twelfth Amendment, even if very expansively construed, in no way prevents two Texans in the White House. It simply limits the ability of *Texas's electors* to vote for two Texans. And because of the obvious textual narrowness of the Twelfth Amendment's inhabitant clause, the JFK-LBJ Amendment points the way to easy workarounds that would enable a Bush-Cheney team in the White House if this be the will of the national electorate.

So let's imagine—contrary to what actually happened—that Cheney had not moved to Wyoming; that he had remained a proud Texan even as he teamed up with another proud Texan; and that Texas's electors were thus barred, à la Levinson, from giving their electoral votes to both Bush and Cheney as their constituents plainly would have liked. And let's imagine further—again, contrary to what really happened, which was far stranger than any hypothetical that a law professor might dream up—that Bush in fact won the national electoral college vote fair and square, and handily, with no Florida nonsense, but that Joe Lieberman had managed to become Bush's vice president on Inauguration Day, because the Texas electors were barred by the Twelfth Amendment from casting their votes for Cheney.

In this scenario, the obvious path of political honor and of good-faith adherence to the deep principles of the JFK-LBJ Amendment would have been for Lieberman to do what Carl Albert should have done in our earlier hypothetical. Thus, Lieberman should have stepped down immediately after Inauguration, thereby enabling Bush to name Cheney as his vice president under section 2 of the JFK-LBJ Amendment. And Congress should then have confirmed Cheney in a heartbeat, because Cheney, in our hypothetical, did have a proper Election Day mandate to serve as Bush's wingman.

Had George W. Bush entertained even the slightest doubt that Lieberman would do the right thing on Inauguration Day, here is what the Bush-Cheney team itself could have done to work around the residence rules of the Twelfth Amendment. After winning 270 or more electoral votes on Election Day, Bush could have instructed all his electors, in Texas and everywhere else, to vote for some non-Texan Republican—let's call him Steve Strawman—for vice president. Strawman would have needed only to be eligible—thirty-five years old, natural born, and so on—and loyal to Bush. Formally, Bush and Strawman would have been announced as the electoral college winners for the presidency and vice presidency, respectively. One nanosecond after taking office on Inauguration Day, Strawman would have resigned—having no real popular mandate to do anything but step aside. Bush would have thereupon named Cheney—his true first choice and the true first choice of the voters on Election

Day—to the vice presidency under section 2 of the JFK-LBJ Amendment. And Congress, in this scenario, should then have immediately confirmed Cheney, because the Twelfth Amendment's inhabitant clause is, by its express terms, wholly inapplicable here; because this clause no longer vindicates any important constitutional principle worthy of broad construction; because Cheney was in fact the man with the Election Day mandate to serve as vice president; and because the JFK-LBJ Amendment was designed to ensure a close working relationship between a president and his competent first choice for vice president.

Put another way, in sharp contrast to the focus on state of residence in the Founding-era's Twelfth Amendment, the more recent JFK-LBJ Amendment pointedly omits any requirement that a president, when filling a vice presidential vacancy under section 1, must name someone from a state different from his own. The amendment purposefully gives a president very broad freedom to pick the person who will be the best fit for the vacant office and the best working helpmate, regardless of state of residence; and Congress should approve the president's first pick, so long as that pick is legally eligible and a person of genuine presidential competence and character.

OF COURSE, WHAT IS fair play for Republicans is also fair play for Democrats. Having just imagined an alternative universe in 2000 in which the JFK-LBJ Amendment could have been used to help Bush, Cheney, Texas, and the Republicans, let's now imagine a different alternative universe in 2000 in which the JFK-LBJ Amendment could have been deployed on behalf of the Democrats in the race—neither of whom, of course, was a Texan.

Recall that as events actually unfolded, Bush-Cheney did not exactly win in a fair and square way. Florida was a fiasco. Thousands of Democratic voters, many of them African Americans, were illegally purged from the voting rolls. Long lines in poor black and brown precincts drove away lots of would-be voters, mainly Democrats. Chad buildup and malfunctioning machines ended up spoiling a ridiculously large number of presidential ballots, most of which would have gone to Al Gore and Joe Lieberman. Misleading ballots were yet another problem, and statewide election officials dramatically failed in their obligations to run a fair, impartial election and vote count. (And let's not forget that the governor of Florida who presided over this electoral debacle was none other than Texas-born Jeb Bush, the brother of candidate George W.)

And then, to top it all off, the United States Supreme Court embarrassed itself in *Bush v. Gore*, wrongly ending a recount that was then under way and improperly snatching various legal issues away from the Florida courts.

But the Supreme Court is final, you say. There was nothing that could be done after the justices had pronounced their last word.

Not so. Presidents, too, are constitutional interpreters and decision-makers. And here is what President Bill Clinton could have done to express his solidarity with his loyal wingman, Al Gore, and his contempt for this appalling Supreme Court decision. He could have invoked section 3 of the JFK-LBJ Amendment, proclaimed himself disabled—heartsick!—and thereby officially made Gore America's "acting president."[11]

Clinton might even have gone a step further and resigned in protest of the Court's decision—a resignation that would have made Al Gore the president of the United States, full-stop, under section 1 of the JFK-LBJ Amendment, thereby placing Gore in a better position to challenge Bush 43 in 2004 in a rematch on a more level rhetorical playing field—ex-president against sitting president. (Recall from the previous chapter that in 1892 a somewhat similar rematch in fact occurred between ex-president Grover Cleveland and sitting president Benjamin Harrison, a rematch won by the ex-president, a Democrat, who thereby avenged his weird electoral college defeat at the hands of the Republican four years earlier.)

Of course, history didn't happen that way—in part, I suggest, because politicians, pundits, and the public have tended to overlook the many interesting possibilities created by the seemingly minor adjustment known as the Twenty-fifth Amendment.

As HISTORY ACTUALLY unfolded, the first formal invocation of section 3 occurred not because Bill Clinton was heartsick in 2000 but because George W. Bush underwent a scheduled colonoscopy in June 2002, and temporarily handed off power to Dick Cheney. For several hours, Cheney was officially acting president. In June 2007, Bush had another scheduled colonoscopy, and once again he used section 3 of the JFK-LBJ Amendment to effect a temporary handoff to Cheney. These handoffs were altogether admirable—in perfect harmony with the JFK-LBJ Amendment's letter, spirit, and intent.

Alas, at the very end of his time in office, our most recent Texan in the White House missed an opportunity to dramatize another sensible application of the JFK-LBJ Amendment. Recall that Barack Obama and Joe Biden beat John McCain and Sarah Palin quite handily in November 2008, even though the Democratic duo lost Texas. Officially, no Texan was on the ballot that year. But in political reality, there were two enormous Texan elephants in the room—or, to be more precise, one Texan elephant, and one ex-Texan elephant. Presidential elections are often referenda on the incumbent, whether or not the incumbent is formally on the ballot. Obama and Biden were running not just against McCain and Palin, but also against the Bush-Cheney record.

As returns came in on Election Night, it was clear to all that Obama and Biden had not just won, but won handily. In the popular vote, the only Democrat in the previous sixty years who had won by a bigger margin was LBJ himself in 1964, when he truly was landslide Lyndon. And, to repeat, the losers that night were not just John McCain and Sarah Palin, but also Bush and Cheney. America that night had voted to break with their vision, to try a new path.

And the economy was in freefall.

Yet even after the people had spoken on Election Night, Bush and Cheney remained in power, awkwardly, for the next two and half months. In effect, these men had suffered a national vote of no confidence; they had no mandate; and the economy continued to slide downward.

In other countries, once the election has occurred, or once a vote of no confidence has carried, incumbents leave office in a hurry, and the winners, with a fresh mandate, take the helm in speedy fashion. And Americans could have done the same thing in early November 2008—thanks to the JFK-LBJ Amendment. Cheney could have resigned the day after the election, Agnew-style; Bush could have named Barack Obama his new vice president under section 2 of the JFK-LBJ Amendment; the Congress could have voted its assent in minutes; Bush would then have been free to step aside in favor of President Obama, whose first act would have been to nominate Biden to be his Number 2 under section 2. In short, there was no need to have waited two and a half months to effect the people's verdict on presidential Election Day.[12]

Perhaps Obama himself did not want to start early—and if so, this would be a good reason why the JFK-LBJ Amendment was in fact not used in the way that I am imagining. Perhaps the amendment should be used in this way only when the American people are told in advance of the election that the winners will take over immediately. But as we think about future elections, we should think about all the ways that the JFK-LBJ Amendment might be creatively used in a variety of scenarios beyond scheduled colonoscopies.[13]

TEXAS AGAIN—AND BUSH 45?

Which brings me, finally, to the upcoming presidential election of 2016. Just for fun, let me spin out an entirely fanciful scenario illustrating yet another way in which the JFK-LBJ Amendment could be used in the future. I will try to steer my flight of fancy in a way that enables me, one last time, to bring Texas into the picture.[14]

Imagine that the Republicans cannot decide between Texas senator Ted Cruz and Texas-born Jeb Bush, formerly the governor of Florida. Republicans want both Texans. And as a team, the two would make a powerful ticket—a diehard and a moderate, highly likely to win both Texas and Florida, two big cornerstones of a winning electoral strategy. But neither wing of the Republican Party is willing to allow the other wing to monopolize the top spot. Moderates insist that Bush must top the ticket, whereas diehards will be satisfied only if Cruz controls.

So at the Republican National Convention, the candidates devise a clever compromise. It will take a village, or at least a tag team, to beat the formidable Hillary Clinton, the Democratic nominee in our playful scenario. So Cruz and Bush flip a coin; and the winner of this coin flip tops the ticket—but only for now. In their acceptance speeches, Bush and Cruz jointly announce that they intend to alternate in power. For example, they could tell the voters that Bush, as the coin-flip winner, will nominally top the ticket and will, if elected, take office in January 2017, but will serve as president for only the first three years of the four-year term. In January 2020, the teammates will use the Twenty-fifth Amendment to switch places—to flip the ticket (in a process I will explain momentarily). Thus, beginning on January 20, 2020, Cruz will be the president and Bush 45 the vice president.

There is nothing magical about this January 20, 2020, date. Many other dates would do. But for maximal democratic legitimacy, Bush and Cruz would need to tell 2016 voters long before Election Day about the details of their planned ticket flip.

If this Republican dream team won in 2016 and proved popular in office, the teammates could run for reelection in 2020, but this time, sitting president Cruz could top the ticket. If reelected, Cruz might then serve until, say, January 20, 2024—four consecutive years in all—and then Bush 45 would resume the top spot for the final year of the second term. Thus, Bush 45 would also end up serving four years, albeit not consecutively.

Nothing in the Constitution would prevent our tag team from presenting themselves to the electorate in similar fashion in 2024. If the voters were to endorse the pair yet again, then at this point Bush 45 would have been elected twice as president and would become ineligible in any future presidential race; but Cruz would remain fully eligible to run in 2028. Thus, so long as the electorate continued to back our dynamic duo, these teammates could, between themselves, share power for a total of four full terms. (Under the Twenty-second Amendment, no person can be elected to the presidency more than twice; and under the Twelfth Amendment, vice presidents must meet the same eligibility and electability rules as presidents.)

Ticket-flipping and tag-team alternation, then, would enable our Texan and ex-Texan duo to leverage the advantages of incumbency well into the future—to stretch their potential presidential tenure over sixteen years rather than the standard eight. Variants of the tag-team approach have operated in other leading democracies. Consider, for example, England's Tony Blair and Gordon Brown (although their alleged gentleman's agreement to alternate in power was never made public) and Israel's mid-1980s alternation agreement between Shimon Peres and Yitzhak Shamir.

Exactly how does the Constitution enable a sitting president and vice president to trade places? Simple: On January 20, 2020 (or whenever), Bush 45 resigns, making Cruz the president full-stop under section 1 of the JFK-LBJ Amendment. Cruz in turn immediately names Bush to be vice president under section 2, and Congress immediately approves. Voilà—the ticket, flipped! As long as the Congress approves, the JFK-LBJ Amendment would thus enable the president and vice president to switch seats in a nimble transaction that could be completed in less time than it takes to eat a taco.

And as a matter of democratic principle, Congress should approve such a deal, given that the American voters would have blessed it long in advance, in the 2016 presidential election itself. But suppose a recalcitrant Congress refused to play along. (Imagine it was controlled by Democratic naysayers and slow-walkers.) No matter. Instead of formally resigning, Bush could accomplish the flip on his own, simply by transferring presidential power to Cruz under section 3 of the JFK-LBJ Amendment, making Cruz the acting president—just as his big brother Bush 43 had made Dick Cheney the acting president, briefly, in 2002 and again in 2007.

One obvious difference would be that the 2002 and 2007 transfers of presidential power were effected for more obviously medical reasons, whereas our imagined uses of the JFK-LBJ Amendment in the Bush–Cruz scenario are more political in nature. But nothing in the amendment limits transfers to purely medical disabilities, and a broader understanding of section 3 is in keeping with the amendment's largest purpose, that of facilitating teamwork and handoffs between America's top two executive officials.[15]

Of course, at every instant, America would have one and only one person acting as president and formally in charge. Handoffs of power between teammates would occur much as they have when incumbents traditionally leave office, as when Reagan yielded in 1989, at the end of his second term, to his own handpicked running mate, Bush 41. As we have seen, the JFK-LBJ Amendment was specially designed to facilitate easy transfers of power back and forth between presidents and vice presidents. However, the amendment's full potential to create a different kind of teamwork at the top—and to launch a new kind of presidential election strategy—has yet to be fully understood.

MY FIRST TELEVISION MEMORY, associated with one Texas city, is counterbalanced by my most vivid early television memory, as a ten-year-old boy, when mankind reached the moon, and astronauts spoke directly to and about another Texas city. The first word uttered on the lunar surface was "Houston."* This was a reference to the Houston Space Center and thus a tribute to the NASA man-on-the-moon-in-this-decade program brilliantly launched by the great John Kennedy and brilliantly carried forward by JFK's great wingman, LBJ—in perfect keeping with the Handpicked Succession, National Democracy, Competence, Party Continuity,

---

* When Apollo 11 touched down on the moon, Neil Armstrong immediately relayed the news: "Houston, Tranquility Base here. The Eagle has landed."

No Vacancy, and Anti-Assassination Principles that I have sought to describe in this chapter.

Americans are a profoundly imaginative people, and "Houston" should remind us that we must never stop imagining. In that spirit, I have in this chapter tried to offer up an imaginative overview of an amendment that, like the Houston Space Center itself, will be forever linked in American memory to two of America's most imaginative presidents, John Fitzgerald Kennedy of Massachusetts and Texas's own native son, Lyndon Baines Johnson.

CHAPTER 10

WYOMING:

A ROCKY-MOUNTAIN VIEW OF

THE SECOND AMENDMENT

Having just considered the relationship between gunmen and *Article* II—how America's presidents and presidency have been affected by assassins and would-be assassins—let us now ponder the relationship between gun-toting and *Amendment* II, more commonly known as the Second Amendment.

In the previous chapter, I suggested that certain Article II issues might be profitably viewed from the distinct perspective of central Texas. In this chapter, I shall similarly suggest that Amendment II appears in a particularly interesting light when seen from a special spot. For reasons that will become clear by the end of this chapter, I invite you to accompany me, in your mind's eye, to the general region of the Rocky Mountain West, and in particular to the great state of Wyoming—widely known as the Cowboy State. (If it seems in any way jarring for you to imagine yourself journeying directly from Texas to Wyoming, just recall Dick Cheney's path to power, as recounted in the previous chapter.)

THE ROCKY MOUNTAIN WEST is gun country in popular folklore and probably also in fact. As for folklore, try to think about cowboys without somehow thinking about guns. As for fact, although reliable numbers are hard to come by, in one relatively recent survey estimating the percentage of households with handguns, the mountain states ranked well above the national average—and this in a nation with one of the highest per capita gun ownership rates in the world.[1]

The US Constitution does not explicitly speak of "guns," but it does contain some notable language in its Second Amendment, which reads as follows: "A well regulated Militia being necessary to the security of a free State, the right of the people to keep and bear Arms shall not be infringed."

I suspect that a high percentage of Wyomingites, in particular, and Rocky Mountaineers, in general, could recite this amendment by heart—or at least part of the amendment, and there's the rub. Many gun fans stress the amendment's "right of the people to keep and bear Arms" language while slighting other words in the amendment, such as "well-regulated" and "Militia." Even the phrase "bear Arms" and the words "the people" did not quite mean the same thing to the Founders as they do to today's National Rifle Association (NRA). To understand the Second Amendment, we must widen our interpretive field of vision.

To begin with, we must see the amendment as a syntactical whole, and note the distinctive grammatical linkage between its opening ode and its closing command. But even this is far too narrow a lens. We must consider the amendment alongside its companion amendments—the First and Third, in particular, and the Bill of Rights more generally. For example, we must see how the Second Amendment resembles the Fifth, Sixth, and Seventh Amendments, and even the Tenth Amendment. More broadly still, we must read the Second Amendment alongside similarly worded provisions of state constitutions, and against the backdrop of earlier English charters of liberty, such as the English Bill of Rights of 1689. Perhaps most important, we must confront later constitutional amendments, such as the Fourteenth and even the Nineteenth, and consider how these later texts place the earlier one in a different light.

The results of this holistic study may surprise folks on both sides of the aisle. Contrary to NRA ideology, the Founders' Second Amendment, by itself, provides only slender support for a robust individual right to own all manner of guns. Later constitutional developments—in particular, the words of and the history surrounding the Fourteenth Amendment—do in fact, when read in conjunction with the Second Amendment, strongly support an individual right to have a gun in one's home for self-protection. But later developments also support other readings of the Second Amendment on topics far removed from the gun-control debate. For example, when read in the light of our entire constitutional structure, including post-Founding amendments, the Second Amendment has some rather remarkable egalitarian implications for issues such as women in combat. And so, to both conservatives who now love the Second Amendment and liberals who now loathe it, I say, think again: the amendment may not quite mean what you thought.

READING THE CONSTITUTION: SUBSTANCE

So what *does* the Second Amendment mean? A lot, says the NRA. Not much, say gun-control groups. In the waning years of the twentieth century, it didn't much matter who was right. On all but the mildest of gun-control measures, the NRA had the votes (and the cash), and that was that. Then came the 1999 massacre at Columbine High School, in the Rocky Mountain West. Since then, various proposals for serious federal gun controls have often been in the air, though very little has reached the congressional floor. Some proposals aim to limit the amount and type of ammunition that may be purchased; others seek to restrict the number of guns a person can buy in a given week; and still others would require universal loophole-free background checks and the licensing of all new guns (and perhaps old ones as well) on the model of automobile licensing, with gun owners obliged to pass both a written gun-safety test and a practical safety and competence exam. If adopted, would such measures violate the federal Constitution?[2]

Let's begin by returning to the language of the amendment itself: "A well regulated Militia being necessary to the security of a free State, the right of the people to keep and bear Arms shall not be infringed." This curious syntax has confounded many modern readers. How do the two main clauses with different subject-nouns fit together? Do these words guarantee a right of *militias*, as the first clause seems to suggest, or a right of *people*, as the second clause seems to say? On one side of the debate, today's gun controllers embrace a narrow, statist reading. They argue that the amendment merely confers a right on state governments to establish professional state militias like the National Guard. On the other side of the aisle, today's gun-rights groups read the amendment in a broad, libertarian way. They claim that the amendment protects a sweeping right of every individual to have guns for self-protection, for hunting, and for sport. Both readings are problematic.

The statist reading glosses over the obvious fact that the amendment's operative command—"shall not be infringed"—appears in its second clause, which speaks of "the people" and not "the States." What's more,

the eighteenth-century "Militia" referred to by the first clause was not re-
motely like today's National Guard. The Framers' militia comprised virtually all voters—rather like today's Swiss militia—rather than a small
group of paid, semiprofessional volunteers.

But the libertarian reading is also imperfect. The amendment does
not speak of "persons" individually. It speaks of a right of "the people"—a
word with collective connotations in many contexts. And the amendment
uses a pointedly military phrase, "bear Arms"—a phrase tightly wedged
between a clause that talks about the "Militia" and a clause (in the Third
Amendment) that regulates the quartering of "Soldiers" in times of "war"
and "peace." State constitutions on the books in 1789 consistently used
the phrase "bear arms" only in military contexts.[3]

Ultimately, we must understand how all the words of the amendment
cohere, and how they, in turn, mesh with other language in the Constitution. The amendment's syntax perplexes because modern readers routinely
misread the words "Militia" and "people," imposing modern-day assumptions and linguistic usages on an eighteenth-century text. At the Founding, the now-confounding subject-nouns were simply different ways of
saying the same thing: the militia were the people and the people were
the militia. An earlier draft of the amendment linked the two clauses with
language speaking of "a well regulated militia, composed of the body of
the people," but the verbose linchpin was later removed. Even without the
linchpin, the very syntax of the amendment as ratified equates the "Militia" of the first clause with "the people" of the second. In a sound republic,
the "people" and the "Militia" are, broadly speaking, one and the same:
those who vote serve in the military, and those who serve in the military
vote.[4]

Underlying these words was a deep distrust of a professional and
authoritarian standing army that might not truly look like America but
might instead embody a dangerous culture within a culture, a military
complex threatening republican equality and civilian supremacy. The
amendment's big idea is not guns, as such. It is not hunting. It is not target
practice. It is that the military must subserve democracy. We the People
must rule: our military must do what We say, not what it wants. To ensure
this, the amendment valorizes a military that represents and embodies
us—the people, the voters, the democratic rulers of a "free State." Rather
than reposing full confidence in a standing army that might be filled with
aliens, convicts, vagrants, and mercenaries—with men who might not
truly represent the electorate, and who might pursue their own dreams

and schemes—a sound republic should rely on its own armed citizens: a "Militia" of "the people."

Call this the republican reading, as opposed to the statist and libertarian readings that dominate modern discourse. Statists anachronistically read the "Militia" to mean the government (the paid professional officialdom) rather than the people (the ordinary citizenry). Equally anachronistically, libertarians read "the people" to mean atomized private persons, each hunting in his own private Idaho (or Wyoming), rather than the citizenry acting collectively.

When the Constitution speaks of "the people" rather than "persons," the collective connotation is often primary. In the Preamble, "We the People . . . do ordain and establish this Constitution" as public citizens meeting together in conventions and acting in concert, not as private individuals pursuing our respective hobbies. The only other reference to "the people" in the Philadelphia Constitution of 1787 appears very close to the Preamble, at the outset of Article I, and here, too, the meaning is public and political, not private and individualistic: every two years, "the people"—that is, the voters—elect the House of Representatives.

Here is another way to see this key distinction: we must heed Abigail Adams's admonition to "[r]emember the Ladies." Free women in 1787 had the rights of "persons" (such as the freedom to practice their religion and the right to enjoy the protections of privacy in their homes), but women did not directly participate in various political acts of "the people." Women back then did not, as a rule, vote in constitutional conventions or for state lawmakers or for Congress; nor did they serve on juries; nor were women part of the militia/people at the heart of the Second Amendment.[5]

The rest of the Bill of Rights buttresses this republican reading. The core of the First Amendment's assembly clause, which textually abuts the Second Amendment, is the right of "the people"—in essence, voters—to "assemble" in constitutional conventions and other political conclaves. Likewise, the core rights retained and reserved to "the people" in the Ninth and Tenth Amendments were rights of the people collectively to govern themselves democratically.[6]

Of course, we need not and should not insist that these amendments refer only to voters and to "the people" collectively; words and phrases in the Constitution (and in language generally) are often properly applied beyond their core, paradigmatic applications. And we should also take note of the wording of the Fourth Amendment: "The right of the people to be secure in their persons, houses, papers, and effects, against unreasonable searches and seizures, shall not be violated . . . " Here, in contrast to the Second Amendment, the collective "people" wording is expressly paired with the more individualistic language of "persons"—a word pointedly repeated later in this amendment, which obviously focuses on the private domain. Plainly, the Fourth Amendment aims to protect individuals—both voters and nonvoters, women as well as men—in their private homes more than in the public square. Why, then, did the Fourth use the words "the people" at all? Perhaps to spotlight the role that jurors—acting collectively and representing the electorate, *the people*—would play in deciding which searches were reasonable and how much to punish government officials who searched or seized improperly.[7]

If we want a useful image of the people's militia at the Founding, we should begin by envisioning the militia's first cousin, the jury. Whereas the Second Amendment highlights the militia, the Fifth, Sixth, and Seventh Amendments, along with the Fourth, feature the jury. (The Fifth protects grand juries; the Sixth, criminal juries; and the Seventh, civil juries.) Like the militia, the jury was a local body countering imperial power—summoned by the government but standing outside it, representing the people, collectively. Like jury service, militia participation was both a right and a duty of qualified voters, who were regularly summoned to discharge their public obligations. (Nonvoters—women, children, aliens—were in general excluded from both the jury and the militia.) Like the jury, the militia was composed of amateurs arrayed against, and designed to check, permanent and professional government officials (judges and prosecutors, in the case of the jury; a standing army, in the case of the militia). Like the jury, the militia embodied collective political action rather than private pursuits.

Historical materials from the Founding generally confirm this republican reading of militias, juries, and the Second Amendment. State constitutions from this era consistently interwove arms-bearing and militia clauses with rules governing standing armies, troop-quartering, martial law, and civilian supremacy. In the English Bill of Rights of 1689, language concerning the right to arms immediately followed language condemning unauthorized standing armies in peacetime.[8] Libertarians today cannot explain this clear pattern, which has everything to do with the military and nothing to do with hunting. Conversely, statists also make a hash of these state constitutional provisions, many of which use language very similar to the Second Amendment to affirm rights *against* state governments.

Keeping the jury-militia analogy in mind, we can see the nugget of truth in these competing accounts and also what's missing from each. On one side, statists are right to see the amendment as localist and to note that law and government help bring the militia together. So, too, with the jury. But what the statist reading misses is that, when the law summons the citizenry together, these citizens, in an important sense, act as the people outside of government, rather than as a professional and permanent government bureaucracy. Just as the bureaucratic IRS is obviously not a true jury, so, too, the semiprofessional National Guard is not a general militia. On the other side, libertarians rightly recoil at the authoritarianism of their opponents in the debate, but wrongly privatize what is an inherently collective and political right. Individuals who choose to hunt or target-shoot together are a gun club, not a general militia.

But to see all this is to see what makes the Second Amendment so slippery today: the legal and social structure on which the amendment was built no longer exists. The Founders' juries—grand, petit, and civil—are still around today, but the Founders' militia is not. America is not Switzerland. Voters no longer muster for militia practice in the town square.

We are free today to read the Second Amendment more broadly if we choose. Thoughtful legal scholars of all stripes—from Sanford Levinson on the left to Eugene Volokh on the right—have reminded us that other amendments have been read generously and therefore ask why the Second should not also be read generously.

Given that a broad reading is an interpretive and policy choice rather than a clear constitutional command, we are entitled to ask ourselves whether a given broad reading makes good sense as a matter of principle and practice. The mere fact that, say, the First Amendment has been read expansively is not an automatic argument for equal treatment for the Second. For example, violent felons—even while in prison, and especially after their release—obviously have a First Amendment right to print their opinions in newspapers. Yet such felons have never had a Second Amendment right to own guns. Even the NRA accepts this double standard. But what underlies it? The obvious commonsensical idea is that guns in the hands of dangerous felons can hurt others in ways that their words cannot.

Especially today's guns. At the Founding, single-fire muskets had certain attractively democratic properties. A person often had to get close to you to kill you, and in getting close, he usually rendered himself vulnerable to counterattack. The musket took time to reload, so one person could not typically mow down dozens in a few seconds. One person, one gun, one shot was not as perfect a system of majority rule as one person, one vote, but the side with the most men often won; and there was a rough proportionality of capacity to kill and be killed. What's more, madmen were constrained by the strong social network of the well-regulated militia. Today, social strictures have loosened, and commonly available weapons are far more lethal than those that were available in the past, a combination rendering isolated madmen vastly more dangerous.

It may be countered that the federal government today is also more dangerous, given vast improvements in military technology. True enough, but today's federal government is also less likely to use this military technology to tyrannize its citizens than many at the Founding feared. The Founders acted and wrote in a world where democratic self-government had never truly existed on a continental scale. The conventional wisdom of the time associated liberty and democracy with localism, and linked geographically expansive regimes with empire and tyranny. If the Framers were slightly paranoid about the potential evil of a central Leviathan, they had good reason for this paranoia in light of their lived experience with the British Empire and the history of the world before 1800. But the past two centuries have shown that America's central government has redeemed the hopes of its friends more than it has confirmed the fears of its enemies. To rail against central tyranny today is to be rather more paranoid than were the Founders, given the track record of the United States since 1787. Put another way, because ballots and the First Amendment have prevented full-blown federal tyranny, bullets and the Second Amendment need not bear as much weight today as some pessimists anticipated two centuries ago.

Above and beyond the original meaning of the Second Amendment, today's interpreters must read this amendment in light of later constitutional words and deeds. After the experience of the Civil War, the strong localism of the original Second Amendment seems more problematic. Constitutionally speaking, the heroes of the Civil War fought for the Union Army, not the rebel militias. In the wake of this war and the amendments it produced, we need to rethink the vision of Union armies and state militias in our constitutional order. Moreover, various post-Founding amendments have dramatically expanded American suffrage. How might these constitutional redefinitions of the electorate affect our understanding of "the people" and the "Militia" at the heart of the Second Amendment?

IF WE SEEK BROAD READINGS of the amendment faithful to the core values of the Founding, yet attentive to subsequent legal and factual developments, here are two that the NRA hasn't proposed but that are as plausible as that organization's preferred broad readings.

First, we could take the military out of the militia. Transcending the typical statist-versus-libertarian debate, some modern scholars have emphasized how the Founders' militia bound citizens together in a common venture. The militia played an important social function in the community and embodied a democratic culture in which rich and poor citizens from all walks of life came together as equals—as with the jury.[9]

Without some forms of democratic glue, our culture risks disintegration, especially in today's world of increasing demographic diversity and specialization of labor. Thus, a broad modern reading of the Second Amendment would call for compulsory or quasi-compulsory national service, with both military and nonmilitary alternatives, such as VISTA or the Civilian Conservation Corps, available as options. (Early militias also performed important nonmilitary functions, such as disaster relief.) Instead of bowling alone, Americans would band together, building a more solid base of social capital and civic virtue.[10]

Second, we could create an army that truly looks like America. At the Founding, a standing army in peacetime was viewed with dread and seen as embodying not ordinary virtuous citizens but a motley assortment of outcasts—mercenaries, convicts, vagrants, and aliens. Today, we view our professional armed forces with pride. These forces represent Us, not Them. Thus, the Founders' militia has begun to morph into today's army, navy, air force, and Marine Corps. Given this development, women should play as equal a role as possible in today's institutions of collective self-defense. The militia lauded by the Second Amendment should reflect the people, just as the jury should.

To put the point another way, the Second Amendment says that voters should bear arms and that arms-bearers should vote: the voting electorate ("the people") and the democratic military ("the Militia") should in republican principle be one and the same. Since the Nineteenth Amendment has made women equal voters, the Second Amendment demands that they be given equal status in arms. Allowing women to buy guns at the local sporting goods store might make them equal in libertarian gun-toting, but it does not make them equal in republican arms-bearing; it fails to include them on equal terms in modern America's militia-substitute.

Great strides have occurred in recent years, but America's military policies are still laced with sex-based rules. Only men must register for selective service, and long-standing bans on women in combat have yet to be entirely phased out. Some types of formal sex discrimination can be justified in some cases, but all sex-based legal distinctions should be closely interrogated. For example, separate bathrooms for men and women are, formally, a kind of sex discrimination, but this arrangement is widely seen as justified by legitimate privacy concerns. So, too, certain sex-based exclusions in military policy might be justifiable, where these exclusions reflect real physical differences relevant to modern warfare. However, where exclusions of women are justified merely by the need to maintain "morale" and "unit cohesion," we should be wary: similar arguments were once used to maintain racial discrimination in our armed forces.[11]

BUT IS THERE NOTHING to be said for the strong libertarian view of guns put forth by the NRA? In fact, there is a great deal to say on behalf of an individual right to keep a gun in one's home for self-defense. The best constitutional arguments for this view come not from the Founding but from the Reconstruction some fourscore years later.

Even with regard to the Founding, it is simplistic to deny any link between collective security and individual self-defense. Somewhat like standing armies, roving bands of thugs and pirates posed a threat to law-abiding citizens, and trusty weapons in private homes were part of a system of community policing against predators. (Note that the amendment encompasses the right to "keep" as well as "bear" arms.)[12]

But this was not the main concern of the Second Amendment at the Founding. Rather, the amendment's big idea was epitomized by Lexington and Concord and Bunker Hill. *When arms were outlawed, only the king's men would have arms.* The amendments forged in the afterglow of the Revolution reflected obvious anxiety about a standing army controlled by the new imperial government, and affection for the good old militia.

Things looked different to Americans after a bloody Civil War. Massachusetts militiamen had once died for liberty at Bunker Hill, but more recently, Mississippi militiamen had killed for slavery at Vicksburg. The imperial Redcoats at the Founding were villains, but the boys in blue who had won under Grant and Sherman were heroes—at least in the eyes of Reconstruction Republicans who governed after the war. Thus, when Lincoln's generation took its turn rewriting the Constitution, it significantly recast the right to weapons. Textually, the Fourteenth Amendment proclaimed the need to protect fundamental "privileges" and "immunities" of citizens.[13]

As scholars from right to left have documented in great detail, the framers of the Fourteenth Amendment strongly believed in an individual right to own and keep guns in one's home for self-protection. Most obviously, blacks and Unionists down south could not always count on the local police to keep roving bands of hooded white terrorists at bay. *When guns were outlawed, only Klansmen would have guns.* Thus, the Reconstruction Congress made quite clear that a right to keep a gun at home for self-protection was a constitutional right—a true "privilege" or "immunity" of citizens.[14]

Although many speeches to this effect may be found in the 1866 floor debates, the most dramatic evidence comes not from individual Congressmen, but from Congress itself. Section 1 of the Fourteenth Amendment was importantly linked to the Civil Rights Act of 1866, which in turn was closely connected to the Freedman's Bureau Bill of 1866. This latter statute explicitly provided that "*personal* liberty, *personal* security, and the acquisition, enjoyment, and disposition of estate, real and *personal, including the constitutional right to bear arms*, shall be secured to and enjoyed by *all the citizens.*" This language made it clear that, according to the Reconstruction Congress that drafted the Fourteenth Amendment, a personal right to firearms ranked among the privileges and immunities of all citizens—both males and females, voters and nonvoters, soldiers and civilians. The statutory language linking this personal arms right to "personal liberty," "personal security," and private property derived directly from William Blackstone's canonical chapter on the right of individual self-protection and self-preservation, a chapter having nothing to do with military and collective self-defense issues, and everything to do with the "personal" rights of every individual, whether or not that individual was a voter or a militiaman.[15]

Nor was this a view unique to Reconstruction Republicans. A decade earlier, Chief Justice Roger Taney's lead opinion in the *Dred Scott* case had proclaimed that if blacks ever became citizens, it would necessarily follow that they would enjoy all the "privileges and immunities" of "citizens," including "full liberty of speech in public and in private upon all subjects upon which [a state's] citizens might speak; [liberty] to hold public meetings upon political affairs, and to keep and carry arms wherever they went."[16]

For Taney and company, this of course meant that blacks, even if free, could never be deemed citizens. The Reconstruction Congress obviously disagreed, and said so in the first sentence of the Fourteenth Amendment, affirming the citizenship of all persons—black and white, male and female, rich and poor—born in America. But in certain key respects, Reconstruction Republicans agreed with Taney on what citizenship implied: a right to have a gun for self-defense.

In contrast to the image of arms at the Founding—a right of the people as a collectivity to organize themselves militarily—both *Dred Scott* and the Freedman's Bureau Bill tended to privatize and demilitarize the image of gun-toting, the former by speaking of an individual's right to "carry arms" rather than "bear arms," and the latter with its repeated use of the word "personal" in contrast to the Founders' collectivist "people."

Thus, the Fourteenth Amendment, when read in the light of its history, does support an individual right to have a gun in one's home for self-protection. Yet today's NRA tends to stress the Second Amendment far more than the Fourteenth. This is supremely ironic. The NRA itself was born after the Civil War, sired by a group of ex-Union officers; its swaddling clothes come from the Reconstruction more than the Founding, as does its individual rights ideology.[17]

IF WE TAKE THE Reconstruction vision of the Second Amendment seriously, this individual right should apply not just against federal officials but also against state and local governments. In legal jargon, the Second Amendment right to arms is properly "incorporated" against the states.[18]

That's the good news for the NRA. But the bad news, at least for the most ardent gun lovers, is that whatever Fourteenth Amendment right exists is a limited one. Most current gun-control proposals seek to regulate rather than prohibit—for example, limiting the amount and type of guns and ammunition one can buy. Requiring loophole-free background checks, registration of guns, and licenses with practical and book tests on the model of automobile licensing horrifies some gun lovers—the first step toward confiscation, they predict in dire tones. But this is hard to take seriously. The authors of the Second Amendment, after all, were perfectly comfortable knowing that the government would know who had weapons—every voter—and also were perfectly comfortable requiring those who owned guns to be properly trained and monitored in their use: Training and monitoring were at the heart of militia musters. Reasonable gun-control laws of the sort I have mentioned may not be exactly what the Framers had in mind when they said that the armed citizenry should be "well regulated." But—at least in a world that is so distant from the Founders—they are close enough.

READING THE CONSTITUTION: METHOD

Now for a few words about interpretive method. One reason that I have chosen the Second Amendment for exposition in this chapter is that this tiny but fraught patch of text so vividly illustrates many of the difficulties that accompany good-faith efforts at modern constitutional interpretation.

Proper constitutional interpretation begins with the text of the Constitution itself. Textual interpretation, however, can be done well or badly, and even when done well it is only the first step of analysis. As James Madison, writing as "Publius," reminded his readers in *The Federalist* No. 37, the natural and social universe is often blurry, lacking clean joints; and language itself introduces further complexities. Words sometimes have relatively clear core meanings but then shade off gradually when we move away from the core. In law, we often seek the meaning of a phrase or an entire sentence in which the legal whole may be more or less than the sum of the linguistic parts, especially when we deal with legal terms of art and metaphors more generally. Consider, for example, the Fifth Amendment command that "no person shall . . . be subject for the same offence to be twice put in jeopardy of life or limb." Should the words "life or limb" here be read literally, allowing the government to try me again after I have been acquitted in a fair trial, so long as the punishment at issue is neither death nor dismemberment? (Suppose the government merely seeks to imprison me for twenty years and subject me to occasional solitary confinement.) Here, it seems clear that the "life or limb" phrase is best read as a poetic pairing, a graphic synecdoche for all serious criminal punishment.

The Second Amendment presents a similar challenge. Though the word "bear" is roughly synonymous with "carry," and the word "Arms" encompasses "guns," there is, I have argued, a subtle difference between the phrases "bear Arms" and "carry guns"—especially when the "bear Arms" phrase is surrounded by other military language. My claim is not, however, that no one at the Founding ever used the phrase "bear Arms" to encompass, say, hunting. In fact, we can find such uses—but they were not the dominant legal usages of this phrase at the Founding.[19]

Further complications arise as language evolves. Today, the phrase "bear Arms" has for many Americans lost its overwhelmingly military meaning and has become more synonymous with gun-toting in general. A great many modern state constitutions use the "bear arms" phrase outside a strictly military and collective context. A significant number of states—including Delaware, Nebraska, Nevada, New Mexico, North Dakota, West Virginia, and Wisconsin—explicitly link the "bear arms" phrase to hunting and/or recreation. Many of these state constitutional references to hunting and recreation are of a distinctly recent vintage, enacted in the 1980s and 1990s.[20]

But sound interpretation of the Constitution often seeks to read the text as it was understood by the people who framed and ratified the language in question, or who reglossed it when adopting a later amendment. When real people have lived through real evils and carefully crafted language to prohibit these evils from recurring, their posterity would be wise to read their language in light of the historical mischief they aimed to banish—the core historical evil, the "paradigm case" underlying many a constitutional prohibition. In reminding readers of the evils of an imperial standing army in the late 1700s, and conjuring up images of Lexington and Concord and Bunker Hill, I have tried to be faithful to this mode of textual and historical interpretation.[21]

A different approach, which sought only the modern meanings of words, would risk constitutional command by pun. If a public school prohibited students from wearing tank tops, surely nothing should turn on whether some clever plaintiff characterizes this dress code as infringing his right to "bare arms." This would remain true even if some trendy back-to-phonics movement had somehow succeeded in convincing most ordinary Americans to spell "bear" and "bare" the same way: bAr.

In seeking out the core meaning of a constitutional prohibition and the historical paradigm case that prompted the prohibition, good textualists have many tools at hand. I have highlighted the significance of language quite similar to the Second Amendment's in antecedent state constitutions, and in other landmark texts, such as the English Bill of Rights. The historical and linguistic links between these documents and the Second Amendment are relatively clear.

Others have suggested that the Founders' Second Amendment borrowed from Blackstone's account of the right to have arms for individual self-defense; but these scholars have not shown any tight linguistic linkage between the Second Amendment's phraseology and Blackstone's, or any specific historical evidence suggesting that the Founders had Blackstone primarily in mind here.[22] (Considerable evidence does exist, however, to confirm that Blackstone's individualistic view of arms was quite influential for the later Reconstruction generation.)[23]

Unlike Blackstone, the Founding generation highlighted the military, political, and populist nature of collective arms bearing rather than its individualistic dimension. Here is where the words of adjoining clauses—the opening ode to the militia, and the neighboring Third Amendment—seem decisive, especially when read against the general backdrop of the American Revolution itself. Attention to contiguous clauses in the Constitution is an interpretive technique that one finds on prominent display in classic Marshall Court opinions authored by Chief Justice Marshall himself and his towering Supreme Court colleague Justice Joseph Story, the Dane Professor of Law at Harvard, and by acclamation the greatest constitutional scholar of his age.[24]

Another technique visible in classic Marshall Court opinions is what is sometimes called "intratextualism"—reading a constitutional word or phrase in light of other uses of that phrase elsewhere in the document. In this tradition, I have emphasized that the words "the people" in the Second Amendment should be read alongside the use of these words in the Preamble and Article I, and their later appearance in the First, Ninth, and Tenth Amendments. I have also explained how the Fourth Amendment's usage is more complicated, because it features the word "person" alongside the more collective-sounding "the people."[25]

A skeptic might wonder if I am simply fabricating a linguistic distinction without a difference: Aren't "the people" just individual "persons" added up, one by one? No. To start with, some "persons" are not within the core meaning of "the people" as the Constitution uses the term. As a general matter, aliens were not part of those who ordained the Constitution, or who vote in congressional elections, or who serve on juries or militias. So, too, with women (prior to the Nineteenth Amendment) and children.[26]

Furthermore, the phrase "the people" suggests an interactivity among persons whereby the whole group is more than simply the parts added together. A militia has an interactive social structure, as does a jury, and as does (ideally) an electorate. A world in which everyone has a gun for sport but never musters with others is not the milieu of a militia: these gun owners are acting as private persons, not a collective people.[27]

Intratextual analysis is also useful in understanding the people's Second Amendment counterpart: the "Militia." Several provisions of Article I, section 8, address the militia, and a complete analysis of the Second Amendment should explain how its words mesh with those earlier provisions. The result of this analysis is plain to see: just as Article I aimed to counterbalance the *military* role of localist militias of ordinary citizens against the *military* role of a paid, professional, centralized standing army, so, too, the Second Amendment was primarily a provision focused on *military* arms-bearing. Contrary to libertarian ideology and the NRA credo, neither hunting nor individual self-defense lay at the core of the Founders' Second Amendment.[28]

None of this means that individual self-defense cannot be recognized as a constitutional right. Not all constitutional rights are strictly textual, and even texts may often be properly read as radiating beyond their core command. If "life or limb" can be read poetically and metaphorically beyond the literalistic core of death and dismemberment, so can the words "bear Arms," especially if we stress the additional word "keep." The question thus becomes, What reasons do we have for reading the words broadly, beyond the core case?

The Ninth Amendment is suggestive here: "The enumeration in the Constitution of certain rights shall not be construed to deny or disparage others retained by the people." Thus, the mere fact that a given right is not explicitly enumerated—not textually specified—should not lead us automatically to conclude that the right does not exist. Rights may exist even if textually unspecified. But the Ninth is better at telling us what not to do than at providing detailed guidance about where, how, and why to find nontextual rights.

HERE, THEN, ARE a few thoughts on the much-discussed topic of unenumerated rights. Even though the text may not enumerate a right, it might nonetheless imply it. For example, although the Constitution's text does not quite enumerate it, surely a defendant has the right to confront physical evidence introduced against him and to introduce reliable physical evidence in his favor—by subpoena if necessary—because the whole point of a wide range of enumerated criminal procedure rights is to guarantee a fair trial giving the defendant a fair chance to show that he is innocent.[29]

As another example, consider whether Congress may punish the author of a handwritten political tract criticizing federal policy. Strictly speaking, the tract is neither oral "speech" nor the product of a printing "press." Yet the enumerated rights of "speech" and "press," and the broader structural logic of the Constitution's scheme of republican self-government, surely imply that this nonenumerated form of political expression must likewise be a right retained by members of the self-governing citizenry.

Sometimes, we should read a textual right more broadly than its core command might demand because these extra applications of the right can provide a buffer zone protecting the core. Buffer zones are especially apt if, in application, it is hard to demarcate crisply the outer boundaries of a given enumerated right.

Consider, once again, the First Amendment. Recall that the core idea underlying the Founders' freedom-of-speech clause was a right to engage in political expression, especially anti-government speech. Intratextual and historical analysis confirms that this was the core idea: the phrase "freedom of speech" derives from the English Bill of Rights protecting "freedom of speech, and debates . . . in parliament."[30]

Moreover, the First Amendment phrase "Congress shall make no law" suggested that Congress simply lacked enumerated federal power to regulate speech. This phrase confirms that the Founders were thinking of political speech, rather than, say, interstate commercial advertising or interstate commercial contracting, both of which are also done with words, but with words that do fall within Congress's enumerated power to regulate interstate commerce. It thus makes sense to say that political speech is the core right in the First Amendment, and that commercial speech is not.

In today's world, however, it may not be possible to sharply distinguish between the two in all contexts. Is a newspaper ad only commercial speech? Even if it criticizes government policy? This is no mere professorial hypothetical: it is the basic set of facts underlying *New York Times v. Sullivan*, which (as we saw in our Hugo Black chapter) stands as one of the most important free-speech cases of the modern era. Given the difficulty of sharply distinguishing between political and commercial speech in some situations, a strict regime in which commercial speech got no protection at all might threaten our core right; we might be better off with a kind of graduated or prophylactic approach protecting some commercial speech in order to maintain a buffer zone around the core right of political expression.

Similarly, even if the core right of "the people" to assemble in the First Amendment focused on political conclaves of voters—constitutional conventions and the like—we have eminently sound structural reasons to read the amendment far beyond this core, protecting even nonvoters' rights to get together for a variety of noncommercial and expressive purposes—prayer, fellowship, parades, and so on. Such a broad right would cohere with other rights affirmed by the First Amendment—freedom of religion, for example—and this broad right also draws historical support from the Fourteenth Amendment, which reflected a strong commitment to the associational rights even of nonvoters (paradigmatically, blacks and women).[31]

NOW LET'S RETURN to the Second Amendment, and ask whether there are comparably good reasons to read the "bear Arms" right broadly, outside its original core meaning. Given that the militia no longer exists as a genuine institutional reality, an individual right serves little purpose as a buffer zone around the core collective right. The core itself has melted away. Nor do general structural arguments that counsel broad readings of the First Amendment on behalf of churches, fellowship groups, fraternal societies, and a wide assortment of other expressive organizations and intermediate associations that enrich American democracy provide comparable support for a broad libertarian reading of the Second Amendment. America's vast collection of clubs, charities, fellowship circles, debating societies, Bible studies, reading groups, service organizations, neighborhood block parties, and the like undoubtedly widen and deepen our democratic culture, but it is doubtful that having lots of guns in lots of places accomplishes any similar democratic enrichment.

History does provide support for a broad libertarian reading of the right to "keep and bear Arms," but as we have seen, the best historical argument for libertarians comes not from the Founding but from Reconstruction. The Fourteenth Amendment's framers emphatically proclaimed their intent to make the Bill of Rights applicable against states.[32] In effect, they readopted the Bill, glossing it with their own understandings. Although the Founders fused together arms-bearing with militias, the key Reconstruction statute, the Freedman's Bureau Bill of 1866, drove a wedge between the two, severing the idea of individual gun ownership for self-protection from militia service. Concretely, the Fourteenth Amendment affirmed the civil right of black men—and of black women and white women, for that matter—to have a gun for self-protection even though these persons did not (yet) enjoy the distinct political right to be part of the militia.

If it seems overly clever to read the 1789 "bear Arms" phrase in light of 1868 understandings that reglossed that phrase in the course of formally rewriting the Constitution, consider an even simpler textual and historical argument for gun rights. For now, put the Second Amendment aside. The Fourteenth Amendment itself says that "[n]o state shall make or enforce any law which shall abridge the privileges or immunities of citizens of the United States." The amendment also presupposes that the federal government may not interfere with these privileges and immunities either. These privileges and immunities inhere in American citizenship itself and are protected from federal abridgment by the amendment's first sentence declaring national birthright citizenship. (The amendment's second sentence explicitly barred *states* from violating these rights of citizenship; this was in direct response to the 1833 Supreme Court case *Barron v. Baltimore*, which had seemed to insist on special Simon Says language where states were concerned.) One of these privileges and immunities is a right to have gun in one's home for self-protection.[33]

The boundaries of this right may be blurry and fluid—reasonable regulations are permissible, total prohibitions more suspect—but it is quintessentially an individual, libertarian right, as highlighted by the text, logic, and history of the Fourteenth Amendment. The text speaks of a "privilege"—a kind of private right—of "citizens." Black men and women of all races are citizens covered by this clause, even if they don't vote, serve on juries or militias, or wield other political rights. And given the paradigm evil of Klan-style thuggery in the minds of Reconstruction Republicans, the right to a gun in one's home was a core component of the original vision of the Fourteenth Amendment.

Yet another Fourteenth Amendment approach might say that judges seeking to identify unenumerated "privileges" and "immunities" deserving federal constitutional protection should look not merely to Reconstruction history, but also to the American tradition more broadly and to modern state constitutional law. On this approach, it is supremely noteworthy that many state constitutions have been written or construed to protect private gun ownership, and that, like it or not, a gun in one's home for self-protection is deeply rooted in the American ethos. There are nearly as many guns in America as persons, and any sustained effort to locate and confiscate the great mass of these ordinary private weapons in ordinary homes would be a civil libertarian nightmare. Of course, on this view as well, the libertarian right would not be an absolutist one. The American tradition has encompassed many reasonable regulations of weapons short of total confiscation, and state judges in the modern era have rarely used state constitutions to strike down moderate gun controls.[34]

So much for constitutional text, constitutional history, and American tradition more broadly.* Even after all these have been considered, our constitutional analysis is still incomplete. Given that the world of 1789 and the world of 1866 are very different from our own, how are we to "translate" these old commands into rules and principles that make constitutional sense today?[35]

The Founders' militia no longer exists. What, then, are we to make of an amendment built on that rock? The slightly paranoid anti-central-government ideology underlying the original Second Amendment seems less justified in the twenty-first century. Is it permissible to disavow paranoia in applying the amendment today? Or is this disavowal simply disagreement with Founding values—which might justify openly amending the Second out of the document, but which cannot justify undermining it via hostile "interpretation"? Let's also bear in mind that guns are far more deadly today than they were in these earlier times. Is this point relevant to proper constitutional interpretation?

My answers to all these questions travel through the Fourteenth Amendment. The very existence of this amendment was publicly predicated on a profoundly un-Founding-like understanding of the central army and local militias. Bluntly, the Fourteenth Amendment was adopted in part because the Union Army helped suppress rebel militias. The Reconstruction Act of 1867 provided for federal military occupation and

---

*As for constitutional precedent: In recent years the Supreme Court has decided two major cases interpreting the Second Amendment and the rights of gun owners. Readers interested in my detailed thoughts about the first of these major cases, *Heller v. United States* (2008), are warmly invited to consult my review essay, "*Heller*, HLR, and Holistic Legal Reasoning," *Harvard LR* 122 (2008): 145. Although I have not publicly commented on the second major opinion, *McDonald v. City of Chicago* (2010), the justices in that case did publicly comment on my opinions—favorably, thank goodness! My views on the meaning of the Second Amendment—views comprehensively summarized and synthesized in the chapter you are now reading—were generously cited six times in Justice Alito's opinion on behalf of the Court majority, twice in Justice Thomas's concurrence, and once in Justice Breyer's dissent (which was joined by Justices Ginsburg and Sotomayor; Justice Stevens also dissented in a separate opinion).

governance of the unreconstructed South, and in effect told Confederate states to ratify the Fourteenth Amendment (and comply with various other conditions) as the best way to gain readmission to Congress and resume their regular role within the Union. Although the Fourteenth Amendment's text did not explicitly rewrite the Founders' elaborate rules about militias and armies, the simple fact of amendment itself invites a new constitutional understanding in which local militias are no longer the unambiguous heroes, and the Union's army is no longer the presumed villain, of America's epic constitutional narrative.[36]

The American *constitution* is an act as well as a text—it is a doing, a constituting. "We the people *do* ordain and establish . . . " So, too, with *amendments*, which are deeds as well as words. And the deed of the Fourteenth Amendment—encompassing the brute fact of its enactment and the public exertions and actions (on the part of America's military and others) through which that enactment did in fact occur—is part of the Constitution itself. To read and follow the text is necessarily, I think, to accept the general validity of the exertions, procedures, and protocols that made the text law. The things publicly done to get various texts adopted are unenumerated (that is, unwritten) aspects of the Constitution, but these public actions are inextricable parts of the Constitution nonetheless.[37]

On this view, the Fourteenth Amendment itself and the key role played by the central army in securing that amendment—implicitly and nontextually, but publicly and emphatically—modified some of the Founders' military provisions. Thus, the death of the Founders' militia is not something, like an erroneous judicial precedent, that faithful constitutionalists must seek to undo if at all possible. (That is why one possible and legitimate response today to an obviously military Second Amendment is an interpretation that seeks to "take the military out of the militia" by encouraging or even requiring Americans to engage in civic, as opposed to military, service.) A less paranoid view of the federal government is implicit in the Fourteenth Amendment itself; it is not merely some extraconstitutional fact about modern American society.

Also, the increased deadliness of weaponry is one among several relevant considerations that modern judges may properly take into account in defining the boundaries of the unenumerated privilege of gun ownership, or (to put the point a different way) the Reconstructed right of individuals to "bear Arms" (read broadly) far outside the bounds of the Founders' militias. The Fourteenth Amendment does not textually specify the precise boundaries of this right, and today's interpreters may legitimately note important differences between nineteenth-century firearms, on the one hand, and twenty-first-century weapons, on the other.

MY TONE HAS BEEN tentative at several points in this chapter because the many intervening changes of fact and law make it difficult to identify with perfect confidence the uniquely best modern interpretation and synthesis of the Founding and Reconstruction texts, as opposed to the range of plausible and responsible readings.

In this vein, one final modern development deserves mention as we seek sensible ways of "translating" Founding and Reconstruction visions into twenty-first-century doctrines. The Reconstruction generation embraced private gun ownership because local police officials in the South could not be trusted to protect blacks. If in some places today this distrust is no longer warranted, might private gun ownership be given less protection? Is the real "privilege" best understood as a gun itself, or the underlying security from thugs? If the latter, perhaps an alternative, or at least an accompanying, translation of the Reconstruction vision would seek to ensure that local police departments provide far better protection to minority communities. A complementary translation of the Founding vision might demand that today's local militia-substitute—the local police department—genuinely reflect the demographic diversity of the local community it serves. Those wielding guns and enforcing local laws (the Founders' militia, and today's police departments) should truly be composed of the body of the people (white men at the Founding, all adults today).

THIS LAST SUGGESTION—that our police departments should truly look like America, with blacks alongside whites, men alongside women, and gays alongside straights—takes us back to my similar claims about America's national armed forces. In essence, the Founders' militia has been replaced by two sets of twenty-first-century institutions. Locally, law enforcement has shifted to police departments; nationally, collective military defense is now headed up by a professional army, navy, air force, and Marine Corps. The deepest idea of the Second Amendment, I have argued, is that these collective arms-bearing entities should reflect the American electorate they are supposed to serve and protect. And, after the Fifteenth and Nineteenth Amendments, that electorate has become more diverse than it was in previous eras. If race discrimination and sex discrimination are suspect at the ballot box, they are likewise troubling in the jury room and in our defense forces.

In support of that constitutional vision, I have highlighted the text of the Second Amendment, but that text is merely the tip of a constitutional iceberg. Now let me try to outline the underlying bulk of the iceberg, and in the process, offer up an illustration of what is meant by structural interpretation of the Constitution—a technique that views various clauses as parts of a coherent whole proclaiming and embodying grand themes.

In word and deed, the Constitution's biggest idea is popular sovereignty. Here, the people rule. In word, We the People ordained the Constitution. In deed, too: despite all the exclusions that blemished the process of ratifying the document in the 1780s, this process was more inclusive than any of its predecessors in world history; never before had so many been allowed to vote on how they and their posterity were to be governed. In word, the document proclaimed that states must feature "republican" as opposed to aristocratic or monarchical forms of government. In deed, the Fourteenth Amendment embodied and expanded this promise, excluding from Congress various southern states that failed to allow large numbers of their free male population (who happened to be black) from voting. With later amendments, such as the Fifteenth and Nineteenth, the grand theme of democracy has been strengthened and deepened in both word and deed.

In order to rule, the people must retain ultimate control over all institutions of government. Ideally, the people should participate in all branches of government. They should directly elect the House of Representatives—the people's house—every two years. They should participate in executive law enforcement. At the Founding, this occurred via militias and posses; today it should occur via citizen review boards overseeing the police. The people should also form part of the judiciary, via the jury. Popular participation is the grand unifying idea underlying many separate provisions of the original Constitution, the Founders' Bill of Rights, and still later amendments.

This chapter has tried to highlight links between jury service, military service, and voting. The Second Amendment's grammar implicitly links two of these; but many other parts of the Constitution reinforce the point. At the Founding, various states allowed patriot militiamen to vote even if they failed to meet ordinary property qualifications. Section 2 of the Fourteenth Amendment defined a state's presumptive electorate as roughly coterminous with its presumptive arms-bearers: male citizens over twenty-one. The Fifteenth Amendment gave black men the vote ahead of white women in part because these black men had proved their valor—and had helped win the war—on the battlefield of glory. Woodrow Wilson endorsed the Nineteenth Amendment in recognition of the role women were playing on the home front in World War I. The Twenty-sixth Amendment gave young adults the vote on the theory that those old enough to fight and die in Vietnam should be allowed to vote on the wisdom of that war, and all other important matters. (The reverse is also true: if women are excluded from military equality, their voices might be given less weight in national debates about military policy, and they are less likely to win high positions of political power that have so often gone to those who have served in America's military.)

In talking about gender issues in the military, I of course am relying on the Nineteenth Amendment in tandem with the Second. The Nineteenth at its core protects a right to vote in ordinary elections, but there are sound historical and structural reasons for reading it broadly beyond its narrow core. The amendment should be understood to protect not just a right to vote, but a right to be voted for—that is, a right to seek and hold office. It should be read to guarantee a right to vote in the judicial branch as well as for the legislature—that is, a right to vote and serve on juries. And finally, in tandem with the Second, it should be read to affirm a right to political equality in modern America's militia substitutes.

THE ROCKY MOUNTAIN WEST is not merely cowboy country and gun country, but also a region with a unique if unsung role in the history of woman suffrage. In 1869–1870, the Wyoming territory embraced women's political equality—encompassing voting, jury service, and office-holding—and in 1890 Wyoming entered the Union as the first state with full suffrage for women. Over the next six years, and long before any other state followed suit, Wyoming's neighboring states of Colorado, Utah, and Idaho also enacted full woman suffrage.[38]

The next state to join the full suffrage club did so in 1910, and by the end of 1914 seven sister states had joined the pioneering four. Interestingly enough, these seven—Washington, California, Oregon, Arizona, Kansas, Nevada, and Montana—form a circle roughly revolving around the Wyoming Rockies.[39]

And here are a few more facts about Wyoming: Unique among the fifty states, Wyoming has two official nicknames. According to its official state website, Wyoming is not just the "Cowboy State," but also the

"Equality State," in remembrance of the state's historic leadership on the rights of women "to vote, serve on juries, and hold office." Wyoming's official motto is "Equal Rights," and the state's website reminds visitors that in 1925 Wyoming became the first state to elect and install a woman as governor, Nellie Tayloe Ross.

On the topic of women's rights, then, Wyoming and its neighboring states in the Rocky Mountain West were once way ahead of their time. Some of what I have said in this chapter about women's rights may also be ahead of its time. But a chapter on this special state and this beautiful region seems the right place to make the case. In fact and folklore, Wyoming, the Cowboy State, may well be Second Amendment country; but let us not forget that Wyoming, the Equality State, is also the mother of the Nineteenth Amendment.

CHAPTER 11

MASSACHUSETTS:
A BAY-STATE VIEW OF
THE FOURTH AMENDMENT

I t is hard to think about the Second Amendment and its original vision without also thinking about greater Boston. The Minutemen of Lexington and Concord epitomized the "well regulated militia" at the heart of the amendment—a locally organized body of yeomen guarding fellow citizens against central tyranny. In the 1770s, that tyranny came from London, and in the 1780s and 1790s, many feared that the new federal capital city might take up where London had left off. So, too, it is hard to reflect upon the Third Amendment and its rules regarding troop quartering without calling to mind colonial Boston. That amendment renounced the principles underlying the 1774 Quartering Act—one of several coercive measures enacted by the British Parliament in direct response to the Boston Massacre of 1770 and the Boston Tea Party of 1773.

But the relationship between Boston and the *Fourth* Amendment is more complicated. In some two dozen cases over the past century and a half, various justices have claimed or assumed that the amendment was drafted with the 1761 Boston writs-of-assistance case, argued by the Boston lawyer James Otis, centrally in mind. Most recently, in a closely watched 2014 Fourth Amendment lawsuit involving police searches of cellphones found upon the persons of arrested suspects, Chief Justice Roberts, who went to college and law school in the Boston area, chose to end his graceful opinion for the Court with a grand rhetorical flourish invoking Otis and the 1761 litigation. This flourish built on foundations laid by Justices Louis Brandeis and Felix Frankfurter, both of whom had also attended law school in the Boston metroplex, and who had invoked Otis and the Boston writs case in a wide range of mid-twentieth-century search and seizure cases. Even justices with no strong ties to Boston or Harvard have at times said similar things, beginning with a high-profile (if also highly problematic) case from 1886, *Boyd v. United States*. But none of these judicial opinions has carefully traced the alleged links between the 1761 controversy and the Fourth Amendment, ratified fully thirty years later.[1]

If you don't know much about the 1761 writs-of-assistance controversy—indeed, if you have never even heard of writs of assistance until this moment—relax. By the end of this chapter, you will know all that you need to know about these arcane eighteenth-century legal instruments. And it turns out that there is a good reason that you may not know a ton about these writs: contrary to what various justices have implied or insisted, the 1761 Boston controversy about writs of assistance may not have loomed all that large in the drafting of the Declaration of Independence in 1776, or in the enactment of the United States Constitution in 1787–1788, or in the creation of America's Bill of Rights in 1789–1791.

Today's Americans thus need not obsess about what happened in Boston in 1761, but we all do need to ponder the Fourth Amendment itself. Properly construed, that amendment prohibits officials from engaging in oppressive search and seizure tactics that would violate the liberty, privacy, and equality rights of ordinary persons. Few provisions of the Constitution come before our courts more often than the Fourth Amendment, and few provisions affect us more directly in our daily lives. For example, may government officials stop and frisk us on the street, or oblige us to walk through a metal detector in an airport, or strip search us in a high school, or force us to submit to fingerprinting in a police station, or search our cars, or rummage through our houses, or hack into our cellphones? And if officials may do these things, when, how, and why may they do so? To answer these and similar questions about government searches and seizures, we must understand the letter and spirit of the Fourth Amendment.

Happily, the amendment really does say what it means and mean what it says. And for what it is worth, the 1761 writs-of-assistance controversy, although hardly the unique golden key to the amendment, in fact confirms that the amendment should be taken at face value.

The Big Questions

Let us begin with the words of the Fourth Amendment itself: "The right of the people to be secure in their persons, houses, papers, and effects, against unreasonable searches and seizures, shall not be violated, and no Warrants shall issue, but upon probable cause, supported by Oath or affirmation, and particularly describing the place to be searched, and the persons or things to be seized."

Modern debate about the Fourth Amendment swirls around three big sets of questions. First, what exactly is the relationship between the Fourth Amendment's first clause, which bans "unreasonable searches and seizures," and its second clause, which addresses warrants? Are all warrantless searches and seizures ipso facto unreasonable? If so, why doesn't the amendment say this explicitly? If, however, the amendment simply means what it says, and does not require warrants, what exactly is the purpose of the warrant clause?

Second, what does the second clause mean when it speaks of "probable cause"? Does the amendment mean what it says in limiting this standard to warrants? If so—and if some warrantless searches are permitted—then does the amendment really mean to authorize some warrantless searches lacking in probable cause? Why should all searches *with* warrants be held to a *higher* standard than some searches *without* warrants? And whenever the "probable cause" standard does apply, how probable must probable be? Fifty-one percent? Does this mean that if there is only a 33 percent likelihood that a suspected terrorist is building a bomb in his house, a warrant may not issue, or a warrantless search would be per se unreasonable? If all searches and seizures must have probable cause, what about metal detectors at airports? And what *kind* of probable cause must the government have? If the government can prove that there is a 70 percent likelihood that I am a terrorist, or that illegal machine guns and bombs are stashed in my house, a warrant to arrest me or to search my house seems sensible. But what if the government merely proves that there is a 70 percent likelihood that I am a professor, or that I have hair on my head, or that skim milk and frozen yogurt are stashed in my house? Seventy percent is probable, but is that *kind* of probable cause enough?

Third, regardless of how we define the Fourth Amendment's rules on the rights side, what should happen as a remedial matter when the government violates these rights? Does the amendment require exclusion of illegally obtained evidence? If so, why doesn't it say so clearly? If not, what remedies are presupposed by the amendment, which proclaims so emphatically that the rights it recognizes "shall not be violated"?

WARRANTS

Having laid out the big questions, let me now try to show how the answers to these three sets of questions are interlinked, how the text of the amendment really does mean what it says, and how what it says makes good common sense.

To begin with, the amendment does not require a warrant for each and every search or seizure. It simply requires that each and every search or seizure be *reasonable*. In the language of the first clause, the amendment affirms the basic "right of the people to be secure . . . against unreasonable searches and seizures." Reading into this wording an implicit warrant requirement for all searches and seizures runs counter to text, Founding-era history, and common sense.

Textually, as we have seen, the amendment contains no third clause explicitly stating that "warrantless searches and seizures are inherently unreasonable," or explicitly barring all "warrantless searches and seizures." Many early state constitutions featured search-and-seizure language rather similar to the Fourth Amendment's, yet none of these constitutions proclaimed an explicit warrant requirement. (Later in this chapter I shall explore in some detail the language of one key state constitutional clause that prefigured the federal Fourth Amendment—the search-and-seizure clause of the celebrated Massachusetts Constitution of 1780.) In cases interpreting early state constitutions, state court after state court after state court explicitly rejected the claim that, by implication, warrants were required for all searches and seizures. No leading English or early American commentator ever claimed that all searches and seizures required a warrant. No leading Framer ever explicitly articulated a global warrant requirement.[2]

Various forms of warrantless searches and seizures were routine at English common law and in early American practice, which combined to form the broad backdrop against which the Fourth Amendment took shape. According to Blackstone—whose treatise on common law was perhaps the single most important item in any Founding-era American lawyer's library—a constable, by dint of his office, had "great original and inherent authority with regard to arrests. He may, *without warrant*, arrest anyone for a breach of the peace, committed in his view, and carry him before a justice of the peace. And, in case of felony actually committed, or a dangerous wounding whereby felony is likely to ensue, he may upon probable suspicion arrest the felon; and for that purpose is authorized (as upon a justice's warrant) to break open doors."[3]

Blackstone clearly says that a constable has inherent arrest powers, by dint of his office, that range beyond the citizen's arrest powers of ordinary folk. Blackstone organizes his discussion of arrest powers as follows: "In general, an arrest may be made four ways: 1. By warrant; 2. By an officer without a warrant; 3. By a private person also without a warrant; 4. By an hue and cry." The entire structure of Blackstone's analysis thus focuses on the special arrest powers of certain officers, such as sheriffs, justices of the peace, coroners, constables, and watchmen, and these special powers are what separate categories 2 and 3. This is what Blackstone means when he speaks of the "great original and inherent authority" of the constable, in contradistinction to the arrest powers of "a private person," powers discussed in a separate passage.[4]

For example, we have seen that a constable could, for felonies, "break open doors"—but a private person generally could not, according to Blackstone.[5] And for more minor breaches of the peace, a private person could intervene to separate combatants, but a constable on the scene had the far greater authority to arrest and imprison the fighters even after the fisticuffs had ended. Thus, in the above-quoted passage, Blackstone affirms the constable's right to, "without warrant, arrest anyone for a breach of the peace committed in his view, and carry him off before a justice of the peace," but he makes clear in his very next paragraph that private persons may generally arrest only for felonies, a much narrower category.[6]

Later English case law powerfully supports and sharpens Blackstone's distinction between the arrest powers of officers and those of citizens. In the 1780 case of *Samuel v. Payne*, the King's Bench held, in the words of the reporter, that "[a] peace officer may justify an arrest on a reasonable charge of felony, without a warrant, although it should afterwards appear that no felony had been committed; but a private individual cannot."[7] The *Samuel* Court invoked and extended the analysis of Sir Matthew Hale's canonical treatise *The History of the Pleas of the Crown*, which, like Blackstone, emphasized the many special ex officio arrest powers enjoyed by certain officers.[8] Five years later, England's Lord Mansfield proclaimed, in *Cooper v. Boot*, that "when a felony has been committed, any person may arrest on reasonable suspicion. When no felony has been committed, an officer may arrest on a charge."[9]

Samuel and *Cooper* were the leading English cases on the subject at the time of the adoption of the Fourth Amendment. Thus we find the New York Supreme Court, in a learned 1829 opinion by Chief Justice John Savage, explicitly invoking *Samuel* and other authorities to make clear that a constable, without warrant, could arrest in situations where private persons could not.[10]

The precise location of the line separating the arrest powers of private citizens from those of officers, by virtue of their office, was at times blurry, as the line gradually shifted over the decades. But the fact that such a line existed—that constables, watchmen, and others had certain special powers of warrantless arrest that ordinary citizens did not—was a basic feature of the leading common-law treatises in the late eighteenth century: Blackstone, Hale, and so on.

When an arrest did occur, the arresting officer was free to search the person of the arrestee for evidence or stolen goods, and to do so without a warrant, even if the arrest was itself warrantless. And, at common law, if a constable without a warrant arrested a person on a mere subjective hunch, rather than objective probable cause, and the person turned out to be a felon, the constable's ex post success was an absolute defense against any trespass or false-imprisonment suit.[11]

Other historical exceptions to a blanket warrant requirement come from the First Congress—the same body that drafted the Fourth Amendment itself. One early congressional statute authorized both warrantless searches of certain ships and warrantless seizures of various items suspected in connection with customs violations. Another early congressional statute authorized warrantless entry into and inspection of all "houses" and buildings that had been registered (as required by law) as liquor storerooms or distilleries. If any member of Congress objected to—or even questioned—these warrantless searches and seizures on Fourth Amendment grounds, modern-day supporters of a warrant requirement have yet to identify him.[12]

So much for text and history, which cut strongly against the notion that each and every search or seizure must be preceded by a warrant. Common sense reinforces the wisdom of text and history on this point. Must warrants issue in cases of hot pursuit, and other exigent circumstances? Or when a wife authorizes police to search her husband's car, and the police reasonably rely upon her authorization? Consider also the case where security agents look unobtrusively for things in plain, public view—say, scanning the crowd at an Olympic event for anything that might be suspicious. Or think about the countless number of real-life, unintrusive, nondiscriminatory—that is to say, reasonable—searches and seizures to which modern-day Americans are routinely subjected: metal detectors at airports, annual auto emissions tests, inspections of closely regulated industries, public school regimens, border searches, and so on.

"BUT IF A WARRANT requirement makes no textual, historical, or practical sense," a critic might respond, "surely the warrant clause of the Fourth Amendment must mean something. What *does* the warrant clause mean, and what is the relationship between it and the earlier reasonableness clause?"

The answer is simple: broad warrants—warrants that fail to meet the various specifications of clause two—are inherently unreasonable under clause one. The amendment in its words and grammar does not require or prefer warrants: it limits them. "No Warrants shall issue, but . . ."

Why did the Framers seek to limit warrants? Because a lawful warrant could immunize the officer who carried it out from the trespass suit that the citizen victim might otherwise have been free to bring. Immunity was part of the very definition—the purpose—of a lawful warrant.

Thus, if an officer searched or seized without a warrant, he could be sued in tort by the citizen whose person, house, papers, or effects had been trespassed upon. In this tort suit, if the officer's intrusion was deemed unreasonable by the court, the intrusion would, under Fourth Amendment clause one, be unconstitutional—and thus any governmental authorization the officer might claim would fall to the ground. But if the officer secured a lawful warrant before searching and seizing, and thereafter acted within the scope of warrant, he could escape this tort liability and after-the-fact judicial review.

Warrants then, were friends of the officer, not the citizen; and so warrants had to be strictly limited under clause two. A valid warrant was not merely a preclearance of a search or seizure, but also a preclusion of later tort suits that an outraged citizen might seek to bring.

And note the many libertarian advantages of the tort suit over the warrant. A tort suit would be presided over by a judge; but, in England and America, various more bias-prone and politically motivated executive officials claimed the authority to issue warrants. Even if issued by a judge, a warrant lacked the traditional judicial safeguards of notice and the opportunity to be heard, and the adversarial presentation of argument and evidence by both sides of a dispute. A warrant issued *ex parte*, without the citizen target or his lawyer in the courtroom to challenge the government's case. Also, in a warrant proceeding, the government could forum-shop by seeking out the most pro-government magistrate to issue the warrant. In a tort suit, by contrast, citizen plaintiffs would have more choice. Moreover, a typical warrant proceeding was secretive—closed to the public—in contrast to the open, public tort trial, with ordinary citizens able to monitor the affair. Finally, in a tort suit, the key question of reasonableness was not always a pure question of law, but at times a question of fact, too, at least in part. And so in our tort suit, key questions about the reasonableness of government conduct might be decided not by a single judge, but by a judge sitting with a local jury, twelve good men and true.[13]

An 1827 King's Bench case, *Beckwith v. Philby*, is telling.* In a trespass suit brought against a constable for a warrantless arrest, Lord Tenterden, the court's chief justice, followed *Samuel v. Payne*, holding that—unlike a private citizen's arrest, where an actual felony must be proved—the constable's warrantless arrest was justified if the constable merely had a "reasonable ground to suspect that a felony had been committed" by the arrestee.[14] The chief justice also proclaimed that: "Whether there was any *reasonable* cause for suspecting that the plaintiff had committed a felony, or was about to commit one, or whether he had been detained in custody an *unreasonable* time, were *questions of fact for the jury*, which they have decided against the plaintiff, and in my judgment most correctly."[15]

Even if a post-search civil suit were tried to a judge rather than a jury, several other reasons that the Framers had for preferring open tort suits to secret warrants still applied. But the jury point is worth emphasizing, for it illustrates how the Fourth Amendment connects to other parts of our Bill of Rights. In previous chapters we have seen that no idea was more central to our Bill of Rights than the idea of the jury—featured explicitly in the Fifth Amendment grand jury clause, the Sixth Amendment petit jury clause, and

---

* Because the Fourth Amendment and its early state constitutional counterparts were crafted against the backdrop of English and American common law, various late eighteenth and early nineteenth-century English cases are highly instructive, even if they postdate the adoption of the Fourth Amendment or its state counterparts. Many of the English cases discussed in this chapter featured prominently in leading early American search-and-seizure cases and commentaries.

the Seventh Amendment civil jury clause, and implicitly in many other provisions, from due process to double jeopardy. On the Founders' view, twelve heads in the jury box would often be better—less idiosyncratic, more representative, less corruptible—than one head on the judicial bench. Juries drawn from local communities might be more skeptical of central-government edicts than might a federal judge appointed in the national capital. Jurors were independent citizens, not on the government payroll. To the extent that "reasonableness" turned on questions of common sense, the jury represented the common sense of common people. To the extent that "reasonableness" implicated legal issues, jurors could learn from judges and help give them feedback that would keep the Constitution in touch with the people. Like the militia of Lexington and Concord, the jury embodied the spirit of the American Revolution as a local, populist institution of ordinary folk checking paid, professional officers of the central government—armies, prosecutors, customs officials, judges, and so on.[16]

Warrants ran counter to this vision and so they had to be limited. Why allow them at all? A good modern-day analogy to the warrant is the temporary restraining order (TRO). Sometimes, emergency action must be taken to freeze the status quo and prevent future harm, and so judges may act ex parte, without the traditional safeguards of adversarial adjudication. But precisely because of the due-process dangers it poses, an ex parte TRO is strictly limited to situations where there is a risk of "immediate and irreparable injury" and a high likelihood of "success on the merits." At common law, a warrant could likewise issue when there was a high likelihood—"probable cause"—that a particular place contained stolen goods. The whole point of the ex parte warrant was to authorize a search that would bring the stolen goods before the magistrate. To give the owner of the hideaway a heads-up in advance of the surprise search might enable him to whisk the goods away—a kind of irreparable injury to the truth, to the justice system, and to the victim of the theft seeking to recover his goods. The need for a surprise search on these facts is obviously strong; but without the absolute guarantee of immunity provided by a warrant, an officer might hesitate to perform the surprise search for fear of a future lawsuit.[17]

But once extended beyond the limited context of the common-law warrant for stolen goods, warrants had the potential for great evil. If authorized on less than probable cause, they would give government henchmen absolute power to round up the usual suspects, rousting political enemies or unpopular groups. And so, too, if warrants were allowed for items other than stolen goods or things closely akin to stolen goods—contraband, smuggled items, dangerous explosives, illegal weapons, and so on. If a warrant could issue because there was probable cause to believe that there was (innocent) skim milk in a given house, then no one would be safe.

Thus, broad warrants had to be banned. This is the meaning of clause two. But warrantless searches did not pose the same threat, because they were not immune from after-the-fact review of the general reasonableness of the government intrusion. If a particular warrantless search were too intrusive; or if the government policy gave officials too much discretion; or if the search threatened other constitutional values, such as freedom of the press; or if the government policies seemed targeted at certain powerless or unpopular minorities; or if, in any number of other ways, the search offended constitutional reasonableness or commonsense reasonableness, judicial review after the fact would invalidate the search under clause one—and trespass damages, compensatory and punitive, would deter future violations. And so, to repeat, the Fourth Amendment did not require warrants; it limited them.

PROBABLE CAUSE AND THE EXCLUSIONARY RULE

Once we see that this is the right answer to our first set of questions, about whether the Fourth Amendment requires warrants, we also see how the right answers to our second and third set of questions, about probable cause and the exclusionary rule, fall into place.

The amendment means what it says: all warrants must have probable cause, and warrantless searches need not always have probable cause, so long as they are reasonable. Ex parte warrants must be limited (just like ex parte TROs), but the limits applicable to warrants do not always sensibly apply to all other searches. Particular description, oath or affirmation, and so on are necessary features of warrants, but not of all searches and seizures. So, too, probable cause is a necessary ingredient for a warrant, but not for all searches and seizures.

To limit warrants, we must insist that a certain *kind* of probable cause exists, as well as a certain level of probability. To support an ex parte warrant without notice to the citizen target, there must be probable cause to believe that a given place contains something very suspicious—such as stolen goods—and that the owner of the premises, if given notice in advance, would spirit away the goods, or defy a subpoena. But even if ex parte warrants should almost never issue for utterly innocent noncriminal items (say, skim milk in refrigerators), often government will properly want to search for or seize various noncriminal items with advance notice—inspecting home wiring for electrical safety, or testing cars for emissions, or checking buildings for possible earthquake damage, or doing a thousand other things involving some sort of justifiable imposition. And so, once again, we see that the "probable cause" test for stolen goods cannot be a global test for all searches and seizures. Of course, in some particular contexts—the inherently intrusive arrest of one's private "person," for example—even a warrantless intrusion might generally call for probable cause, or more, in order to be reasonable overall.

History strongly supports this textual and structural analysis. No leading Framer or Founding-era commentator ever proclaimed that every search or seizure required probable cause. On the contrary, the First Congress clearly authorized various searches of ships and liquor storehouses in situations in which there was not only no warrant, but also no ground for individualized suspicion: these were blanket searches of a sort.

Our reading squares with common sense and modern life. Every day, modern government officials engage in a vast number of relatively unintrusive and nondiscriminatory searches without probable cause and often without individualized suspicion: border searches, metal detectors, Occupational Safety and Health Administration audits, restaurant inspections, and so on. Surely these are not all unconstitutional.

Our analysis of Fourth Amendment rights also clarifies Fourth Amendment remedies. Here, too, the amendment means what it says. It does not call for judges in criminal cases to exclude or suppress illegally found evidence; rather, the amendment presumes the general availability of civil trespass suits. The "right of the people to be secure in their persons, houses, papers, and effects" presupposes tort law, which protects persons and property from unreasonable invasions. This textual analysis is strongly supported by history—no Framer ever argued for exclusion; nor did any early commentator, or judge—and by common sense: unlike tort law, exclusion rewards the guilty but gives nothing to innocent citizens whom the government knows to be innocent but seeks to hassle for some improper reason—say, to intimidate political critics, to oppress disfavored minorities, or merely to flex and flaunt government power.

(If officers expect to find nothing and indeed find nothing, there is nothing to exclude, and thus the exclusionary rule is of absolutely no help here; in this situation, the rule does absolutely nothing to deter government misconduct.)[18]

IF WE SEEK A PARADIGMATIC illustration of all of these themes in action, we should ponder two related English cases handed down in the mid-1760s, *Wilkes v. Wood* and *Entick v. Carrington*. These and several companion cases, decided by Lord Camden, were the most famous search-and-seizure cases in the Anglo-American world, and they undeniably influenced the later drafting of the federal Fourth Amendment and various state constitutional counterparts in the 1770s and 1780s.[19] (We must remember that in the 1760s, American colonists were part of the British Empire. Even though these cases arose in faraway London, they featured a fascinating cast of characters, including the flamboyant plaintiff John Wilkes, and involved intense contestation at the highest level of imperial law and politics. British subjects up and down the American continent followed every twist and turn in these cases—much as Americans far from Florida in December 2000 immersed themselves in the minutiae of the various legal and political spectacles playing out in that state that month.)

Armed with sweeping warrants issued by high officials in the ministry of King George III, various henchmen broke into Englishmen's houses, searched their papers, arrested their persons, and rummaged through their effects in hopes of finding evidence against the authors and publishers of certain anonymous anti-government pamphlets. The Englishmen who had been trespassed upon brought tort suits against the henchmen, who tried to hide behind their sweeping warrants. But Lord Camden found these overbroad warrants—most of which lacked (among other things) probable cause under oath, and all of which had issued for private papers rather than stolen goods—null and void. Since the warrants were illegal, civil juries, aided by Camden's instructions, found the intrusions unjustified and proceeded to pile massive punitive damages upon the henchmen to send a message to the government and deter future abuse. The British government found itself obliged to indemnify the henchmen, who were, after all, merely carrying out ministry policy. All told, it was said that the government paid out some 100,000 pounds (tens of millions of today's US dollars) in connection with the *Wilkes* and *Entick* litigation.[20]

BOSTON

What, it might be asked, does any of this have to do with Boston, Massachusetts, or the writs of assistance? Let me first trace the elements of my story that link up to Boston and Massachusetts generally; and then, in closing, I shall offer a fresh way of thinking about colonial writs of assistance.

Begin with the words of the 1780 Massachusetts Constitution, drafted by a convention that sat first across the Charles in Cambridge and then in Boston proper:

> Every subject has a right to be secure from all unreasonable searches and seizures of his person, his houses, his papers, and all his possessions. All warrants, therefore, are contrary to this right, if the cause or foundation of them be not previously supported by oath or affirmation, and if the order in the warrant to a civil officer, to make search in suspected places, or to arrest one or more suspected persons, or to seize their property, be not accompanied with a special designation of the persons or objects of search, arrest, or seizure; and no warrant ought to be issued but in cases, and with the formalities, prescribed by the laws.

The language, logic, and structure of the Massachusetts Constitution's Article XIV foreshadow the federal Fourth Amendment. (Article XIV itself borrowed from and clarified the language of the Pennsylvania Constitution of 1776.) The first clause of Article XIV affirms a right to be secure against unreasonable intrusions, and later clauses seek to limit warrants, not to require or prefer them. The pivotal word "therefore," logically linking the two halves of Article XIV, clearly says that overbroad warrants—not warrantless searches—are per se unreasonable.

Nowhere is there a third clause in Article XIV requiring warrants for all searches and seizures, and the clear tone of the article seems skeptical toward warrants. "All warrants . . . are contrary to . . . right [unless] . . . ; and no warrant ought to be issued but . . ." Warrants here are heavies, not heroes. And the clear language of the first sentence of Article XIV—a complete and self-contained legal command—gives the lie to those modern scholars who dismiss the clear general rule of "reasonableness" in the federal Fourth as a drafting mistake or an ill-considered textual hiccup.[21]

Massachusetts's Article XIV was borrowed virtually verbatim by the New Hampshire Constitution of 1784, and this article later served as a prototype for early versions of the federal Fourth in various state ratifying conventions. The Virginia convention of 1788 called for a federal amendment affirming that "every freeman has a right to be secure from all unreasonable searches and siezures [*sic*] of his person, his papers and his property." Conventions in New York and North Carolina proposed virtually identical language, and all three states went on to condemn overbroad warrants—not warrantless searches—as "therefore" unreasonable: "grievous," "oppressive," and "dangerous." In his first draft of the federal Fourth in the First Congress, James Madison likewise spoke of the people's right "to be secured in their persons, their houses, their papers, and their other property, from all unreasonable searches and seizures," and he furthermore declared that this right was threatened not by warrantless intrusions but by loose warrants.[22]

The first clause of Article XIV also plainly foreshadows the "persons, houses, papers, and effects" language of the federal Fourth, with "possessions" used as the Massachusetts residual catchall—all other important stuff—instead of its close cousin "effects." This suggests that we should construe "effects" generously, to avoid gaping holes in Fourth Amendment coverage.[23]

If "effects" and "all possessions" really are best read as rather sweeping catchalls, why did both Massachusetts's Article XIV and the federal Fourth bother to specify "persons," "houses," and "papers"? Precisely to remind us of the heightened sensitivity government should show toward searches and seizures of these three specially named items. Houses are often more private than other buildings; diaries and other private papers are often our dearest possessions (and raise large issues of free expression, as do all political papers); and searches and seizures of our bodies—our persons—obviously call for special sensitivity. In *Wilkes* and *Entick*, intrusions occurred against *persons*, *houses*, and *papers*, with bodily arrests and the ransacking of secret cabinets in homes in search of personal and political writings. Here, too, we see how these paradigm cases plainly prefigured both the Massachusetts and the federal constitutions.[24]

WHEN WE TURN FROM the Massachusetts Constitution to nineteenth-century judicial pronouncements in Massachusetts, we find further confirmation of our general story.

In the 1850 case of *Rohan v. Sawin*, the Supreme Judicial Court, meeting in Boston, held that a warrant was not required for arrest under either the US Constitution or the Massachusetts Constitution. The *Rohan* court, presided over by the great chief justice Lemuel Shaw, made clear that the "private" citizen's arrest power was "much more restricted" than the power of "constables, and other peace-officers, acting officially," to effect warrantless arrests. *Rohan* cited the 1780 English case of *Samuel v. Payne*, and quoted with approval as "direct authority" a key passage of Lord Tenterden's opinion in *Beckwith v. Philby*. The *Rohan* court also invoked another English case, one involving a warrantless arrest by a constable, for the proposition that in such cases a jury should consider "whether the circumstances . . . [in the case] afforded the constable *reasonable* ground to suppose that the . . . arrestee had committed a felony." Finally, the *Rohan* court made clear that, as a matter of law, an officer could arrest without warrant even in a case where a warrant would have been easy to get. In other words, case law did not as a rule require or even prefer warrants, even when warrants were practicable.[25]

Six years after *Rohan*, the same Massachusetts high court upheld a warrantless seizure of liquors from a wagon. The statute involved in this case, *Jones v. Root*, vested special warrantless seizure and arrest power in certain officers. The court briskly upheld the statute and affirmed the trial court's instruction that the jury should find for the plaintiff only if it determined that the defendant officers detained the plaintiff's innocent horse and wagon "for a longer time than was *reasonably* necessary" to remove the offending liquors from the wagon.[26]

Three years after that, in 1859, the court reemphasized that Article XIV did not prefer warrants, or require them; it sought to limit them. And so the court rejected the idea that an ex parte warrant could issue based on probable cause to believe that a debtor was concealing assets or property. That *kind* of probable cause, suggested the court, was not close enough to the kind of probable cause supporting ex parte warrants for stolen goods.[27]

Here, then, are the basic rules regarding search-and-seizure rights evident in early Bay State jurisprudence: no global warrant requirement, no global probable-cause requirement, limitations on when warrants can issue and on the kind of probable cause that is necessary to procure a warrant, and a general focus on reasonableness.

On the remedy side, the great justice Joseph Story, who would later become the Dane Professor of Law at Harvard, forcefully rebuffed a plea to exclude illegally obtained evidence in a circuit case decided in Boston in 1822: "In the ordinary administration of municipal law the right of using evidence does not depend, nor, as far as I have any recollection, has ever been supposed to depend upon the lawfulness or unlawfulness of the mode, by which it is obtained. . . . The evidence is admissible on charges for the highest crimes, even though it may have been obtained by a trespass upon the person, or by any other forcible and illegal means."[28]

Nineteen years later, the Massachusetts Supreme Judicial Court, sitting in Boston, also flatly rejected the exclusionary rule: "If the search warrant were illegal, or if the officer serving the warrant exceeded his authority, the party on whose complaint the warrant issued, or the officer, would be responsible for the wrong done; but this is no good reason for excluding the papers seized as evidence."[29]

As late as 1883, the leading evidence treatise in America, published in Boston, proclaimed illegally obtained evidence universally admissible in English and American courts. (The treatise was authored by Cambridge resident Simon Greenleaf, who succeeded Story to the Dane Professorship at Harvard.) And the greatest evidence scholar of the twentieth century—the Harvard-educated giant John Henry Wigmore—led a lifelong crusade against the illogic and injustice of the exclusionary rule. His encyclopedic, multivolume treatise was published in Boston.[30]

WRITS OF ASSISTANCE

More recently, Chief Justice John Roberts and others have tried to put Boston back on the Fourth Amendment map in yet another way, by emphasizing the Fourth Amendment significance of the 1761 writs-of-assistance controversy, which played out in colonial Boston.

A quick refresher on writs of assistance in the 1760s: The general writs and the British parliamentary statutes that underlay them authorized customs officers—without probable cause, or individualized suspicion—to break and enter houses, shops, and "any . . . other place" in search of uncustomed goods (that is, goods as to which proper customs duties had not been paid). In 1761, Boston lawyer James Otis challenged the lawfulness of these intrusive writs in a legal proceeding commonly (if somewhat loosely) known as *Paxton's Case*.[31]

Although many justices today appear to believe that this controversy was central to the thinking that underlay the Fourth Amendment, scholars have uncovered only one major direct reference to *Paxton* in the debates about the ratification of the Constitution and the drafting of the Bill of Rights. And that reference came from a pseudonymous pamphlet that we now know was authored by Mercy Otis Warren, the sister of James Otis.[32]

It is often noted that John Adams wrote the following about Otis's argument: "Then and there was the first scene of the first act of opposition to the arbitrary claims of Great Britain. Then and there the child Independence was born." What is less often noted is that Adams wrote these words more than fifty years after the event, and long after the enactment of the Fourth Amendment. Sometimes, the first act of a grand historical drama is much clearer in retrospect than it was at the time.[33]

Boston has long fancied itself "the Hub"—of Massachusetts; of New England; of the American Revolution; indeed, of the world! But in the early 1760s, before a continental consciousness swept the land, London was America's actual hub. Each American colony had its own unique founding, history, charter or charter-analogue, and relationship with England. Americans in diverse and far-flung British North American colonies were tied together in a hub-and-spoke configuration, with the mother country and king at the center. In the early 1760s, Boston, New York, Philadelphia, and Charleston often followed legal and political events in London (such as the Wilkes affair) far more closely than they followed developments in sister colonies. Of course, all this began to change in the mid-1760s, but the 1761 Boston writs-of-assistance case looms larger in retrospect than it did in its day.

Just as Boston has long seen itself as the Hub, so, too, John Adams at times fancied himself the Hub, the Center of All Things. Surely, the first act of the Revolution, in Adams's mind, had to have taken place not in Jefferson's Virginia but in Adams's beloved Boston, ideally with Adams himself in the room. (Never mind how many others were watching; Adams may have preferred to see himself as one of a select few "in" at the beginning.)[34]

In a similar vein, one historian has noted that Otis's speech "was not reported in the newspapers of the period and circulated to the 99.9 percent of the population that surely did not hear it. Of those present, apparently John Adams was the only one who was sufficiently impressed to take notes on what was said and he gave us the full account of it some fifty years after Otis delivered it."[35]

To be sure, later writs-of-assistance controversies arose in other colonies after the 1767 Townshend Act. These cases were more significant to contemporaries than the 1761 Boston case had been. But all these later cases were powerfully shaped by America's interest in the intervening and far more famous English cases of *Wilkes* and *Entick*.[36]

The words of both the Massachusetts Constitution and the US Constitution seem to track *Wilkes* and *Entick* more than *Paxton*; they speak of "warrants," not "writs," and highlight "persons" and "papers" as well as "houses." Many references to *Wilkes* and *Entick*, and to their principles, appear in debates surrounding the Constitution and Bill of Rights; not so with the writs of assistance. The Declaration of Independence makes no mention of abusive searches and seizures in America—an omission hard to explain if the American *Paxton's Case* was on everyone's mind and lips, but wholly consistent with the fame of the English *Wilkes* and *Entick* cases. Also, as we shall see in our final chapter, the names of "Wilkes" and "Camden" undoubtedly dot the map of early America more than "Otis" does. Yet another clue: in Joseph Story's brief discussion of the Fourth Amendment in his grand 1833 treatise on the Constitution (published in Boston and Cambridge), the great justice (then a Cambridge resident) highlights the 1763 English general warrants controversy involving Wilkes and others, but makes no mention of Otis or the writs of assistance.[37]

It remains to ask two questions about the writs of assistance themselves. First, why did Otis and other Bostonians object so much to these devices? And second, why, in England, did judges strike down general warrants but uphold writs of assistance?

The writs-of-assistance system seems offensive on several counts. First, it provided next to no guidance constraining the discretion of officers, thus inviting discrimination against government enemies and favoritism toward friends. Second, it authorized intrusions into houses—the most private buildings imaginable. Third, the writs-of-assistance scheme theoretically authorized customs officers to commandeer—to dragoon, or impress—ordinary passersby to aid them in their invasions. This "assistance" power added a vague and possibly tyrannical new layer of bodily intrusion and unchecked discretion into the system.[38] Finally, the objects of the search—relatively innocent "uncustomed" goods like tea and sugar—were not nearly so compelling as stolen goods, at least in a town, like colonial Boston, where customs evasion and tax evasion were practically a way of life, implicating a good many otherwise law-abiding folk. In other words, untaxed sugar in homes seems more like skim milk than like bombs. All of the foregoing factors, I suggest, would be relevant to a proper reasonableness analysis under the later-enacted Fourth Amendment.[39]

In light of all this, we must ask ourselves why some of the very same English judges who struck down general warrants upheld writs of assistance. At one level, the answer may be obvious: Parliament had not explicitly authorized general warrants, but it had by statute authorized writs of assistance. English judges, in general, had no authority to invalidate Acts of Parliament. But this merely pushes the question up one level: Why did Parliament continue to permit writs of assistance even after Parliament went on record, shortly after *Wilkes* and *Entick*, as opposed to certain types of warrants?[40]

Part of the answer may be that the *Wilkes* and *Entick* warrants were directly aimed at political dissenters and political papers. Tellingly, two of the three parliamentary resolutions condemning certain warrants after *Wilkes* and *Entick* highlighted issues of papers and expression. As I have already noted, free-expression concerns should loom large in any framework organized around constitutional reasonableness rather than a warrant requirement or a probable-cause requirement.[41]

But if my overall analysis is right, we should also look closely at the immunity issue. For I have suggested that lawful warrants, because they immunized the officer, had to be strictly limited. If, however, the writs of assistance offered less immunity, perhaps this might explain why they were somewhat less offensive.

Evidence from several English cases supports this hypothesis. In the first case, decided in 1769 in the Court of Common Pleas, one Redshaw brought a trespass suit against Brook and other defendants. Defendants were "custom-house officers" who conducted a suspicionless search for prohibited and uncustomed goods in Redshaw's house and came up empty. The jury awarded a whopping two hundred pounds to the plaintiff, and the lord chief justice upheld the verdict: "I cannot say the jury have done wrong."[42]

The brief report in *Redshaw* does not make clear whether defendants sought to hide behind a writ of assistance, but the issue arose again a year later in the Common Pleas case of *Bruce v. Rawlins*. Here, the defendants broke into a house, found nothing, and left saying—and this is a direct quote from the case—"Damn it, there are no goods!" When sued in trespass, they tried to hold up a writ of assistance as a shield, but the jury found for plaintiff and awarded one hundred pounds of damages. The court upheld the verdict, following *Redshaw*. Only Justice Henry Gould explicitly discussed the writ defense, and he stressed that defendants had failed to strictly comply with the writ, since they had not brought a constable along with them.[43]

Neither *Redshaw* nor *Bruce* carefully discussed writs of assistance, but the issue resurfaced and was crisply addressed in a 1785 King's Bench case. In *Cooper v. Boot*, Lord Mansfield observed in dicta that writs—unlike warrants—did not immunize for unsuccessful searches: "We think the Excise officer cannot be guilty of a trespass, either in procuring or executing the warrant. . . . It is a solecism [that is, a contradiction in terms] to say that the regular execution of a legal warrant shall be a trespass. . . . The case of the writ of assistance is not applicable. There is no warrant, and all is left to the discretion of the officer; besides, *which is very material*, there is a positive clause in the Statute of Charles 2, which makes the whole *depend on the actual finding of goods*."[44] As Lord Mansfield pithily put the point earlier, from the bench, "*under a writ of assistance you must find the goods, but not under a warrant*."[45]

This line of analysis was foreshadowed in the argument of Otis's colleague, Oxenbridge Thacher, in *Paxton's Case* itself,[46] and also appeared in a footnote drafted by "Horace Gray, Jr., Esq., of the Boston Bar," in his notes on the writs of assistance published in the 1860s. According to Gray, who would go on to become chief justice of Massachusetts and an associate justice of the United States Supreme Court, "it was well settled law that a person searching under a writ of assistance and finding nothing was not justified."[47] This was, apparently, also Lord Camden's view in an unpublished 1760s case, *Shipley v. Redmain*, which was described by counsel in *Cooper*;[48] and it was the view put forth by Chief Justice William De Grey in the 1773 English case of *Bostock v. Saunders*.[49] By contrast, as Blackstone made clear both in his treatise and on the bench in *Bostock*,[50] a lawful warrant "will at all events indemnify [that is, immunize] the officer."[51]

Now, for the reasons I have already mentioned, this difference between writs and warrants is not, in my view, enough to render the writs of assistance truly reasonable: the writ conferred immunity whenever an officer found untaxed sugar or tea in a home, and I would consider such intrusive, ill-justified, and probably discriminatory searches unreasonable even if successful. (And, of course, no one in America ever voted for the law in the first place.)

But the English cases do explain why general warrants were in one hugely significant way even worse than general writs. This key difference—immunity—fits nicely into our general story about why warrants were dangerous in the Founding era, and about why the Fourth Amendment reads as it does and means what it says.

IT THUS TURNS OUT that Boston and the 1761 writs-of-assistance controversy do cast some light on the Fourth Amendment, although not quite in the way that some modern scholars and judges have assumed. In our next and final state chapter, we shall take one last look at the Fourth Amendment, this time from the perspective of another, rather less glamorous and less Hub-like, eastern city.

CHAPTER 12

NEW JERSEY:
LORD CAMDEN MEETS
FEDERALISM

Philadelphia, Pennsylvania, the City of Brotherly Love, is one of our nation's greatest seats of commerce, industry, philanthropy, and education—and also, of course, the place where the Constitution was drafted and first went public. Just across the Delaware River from Philadelphia, in that Rodney Dangerfield of states, New Jersey, lies the gritty municipality of Camden, which has its own fascinating connection to American constitutionalism.

Many Americans have heard of William Penn, whose statue soars high above Philadelphia's grand city hall. Relatively few modern Americans know anything about Lord Camden, the namesake of Philadelphia's little sister city. Even among those who do know something about Camden's Founding-era contributions, few have given sufficient thought to the profound and provocative implications of his English ideas for American federalism and rights-protection.

Who was this Camden? Why did Founding-era Americans name a New Jersey city (and several other places, too) in his honor? And what does any of this have to do with how federalism can operate to protect constitutional rights in twenty-first-century America? Read on and find out.

CAMDEN:
FROM PERSON TO PLACE TO PRINCIPLES

Born Charles Pratt, Lord Camden was a great lawyer, a lover of liberty, and chief justice of England's Court of Common Pleas. Revolutionary-era

Americans adored him, not only because he championed the American cause in grand speeches in the late 1760s, but also because he decided two great cases in the mid-1760s: *Wilkes v. Wood* and *Entick v. Carrington*. If we seek modern analogues, perhaps we might think of *Wilkes* and *Entick* as the *Brown v. Board of Education* and *Gideon v. Wainwright* of their day; and Chief Justice Camden as the Earl Warren or Hugo Black of his era.[1]

What were *Wilkes* and *Entick* all about? Recall from the previous chapter that when various English critics of King George III and his ministers published anonymous pamphlets sharply attacking government policy and policymakers, the king's ministers ordered their underlings to find out who had authored these pamphlets so that the authors could be prosecuted and punished for their audacity and impertinence. In the *Wilkes* case, the government's underlings proceeded to procure a general warrant, which purported to authorize them to search the homes or the persons of anyone they doubted—to round up the usual anti-government suspects, as it were, including the outspoken John Wilkes. In the *Entick* case, the henchmen got a narrower warrant, identifying the anti-government writer John Entick by name, but purporting to authorize a search of even his most private personal papers at home. John Wilkes and John Entick then brought civil trespass suits against the government henchmen, seeking compensatory and punitive damages for the torts committed upon them. The plaintiffs won, and won big, receiving impressive damage awards from civil juries presided over by Lord Camden.[2]

The structure of these cases was quite simple. Plaintiffs sued in tort claiming that the government's searches and seizures invaded their persons and their property. Defendant government officers, in turn, pointed to the warrants. The defendants conceded that they did in some sense trespass upon person and property, but argued that the government had authorized them to do so via the warrants that they had obtained. And government, of course, can often authorize what would otherwise be an actionable tort. If A reaches into B's pocket and takes money from B's wallet, that's ordinarily a tort. But if A does this with governmental authorization, it's okay. It's not trespass, it's taxes. At this point in the argument, plaintiffs countered that the warrants were themselves illegal because they violated the unwritten British Constitution, based on custom, tradition, and right reason. No parliamentary statute explicitly authorized general warrants—that is, warrants lacking probable cause under oath, and particular specification of the person or thing to be searched or seized. Similarly, no parliamentary statutes authorized warrants for private personal papers, such as diaries. Wilkes and Entick argued that these broad warrants violated deep English traditions of privacy and freedom from unreasonable searches.

In his rulings and his jury instructions, Camden sided with the plaintiffs. On his view, the government warrants were illegal, null and void, not worth the paper they were written on. The defendant officials' defense of government authorization thus collapsed, and they stood as naked tortfeasors liable for both compensatory damages, to make Wilkes and Entick whole, and punitive damages, to teach arrogant government officialdom a lesson and to deter similar unconstitutional conduct in the future.

AMERICAN PATRIOTS IN THE Revolutionary era loved this pair of cases, and loved this man, Camden. For Americans, too, often railed against George III's arrogant ministers. They, too, felt that ministerial policy was violating important traditions of liberty and freedom embodied in an unwritten British Constitution. They, too, cherished juries—for American colonists were eligible to serve on a local jury, but were ineligible to serve in, or even vote for, an English Parliament.

New Jerseyans were not the only early Americans to honor Camden in a geographically memorable way. The residents of a beautiful seaport now known as Camden, Maine, named their township in honor of Lord Camden in the late 1760s, when Maine was still part of Massachusetts. (Today, this township's official seal, chosen in a competition held in June 1994, features a handsome portrait of Lord Camden.) Revolution-era South Carolinians also named a town in Camden's honor; and today's Baltimore Orioles play their home games in historic Camden Yards.[3]

The other major figure in these English proto–Fourth Amendment cases, the plaintiff John Wilkes, also left his mark on this side of the Atlantic. From north to south, Americans adored this advocate of liberty, as any map will show: consider Wilkes-Barre, Pennsylvania; Wilkes County, Georgia; and Wilkes County, North Carolina.

STATE REMEDIES FOR FEDERAL WRONGS

But how, it might be asked, do Lord Camden's legendary rulings in support of plaintiffs Wilkes and Entick connect up to American federalism?

The best way to answer this question is through a series of hypothetical cases building on the principles underlying Lord Camden's storied rulings.

Let's begin by recalling the Fourth Amendment's opening clause affirming citizens' rights to be "secure in their persons, houses, papers, and effects, against unreasonable searches and seizures." This amendment's general prohibition of unreasonable searches and seizures was not, in the Founding era, enforced by any sort of exclusionary rule. The exclusionary rule is a modern-day judicial fabrication. As late as 1876, when America celebrated the centennial of its independence, no court in the land, state or federal, had ever excluded reliable evidence on the grounds of its having been obtained illegally; only in the twentieth century did the rule take deep root—and England has never had an exclusionary rule. *Wilkes* and *Entick* were emphatically not exclusionary-rule cases—they were English tort-law cases.

Similar tort-law principles applied in Founding-era America. If the federal government authorized an outrageous and intrusive search or seizure, the citizen victimized by this intrusion could bring a tort suit against the federal officials who carried out the search. In this civil suit, our American citizen—let's call him John Wilkes Entick—would sue the officers for civil trespass and seek compensatory and punitive damages, just as in England. In turn, government-officer defendants would plead immunity based on the fact that the federal government had authorized the search or seizure. Then the plaintiff would counter that the purported governmental authorization was null and void, because the intrusion was, under the Fourth Amendment, unreasonable, and thus unconstitutional. The federal government, John Wilkes Entick would remind the court, had no power to authorize unconstitutional searches and seizures; any purported authorization, if unreasonable, must be ignored, and defendant officers thus stood exposed as naked tortfeasors.

So far, the case of our hypothetical American, John Wilkes Entick, seems to look just like the real cases of the Englishmen, Wilkes and Entick, with the simple substitution of a written American Constitution for an unwritten English one. That difference, of course, is an important one. In England, judges could rule in favor of ordinary citizens and against government henchmen only in the absence of a clear parliamentary statute authorizing the government officers' actions. So long as Parliament unambiguously expressed its will to abrogate the traditional freedoms of Englishmen, this sovereign legislature could do as it pleased, and English judges would uphold its laws. In America, by contrast, judges could disregard even explicit congressional statutes if such statutes violated the freedoms of Americans set forth in a written Constitution and Bill of Rights.

There remains another more subtle, but for our present purposes more important, difference between our hypothetical American case of John Wilkes Entick and its real-life English forebears. Britain featured a unitary legal system in which the central government had plenary power over every inch of the island, whereas America's Constitution structured a federal system that divided legal authority between state and central governments. Let us now look more closely at our hypothetical American case to see what happens when the lessons of *Entick* and *Wilkes* take root in American soil—when, in effect, Lord Camden meets federalism.

IN OUR HYPOTHETICAL SUIT, John Wilkes Entick is suing federal officers. In order to prevail in the end, he must show that these officials violated the federal Constitution—the Fourth Amendment—and thus lack true governmental immunity. But what law gets J. W. Entick into court in the first place? Trespass law, based on property and tort principles typically grounded in state law.* This state law might take any of several forms. It might simply take shape in common-law opinions—and, as the influential 1938 case of *Erie Railroad v. Tompkins* explains, the common law of property and tort is typically *state* law. These principles might also be codified in local ordinances, or in state statutes, or in state constitutions. Whatever their form, these tort and property rules remind us of a dramatic but often ignored truth about the Founders' scheme: *state* law could provide citizens with remedies against *federal* constitutional violations committed by *federal* agents.

To some, this fact may come as shock: "That can't be right! What about the supremacy clause? What about *McCulloch v. Maryland*? What about the Civil War?"

Actually, nothing in the Article VI supremacy clause, or in the landmark case of *McCulloch v. Maryland*, or in the spirit of Appomattox and

---

* The federal government is a government of enumerated powers, and the Constitution does not give this government plenary power to regulate property law and tort law in the several states. Thus state law typically operates here, in keeping with the Tenth Amendment's reminder that in situations where no federal law applies, state law often fills the vacuum.

the Civil War Amendments, contradicts the dramatic fact of state-law remedies for federal constitutional wrongs committed by federal agents. The supremacy clause does not make federal agents, or even congressional laws, supreme. It makes the Constitution itself supreme. When federal agents, even if backed by federal law, violate the federal Constitution, the supremacy clause itself reminds us that these actions are improper and off limits—not "in pursuance" of the Constitution, in the words of the clause. When federal agents search or seize unconstitutionally, the supremacy clause sides with our J. W. Entick, not against him.[4]

In the 1819 case of *McCulloch v. Maryland*, Chief Justice John Marshall struck down state interference with a federal bank that was a wholly lawful creation of the federal government. We should remember how Marshall structured his analysis. First, he ruled that the creation and maintenance of the bank fell within the federal government's legitimate constitutional powers. Only after deciding this first question did he turn to the second: May a state *nonetheless* tax a federal bank? The clear logic of this overall structure, and of several specific passages in the opinion, suggests that very different principles would have applied to state-law interference with an *unconstitutional* federal bank that could *not* claim bona fide federal immunity. The Civil War, and the amendments that followed it, reinforced the supremacy clause and *McCulloch*, but nowhere freed the federal government from limits of the Constitution itself, limits embodied in clauses like the Fourth Amendment and in the idea of enumerated power.[5]

Note that in stressing the role of state law in countering federal abuses, we have not rejected the centrality of federal courts. Although Mr. J. W. Entick might rely on trespass doctrine laid down by prior state court cases, his own case might well be tried in a federal court. In a series of jurisdictional statutes adopted in the early nineteenth century, Congress provided that damage suits against various categories of federal officers for alleged abuses be removed before trial from state court to federal district court. Even if J. W. Entick's case were somehow tried in state court, the case would necessarily involve federal questions—most importantly, Did the defendants' search or seizure violate the federal Fourth Amendment?—and would thus trigger the Supreme Court's appellate review under section 25 of the Judiciary Act of 1789. (*McCulloch* itself was precisely that kind of case; tried in state court, the case raised federal questions—Was the federal bank constitutional? Could states nonetheless tax it?—that triggered Supreme Court appellate review under section 25.)

In admitting that federal judges would rule on the federal Constitution in the last instance and, if Congress so desired, at trial, too, have we undercut the importance of state law in cases like J. W. Entick's? Not really. For federal judges, too, are obliged to enforce relevant substantive state laws, even in federal-question cases. This is required by the Tenth Amendment, by the famous section 34 of the Judiciary Act of 1789—the so-called "Rules of Decision Act"—and by various notable federal-jurisdiction cases decided over the years, including *Green v. Neal's Lessee* in 1832, *Murdock v. City of Memphis* in 1875, and *Erie v. Tompkins* in 1938.

THERE IS YET ANOTHER dramatic way in which, under the Founders' vision, state law would help ease and shape the vindication of federal constitutional rights against federal officialdom. If, because of federal jurisdictional removal statutes, our friend J. W. Entick were obliged to try his case before a federal trial judge, the Seventh Amendment would guarantee Entick that his right to a civil jury would be "preserved." Remember that in English cases like *Wilkes* and *Entick*, Lord Camden had not acted alone—but in tandem with juries—to vindicate the rights of Englishmen. In America, the Fourth Amendment question would often boil down to the basic reasonableness of a given search or seizure, and the Framers expected that civil juries, working alongside judges, would help breathe life into, and give shape to, this broad standard.

"Reasonableness" in tort law often emerges as an issue of fact, or a mixed issue of law and fact, in which the jury looms large. Beyond its role in helping to determine liability, a civil jury would also often decide whether to sock defendants with punitive damages, and, if so, where to set the award within a broad range marked out by judges.[6]

In short, the Founders saw the ideas underlying the Fourth and Seventh Amendments as tightly linked together—a linkage no doubt forged in their minds by the dramatic cases of *Wilkes* and *Entick*. This linkage was perhaps most visible in the Maryland ratifying convention, where a committee recommended a federal constitutional amendment requiring civil jury trial in "all cases of trespasses"—plainly contemplating government officer trespasses—and prohibiting appellate relitigation of the jury's factual findings.[7]

We have already noted how, substantively, the trespass law underlying the Fourth Amendment was state law. Now consider the intriguing possibility that, procedurally, the jury law underlying the Seventh Amendment was also intended by the Framers to be state law.

What exactly did the Seventh Amendment mean when it required federal courts to "preserve" the right of civil juries, given that this right so obviously varied from state to state, and within a single state also varied over time? Perhaps this: If a state court across the street entertaining a given common-law case would use a civil jury, a federal court hearing the same case (say, because of removal) must follow—must "preserve"—that state-law jury right. In other words, the Seventh Amendment might be a kind of *Erie*-rule for the procedural issue of jury trial, requiring federal courts, at a minimum, to follow state-law jury rules. Federal courts, on this reading, could provide more juries than state courts across the street, but never fewer juries. Thus, Congress would be free to provide for a uniform federal jury rule so long as that rule was at least as protective as the most protective state jury rule. (Anti-Federalists would obviously have liked this incentive scheme, inducing the federal government, if it sought uniformity within the federal system, to be uniformly pro-jury rather than uniformly anti-jury.)[8]

This reading snugly fits with *The Federalist* No. 83, where Alexander Hamilton described various Anti-Federalist proposals to constitutionalize civil juries as follows: "Cases in the federal courts should be tried by jury, if, in the State where the courts sat, that mode of trial would obtain in a similar case in the State courts." Although the Supreme Court has never embraced this approach, Hamilton's understanding draws support from a considerable amount of historical evidence from the Founding era. Compared to the Supreme Court's current approach—which can charitably be called a muddle—the state-law model is rather easy to apply. A federal court would simply look across the street at the current state-law provisions regarding civil juries—provisions embodied in state court cases, state rule and regulations, state statutes, and, of course, state constitutions.[9]

Structurally, once we recall that the Framers expected state law to provide the substantive right to sue (what lawyers call "the cause of action") in trespass suits against overreaching federal officials, it makes some sense that state law should also be able to guarantee a civil jury even in a federal trial court. In the converse situation, where a case based on a federal statute is brought in state court, the basic rule is that in some situations a right to a civil jury is part and parcel of the federal statutory entitlement (part and parcel of the federal substantive "cause of action"), and therefore obligatory even on state judges.[10]

State-law causes of action were at the core of the Seventh Amendment. For the Founders, two types of Seventh Amendment cases were paradigmatic: first, state-law trespass suits against federal officers, and second, state-law contract cases pitting creditor-state plaintiffs against debtor-state defendants. The Seventh Amendment was crafted around these two types of cases and had less bite for causes of action based on federal statutes; a Congress intent on evading civil juries could draft statutes sounding in equity, not law. The centrality of state-law cases to the Seventh Amendment also explains why its jury rules were sensibly keyed to state practice, whereas the grand-jury rules of the Fifth Amendment, and the criminal-jury rules of the Sixth Amendment—dealing mainly with suits under federal law—were not.[11]

Here, too, the notion that state law might play a role in adjudicating federal constitutional rights against federal officers might come as a shock to some: "That can't be right! Surely the federal Constitution does not mean one thing in state A and a different thing in state B. Surely it cannot mean one thing today and a different thing tomorrow. The Constitution lays down a single rule, for all times and all places."

However, these objections miss a deep and dramatic truth about our federal system. As Professors Henry Hart and Herbert Wechsler proclaimed in a canonical passage in their canonical mid-twentieth-century casebook on America's federal system: "Federal law is generally interstitial in its nature. It rarely occupies a legal field completely, totally excluding all participation by the legal systems of the states. . . . Federal legislation . . . builds upon legal relationships established by the states, altering or supplanting them only so far as necessary for the special purpose. Congress acts, in short, against the background of the total *corpus juris* of the states in much the same way that a state legislature acts against the background of the common law, assumed to govern unless changed by legislation."[12]

Here is an example. Copyright law is distinctively federal law; the Constitution explicitly empowers Congress to frame nationwide copyright laws in Article I, section 8, clause 8. Suppose that Congress legislates that, when an author dies, his family should be allowed to renew his copyright, and share in his royalties. But suppose the federal statute does not carefully define who counts as an author's family. Do illegitimate children count? Adopted children? Divorced spouses? The Supreme Court has told us that, typically, gaps like this in federal law are to be filled by state family-law, incorporated into a federal scheme. Thus, the very same federal copyright statute would, in its application, vary somewhat from state to state and from year to year.[13]

What is true of federal laws passed by Congress is true of the federal Constitution itself. It also often incorporates state law, taking on local hues and molding its shape to fit different and changing state-law rules. Consider, for example, the just-compensation clause of the Fifth Amendment. This clause prevents the federal government from taking private property, for public use, without just compensation. But what is property? Property is often a state-law concept, and one that changes over time. Thus, the compensation clause will vary from state to state and from year to year as the state-law-tinged concept of property itself varies.

The point goes even deeper. State law not only helps shape the very meaning of certain constitutional clauses that build on state law, but it does so even for constitutional clauses, like the just-compensation clause, that limit *federal* officers. One of the deepest and most important functions of state law, and of state constitutions, is to help counter abuses of federal officialdom.[14]

This is a point that has been lost by many recent celebrations of federalism and state constitutionalism following in the tradition of one of New Jersey's favorite sons, US Supreme Court Justice William Brennan. In Justice Brennan's vision, state judges can use state constitutions to protect state citizens from abuses perpetrated by *state* governmental officials.[15]

Although his reminder is vitally important, it is incomplete. Brennan's vision nowhere explains why Americans are better off with federalism than without it. A critic of federalism might say that federalism merely creates two sets of governments to bully citizens rather than one. Brennan counters that state constitutions can provide rights against states, but of course, if these potentially abusive states did not exist in the first place, citizens would not need any state constitutional protections against them.

Thus, we need to supplement Justice Brennan's vision of federalism with Madison's and Hamilton's vision, which has recently been embraced by the US Supreme Court in a series of federalism cases, beginning with a 1991 case, *Gregory v. Ashcroft*. In this vision, states, state laws, and state constitutions can help protect Americans not merely against state abuses, but against federal abuses, too. In the words of the *Gregory* Court:

> Perhaps the principle benefit of the federalist system is a check on abuses of government power. . . . Just as the separation and independence of the coordinate branches of the Federal Government serve to prevent the accumulation of excessive power in any one branch, a healthy balance of power between the States and the Federal Government will reduce the risk of

tyranny and abuse from either front. Alexander Hamilton explained to the people of New York, perhaps optimistically, that the new federalist system would suppress completely "the attempts of the government to establish a tyranny."[16]

The *Gregory* Court then proceeded to quote two suggestive passages from *The Federalist*. First came the words of Hamilton's *Federalist* No. 28:

> In a confederacy the people, without exaggeration, may be said to be entirely the masters of their own fate. Power being almost always the rival of power, the general government will at all times stand ready to check usurpations of the state governments, and these will have the same disposition towards the general government. The people, by throwing themselves into either scale, will infallibly make it preponderate. *If their rights are invaded by either, they can make use of the other as the instrument of redress.* (My emphasis.)

Then came a quotation from Madison's *Federalist* No. 51:

> In a single republic, all the power surrendered by the people is submitted to the administration of a single government; and the usurpations are guarded against by a division of the government into distinct and separate departments. In the compound republic of America, the power surrendered by the people is first divided between two distinct governments, and then the portion allotted to each subdivided among distinct and separate departments. Hence a double security arises to the rights of the people. The different governments will control each other, at the same time that each will be controlled by itself.

OUR MR. JOHN WILKES ENTICK is of course fictional, but in countless nonfictional Fourth Amendment cases from the 1790s to the 1970s, real-life Americans did sue federal officers in trespass—and win. In 1971, the Supreme Court handed down its landmark decision in *Bivens v. Six Unknown Named Agents of Federal Bureau of Narcotics*, a decision that made clear that Americans could sue for damages directly under the Fourth Amendment itself, without the need to plead a state-law trespass. However, *Bivens* did not oust the ancient trespass remedy; *Bivens* merely supplemented the old model.

State-law trespass is now no longer the only way to vindicate Fourth Amendment rights of innocent victims of government abuse, but for some aggrieved citizens, it might still be the best way to vindicate these rights. For what the Supreme Court gave with one hand in *Bivens*, it largely took away with the other hand in later cases that created zones of immunity for government officials.[17] So far, these federal judge–made immunities have been used by the Supreme Court only to limit the federal judge–made *Bivens* remedy: what the Supreme Court giveth, the Supreme Court can taketh away. The Court has never said that the Constitution requires these immunities—or that these immunities can lawfully oust *state-law* remedies that seek to hold federal officers strictly liable for constitutional violations perpetrated in "good faith." And because *Bivens* created a national floor, applicable in all fifty states, federal courts may have strictly limited the amount of damages available in *Bivens* actions; but these very same federal courts might permit a given state-law remedy to be more generous than the federal floor. Thus, even after *Bivens*, a modern-day J. W. Entick may sometimes prefer state-law remedies to the federal *Bivens* variety. To put the point a different way, federal courts may well award a more generous recovery to a plaintiff with state law on his side than to a plaintiff without.[18]

HERE IS ANOTHER EXAMPLE. Imagine that our friend J. W. Entick is driving his car down the highway. With no justification whatsoever, federal officers pull him over and start rummaging through his glove compartment. In the compartment, they find a very personal, private letter written to Entick by his friend Camden Lord, who also happens to be a passenger in the car. With no good reason—just for kicks, and to flex their power—the federal officers proceed to read the letter, mocking passenger Lord for some of the more personal passages. Now suppose that Lord sues under *Bivens*. Although there are no Supreme Court *Bivens* cases precisely on point, the Supreme Court has held, in the 1978 exclusionary-rule case of *Rakas v. Illinois*, that car passengers do not have Fourth Amendment standing to challenge car searches, because they lack a "legitimate expectation of privacy in the invaded place." Perhaps, then, by this logic, only owner Entick could bring a *Bivens* action, but passenger Lord could not.

But suppose that the car search occurred in Camden, New Jersey, and suppose further that New Jersey had a legal rule—in a Camden city ordinance, or in a state statute, or in the state constitution, or in New Jersey case law—that passengers of cars, or writers of letters "owned" by others, do have privacy and property rights. Might this New Jersey law give our Mr. Camden Lord "standing" to sue under the Fourth Amendment that he would otherwise lack?

Quite possibly yes! In one passage, the *Rakas* Court noted that the passenger in that case had "neither a property nor a possessory interest in the automobile, nor an interest in the property seized." By contrast, our Mr. Lord could claim a kind of legal interest in the letter seized. In another key passage, the *Rakas* Court noted that

> [l]egitimation of expectations of privacy by law must have a source outside of the Fourth Amendment, either by reference to concepts of real or personal property law or to understandings that are recognized and permitted by society. One of the main rights attaching to property is the right to exclude others . . . and one who owns or lawfully possesses or controls property will in all likelihood have a legitimate expectation of privacy by virtue of this right to exclude. . . . The Court has not altogether abandoned use of property concepts in determining the presence or absence of the privacy interests protected by that Amendment.

Thanks to New Jersey law, Camden Lord would argue, he does have a Fourth Amendment interest—a legitimate expectation of privacy—that he might otherwise lack.[19]*

From Remedies to Rights

In our last hypothetical, we have shifted gears somewhat. We began with Mr. John Wilkes Entick in the Founding era, using state law as a remedy for a (by hypothesis) clear Fourth Amendment violation. But now, with Camden Lord, we are thinking about using state law to confer standing for a (by hypothesis) clear Fourth Amendment violation.[20] Here, too, we might frame the issue as one of additional Fourth Amendment "remedies." For surely the car search violated owner Entick's rights. Thus, the argument goes, if state law could give Entick a more generous recovery than he might get with *Bivens* alone, why can't state law do the same thing for Lord?

---

* In actual fact, the New Jersey Supreme Court has already begun to do what I am calling for here, but has pulled up short. For details, see p. 343n.19.

From another perspective, "standing" could be seen not as an issue of "remedy," but as one of "right": Were Lord's Fourth Amendment rights violated at all? If not, he has no "right," and thus deserves no "remedy." But on this view, the lesson of Lord's case is that state law can not only help remedy a clear Fourth Amendment violation by the feds, but can also help *define* a clear violation in the first place.

Here is an even bolder formulation of the rather startling lesson of this hypothetical: state law can at times transform what would otherwise be constitutional federal conduct into unconstitutional federal conduct.

To test this formulation, consider yet another hypothetical case involving our imaginary friend Camden Lord. Lord lives in—where else?—Camden, New Jersey. Every Sunday night he places a dark green trash bag out on his sidewalk for garbage collection Monday morning. But Lord is a vocal opponent of the federal government, and so the feds don't like him much. Thus, with no good justification, the feds decide to harass Lord by snatching his trash bag early one Monday morning and pawing through it, hoping to find something embarrassing. Outraged, Lord brings a *Bivens* suit.

Alas, Lord may well lose. According to the Supreme Court's opinion in the 1988 case of *California v. Greenwood*, a homeowner lacks a legitimate expectation of privacy in his garbage once he places it out on the sidewalk for trash pickup. To be sure, *Greenwood* was an exclusionary-rule case, and this may have warped the Court's judgment. (To admit that the Fourth Amendment was violated in that case would have possibly obliged the Court to exclude reliable evidence of criminal guilt, something sensible judges are loath to do in close cases.) Yet the logic of *Greenwood* leans heavily against Lord in suggesting that citizens have no Fourth Amendment right to protect their garbage. No right, no remedy.

But suppose Camden, New Jersey, has a local ordinance explicitly vesting homeowners with a "privacy" and "property" right in their garbage, vis-à-vis all the world except local trash collectors themselves, who are allowed to pick up trash, but are forbidden to search it. Wouldn't this local ordinance itself help to give Lord a legitimate expectation of privacy? By the same reasoning, a state statute, or a state court case, or a state constitutional provision, could also help to create a legitimate expectation of privacy. Thus, state law might help to give Lord a Fourth Amendment right against federal officialdom that he might otherwise lack.[21]

True, the Court's opinion in *Greenwood*, in one key, but utterly thoughtless, passage, purports to reject the relevance of California law to the federal question at hand. Yet it does so in a paragraph that explicitly cites to the *Rakas* language that property law is relevant. Earlier in the *Greenwood* opinion itself, the Court seems to rely on local law to construe the Fourth Amendment, by pointing out that trash collectors themselves are free to search through garbage or can allow the police to do so. Even if state law is not always dispositive on the federal reasonableness of a search, surely it is at least relevant to whether a given person's "effects" have been searched and to whether that search was "reasonable." So we are left with a suspicion that *Greenwood* in the end may have been driven more by (sound) doubts about the exclusionary rule than by a proper understanding of Fourth Amendment reasonableness and the structure of our federal Constitution.[22]

Now take this analysis one last step. Suppose that no Camden city ordinance, or New Jersey statute, or New Jersey case or constitutional clause, exists. But suppose that many other states have adopted garbage protection laws. Are not these state laws, at some point, evidence of a national social understanding that must inform the meaning of "legitimate expectations of privacy" under the Fourth Amendment? (In a similar fashion, the Supreme Court has explicitly consulted state death-penalty laws as evidence of national social understandings about cruel and unusual punishment within the meaning of the Eighth Amendment. Thanks in part to the merciful actions of various states, the capacity of the federal government itself to impose the death penalty has been constrained.) In this tally of state laws, perhaps state constitutions should count for more than mere state statutes or local ordinances, as constitutions represent deeper and more considered judgments of the people themselves. So here, too, we see how state constitutions can help counter federal abuses.[23]

HIGH SCHOOL CIVICS STUDENTS are taught that New Jersey's most significant attempted contribution to American federalism was the failed New Jersey Plan at the Philadelphia Convention. Under this plan, states large and small were given equal votes in a Congress with rather limited powers. Much of that plan was, quite sensibly, rejected by James Madison and his fellow big-state nationalists at Philadelphia.

But there is an alternative story worth telling about New Jersey's contributions to American federalism, a story that views states as retaining important powers to protect Americans against federal abuse even within a constitutional system that dramatically differs from the failed New Jersey Plan. This alternative story about federalism, Jersey-style—the story I have told in this chapter—builds on a little-noted but genuinely notable fact: the New Jersey city closest to Independence Hall was named for a great jurist who insisted that judges and juries must always enjoy sufficient power to ensure that fundamental rights remain the law of the land.[24]

CONCLUSION

I t's not true, of course, but that has never stopped me from telling the story of the day when my mom gave me two new shirts. I immediately changed into one of them, at which point my mother looked at me and asked, "Why don't you like the other one?"

Readers should not assume that the fact that only twelve states are showcased in the preceding chapters must mean that I don't like the other ones, which include the state where I was born (Michigan); the state where my first child was born (Connecticut); and, oh yes, the states where, depending on how you look at it, the Constitution itself was born (Pennsylvania and New Hampshire).*

The truth is that I haven't yet visited or studied certain states, and in any event, this book would have swollen to unwieldy proportions had I tried to cram fifty chapters between its covers. I have chosen these twelve states, and these twelve stories, because this particular ensemble will, I hope, enable readers to appreciate three interconnected elements of American constitutional federalism.

GEOGRAPHY

One element, specially emphasized in this book's opening chapter, is brute geography. America's fifty states are *territorial* units, defined by their unique geographic features: their lands and lakes, their mountains and valleys, their rivers and coastlines. Basic topographic features matter for key

---

* Pennsylvania's claim derives from the fact that the document was drafted in Philadelphia during the summer of 1787 and first went public in that city—on September 17, 1787, to be precise. But the document became legally valid only when ratified by the necessary ninth state—New Hampshire, as it turns out—on June 21, 1788.

issues of constitutional law. The wideness of the Atlantic, the flatness of the Midwest, and the centrality of the Mississippi were all important factors influencing the Founders' and Lincoln's views of the secession question.

Natural topography is almost never unaffected by manmade laws and lines. Manmade trade and manmade trade barriers heighten the significance of legal control over critical ports and entrepôts such as New York and New Orleans. Likewise, railroads and canals can profoundly reshape economies and societies. Thus, one of the precipitants of the Civil War was the Kansas-Nebraska Act of 1854, which arose amid intense wrangling over where to locate America's first transcontinental railroad—a vexed question implicating both brute geography (substrata, slopes, rivers, and so on) and laws (free-soil or slave-soil?).

Geography's complex interaction with law and culture lies close to the surface of my opening chapter on Lincoln; but other chapters should also be understood in this light. Consider, for example, the apportionment of the United States Supreme Court—an issue that recurs repeatedly in my New York chapter on Robert Jackson, in which I make note of the remarkable fact that more than half the current Court members come from a single state.

A critic might think this factoid a cheat on my part: John Roberts left the Empire State long ago, as did Antonin Scalia, Ruth Bader Ginsburg, and Elena Kagan. Only Sonia Sotomayor lived continuously in New York until called to the Supreme Court—though we should remember, as even a critic might admit, that Samuel Alito has likewise lived most of his professional life within commuting distance of the Big Apple.

If we take this criticism seriously and focus not on where today's justices were born and raised but instead on where they resided right before they reached the Supremes, our larger geographic puzzle remains. Geographically, the current Court is astonishingly imbalanced, no matter how we slice it. Four justices lived and worked in the vicinity of the District of Columbia; two more came from the New York City metropolitan area; two more arrived from the Boston metroplex; and one was from Northern California. In short: three Amtrak Northeast Corridor cities plus San Francisco.*

---

*While Anthony Kennedy sat on the Ninth Circuit, which met in San Francisco, he lived in nearby Sacramento. I confess that as a former resident of the Bay Area, I am, perhaps imperialistically, inclined to see Sacramento as part of the larger metroplex encompassing San Francisco, Oakland, and San Jose, much as a New York City resident might be wont, imperiously, to view Newark and even New Haven as parts of Greater Gotham.

Such a geographic imbalance could never happen in the Senate. The Constitution expressly mandates that each state get two senators and that each senator come from the state he or she represents. Likewise, a broad geographic distribution is constitutionally hardwired into the House of Representatives. It is inconceivable that all House members would live in four big metropolitan areas, or—bracketing the DC beltway, which raises special complexities—that all lawmakers coming from outside that beltway would hail from only three coastal cities of our vast continent.

In early America, a broad, Congress-like geographic distribution pattern was in fact built into the Supreme Court's apportionment as well. Justices had to ride circuit, and circuits were defined *geographically*. In 1789, there were three territorially defined circuits—a northern one, a mid-Atlantic one, and a southern one—each with two designated justices tasked with presiding over various trials and appeals within the circuit. As the nation spread westward, new geographically defined circuits were created and folded into the system. Though presidents were formally free to nominate justices who resided outside their assigned circuit, practical and political considerations counseled otherwise: a justice, most believed, should ordinarily come from the circuit that he would need to ride, be a member of the bar of one of the states within this circuit, and possess special familiarity with and fluency in the law of that state.

Only after circuit-riding was phased out in the late nineteenth century did the Supreme Court decisively begin to lose its geographically dispersed character. Today, we no longer speak of the "southern seat" on the Court. There is no southern seat! Demography has replaced geography. Hence the more modern idea of Jewish seats, Catholic seats, women's seats, and the like.

This focus on judicial geography, then and now, enables us to see old questions in new ways. For example, how can we explain the Supreme Court's ruling in the 1857 *Dred Scott* case, preposterously proclaiming that federal free-soil laws banning slavery in various federal territories were unconstitutional? Here is one way—a geographic way: five of the Court's nine members in 1857 came from the slaveholding South, even though less than a third of America's free population inhabited that region. Why the gross overrepresentation of Dixie? In part because of brute geography. Southern roads were particularly poor, and southern cities were widely scattered. Circuit-riding in the South was especially hard on the justices doing the riding down there; so circuits were drawn and Supreme Court manpower was allocated with one eye on the number and kinds of acres to be ridden and roads to be traveled, as distinct from the size of the free population to be judicially served.*

Before turning from geography, we should loop back one last time to some remarkable facts about the current Court and the American map. Here is one way of recasting one theme of my New York chapter: As young persons, seven of the nine current justices grew up in or around three great port cities—New York, Philadelphia, and San Francisco. Only two current justices came from anything that could be called the heartland (sometimes referred to by the dismissive term "flyover country"): John Roberts spent much of his childhood near Michigan City, Indiana, and Clarence Thomas hails from Pinpoint, Georgia. But even Roberts was born and spent his early childhood in Buffalo, a major inland port in mid-twentieth-century America, thanks in part to railroads and canals; and Michigan City is less than an hour from another mighty inland port, Chicago, which links the vast Mississippi River system to the Great Lakes and ultimately (via Buffalo) to New York City. And Pinpoint is about 10 miles from the historic southern port city of Savannah.

I believe that this pattern is not entirely coincidental. Ports are places of trade and commerce, where goods and ideas flow freely, where people and peoples intermingle. Even if shipping and trade at some later moment subside, the rich physical and intellectual infrastructure that took root within and around once-vibrant ports often remains. Ports are typically law towns, with lawyers galore. New York City, Philadelphia, and San Francisco in particular are all big-time law towns, lousy with lawyers (as is Washington, DC, of course), and children learn what they live. Thus, it is not entirely random that our highest Court has so many members who came from so few places.

To put the point autobiographically, I grew up right outside San Francisco, and now live right outside New Haven, within commuting distance of four of our nation's six best law schools. Two of these schools are in Manhattan, one is a stone's throw from Boston, and the other— my home school, Yale—lies in the geographic center of this powerful

---

* Another factor in the antebellum Court's malapportionment was the proslavery tilt of the antebellum presidents who got to pick men for the Court, and who were themselves picked via an electoral college system skewed toward slavery by the malodorous three-fifths clause.

law-and-education circle. (The other two top law schools may be found in Chicago and the San Francisco Bay Area.) New Haven has its detractors and drawbacks, as I would be the first to admit; but this old port town has always been close to where the action is, legally and educationally. Perhaps I should have entitled this book, "The Law of the Land—and of the Water."

STATES AS BUILDING BLOCKS

Let us now consider another element of American-style federalism show-cased in this book's general tour. State law at times interacts in a special way with the federal Constitution (big C) and the federal constitution (small c). Specifically, state laws form some of the building blocks of the federal governmental edifice. To a degree that might startle a non-expert, state laws can determine how the federal government is *constituted*.

We have just seen that in the nineteenth-century era of circuit-riding, states claimed informal seats on the US Supreme Court, and that this state-seat system is now largely a thing of the past. But even today, state law plays a large and formal role in constituting the federal executive branch, via the electoral college. It is this state-based system that determines who gets to be the federal president. What matters legally is not how many votes each presidential candidate gets in America as a whole, but where he or she gets these votes. Thus, everything turns on how many states a candidate wins, and on whether these states add up to the necessary 270 electoral votes. And if no one gets to this magic number, the Constitution provides that the House of Representatives will decide, with each state, qua state, casting one vote, regardless of that state's population, in an almost perfect echo of the old state-centered Articles of Confederation, in which each state voted as a unit—one state, one vote.

My Florida chapter on *Bush v. Gore* tries to drive home one clear implication of this idea that states can function as building blocks of the federal edifice: the national 2000 presidential contest, coming down as it did to the verdict of the Sunshine State, should have been decided—at least on certain issues of ordinary election jurisprudence—by Florida law, as construed by Florida courts. The mere fact that Florida law was obviously deciding a national presidential election was no good excuse for the national Supreme Court to do what it did, namely, muscle aside the Florida judiciary from its proper role as the final arbiter of the meaning of Florida election law. Exemplifying the idea of state laws as federal building blocks, the federal

Constitution's Article II vested the Florida state legislature with the power to make key decisions about how Florida presidential elections were to be conducted; and the Florida legislature, in turn—long before Election Day 2000—deputized the Florida judiciary, and not the US Supremes, to interpret and implement the Florida legislature's complex state-law matrix of election rules. To get to the bottom of *Bush v. Gore*, my Florida chapter thus drills down deep into state law as construed by state courts.

While not going so deeply into the details of state law, the two subsequent chapters—on Ohio and Texas—do explore other aspects of the electoral college and presidential-selection process through a state-centered lens, a lens that I find particularly apt given that these two states are, like Florida, especially big parts of the federal presidential-selection process.

Modern-day Republican and Democratic presidential candidates do not compete furiously to win the Upper South or the Ohio Valley as such. Rather, presidential candidates go all out to win Virginia and Ohio as distinct states. In our politically polarized world, many states at the presidential level are deeply red or deeply blue; there are not many truly purple presidential states left, if we define a purple state as one whose presidential race is decided by less than 5 percentage points. Virginia and Ohio were in fact two of only four truly purple states in the 2012 presidential election. (The third and fourth all-important purple states in 2012 were North Carolina and, of course, Florida.)

Likewise, the presidential election game in early America was to win the big swing state of Virginia; and thus most early presidents were in fact not merely Upper South southerners, but Virginians in particular. As America's electoral center of gravity moved north and west over the ensuing decades, Ohio became the big swing state to win, and in the years after the Civil War, many successful presidential candidates had specific and formal ties to Ohio as such, and not merely the Midwest more generally. This is the general backdrop of the tale I tried to tell in my Buckeye State chapter. As the twentieth century wore on and the twenty-first century dawned, and as the American population spread further west and south, California and Texas became key prizes. Hence my determination, when I decided to write about Texas, to focus on issues connected to presidential selection and succession.

Although my California chapter profiles a California justice rather than analyzing the state's role in modern presidential politics, it is worth noting that California's Anthony Kennedy was named to the Court by a former California governor-turned-president, Ronald Reagan; and that Justice Kennedy in his more liberal moments, including the moments highlighted in my chapter, bears some resemblance to an earlier California justice: Earl Warren, who himself came quite close to winning the vice presidency in the electoral college contest of 1948.

As for Texas, the states-as-building-blocks perspective casts strong light on the past century of presidential law and politics. In the 1930s, the Lone Star State was a cornerstone of FDR's New Deal coalition. Not for nothing was his first vice president John Nance Garner—a south Texan nicknamed "Cactus Jack." Aiming to keep FDR's still-powerful coalition intact in 1960, JFK brought LBJ onto the ticket to carry Texas. Kennedy himself was in Dallas in November 1963 to mend political fences in Texas in preparation for his planned 1964 reelection bid, which was, tragically, not to be. Enter LBJ, a Texan whose crucial support for the 1964 Civil Rights Act and the 1965 Voting Rights Act shattered the New Deal coalition.

In the ensuing national political realignment, Texas has generally eluded the grasp of Democratic presidential candidates. Jimmy Carter, a southern Democrat, did eke out a narrow victory in Texas in 1976, but he lost the state by a staggering 14 points to Ronald Reagan four years later. Since then, no Democrat has won Texas's electoral votes. When Michael Dukakis and Lloyd Bentsen in 1988 tried to re-create the Boston-Austin magic of 1960, they lost Bentsen's home state of Texas by 13 points. In six of the last nine presidential elections, Republicans have nominated a Texan for president or vice president—or both, if we see Dick Cheney as being a Texan of sorts, despite his return to Wyoming right before the 2000 election. The GOP won five of these six elections with Republican Texans on the ticket, but in all three elections without Republican Texans on the ballot, the GOP lost. Democrats can no longer count on Texas, so the party of FDR, JFK, and LBJ must offset this loss by focusing all the more intently on Ohio and Florida. (Again, these two states!)

To not understand all this—to misperceive America's presidential selection process as more national and less state-based than it truly is, and to overlook the key constitutional fact that states remain basic legal and political building blocks in presidential races—is to miss much of the real process of presidential selection in the modern era. Hence my invitation in this book to think about states in general—and about the key states of Florida, Ohio, and Texas in particular—in pondering various issues related to presidential selection and succession.

My imagined Cruz–Bush 2016 tag-team was admittedly whimsical—designed merely to illustrate various political maneuvers and strategies that the Twenty-fifth Amendment makes possible. But here is a less whimsical handicapping of the 2016 presidential race using the ideas and framework of the preceding pages:

On the Republican side, Jeb Bush, Ted Cruz, Rand Paul, and Rick Perry all have strong Texas ties—a plus for any Republican—and Bush is of course also the former governor of Florida. (Bush was born and raised in Texas and went to college in Texas; Cruz is a senator from Texas; Paul was raised in Texas, and his father, who ran repeatedly for president, was a long-serving member of Congress from Texas; and Rick Perry was the governor of the Lone Star State for more than a dozen years.) Bush also has important northeastern credentials as the scion of a prominent Yale family and an alum of a prestigious New England prep school (Phillips Andover). Cruz, too, boasts impressive Ivy League and northeastern educational credentials as a graduate of both Princeton and Harvard Law School. But Cruz's brooding personality is very far from the sunny western openness epitomized by Ronald Reagan and Earl Warren. (Shades of Richard Nixon, perhaps?) Rick Perry is emphatically not an Ivy League graduate, and over the years, he has said truly stupid things about secession. Though this know-nothing rhetoric may play well in some small southern circles, it is a genuine embarrassment on a national stage. (Recall that all America is, in profound ways, the land of Lincoln.)

As for other Republicans: Rob Portman is a senator from the all-important bellwether state of Ohio, and he is a graduate of a New England Ivy League School (Dartmouth) to boot. He has backed gay marriage, putting him closer to the emerging American consensus than are many other leading members of the GOP, including Ohio's governor, John Kasich. Marco Rubio is a senator from another large bellwether state, Florida. Though his ethnic success story is broadly similar to Obama's, he lacks Obama's notable northeastern educational achievements. (Obama graduated with top grades from Columbia College and Harvard Law School. In these respects, the Republican presidential wannabe who most resembles him is the Indian American governor of Louisiana, Bobby Jindal, a Rhodes Scholar graduate of Brown University.) Chris Christie, Sarah Palin, Mike Pence, Paul Ryan, Scott Walker, and many other Republican aspirants have no special ties to Ohio, Florida, or Texas, or to the Ivy League schools that play an outsized role in producing America's leadership class; were any of them to prevail, this would be something new under the sun.

On the Democratic side, Hillary Clinton likewise lacks special ties to the key states of Ohio, Florida, and Texas. Nevertheless, she is a genuine regional triple-threat, having grown up in the Midwest, served as the First Lady of a southern state, and later represented a northeastern state in the US Senate. She also has impeccable northeastern educational credentials (Wellesley, Yale Law), and she has spent more political time in more states than just about anyone alive. And, of course, she is the living embodiment of the robust Nineteenth Amendment vision I tried to elaborate in my Wyoming chapter.

In some respects, Hillary Clinton is reminiscent of Mitt Romney, who was born in the Midwest, has strong ties to the West, and served as a northeastern governor; and who also has sterling Ivy League credentials; and has also spent an enormous amount of political time in many distinct states. Both are from political families: she is a political wife and he is a political son. However, one of Romney's biggest problems is that his party is based in the South, and he lacks strong southern connections and sensibilities. Clinton does not share any comparable geographic weakness. Though she herself has never lived on the Pacific Coast—a Democratic stronghold—her only child, who promises to be a strong force in the campaign, was educated at Stanford; and as president, her husband visited California more than seventy times.

A brief aside on my perhaps off-putting emphasis on fancy educational credentials in the foregoing analysis: Beginning with Theodore Roosevelt, ten of our most recent nineteen presidents attended Harvard, Yale, Princeton, or Columbia for college or graduate study or both. Five others attended other academic powerhouses—Amherst, Stanford, West Point, Duke, and the Naval Academy—and one of these five (Eisenhower) also served as president of Columbia University. (Before Ike, Woodrow Wilson, a Princeton graduate, had served as Princeton's president.) In a whopping twenty of the last twenty-eight presidential elections (beginning with Teddy Roosevelt in 1904), one or both of the major-party candidates for the presidency had a degree from one or more of these four schools.[1]

In recent years, the presidentially rich schools, like the judicially rich schools, have gotten even richer, as is evident if we narrow our focus to the two leadership factories highlighted in several of my chapters. Each of our four most recent presidents attended Harvard or Yale or both, as did five of the seven most recent runners up (Michael Dukakis, George H. W. Bush, Al Gore, John Kerry, and Mitt Romney). The last time Americans voted for president without a Harvard or Yale graduate on the ballot as a major-party presidential candidate was 1984. If we include vice presidential candidates in our tally, we have to go all the way back to 1968 to find a year when none of the top four candidates went to one of these two schools. (Although the victor in 1968, Richard Nixon, had won admission to Harvard as a young man, family financial concerns had obliged him to turn Harvard down and study elsewhere.)[2]

IF TODAY'S STATES REMAIN hugely important *presidential* building blocks, even though they no longer serve as comparably significant building blocks in the *Supreme Court* selection process, what about the constitution (small c) of *Congress*? Are today's states important building blocks in the process of selecting federal legislators?

If you blinked, you may have missed it, but this book does address this question, in the middle of my Alabama chapter on Hugo Black. Recall that before Black joined the Court, state delegations to the House of Representatives were often grossly malapportioned, pursuant to state law. Pre-Black, each state legislature was seen as having wide authority, under the federal Constitution's Article I, section 4, to apportion that state's congressional districts as it saw fit, unless Congress by law said otherwise.* And Congress, chosen as it was in malapportioned ways by many states, never said otherwise, and never did anything to stop malapportionment within state legislatures themselves. Each hand, Congress and state legislatures, washed the other.

Hugo Black smashed this state-building-block system of House apportionment—first by dissenting in the 1946 case of *Colegrove v. Green*, where he read the Constitution to require that each House district within a given state be of equal size; next by authoring the Court's 1964 majority opinion in *Wesberry v. Sanders*, which turned his *Colegrove* dissent into enduring Court doctrine; and then, a few months later, by joining the Court's opinion in *Reynolds v. Sims*, which built on *Wesberry* and ended malapportionment within state legislatures themselves. Here, in microcosm, we glimpse the significance of Black to modern constitutional law.

---

* The relevant constitutional language reads as follows: "The Times, Places, and Manner of holding Elections for Senators and Representatives, shall be prescribed in each State by the Legislature thereof; but the Congress may at any time by Law make or alter such Regulations, except as to the Places of chusing Senators."

Black's most important constitutional legacy—the centerpiece of my chapter on him—can also be seen as closely related to the idea of the states as building blocks. Black's big idea of incorporating the Bill of Rights against states made sense for many reasons, not the least of which is the fact that virtually all the rights in the federal Bill also appear in most state constitutions, which in 1789 were themselves building blocks of sorts for the federal Bill itself. Much as James Madison and his fellow delegates at Philadelphia in 1787 had canvassed state constitutions and borrowed the best features of these state documents in drafting their proposed federal Constitution, so Madison and his fellow congressmen in 1789 combed through state bills of rights in composing their proposed federal Bill.

My Massachusetts chapter showcases one particularly notable example. Because the search-and-seizure clause of the 1780 Massachusetts state constitution was an obvious precursor of the federal Fourth Amendment, a careful examination of this particular state building block can deepen our understanding of its federal counterpart. Here, too, we must drill down deep into state law to get to the bottom of an issue that at first might seem wholly federal.

Also, when we look into the details of the Bill of Rights, we at times discover yet another type of state building block, as I elaborate in my New Jersey chapter. State law at times defines who has property rights against the federal government under the federal Fifth Amendment, who has reasonable expectations of privacy against the feds under the Fourth Amendment, and so on. Various amendments might have more bite against the feds in State A or City B, which have robust property and privacy laws and ordinances, than in State C or City D, which have more lax state and local protections. Thus we have specific confirmation in this chapter of one of this book's general themes: despite surface appearances of perfect national uniformity, our federal Constitution does vary slightly from place to place and state to state.

LOCAL, STATE, AND REGIONAL IDENTITY

States are geographic locations, and states are legal and political building blocks for federal institutions and ideas. These are two of the main themes of the preceding chapters. A final theme tying these chapters together involves cities, states, and regions as shapers of their inhabitants' identities—their self-understandings, their affiliations and attachments, their commitments, and the ways these inhabitants are perceived by others.

One key thing to understand about Alabama, I submit, is that it is part of the Deep South. The point is not merely a claim about brute topography and pre-political geography. Alabama in my narrative has more in common with Virginia and Texas than with Kentucky, even though Kentucky is closer as the crow flies. But Lincoln's birth-state of Kentucky did not secede in 1860–1861, whereas these other states did; and these facts matter hugely in American law, memory, and culture. On this view, Hugo Black grew up not merely in Alabama, but in the former Confederacy, and this basic fact shaped his understanding of his own identity as well as others' perceptions of him; smug Yankees underestimated him, and continue to underestimate him, because he came from the southland. My Alabama chapter is thus less about Alabama as such and more about the region of the Deep South generally.

My Wyoming chapter on the Second Amendment is likewise a regional meditation. Although I do draw attention to Wyoming in particular as both the Cowboy State and the Equality State, I also call attention to the wider regional culture, history, and identity of the Rocky Mountain West and note the early woman suffrage experiences of Wyoming's neighboring mountain states of Colorado, Idaho, and Utah.

Readers seeking detailed state-specific observations about Kansas and Iowa may feel disappointed, for in truth, I offer only a few such nuggets in my chapters on these states. As I note in my opening paragraphs of the Kansas chapter, the issues of educational segregation in *Brown v. Board* were hardly unique to Topeka; and as I note in my closing passages of that chapter, Kansas is not the only state that remains hostile to same-sex marriage. Similarly, facts akin to those in *Tinker* could have arisen in many states other than Iowa.

But the Court's ruling in *Brown* did put Topeka front and center; and *Tinker* did arise in Des Moines. These are mere contingent facts—but what would history be without contingency? Had Lincoln never been born, perhaps there would be no United States today. As history actually happened, however, Lincoln *was* born, and he *did* save the Union, and these contingent facts have profoundly shaped America's memory and identity.

So, too, with *Brown* and *Tinker*, which have profoundly influenced the culture, the memories, and the identities of local residents. Whoever visits

Topeka cannot but be impressed by how its residents have organized important public spaces to commemorate the Court's ruling. Similarly, the good people of Des Moines self-consciously help keep the memory of the *Tinker* case alive in ways that the good people of, say, Duluth do not. My Iowa chapter was, in fact, prompted by a Des Moines–based conference specifically organized to celebrate a major anniversary of *Tinker*.

Thus we return yet again to a basic claim of this book: America's Constitution looks slightly different in each of the cities, states, and regions that make up this great land.

EVEN AS AMERICA'S CITIES, states, and regions vary, they also unite to form one nation, one constitutional system. Lincoln, of course, grasped this great truth, as did the Founders before him. Writing as "Publius" in *The Federalist* No. 11—the same essay in which he stressed the need for a "strict and indissoluble union"—Alexander Hamilton elaborated the comparative advantages of different regions for building a strong American navy. The South, Hamilton observed, could produce abundant timber and pitch; the Mid-Atlantic had superior iron; and seamen would be drawn chiefly from "the Northern hive."

In today's America, the regions continue to complement each other in fascinating ways. Whereas the South furnishes more than its fair share of America's volunteer warriors, I have suggested in this book that northeastern Ivy League schools play an outsized role in training justices (and presidents, for that matter); and that Ohio, Florida, Texas, and California have been particularly important to the modern presidency. The Warren Court was a strong alloy of Earl Warren from the West, Hugo Black from the South, and William Brennan from the Northeast. Today's regime of rights protection is likewise the joint product of our different regions. The key text, the Fourteenth Amendment, was generated by men from the Old Northwest allied with the likes of Abe Lincoln and John Bingham; was later reclaimed and redeemed by a deep southerner, Hugo Black; and is now kept fresh by a sunny westerner, Anthony Kennedy, on a Court where almost everyone was schooled in the Northeast.

To see the big picture from another angle: Our sacred Bill of Rights, though conceived in the 1700s in East Coast venues such as Massachusetts and New Jersey, was reborn, reglossed, and reshaped in the 1800s and 1900s by later sacred texts, such as the Fourteenth and Nineteenth Amendments, which were in turn powerfully influenced by the experiences of western lands such as Illinois, Kansas, Iowa, and Wyoming. Modern

America's Constitution is thus the child of multiple centuries, multiple branches and levels of government, and multiple regions. *E pluribus unum.*

HAVE CONSTITUTION, WILL TRAVEL

The Law of the Land: A Grand Tour of Our Constitutional Republic is the third book in a still-unfolding series. Each book in this series aims to give general readers a panoramic perspective on the American constitutional project, but each does so along a different axis. The first book, *America's Constitution: A Biography* (2005) was organized *textually*—walking the reader through the written Constitution in textual order, article by article and amendment by amendment. The next book, *America's Unwritten Constitution: The Precedents and Principles We Live By* (2012), was organized by *interpretive method*. Each chapter offered a different interpretive tool or technique for going beneath, behind, or beyond the Constitution's written words while still harmonizing with the terse text. The current volume has been organized *geographically*, state by state, for the reasons just explained. I hope soon to begin work on the next panoramic book in this series, *Twelve Score: America's Constitutional Conversation, 1761–2000*, which will be organized *chronologically*, offering readers a detailed account of America's constitutional discourse decade by decade, both in and out of court, from the Revolution to the Reagan era. After that book, who knows? I have a few half-baked ideas, but nothing definite.

Oh, and I haven't given up on the idea of writing more state-based stories about places that I have yet to visit and study, if there is any local interest. In particular, if there is anyone out there who would like to invite me to spend some time in Hawaii, please let me know! I'm pretty sure I could figure out something to write about the Aloha State's special relationship to American constitutionalism. And did I mention that my wife and kids have been begging to see Mauna Loa?

ACKNOWLEDGMENTS

This book has been nearly two decades in the making. I conceived the animating idea—a series of constitutional-law chapters highlighting special persons, cases, principles, and events closely associated with the various and distinct states and regions—in the late 1990s. But only recently was I able to complete my envisioned constitutional tour in proper fashion. Among other things, I always wanted to have America's four most populous states—California, Texas, Florida, and New York—represented in the book. I am thus particularly grateful to my dear friends and sometime co-teachers Ken Starr and Philip Bobbitt for recently inviting me to spend time not just in Texas, but in that part of Texas where the South meets the West. (My detailed reasons for wanting to journey to and think about this precise spot are made clear in the Texas chapter itself.) I also owe thanks to Bruce Ackerman, Vik Amar, Hadley Arkes, Richard Aynes, Ian Ayres, Jack Balkin, Aharon Barak, Randy Barnett, John Barrett, Will Baude, Emily Bazelon, Les Benedict, David Bernstein, Charles Black, Jon Blue, Philip Bobbitt (again), Todd Brewster, Rick Brookhiser, Jennifer Brown, Guido Calabresi, Steve Calabresi, Linc Caplan, Steve Carter, Josh Chafetz, Dan Coenen, Mike Cocnen, Stephen Colbert, David Currie, Michael Kent Curtis, Walter Dellinger, Alan Dershowitz, Neal Devins, John Dinan, Justin Driver, Chris Eisgruber, John Ely, Bill Eskridge, Richard Fallon, Dan Farber, Noah Feldman, Paul Finkelman, Owen Fiss, Stanley Flink, Eric Foner, James Forman, Joanne Freeman, Barry Friedman, Josh Geltzer, Mike Gerhardt, Heather Gerken, Paul Gewirtz, Abbe Gluck, Joe Goldstein, Jamal Green, Linda Greenhouse, Dale Gregory, Henry Hansmann, Gary Hart, Oona Hathaway, Rick Hills, Peter Jennings, Paul Johnson, Neal Katyal, Doug Kendall, Randy Kennedy, Orin Kerr, Alexander Keyssar, Mike Klarman, Doug Kmiec, Harold Koh, Andy Koppelman, John Langbein, Ed Larson, Kurt Lash, Sandy Levinson, Eric Liu, Chip Lupu, Gerard Magliocca, Pauline Maier, John Manning, Burke Marshall, Jerry Mashaw, David Mayhew, Michael McConnell, David McCullough, John McGinnis, Tracey Meares, Michael Medved, Chris Michel, Edmund Morgan, Trevor Morrison, Victoria Nourse, Jim Oakes, Norm Ornstein, Vinita Parkash, Nick Parrillo, Mike Paulsen, Robert Post, Scot Powe, Sai Prakash, Richard Primus, Bob Pushaw, Jack Rakove, Mike Rappaport, Diane Rehm, Charles Reich, Judith

Resnik, Aniko Richheimer, Kim Roosevelt, Charlie Rose, Jeff Rosen, Nick Rosenkranz, Jed Rubenfeld, Steve Sachs, Larry Sager, Adam Samaha, Tom Schmidt, Peter Schuck, Jon Siegel, Neil Siegel, Reva Siegel, Jim Simon, David Sklansky, Stephen Skowronek, Rogers Smith, Ken Starr (again), Kate Stith, Geoff Stone, David Strauss, Nadine Strossen, Bill Stuntz, Jake Sullivan, Kathleen Sullivan, Cass Sunstein, Steve Susman, Alan Tarr, Jeff Toobin, Nina Totenberg, Larry Tribe, Mark Tushnet, Adrian Vermeule, Eugene Volokh, Bruce Wessel, William Wiecek, George Will, Owen Williams, Garry Wills, Adam Winkler, John Fabian Witt, Evan Wolfson, Gordon Wood, Lindsey Ohlsson Worth, Ron Wright, and John Yoo for writings and conversations that stimulated many of the ideas in this book, large and small. Professor Steve Calabresi's many and subtle ideas about American federalism and regionalism have exerted a particularly profound influence on my thinking.

Several of the chapters in this book began as endowed lectures delivered in various university settings. When one is invited to deliver such a lecture, it is often customary to publish a version of the lecture—sometimes the entirety of the lecture as delivered, sometimes an abridged version—in the host-school's law journal to memorialize the event. Early versions of chapters 1–2, 4–8, and 10–12 thus appeared in the following venues: *U. of Illinois LR* (2001): 1109; *Alabama LR* 53 (2002): 1221; *Pacific LR* 28 (1997): 515; *Washburn LJ* 40 (2000): 1; *Drake LR* 48 (2000): 507; *Florida LR* 61 (2009): 945; *U. of Cincinnati LR* 67 (1999): 375; *Utah LR* (2001): 889; *Suffolk U. LR* 30 (1996): 53; *Rutgers LJ* 27 (1996): 845. All of these early versions have been very substantially revised in connection with this book.

And speaking of revisions . . . I owe an enormous debt to my wise literary agents, Glen Hartley and Lynn Chu, and to my incomparably brilliant editors, Lara Heimert and Dan Gerstle, for their great suggestions about how to put this book together in the right way. Special thanks also to several special friends—Sundeep Iyer, Jaclyn Delligatti, Nick Crown, Bradley Silverman, Kathy Streckfus, and Meng Jia Yang—for their astute editorial assistance in the final stages of this project. Professor Ed Larson also provided superb suggestions for my final rewrite. As his many prize-winning books attest, he sure knows how to write, and I am especially grateful to him for sharing with me his many authorial insights, large and small.

My fondness for road trips and my interest in local color began in childhood, thanks to my parents, who organized countless interstate family travel adventures for me and my sibs. I also recall with great affection my childhood scoutmaster, Kenneth Harmon, Sr., who made me a part of his family, and one year took us all on a summer road trip from the San Francisco Bay Area to the Rocky Mountains and back. My Rocky Mountain lecture, as originally delivered, was dedicated to Mr. Harmon—"for all that he taught me about guns, and about life."

In the spirit of paying things forward, I am now trying to drag my own spouse and kids all across the country. Sometimes they have even enjoyed it. Or at least, so I have convinced myself—aided, perhaps, by memory's selective fog. In any event, I hope they will remember the places we saw and the things we did.

APPENDIX:

THE CONSTITUTION OF

THE UNITED STATES

WE THE PEOPLE of the United States, in Order to form a more perfect Union, establish Justice, insure domestic Tranquility, provide for the common defence, promote the general Welfare, and secure the Blessings of Liberty to ourselves and our Posterity, do ordain and establish this Constitution for the United States of America.

ARTICLE I.

SECTION 1. All legislative Powers herein granted shall be vested in a Congress of the United States, which shall consist of a Senate and House of Representatives.

SECTION 2. The House of Representatives shall be composed of Members chosen every second Year by the People of the several States, and the Electors in each State shall have the Qualifications requisite for Electors of the most numerous Branch of the State Legislature.

No Person shall be a Representative who shall not have attained to the Age of twenty five Years, and been seven Years a Citizen of the United States, and who shall not, when elected, be an Inhabitant of that State in which he shall be chosen.

Representatives and direct Taxes shall be apportioned among the several States which may be included within this Union, according to their respective Numbers, which shall be determined by adding to the whole Number of free Persons, including those bound to Service for a Term of Years, and excluding Indians not taxed, three fifths of all other Persons. The actual Enumeration shall be made within three Years after the first Meeting of the Congress of the United States, and within every subsequent Term of ten Years, in such Manner as they shall by Law direct. The Number of Representatives shall not exceed one for every thirty Thousand, but each State shall have at Least one Representative; and until such enumeration shall be made, the State of

New Hampshire shall be entitled to chuse three, Massachusetts eight, Rhode-Island and Providence Plantations one, Connecticut five, New-York six, New Jersey four, Pennsylvania eight, Delaware one, Maryland six, Virginia ten, North Carolina five, South Carolina five, and Georgia three.

When vacancies happen in the Representation from any State, the Executive Authority thereof shall issue Writs of Election to fill such Vacancies.

The House of Representatives shall chuse their Speaker and other Officers; and shall have the sole Power of Impeachment.

SECTION 3. The Senate of the United States shall be composed of two Senators from each State, chosen by the Legislature thereof, for six Years; and each Senator shall have one Vote.

Immediately after they shall be assembled in Consequence of the first Election, they shall be divided as equally as may be into three Classes. The Seats of the Senators of the first Class shall be vacated at the Expiration of the second Year, of the second Class at the Expiration of the fourth Year, and of the third Class at the Expiration of the sixth Year, so that one third may be chosen every second Year; and if Vacancies happen by Resignation, or otherwise, during the Recess of the Legislature of any State, the Executive thereof may make temporary Appointments until the next Meeting of the Legislature, which shall then fill such Vacancies.

No Person shall be a Senator who shall not have attained to the Age of thirty Years, and been nine Years a Citizen of the United States, and who shall not, when elected, be an inhabitant of that State for which he shall be chosen.

The Vice President of the United States shall be President of the Senate, but shall have no Vote, unless they be equally divided.

The Senate shall chuse their other Officers, and also a President pro tempore, in the Absence of the Vice President, or when he shall exercise the Office of President of the United States.

The Senate shall have the sole Power to try all Impeachments. When sitting for that Purpose, they shall be on Oath or Affirmation. When the President of the United States is tried, the Chief Justice shall preside: And no Person shall be convicted without the Concurrence of two thirds of the Members present.

Judgment in Cases of Impeachment shall not extend further than to removal from Office, and disqualification to hold and enjoy any Office of honor, Trust or Profit under the United States: but the Party convicted shall nevertheless be liable and subject to Indictment, Trial, Judgment and Punishment, according to Law.

SECTION 4. The Times, Places and Manner of holding Elections for Senators and Representatives, shall be prescribed in each State by the Legislature thereof; but the Congress may at any time by Law make or alter such Regulations, except as to the Places of chusing Senators.

The Congress shall assemble at least once in every Year, and such Meeting shall be on the first Monday in December, unless they shall by Law appoint a different Day.

SECTION 5. Each House shall be the Judge of the Elections, Returns and Qualifications of its own Members, and a Majority of each shall constitute a Quorum to do Business; but a smaller Number may adjourn from day to day, and may be authorized to compel the Attendance of absent Members, in such Manner, and under such Penalties as each House may provide.

Each House may determine the Rules of its Proceedings, punish its Members for disorderly Behaviour, and, with the Concurrence of two thirds, expel a Member.

Each House shall keep a Journal of its Proceedings, and from time to time publish the same, excepting such Parts as may in their Judgment require Secrecy; and the Yeas and Nays of the Members of either House on any question shall, at the Desire of one fifth of those Present, be entered on the Journal.

Neither House, during the Session of Congress, shall, without the Concent of the other, adjourn for more than three days, nor to any other Place than that in which the two Houses shall be sitting.

SECTION 6. The Senators and Representatives shall receive a Compensation for their Services, to be ascertained by Law, and paid out of the Treasury of the United States. They shall in all Cases, except Treason, Felony and Breach of the Peace, be privileged from Arrest during their Attendance at the Session of their respective Houses, and in going to and returning from the same; and for any Speech or Debate in either House, they shall not be questioned in any other Place.

No Senator or Representative shall, during the Time for which he was elected, be appointed to any civil Office under the Authority of the United States, which shall have been created, or the Emoluments whereof shall have been encreased during such time; and no Person holding any Office under the United States, shall be a Member of either House during his Continuance in Office.

SECTION 7. All Bills for raising Revenue shall originate in the House of Representatives; but the Senate may propose or concur with Amendments as on other Bills.

Every Bill which shall have passed the House of Representatives and the Senate, shall, before it become a Law, be presented to the President of the United States; If he approve he shall sign it, but if not he shall return it, with his Objections to that House in which it shall have originated, who shall enter the Objections at large on their Journal, and proceed to reconsider it. If after such Reconsideration two thirds of that House shall agree to pass the Bill, it shall be sent, together with the Objections, to the other House, by which it shall likewise be reconsidered, and if approved by two thirds of that House, it shall become a Law. But in all such Cases the Votes of both Houses shall be determined by yeas and Nays, and the Names of the Persons voting for and against the Bill shall be entered on the Journal of each House respectively. If any Bill shall not be returned by the President within ten Days (Sundays excepted) after it shall have been presented to him, the Same shall be a Law, in like Manner as if he had signed it, unless the Congress by their Adjournment prevent its Return, in which Case it shall not be a Law.

Every Order, Resolution, or Vote to which the Concurrence of the Senate and House of Representatives may be necessary (except on a question of Adjournment) shall be presented to the President of the United States; and before the Same shall take Effect, shall be approved by him, or being disapproved by him, shall be repassed by two thirds of the Senate and House of Representatives, according to the Rules and Limitations prescribed in the Case of a Bill.

SECTION 8. The Congress shall have Power To lay and collect Taxes, Duties, Imposts and Excises, to pay the Debts and Provide for the common Defence and general Welfare of the United States; but all Duties, Imposts and Excises shall be uniform throughout the United States;

To borrow Money on the credit of the United States;

To regulate Commerce with foreign Nations, and among the several States, and with the Indian Tribes;

To establish an uniform Rule of Naturalization, and uniform Laws on the subject of Bankruptcies throughout the United States;

To coin Money, regulate the Value thereof, and of foreign Coin, and fix the Standard of Weights and Measures;

To provide for the Punishment of counterfeiting the Securities and current Coin of the United States;

To establish Post Offices and post Roads;

To promote the Progress of Science and useful Arts, by securing for limited Time to Authors and Inventors the exclusive Right to their respective Writings and Discoveries;

To constitute Tribunals inferior to the supreme Court;

To define and punish Piracies and Felonies committed on the high Seas, and Offences against the Law of Nations;

To declare War, grant Letters of Marque and Reprisal, and make Rules concerning Captures on Land and Water;

To raise and support Armies, but no Appropriation of Money to that Use shall be for a longer Term than two Years;

To provide and maintain a Navy;

To make Rules for the Government and Regulation of the land and naval Forces;

To provide for calling forth the Militia to execute the Laws of the Union, suppress Insurrections and repel Invasions;

To provide for organizing, arming, and disciplining, the Militia, and for governing such Part of them as may be employed in the Service of the United States, reserving to the States respectively, the Appointment of the Officers, and the Authority of training the Militia according to the discipline prescribed by Congress;

To exercise exclusive Legislation in all Cases whatsoever, over such District (not exceeding ten Miles square) as may, by Cession of Particular States, and the Acceptance of Congress, become the Seat of the Government of the United States, and to exercise like Authority over all Places purchased by the Consent of the Legislature of the State in which the Same shall be, for the Erection of Forts, Magazines, Arsenals, dock-Yards, and other needful Buildings;—And

To make all Laws which shall be necessary and proper for carrying into Execution the foregoing Powers, and all other Powers vested by this Constitution in the Government of the United States, or in any Department or Officer thereof.

SECTION 9. The Migration or Importation of such Persons as any of the States now existing shall think proper to admit, shall not be prohibited by the Congress prior to the Year one thousand eight hundred and eight, but a Tax or duty may be imposed on such Importation, not exceeding ten dollars for each Person.

The Privilege of the Writ of Habeas Corpus shall not be suspended, unless when in Cases of Rebellion or Invasion the public Safety may require it.

No Bill of Attainder or ex post facto Law shall be passed.

No Capitation, or other direct, Tax shall be laid, unless in Proportion to the Census or Enumeration herein before directed to be taken.

No Tax or Duty shall be laid on Articles exported from any State.

No Preference shall be given by any Regulation of Commerce or Revenue to the Ports of one State over those of another: nor shall Vessels bound to, or from, one State, be obliged to enter, clear, or pay Duties in another.

No Money shall be drawn from the Treasury, but in Consequence of Appropriations made by Law; and a regular Statement and Account of the Receipts and Expenditures of all public Money shall be published from time to time.

No Title of Nobility shall be granted by the United States: And no Person holding any Office of Profit or Trust under them, shall, without the Consent of the Congress, accept of any present, Emolument, Office, or Title, of any kind whatever, from any King, Prince, or foreign State.

SECTION 10. No State shall enter into any Treaty, Alliance, or Confederation; grant Letters of Marque and Reprisal; coin Money; emit Bills of Credit; make any Thing but gold and silver Coin a Tender in Payment of Debts; pass any Bill of Attainder, ex post facto Law, or Law impairing the Obligation of Contracts, or grant any Title of Nobility.

No State shall, without the Consent of the Congress, lay any Imposts or Duties on Imports or Exports, except what may be absolutely necessary for executing it's inspection Laws: and the net Produce of all Duties and Imposts, laid by any State on Imports or Exports, shall be for the Use of the Treasury of the United States; and all such Laws shall be subject to the Revision and Controul of the Congress.

No State shall, without the Consent of Congress, lay any Duty of Tonnage, keep Troops, or Ships of War in time of Peace, enter into any Agreement or Compact with another State, or with a foreign Power, or engage in War, unless actually invaded, or in such imminent Danger as will not admit of delay.

ARTICLE II.

SECTION 1. The executive Power shall be vested in a President of the United States of America. He shall hold his Office during the Term of four Years, and, together with the Vice President, chosen for the same Term, be elected, as follows.

Each State shall appoint, in such Manner as the Legislature thereof may direct, a Number of Electors, equal to the whole Number of Senators and Representatives to which the State may be entitled in the Congress: but no

Senator or Representative, or Person holding an Office of Trust or Profit under the United States, shall be appointed an Elector.

The Electors shall meet in their respective States, and vote by Ballot for two Persons, of whom one at least shall not be an Inhabitant of the same State with themselves. And they shall make a List of all the Persons voted for, and of the Number of Votes for each; which List they shall sign and certify, and transmit sealed to the Seat of the Government of the United States, directed to the President of the Senate. The President of the Senate shall, in the Presence of the Senate and House of Representatives, open all the Certificates, and the Votes shall then be counted. The Person having the greatest Number of Votes shall be the President, if such Number be a Majority of the whole Number of Electors appointed; and if there be more than one who have such Majority, and have an equal Number of Votes, then the House of Representatives shall immediately chuse by Ballot one of them for President; and if no Person have a Majority, then from the five highest on the List the said House shall in like Manner chuse the President. But in chusing the President, the Votes shall be taken by States, the Representation from each State having one Vote; A quorum for this Purpose shall consist of a Member or Members from two thirds of the States, and a Majority of all the States shall be necessary to a Choice. In every Case, after the Choice of the President, the Person having the greatest Number of Votes of the Electors shall be the Vice President. But if there should remain two or more who have equal Votes, the Senate shall chuse from them by Ballot the Vice President.

The Congress may determine the Time of chusing the Electors, and the Day on which they shall give their Votes; which Day shall be the same throughout the United States.

No Person except a natural born Citizen, or a Citizen of the United States, at the time of the Adoption of this Constitution, shall be eligible to the Office of President; neither shall any Person be eligible to that Office who shall not have attained to the Age of thirty five Years, and been fourteen Years a Resident within the United States.

In Case of the Removal of the President from Office, or of his Death, Resignation, or Inability to discharge the Powers and Duties of the said Office, the Same shall devolve on the Vice President, and the Congress may by Law provide for the Case of Removal, Death, Resignation or Inability, both of the President and Vice President, declaring what Officer shall then act as President, and such Officer shall act accordingly, until the Disability be removed, or a President shall be elected.

The President shall, at stated Times, receive for his Services, a Compensation, which shall neither be encreased nor diminished during the Period for which he shall have been elected, and he shall not receive within that Period any other Emolument from the United States, or any of them.

Before he enter on the Execution of his Office, he shall take the following Oath or Affirmation:—"I do solemnly swear (or affirm) that I will faithfully execute the Office of President of the United States, and will to the best of my Ability, preserve, protect and defend the Constitution of the United States."

SECTION 2. The President shall be Commander in Chief of the Army and Navy of the United States, and of the Militia of the several States, when called into the actual Service of the United States; he may require the Opinion, in writing, of the principal Officer in each of the executive Departments, upon any Subject relating to the Duties of their respective Offices, and he shall have Power to grant Reprieves and Pardons for Offences against the United States, except in Cases of Impeachment.

He shall have Power, by and with the Advice and Consent of the Senate, to make Treaties, provided two thirds of the Senators present concur; and he shall nominate, and by and with the Advice and Consent of the Senate, shall appoint Ambassadors, other public Ministers and Consuls, Judges of the supreme Court, and all other Officers of the United States, whose Appointments are not herein otherwise provided for, and which shall be established by Law: but the Congress may by Law vest the Appointment of such inferior Officers, as they think proper, in the President alone, in the Courts of Law, or in the Heads of Departments.

The President shall have Power to fill up all Vacancies that may happen during the Recess of the Senate, by granting Commissions which shall expire at the End of their next Session.

SECTION 3. He shall from time to time give to the Congress Information of the State of the Union, and recommend to their Consideration such Measures as he shall judge necessary and expedient; he may, on extraordinary Occasions, convene both Houses, or either of them, and in Case of Disagreement between them, with Respect to the Time of Adjournment, he may adjourn them to such Time as he shall think proper; he shall receive Ambassadors and other public Ministers; he shall take Care that the Laws be faithfully executed, and shall Commission all the Officers of the United States.

SECTION 4. The President, Vice President and all civil Officers of the United States, shall be removed from Office on Impeachment for, and conviction of, Treason, Bribery, or other high Crimes and Misdemeanors.

ARTICLE III.

SECTION 1. The judicial Power of the United States, shall be vested in one supreme Court, and in such inferior Courts as the Congress may from time to time ordain and establish. The Judges, both of the supreme and inferior Courts, shall hold their Offices during good Behaviour, and shall, at stated Times, receive for their Services, a Compensation, which shall not be diminished during their Continuance in Office.

SECTION 2. The judicial Power shall extend to all Cases, in Law and Equity, arising under this Constitution, the Laws of the United States, and Treaties made, or which shall be made, under their Authority;—to all Cases affecting Ambassadors, other public Ministers and Consuls;—to all Cases of admiralty and maritime Jurisdiction;—to Controversies to which the United States shall be a Party;—to Controversies between two or more States;—between a State and Citizens of another State;—between Citizens of different States,—between Citizens of the same State claiming Lands under Grants of different States, and between a State, or the Citizens thereof, and foreign States, Citizens or Subjects.

In all Cases affecting Ambassadors, other public Ministers and Consuls, and those in which a State shall be Party, the supreme Court shall have original Jurisdiction. In all the other Cases before mentioned, the supreme Court shall have appellate Jurisdiction, both as to Law and Fact, with such Exceptions, and under such Regulations as the Congress shall make.

The Trial of all Crimes, except in Cases of Impeachment, shall be by Jury; and such Trial shall be held in the State where the said Crimes shall have been committed; but when not committed within any State, the Trial shall be at such Place or Places as the Congress may by Law have directed.

SECTION 3. Treason against the United States, shall consist only in levying War against them, or in adhering to their Enemies, giving them Aid and Comfort. No Person shall be convicted of Treason unless on the Testimony of two Witnesses to the same overt Act, or on Confession in open Court.

The Congress shall have Power to declare the Punishment of Treason, but no Attainder of Treason shall work Corruption of Blood, or Forfeiture except during the Life of the Person attainted.

ARTICLE IV.

SECTION 1. Full Faith and Credit shall be given in each State to the public Acts, Records, and judicial Proceedings of every other State. And the Congress may by general Laws prescribe the Manner in which such Acts, Records and Proceedings shall be proved, and the Effect thereof.

SECTION 2. The Citizens of each State shall be entitled to all Privileges and Immunities of Citizens in the several States.

A Person charged in any State with Treason, Felony, or other Crime, who shall flee from Justice, and be found in another State, shall on Demand of the executive Authority of the State from which he fled, be delivered up, to be removed to the State having Jurisdiction of the Crime.

No Person held to Service or Labour in one State, under the Laws thereof, escaping into another, shall, in Consequence of any Law or Regulation therein, be discharged from such Service or Labour, but shall be delivered up on Claim of the Party to whom such Service or Labour may be due.

SECTION 3. New States may be admitted by the Congress into this Union; but no new State shall be formed or erected within the Jurisdiction of any other State; nor any State be formed by the Junction of two or more States, or Parts of States, without the Consent of the Legislatures of the States concerned as well as of the Congress.

The Congress shall have Power to dispose of and make all needful Rules and Regulations respecting the Territory or other Property belonging to the United States; and nothing in this Constitution shall be so construed as to Prejudice any Claims of the United States, or of any particular State.

SECTION 4. The United States shall guarantee to every State in this Union a Republican Form of Government, and shall protect each of them against Invasion; and on Application of the Legislature, or of the Executive (when the Legislature cannot be convened) against domestic Violence.

ARTICLE V.

The Congress, whenever two thirds of both Houses shall deem it necessary, shall propose Amendments to this Constitution, or, on the Application of the Legislatures of two thirds of the several States, shall call a Convention for proposing Amendments, which, in either Case, shall be valid to all Intents and Purposes, as Part of this Constitution, when ratified by the Legislatures of three fourths of the several States, or by Conventions in three fourths thereof, as the one or the other Mode of Ratification may be proposed by the Congress; Provided that no Amendment which may be made prior to the Year One thousand eight hundred and eight shall in any

Manner affect the first and fourth Clauses in the Ninth Section of the first Article; and that no State, without its Consent, shall be deprived of its equal Suffrage in the Senate.

ARTICLE VI.

All Debts contracted and Engagements entered into, before the Adoption of this Constitution, shall be as valid against the United States under this Constitution, as under the Confederation.

This Constitution, and the Laws of the United States which shall be made in Pursuance thereof; and all Treaties made, or which shall be made, under the Authority of the United States, shall be the supreme Law of the Land; and the Judges in every State shall be bound thereby, any Thing in the Constitution or Laws of any State to the Contrary notwithstanding.

The Senators and Representatives before mentioned, and the Members of the several State Legislatures, and all executive and judicial Officers, both of the United States and of the several States, shall be bound by Oath or Affirmation, to support this Constitution; but no religious Test shall ever be required as a Qualification to any Office or public Trust under the United States.

ARTICLE VII.

The Ratification of the Conventions of nine States, shall be sufficient for the Establishment of this Constitution between the States so ratifying the Same.

Done in Convention by the Unanimous Consent of the States present the Seventeenth Day of September in the Year of our Lord one thousand seven hundred and Eighty seven and of the Independence of the United States of America the Twelfth In witness whereof We have hereunto subscribed our Names,

Attest William Jackson Secretary

G°. Washington
Presidt. and deputy from Virginia

New Hampshire	John Langdon
	Nicholas Gilman
Massachusetts	Nathaniel Gorham
	Rufus King

Connecticut	Wm. Saml. Johnson
	Roger Sherman
New York	Alexander Hamilton
New Jersey	Wil: Livingston
	David Brearley
	Wm. Paterson
	Jona: Dayton
Pennsylvania	B Franklin
	Thomas Mifflin
	Robt Morris
	Geo. Clymer
	Thos. FitzSimons
	Jared Ingersoll
	James Wilson
	Gouv Morris
Delaware	Geo: Read
	Gunning Bedford jun
	John Dickinson
	Richard Bassett
	Jaco: Broom
Maryland	James McHenry
	Dan of St Thos. Jenifer
	Danl. Carroll
Virginia	John Blair
	James Madison Jr.
North Carolina	Wm. Blount
	Richd. Dobbs Spaight
	Hu Williamson
South Carolina	J. Rutledge
	Charles Cotesworth Pinckney
	Charles Pinckney
	Pierce Butler
Georgia	William Few
	Abr Baldwin

AMENDMENT I [1791]

Congress shall make no law respecting an establishment of religion, or prohibiting the free exercise thereof; or abridging the freedom of speech, or of the press; or the right of the people peaceably to assemble, and to petition the Government for a redress of grievances.

AMENDMENT II [1791]

A well regulated Militia, being necessary to the security of a free State, the right of the people to keep and bear Arms, shall not be infringed.

AMENDMENT III [1791]

No Soldier shall, in time of peace be quartered in any house, without the consent of the Owner, nor in time of war, but in a manner to be prescribed by law.

AMENDMENT IV [1791]

The right of the people to be secure in their persons, houses, papers, and effects, against unreasonable searches and seizures, shall not be violated, and no Warrants shall issue, but upon probable cause, supported by Oath or affirmation, and particularly describing the place to be searched, and the persons or things to be seized.

AMENDMENT V [1791]

No person shall be held to answer for a capital, or otherwise infamous crime, unless on a presentment or indictment of a Grand Jury, except in cases arising in the land or naval forces, or in the Militia, when in actual service in time of War or public danger; nor shall any person be subject for the same offence to be twice put in jeopardy of life or limb; nor shall be compelled in any criminal case to be a witness against himself, nor be deprived of life, liberty, or property, without due process of law; nor shall private property be taken for public use, without just compensation.

AMENDMENT VI [1791]

In all criminal prosecutions, the accused shall enjoy the right to a speedy and public trial, by an impartial jury of the State and district wherein the crime shall have been committed, which district shall have been previously ascertained by law, and to be informed of the nature and cause of the accusation;

to be confronted with the witnesses against him; to have compulsory process for obtaining witnesses in his favor, and to have the Assistance of Counsel for his defence.

AMENDMENT VII [1791]

In Suits at common law, where the value in controversy shall exceed twenty dollars, the right of trial by jury shall be preserved, and no fact tried by a jury, shall be otherwise re-examined in any Court of the United States, than according to the rules of the common law.

AMENDMENT VIII [1791]

Excessive bail shall not be required, nor excessive fines imposed, nor cruel and unusual punishments inflicted.

AMENDMENT IX [1791]

The enumeration in the Constitution, of certain rights, shall not be construed to deny or disparage others retained by the people.

AMENDMENT X [1791]

The powers not delegated to the United States by the Constitution, nor prohibited by it to the States, are reserved to the States respectively, or to the people.

AMENDMENT XI [1795]

The Judicial power of the United States shall not be construed to extend to any suit in law or equity, commenced or prosecuted against one of the United States by Citizens of another State, or by Citizens or Subjects of any Foreign State.

AMENDMENT XII [1804]

The Electors shall meet in their respective states and vote by ballot for President and Vice-President, one of whom, at least, shall not be an inhabitant of the same state with themselves; they shall name in their ballots the person voted for as President, and in distinct ballots the person voted for as Vice-President, and they shall make distinct lists of all persons voted for as President, and of all persons voted for as Vice-President, and of the number of votes for each, which lists they shall sign and certify, and transmit sealed to the seat of the government of the

United States, directed to the President of the Senate;—The President of the Senate shall, in the presence of the Senate and House of Representatives, open all the certificates and the votes shall then be counted;—The person having the greatest Number of votes for President, shall be the President, if such number be a majority of the whole number of Electors appointed; and if no person have such majority, then from the persons having the highest numbers not exceeding three on the list of those voted for as President, the House of Representatives shall choose immediately, by ballot, the President. But in choosing the President, the votes shall be taken by states, the representation from each state having one vote; a quorum for this purpose shall consist of a member or members from two-thirds of the states, and a majority of all the States shall be necessary to a choice. And if the House of Representatives shall not choose a President whenever the right of choice shall devolve upon them, before the fourth day of March next following, then the Vice-President shall act as President, as in the case of the death or other constitutional disability of the President.—The person having the greatest number of votes as Vice-President, shall be the Vice-President, if such number be a majority of the whole number of Electors appointed, and if no person have a majority, then from the two highest numbers on the list, the Senate shall choose the Vice-President; a quorum for the purpose shall consist of two-thirds of the whole number of Senators, and a majority of the whole number shall be necessary to a choice. But no person constitutionally ineligible to the office of President shall be eligible to that of Vice-President of the United States.

AMENDMENT XIII [1865]

SECTION 1. Neither slavery nor involuntary servitude, except as a punishment for crime whereof the party shall have been duly convicted, shall exist within the United States, or any place subject to their jurisdiction.

SECTION 2. Congress shall have power to enforce this article by appropriate legislation.

AMENDMENT XIV [1868]

SECTION 1. All persons born or naturalized in the United States and subject to the jurisdiction thereof, are citizens of the United States and of the State wherein they reside. No State shall make or enforce any law which shall abridge the privileges or immunities of citizens of the United States; nor shall any State deprive any person of life, liberty, or property, without due process of law; nor deny to any person within its jurisdiction the equal protection of the laws.

SECTION 2. Representatives shall be apportioned among the several States according to their respective numbers, counting the whole number of persons in each State, excluding Indians not taxed. But when the right to vote at any election for the choice of electors for President and Vice President of the United States, Representatives in Congress, the Executive and Judicial officers of a State, or the members of the Legislature thereof, is denied to any of the male inhabitants of such State, being twenty-one years of age, and citizens of the United States, or in any way abridged, except for participation in rebellion, or other crime, the basis of representation therein shall be reduced in the proportion which the number of such male citizens shall bear to the whole number of male citizens twenty-one years of age in such State.

SECTION 3. No person shall be a Senator or Representative in Congress, or elector of President and Vice President, or hold any office, civil or military, under the United States, or under any State, who, having previously taken an oath, as a member of Congress, or as an officer of the United States, or as a member of any State legislature, or as an executive or judicial officer of any State, to support the Constitution of the United States, shall have engaged in insurrection or rebellion against the same, or given aid or comfort to the enemies thereof. But Congress may by a vote of two-thirds of each House, remove such disability.

SECTION 4. The validity of the public debt of the United States, authorized by law, including debts incurred for payment of pensions and bounties for services in suppressing insurrection or rebellion, shall not be questioned. But neither the United States nor any State shall assume or pay any debt or obligation incurred in aid of insurrection or rebellion against the United States, or any claim for the loss or emancipation of any slave; but all such debts, obligations and claims shall be held illegal and void.

SECTION 5. The Congress shall have power to enforce, by appropriate legislation, the provisions of this article.

AMENDMENT XV [1870]

SECTION 1. The right of citizens of the United States to vote shall not be denied or abridged by the United States or by any State on account of race, color, or previous condition of servitude.

SECTION 2. The Congress shall have power to enforce this article by appropriate legislation.

AMENDMENT XVI [1913]

The Congress shall have power to lay and collect taxes on incomes, from whatever source derived, without apportionment among the several States, and without regard to any census or enumeration.

AMENDMENT XVII [1913]

The Senate of the United States shall be composed of two Senators from each State, elected by the people thereof, for six years; and each Senator shall have one vote. The electors in each State shall have the qualifications requisite for electors of the most numerous branch of the State legislatures.

When vacancies happen in the representation of any State in the Senate, the executive authority of such State shall issue writs of election to fill such vacancies: Provided, That the legislature of any State may empower the executive thereof to make temporary appointments until the people fill the vacancies by election as the legislature may direct.

This amendment shall not be so construed as to affect the election or term of any Senator chosen before it becomes valid as part of the Constitution.

AMENDMENT XVIII [1919]

SECTION 1. After one year from the ratification of this article the manufacture, sale, or transportation of intoxicating liquors within, the importation thereof into, or the exportation thereof from the United States and all territory subject to the jurisdiction thereof for beverage purposes is hereby prohibited.

SECTION 2. The Congress and the several States shall have concurrent power to enforce this article by appropriate legislation.

SECTION 3. This article shall be inoperative unless it shall have been ratified as an amendment to the Constitution by the legislatures of the several States, as provided in the Constitution, within seven years from the date of the submission hereof to the States by the Congress.

AMENDMENT XIX [1920]

The right of citizens of the United States to vote shall not be denied or abridged by the United States or by any State on account of sex.

Congress shall have power to enforce this article by appropriate legislation.

AMENDMENT XX [1933]

SECTION 1. The terms of the President and Vice President shall end at noon on the 20th day of January, and the terms of Senators and Representatives at noon on the 3d day of January, of the years in which such terms would have ended if this article had not been ratified; and the terms of their successors shall then begin.

SECTION 2. The Congress shall assemble at least once in every year, and such meeting shall begin at noon on the 3d day of January, unless they shall by law appoint a different day.

SECTION 3. If, at the time fixed for the beginning of the term of the President, the President elect shall have died, the Vice President elect shall become President. If a President shall not have been chosen before the time fixed for the beginning of his term, or if the President elect shall have failed to qualify, then the Vice President elect shall act as President until a President shall have qualified; and the Congress may by law provide for the case wherein neither a President elect nor a Vice President elect shall have qualified, declaring who shall then act as President, or the manner in which one who is to act shall be selected, and such person shall act accordingly until a President or Vice President shall have qualified.

SECTION 4. The Congress may by law provide for the case of the death of any of the persons from whom the House of Representatives may choose a President whenever the right of choice shall have devolved upon them, and for the case of the death of any of the persons from whom the Senate may choose a Vice President whenever the right of choice shall have devolved upon them.

SECTION 5. Sections 1 and 2 shall take effect on the 15th day of October following the ratification of this article.

SECTION 6. This article shall be inoperative unless it shall have been ratified as an amendment to the Constitution by the legislatures of three-fourths of the several States within seven years from the date of its submission.

AMENDMENT XXI [1933]

SECTION 1. The eighteenth article of amendment to the Constitution of the United States is hereby repealed.

SECTION 2. The transportation or importation into any State, Territory, or possession of the United States for delivery or use therein of intoxicating liquors, in violation of the laws thereof, is hereby prohibited.

SECTION 3. This article shall be inoperative unless it shall have been ratified as an amendment to the Constitution by conventions in the several States, as provided in the Constitution, within seven years from the date of the submission hereof to the States by the Congress.

AMENDMENT XXII [1951]

SECTION 1. No person shall be elected to the office of the President more than twice, and no person who has held the office of President, or acted as President, for more than two years of a term to which some other person was elected President shall be elected to the office of the President more than once. But this Article shall not apply to any person holding the office of President, when this Article was proposed by the Congress, and shall not prevent any person who may be holding the office of President, or acting as President, during the term within which this Article becomes operative from holding the office of President or acting as President during the remainder of such term.

SECTION 2. This Article shall be inoperative unless it shall have been ratified as an amendment to the Constitution by the legislatures of three-fourths of the several States within seven years from the date of its submission to the States by the Congress.

AMENDMENT XXIII [1961]

SECTION 1. The District constituting the seat of Government of the United States shall appoint in such manner as the Congress may direct:

A number of electors of President and Vice President equal to the whole number of Senators and Representatives in Congress to which the District would be entitled if it were a State, but in no event more than the least populous State; they shall be in addition to those appointed by the States, but they shall be considered, for the purposes of the election of President and Vice President, to be electors appointed by a State; and they shall meet in the District and perform such duties as provided by the twelfth article of amendment.

SECTION 2. The Congress shall have power to enforce this article by appropriate legislation.

AMENDMENT XXIV [1964]

SECTION 1. The right of citizens of the United States to vote in any primary or other election for President or Vice President, for electors for President or Vice President, or for Senator or Representative in Congress, shall not be denied or abridged by the United States or any State by reason of failure to pay any poll tax or other tax.

SECTION 2. The Congress shall have power to enforce this article by appropriate legislation.

AMENDMENT XXV [1967]

SECTION 1. In case of the removal of the President from office or of his death or resignation, the Vice President shall become President.

SECTION 2. Whenever there is a vacancy in the office of the Vice President, the President shall nominate a Vice President who shall take office upon confirmation by a majority vote of both Houses of Congress.

SECTION 3. Whenever the President transmits to the President pro tempore of the Senate and the Speaker of the House of Representatives his written declaration that he is unable to discharge the powers and duties of his office, and until he transmits to them a written declaration to the contrary, such powers and duties shall be discharged by the Vice President as Acting President.

SECTION 4. Whenever the Vice President and a majority of either the principal officers of the executive departments or of such other body as Congress may by law provide, transmit to the President pro tempore of the Senate and the Speaker of the House of Representatives their written declaration that the President is unable to discharge the powers and duties of his office, the Vice President shall immediately assume the powers and duties of the office as Acting President.

Thereafter, when the President transmits to the President pro tempore of the Senate and the Speaker of the House of Representatives his written declaration that no inability exists, he shall resume the powers and duties of his office unless the Vice President and a majority of either the principal officers of the executive department or of such other body as Congress may by law provide, transmit within four days to the President pro tempore of the Senate and the Speaker of the House of Representatives their written declaration that the President is unable to discharge the powers and duties of his office. Thereupon

Congress shall decide the issue, assembling within forty-eight hours for that purpose if not in session. If the Congress, within twenty-one days after receipt of the latter written declaration, or, if Congress is not in session, within twenty-one days after Congress is required to assemble, determines by two-thirds vote of both Houses that the President is unable to discharge the powers and duties of his office, the Vice President shall continue to discharge the same as Acting President; otherwise, the President shall resume the powers and duties of his office.

AMENDMENT XXVI [1971]

SECTION 1. The right of citizens of the United States, who are eighteen years of age or older, to vote shall not be denied or abridged by the United States or by any State on account of age.

SECTION 2. The Congress shall have the power to enforce this article by appropriate legislation.

AMENDMENT XXVII [1992]

No law varying the compensation for the services of the Senators and Representatives shall take effect, until an election of Representatives shall have intervened.

NOTES

ABBREVIATIONS AND WORKS FREQUENTLY CITED

Amar, *ACAB*. Akhil Reed Amar, *America's Constitution: A Biography* (2005)

Amar, *AUC*. Akhil Reed Amar, *America's Unwritten Constitution: The Precedents and Principles We Live By* (2012)

Amar, *Bill of Rights*. Akhil Reed Amar, *The Bill of Rights: Creation and Reconstruction* (1998)

Amar, *CCP*. Akhil Reed Amar, *The Constitution and Criminal Procedure: First Principles* (1997)

Elliot's Debates.[†] Jonathan Elliot, ed., *The Debates in the Several State Conventions on the Adoption of the Federal Constitution. . . .* (1888), 5 vols.

***LJ*.** Law Journal

***LR*.** Law Review

Stat.[†] Statutes at Large

CHAPTER 1: ILLINOIS
ABRAHAM LINCOLN AND THE AMERICAN UNION

1. Farewell Address at Springfield, Illinois (Feb. 11, 1861). Several versions of this address exist; here I quote from the version written out by Lincoln as the train was leaving Springfield. The manuscript begins in Lincoln's handwriting, but concludes with that of

---

[†]Available online on the Library of Congress website, "A Century of Lawmaking." Many LOC databases are word-searchable. Detailed citations are generally omitted for other easily web-searchable materials such as the *Federalist* essays, the Collected Works of Abraham Lincoln, and modern-day Supreme Court opinions.

his secretary, John G. Nicolay. Perhaps its most haunting phrase to modern readers (who know, as no one could that day, the rest of Lincoln's story)—"or whether ever, I may return"—is in Nicolay's hand. A version published in an Illinois paper on February 12, 1861, does contain the following: "With these few words, I must leave you—for how long I know not." This newspaper version, with minor punctuation changes, appears on a plaque at Lincoln's tomb in Springfield.

2. For a different reading of this address, stressing its tactical flexibility, see David M. Potter, *Lincoln and His Party in the Secession Crisis* (1942), 318–333.

3. Buchanan's Annual Message (Dec. 3, 1860) (summarizing but rejecting this view). Emphasis added to Article VII.

4. U.S. Const. art. V ("[N]o State, without its Consent, shall be deprived of its equal Suffrage in the Senate."). See also Lincoln's Speech at Galena, Illinois (July 23, 1856) ("We don't want to dissolve [the Union] and if you attempt it, *we won't let you*.") (emphasis in original); Letter of Dec. 17, 1860, to Thurlow Weed ("I believe you can pretend to find but little, if any thing, in my speeches, about secession; but my opinion is that no state can, in any way lawfully, get out of the Union, without the consent of the others."). Read broadly, these statements might seem to insist that every state must agree to secession; read narrowly, they merely reject the idea that each state may unilaterally secede without the general (though not necessarily unanimous) consent of sister states and the American people as a whole.

5. On Lincoln's rejection of the compact theory, see infra pp. 14–15.

6. For more discussion of the implications of Lincoln's allusion to the Union's "territorial integrity," see infra pp. 23–25. For more discussion of the implications of Lincoln's allusion to "succeeding elections," see infra text accompanying nn. 13–14.

7. Gettysburg Address. See also Letter of January 11, 1861, to James T. Hale ("We have just carried an election on principles fairly stated to the people. Now we are told in advance, the government shall be broken up, unless we surrender to those we have beaten, before we take the offices. . . . [I]f we surrender, it is the end of us, and of the government.").

8. For more discussion of why the document has been read so as not to require presidential presentment of congressionally proposed amendments, see Amar, *ACAB*, 594–595n.7; Amar, *AUC*, 573n.9.

9. For discussion, see Bruce Ackerman, *We the People: Transformations* (1998), 128–129; Herman Ames, *The Proposed Amendments to the Constitution of the United States* (1896), 293–294; Potter, *Lincoln and His Party*, 101–111; Stephen Keogh, "Formal and Informal Constitutional Lawmaking in the United States in the Winter of 1860–61," *J. Legal Hist*. 8 (1987): 275, 280. Lincoln did not support Crittenden's call for a national referendum, but his reasons were more substantive than procedural: he strongly disagreed with the specific compromises with slavery that Crittenden was seeking to enshrine in the Constitution.

10. On the hoped-for moral authority of the envisioned Crittenden referendum, see *Congressional Globe*, 36th Cong., 2nd sess. (1861): 237 (Crittenden, Jan. 3, 1861) ("I do hope that the representatives will respect and regard and give a proper influence to the sense of the people."). On various "beauty contest" precursors to the Seventeenth Amendment, see Ronald D. Rotunda, "The Aftermath of Thornton," *Constitutional Commentary* 13 (1996): 201, 206–209; see also George H. Haines, *The Election of Senators* (1906); Vikram David Amar, "The People Made Me Do It: Can the People of the States Instruct and Coerce Their State Legislatures in the Article V Constitutional Amendment Process?," *William & Mary LR* 41 (2000): 1037, 1068–1071. On the Lincoln-Douglas debates

as a forerunner of the Seventeenth Amendment, see Haines, supra, at 99; Don E. Fehren-bacher, *Prelude to Greatness: Lincoln in the 1850's* (1962), 49.

11. Even in South Carolina, the consensus among "duly qualified voters" of course excluded black folk from the conversation and the voting tally. The exclusion of both slaves and free blacks from southern deliberations, and the proslavery rules of polit-ical apportionment within many southern states—rules that gave more clout to dis-tricts with large slave populations—should remind us that we must be careful not to equate the views of politically dominant forces in the South with the views of "the South" itself. In most southern states, blacks accounted for between a quarter and a half of the total population. If we count all the people within states, it becomes much harder to say that Confederate governments really reflected the views of their respective state peoples. In addition, antebellum southern governments criminalized antislavery speech, rendering suspect any claim that these governments were genu-inely "democratic" by the standards of today or even by the standards of antebellum northern states. For more discussion, see Akhil Reed Amar, "The Central Meaning of Republican Government: Popular Sovereignty, Majority Rule, and the Denominator Problem," *U. of Colorado LR* 65 (1994): 749.

12. But see *Geofroy v. Riggs*, 133 U.S. 258, 267 (1890) (dictum) (casting doubt upon the power of a treaty to cede state territory absent state consent).

13. See U.S. Const. art. IV, sec. 3 ("[N]o new State shall be formed or erected within the Jurisdiction of any other State; nor any State be formed by the Junctions of two or more States, or Parts of States, without the Consent of the Legislatures of the States con-cerned as well as of Congress."); ibid., sec. 4 ("The United States . . . shall protect each of [the States] against Invasion.").

14. Emphasis added. See also supra n. 6.

15. For powerful reminders of the enormous importance of the very fact of a regular election in 1864, see Herman Belz, *Abraham Lincoln, Constitutionalism, and Equal Rights in the Civil War Era* (1998), 33–34; Philip Shaw Paludan, *The Presidency of Abraham Lin-coln* (1994), 290–292.

It is interesting to note that, between 1939 and 1945, America held three regular federal elections—two of them presidential elections. Lincoln's 1864 precedent made any deviation unthinkable, even in the midst of an all-out world war. In marked contrast, En-gland held no general parliamentary elections between November 1935 and July 1945. The general election scheduled for 1940 was postponed by amendments to the Septennial Act of 1716. As Winston Churchill himself acknowledged to Commons in October 1944, "no one under thirty has ever cast a vote at a General Election, or even at a by-election, since the registers fell out of action at the beginning of the war." Winston S. Churchill, *Triumph and Tragedy* (1953), 586–587. For a rich discussion of the difference between fixed electoral timetables in America and the more fluid electoral timetables characteristic of parliamentary systems, see Bruce Ackerman, "The New Separation of Powers," *Harvard LR* 113 (2000): 633.

For Lincoln's midsummer assessment of his reelection prospects, see Lincoln's Secret Memorandum Concerning His Probable Failure of Re-election (Aug. 23, 1864), in which he thought it "exceedingly probable" that he would be defeated by an administration that would likely undo his stance toward the Confederacy. In such an event, he deemed it his duty to preserve the Union as best he could until the end of his constitutional term, and thereafter surrender his office.

16. Cf. Lincoln's Speech at White House Serenade (Nov. 10, 1864): "We can not have free government without elections; and if the rebellion could force us to forego, or postpone a national election, it might fairly claim to have already conquered and ruined us. . . . [The election] has demonstrated that a people's government can sustain a national election, in the midst of a great civil war. Until now it has not been known to the world that this was a possibility." These words, of course, came after electoral victory was his; but Lincoln had committed himself to a regular election long before he had any strong assurance that he would win.

True, Lincoln-haters in Confederate states generally did not vote in the 1864 Union elections; but it was hardly Lincoln's fault that lawless rebels in effect boycotted the Union election, or that true Unionists down south could not register their views in a fair and proper election conducted by a proper loyal and republican state government. In any event, Lincoln would have won an electoral college victory in 1864 even if southern electoral votes had been fully counted; as in 1860, Lincoln's near-sweep of the northern states sufficed to give him the win under any scenario, and in fact he received more electoral votes the second time around.

17. For a more extended analysis of presidents without mandates, see infra Chapters 8 and 9.

18. On the 1858 election, see Fehrenbacher, *Prelude to Greatness*, 114–120.

19. For more discussion of my claim that the three-fifths clause gave the South extra clout, and the baseline issues implicated by that claim, see infra Chapter 9, n. 1, and sources cited therein.

20. This background might help explain the meaning of Lincoln's pointed suggestion in his First Inaugural that just as northern states should respect southern rights by allowing the Article IV fugitive-slave clause to be enforced, so southern states should likewise respect the Article IV "privileges" and "immunities" of northern "citizens." Such immunities encompassed freedom of speech, press, petition, assembly, and worship, in the minds of most Republican Party leaders; this ideology would eventually culminate in the language of the Fourteenth Amendment's privileges-or-immunities clause, designed to protect free speech and other fundamental rights against state abridgment. See, generally, Amar, *Bill of Rights*, and the myriad works of Professor Michael Kent Curtis cited therein.

Another possible reason for the Slave Power's fear of Lincoln in 1861 was that Lincoln could, as president, appoint territorial governors who might try to enforce antislavery policies in the territories, thereby constricting slavery's expansion. However, such policies were likely to face tough sledding before the Taney Court, which in the 1857 case of *Dred Scott v. Sanford* had proclaimed that antislavery laws in federal territories were unconstitutional. Moreover, although Lincoln's anticipated territorial policies may have threatened slaveowners' long-term interests, these policies did not pose any immediate threat to the Slave Power's dominant power base in the South.

21. Don E. Fehrenbacher, "The Post Office in Illinois Politics of the 1850's," *J. Illinois State Historical Society* 46 (1953): 60, 70.

22. See, generally, Jefferson Davis, *The Rise and Fall of the Confederate Government*, rev. ed. (1958).

23. Emphasis altered.

24. On May 10, 1776, the Second Continental Congress resolved that "it be recommended to the respective assemblies and conventions of the United Colonies, where no government sufficient to the exigencies of their affairs have been hitherto established, to

adopt such government as shall, in the opinion of the representatives of the people, best conduce to the happiness and safety of their constituents in particular, and America in general." *Journals of the Continental Congress* 4 (1776): 342. See also the related resolution of May 15, ibid., 357–358. The word *recommended* says it all: the continental center is playing a recommendatory and interstate synchronization role, but the final and binding decisions about each state constitution are to be made by the "representatives of the people" of each state, acting as a distinct state and without any need for further continental approval or ratification of the locally produced constitution.

25. Emphasis added to quotations. My brief sketch in the preceding paragraphs represents a composite of arguments I have elsewhere presented. See, e.g., Akhil Reed Amar, "Of Sovereignty and Federalism," *Yale LJ* 96 (1987): 1425, 1442–1462; Akhil Reed Amar, "The Consent of the Governed: Constitutional Amendment Outside Article V," *Columbia LR* 94 (1994): 457, 462–469 & n. 37; Amar, *Bill of Rights*, 5–6, 156–158. For still more elaboration, see Chapter 1 of Amar, *ACAB*. Both today and in previous writings I sharply distinguish between "sovereignty" for the purposes of external and foreign relations, and internal sovereignty issues—the crux of the secession question.

26. An Act for rendering the Union of the Kingdoms more intire and complete, 1707, 6 Anne, ch. 6; William Blackstone, *Commentaries on the Laws of England*, 1:*98, n. e (added in 1766 edition); *Elliot's Debates*, 2:463 (emphasis added); Letter of July 20, 1788, in Robert A. Rutland and Charles F. Hobson, eds., *The Papers of James Madison* 11 (1977): 189 (emphasis altered). I have also added emphasis to my quotation from *The Federalist* No. 11.

27. Emphasis added.

28. For a sustained effort to see certain modern constitutional issues from a Texas-centered perspective, see infra Chapter 9.

29. On Lincoln's American ancestors, see his Letter of Dec. 20, 1859, to Jesse W. Fell.

30. First Inaugural Address (March 4, 1861); Special Session Address (July 4, 1861).

31. Douglass Adair, *Fame and the Founding Fathers*, Trevor Colbourn, ed. (1974), 75–76.

32. The paraphrase of Publius in the preceding paragraphs borrows from an earlier piece of mine, which attempts to present these ideas with far more elaboration and documentation. See Akhil Reed Amar, "Some New World Lessons for the Old World," *U. of Chicago LR* 58 (1991): 483. A similar paraphrase appears in Amar, *ACAB*, 44–47.

33. For details, see Amar, "Some New World Lessons."

34. This paragraph closely tracks Amar, *ACAB*, 52–53. For a rich discussion of federalism and secession, see Steven G. Calabresi and Nicholas Terrell, "The Number of States and the Economics of American Federalism," *Florida LR* 63 (2011): 1. This article thoughtfully analyzes the collective-action challenges faced by the slaveholding states among themselves.

35. Letter of Aug. 26, 1863, to James C. Conkling.

36. See, generally, Garry Wills, *Inventing America* (1978), xv–vi; Garry Wills, *Lincoln at Gettysburg* (1992), 57, 77–79.

37. See Eric Foner, *Reconstruction* (1988), 49, 74, 180, 183. Privately, Lincoln continued to muse about compensation schemes, even after congressional passage of the Thirteenth Amendment. (Lincoln, of course, did not live to see the amendment ratified by the requisite number of states.)

38. Letter to James S. Wadsworth (Jan. 1864?).

39. Last Public Address (Apr. 11, 1865).

CHAPTER 2: ALABAMA
Hugo Black and the Hall of Fame

1. See Robert M. Cover, "Your Law-Baseball Quiz," *NY Times*, Apr. 5, 1979, A23.

2. Letter from James Madison to Richard Peters (Aug. 19, 1789), in Robert A. Rutland and Charles F. Hobson, eds., *The Papers of James Madison* 12 (1979): 346.

3. Robert J. Reinstein, "Completing the Constitution: The Declaration of Independence, Bill of Rights and Fourteenth Amendment," *Temple LR* 66 (1993): 361, 365n.25.

4. We shall revisit these issues in later chapters. For more on the federalism aspects of the original First Amendment, see Chapter 6, pp. 126–128. For more on federalism and the Second Amendment, see Chapter 10, pp. 206–210. For more on the Founders' views regarding the powers of civil juries under the Fourth and Fifth Amendments, see Chapters 11 and 12, pp. 236–237, 256–258.

5. The *Dred Scott* Court had appeared to hold that most blacks, even if free, could never be American citizens. The first sentence of the Fourteenth Amendment repudiates that apparent holding: "All persons born or naturalized in the United States and subject to the jurisdiction thereof, are citizens of the United States and of the State wherein they reside."

6. If the framers of the Fourteenth Amendment meant to hold states to the Bill of Rights, no more and no less, why, it might be asked, didn't they say so more directly? My answer is that, strictly speaking, Reconstruction Republicans meant both more and less than the first eight amendments as such. See Amar, *Bill of Rights*, 174–180; Amar, *AUC*, 151–172. On applying the amendment to protect fundamental rights beyond those specified in the Bill itself, consider the views of Justices Murphy and Rutledge, discussed supra p. 37. And on the ways in which the Fourteenth Amendment might incorporate something less than the Bill of Rights as such, see infra n. 13 (discussing "refined incorporation"). For a powerful reminder that state constitutions are also proper sources from which judges may mine federal "privileges" and "immunities," see Steven G. Calabresi and Sarah Agudo, "Individual Rights Under State Constitutions When the Fourteenth Amendment Was Ratified in 1868: What Rights Are Deeply Rooted in American History and Tradition?," *Texas LR* 87 (2008): 7.

7. Emphasis added to constitutional quotations. For general theoretical discussions about how a given text or other sign can come to mean different things in different historical contexts, see J. M. Balkin, "Deconstructive Practice and Legal Theory," *Yale LJ* 96 (1987): 743; J. M. Balkin, "Ideological Drift and the Struggle over Meaning," *Connecticut LR* 25 (1993): 869; Lawrence Lessig, "Fidelity in Translation," *Texas LR* 71 (1993): 1165.

8. Justice Black would later identify some of the obvious procedural problems with this kind of judicial contempt. See infra n. 27. On why I believe Holmes is overrated, see infra Chapter 3, n. 2.

9. See, e.g., *Stromberg v. California*, 283 U.S. 359 (1931); *Near v. Minnesota*, 283 U.S. 697 (1931); *De Jonge v. Oregon*, 299 U.S. 353 (1937).

10. Is this an attractive assumption? Why should our criminal justice system allow appellate courts to review and correct a legal error made by the trial judge if and only if that legal error leads to an erroneous conviction, as opposed to an erroneous acquittal? If the defendant is entitled to appeal a legal error made against him, why shouldn't the prosecutor have the same entitlement? Note that the issue here is different from, say, rules concerning doubt about factual guilt; although reasonable factual doubts are to be resolved

in a defendant's favor, are legal errors the same as factual doubts? For more discussion and analysis, see Akhil Reed Amar, "Double Jeopardy Law Made Simple," *Yale LJ* 106 (1987): 1807, 1838–1848.

11. Note that Frankfurter's test is, in essence, the same test that the Court has often applied generally to so-called substantive-due-process cases. This similarity should not be surprising once we recall that incorporation of the Bill of Rights was itself viewed by many as a kind of substantive due process, in which judges used the language of the due-process clause to protect what were often substantive—that is, nonprocedural—rights, such as freedom of expression and freedom of religion.

12. This paragraph borrows heavily from Amar, *Bill of Rights*, 139–140. In the case law, see, e.g., *In re Oliver*, 333 U.S. 257 (1948) (Sixth Amendment right to public trial); *Wolf v. Colorado*, 338 U.S. 25 (1949) (Fourth Amendment right against unreasonable searches and seizures); *Mapp v. Ohio*, 367 U.S. 643 (1961) (exclusionary rule); *Robinson v. California*, 370 U.S. 660 (1962) (Eighth Amendment right against cruel and unusual punishment); *Gideon v. Wainwright*, 372 U.S. 335 (1963) (Sixth Amendment right to counsel); *Malloy v. Hogan*, 378 U.S. 1 (1964) (Fifth Amendment right against compelled self-incrimination); *Pointer v. Texas*, 380 U.S. 400 (1965) (Sixth Amendment right to confront opposing witnesses); *Klopfer v. North Carolina*, 386 U.S. 213 (1967) (Sixth Amendment right to speedy trial); *Washington v. Texas*, 388 U.S. 14 (1967) (Sixth Amendment right to compulsory process); *Duncan v. Louisiana*, 391 U.S. 145 (1968) (Sixth Amendment right to jury trial); *Benton v. Maryland*, 395 U.S. 784 (1969) (Fifth Amendment right against double jeopardy); *Schilb v. Kuebel*, 404 U.S. 357 (1971) (Eighth Amendment right against excessive bail) (dictum); *City of Chicago v. McDonald*, 561 U.S. 3025 (2010) (Second Amendment right to have a gun in the home for self-protection).

Apodaca v. Oregon, 406 U.S. 404 (1972), offers an interesting counterpoint. In *Apodaca*, four justices (White, Burger, Blackmun, and Rehnquist) argued that the Sixth Amendment does not require that a criminal jury be unanimous to convict, while four others (Douglas, Brennan, Stewart, and Marshall) claimed that the Sixth Amendment does require unanimity. Justice Powell cast the deciding vote to uphold Oregon's law, on the theory that although the Sixth Amendment does require unanimity, this aspect of Sixth Amendment doctrine should not be incorporated against states jot-for-jot.

13. For famous commentary harshly critical of Justice Black's position, see Charles Fairman, "Does the Fourteenth Amendment Incorporate the Bill of Rights?," *Stanford LR* 2 (1949): 5. Fairman's scholarship was, in turn, sharply attacked in William Winslow Crosskey, "Charles Fairman, 'Legislative History,' and the Constitutional Limitations on State Authority," *U. of Chicago LR* 22 (1954): 1; Michael Kent Curtis, *No State Shall Abridge: The Fourteenth Amendment and the Bill of Rights* (1984); and Richard Aynes, "On Misreading John Bingham and the Fourteenth Amendment," *Yale LJ* 103 (1997): 57. Elsewhere, I have attempted to synthesize the competing positions as follows:

> This synthesis, which I shall call "refined incorporation," begins with Black's insight that *all* of the privileges and immunities of citizens recognized in the Bill of Rights became "incorporated" against states by dint of the Fourteenth Amendment. But not all of the provisions of the original Bill of Rights were indeed rights of citizens. Some instead were at least in part rights of states, and as such, awkward to fully incorporate *against* states. Most obvious, of course, is the Tenth Amendment, but other provisions of the first eight amendments resembled the Tenth much more than Justice

Black admitted. Thus there is deep wisdom in Justice Brennan's invitation to consider incorporation clause by clause—or more precisely still, right by right—rather than wholesale. But having identified the right unit of analysis, Brennan posed the wrong question: Is a given provision of the original Bill really a *fundamental* right? The right question is whether the provision really guarantees a privilege or immunity of *individual citizens* rather than a right of *states* or the *public* at large. And when we ask this question, clause by clause and right by right, we must be attentive to the possibility, flagged by Frankfurter, that a particular principle in the Bill of Rights may change its shape in the process of absorption into the Fourteenth Amendment. This change can occur for reasons rather different from those that Frankfurter offered. (He, more than Black and Brennan, diverted attention from the right question by his insistence on abstract conceptions of "fundamental fairness" and "ordered liberty" as the sole Fourteenth Amendment litmus tests, and by his disregard of the language and history of the privileges-or-immunities clause.) Certain alloyed provisions of the original Bill— part citizen right, part state right—may need to undergo refinement and filtration before their citizen-right elements can be absorbed by the Fourteenth Amendment. And other provisions may become less majoritarian and populist, and more libertarian, as they are repackaged in the Fourteenth Amendment as liberal civil rights—"privileges or immunities" of individuals—rather than republican political "right[s] of the people," as in the original Bill.

Amar, *Bill of Rights*, xiv–xv.

14. On Black's oversimplification: First, the dissent failed to offer a careful account of the respective roles of the privileges-or-immunities clause and the due-process clause (see supra p. 34, n.*). Second, the dissent never directly explained why, if the Fourteenth Amendment meant no more and no less than incorporating Amendments One through Eight, it did not say so more directly. (The best answer is that the amendment meant both somewhat more and somewhat less than Black suggested, though the core of his account remains right in application—see supra nn. 6, 13.) Finally, Black's mechanical approach to incorporation tended to downplay important ways in which the Fourteenth Amendment helped redefine the meaning of the original provisions of the Bill of Rights. For examples and illustrations of this redefinition, see, generally, Amar, *Bill of Rights*. See also infra Chapters 6, 10.

15. For my own efforts to follow in Justice Black's footsteps here, see Akhil Reed Amar, "The Supreme Court, 1999 Term—Foreword: The Document and the Doctrine," *Harvard LR* 114 (2000): 26. For an earlier exposition of the significance of Black's methodological leadership, see Philip Bobbitt, *Constitutional Fate* (1982), 26–27, 31:

Black had one thing none of his colleagues had: Black had genius, a grasp of the effect of simplicity in the law and of the need for it and an understanding of how to make his contemporaries feel that need. It was this understanding that animated and gave to textualism a power that it had not had since the Marshall Court. It was Hugo Black who led constitutional argument out of the wilderness of legal realism. He accomplished this by his remarkable use of textual argument and his creation of a constitutional grammar for this use.

. . .

> Black developed the textual argument, and a set of supporting doctrines, with a simplicity and a power they had never before had. . . . [A Blackian judge interprets the Constitution] on a basis readily apprehendable by the people at large, namely, giving the common-language meanings to constitutional provisions. This allowed Black to restore to judicial review the popular perception of legitimacy which the New Deal crisis had jeopardized.

16. For a fascinating exploration of similarities and differences between biblical Protestantism and constitutional fundamentalism, see Sanford Levinson, *Constitutional Faith* (1988). It is worth noting that Black's own very short 1968 book about his constitutional philosophy is entitled *A Constitutional Faith*. See also Noah Feldman, *Scorpions: The Battles and Triumphs of FDR's Great Supreme Court Justices* (2010), 145 ("Before going on the Court, Black's main experience with interpreting texts was his weekly job of reading Bible passages and applying them to ordinary life for the benefit of a large audience of adult men. The deep wellspring of Black's originalism was the distinctively Protestant method of biblical interpretation that he had used for two decades as a Sunday school teacher in Birmingham."). My geographic tally does not treat the DC beltway as a genuine part of Dixie, even though some of the beltway is of course formally in Virginia.

17. See, generally, Lucas A. Powe, Jr., *The Warren Court and American Politics* (2000); Harry Kalven, Jr., *The Negro and the First Amendment* (1965).

18. Other justices may have been tempted to enlist proxies in the fight, but this was not Black's style. In 1992, Federal District Judge Louis Oberdorfer (himself a native Alabamian and a Yale Law School graduate) recounted the following story to me, which illuminates several features of Black's character:

> I was Justice Black's law clerk in the 1946 term when he wrote his dissent in *Adamson*. Although I don't claim any credit for the *Adamson* dissent (it was entirely the Justice's production), I was in a position to correct errors in it and the Justice would have been very receptive to my suggestions. I thought and still think that, given the limitations, the dissent was a monumental and accurately documented achievement. So you can imagine my chagrin when, two years later, I read Fairman's attack on the integrity of the dissent and its author. After reading Fairman, I went to see Justice Black and offered to respond. He firmly asked me not to do so. I have honored the request.

Letter from Louis F. Oberdorfer to Akhil Reed Amar, May 21, 1992. For my own efforts to rebut Fairman's attacks on Black, see Amar, *Bill of Rights*, 188–193, 198–207. For more background on the Fairman-Frankfurter-Harvard connection, see Richard L. Aynes, "Charles Fairman, Felix Frankfurter, and the Fourteenth Amendment," *Chicago-Kent LR*, 70 (1995): 1197.

19. Thus, despite Black's disagreement with certain features of Justice Byron White's opinion for the Court in *Duncan v. Louisiana*, 391 U.S. 145 (1968), which incorporated the Sixth Amendment jury right against states, Black joined White and dismissed their zone of disagreement as "dictum." Had Black and fellow incorporationist William Douglas forced the issue, the case might have been resolved without a majority opinion, which would have left it a weaker precedent for the general idea of incorporation. For details, see Amar, *Bill of Rights*, 289 and n.*.

20. See, e.g., *Adamson v. California*, 332 U.S. 46, 70–71 (1947) (Black, J., dissenting); *Green v. United States*, 356 U.S. 165, 209 (1958) (Black, J., dissenting). For an example of Frankfurter's thin skin, see, e.g., his famously overwrought dissent in the 1943 *West Virginia State Board of Education v. Barnette*, which overruled an earlier, and today widely discredited, opinion for the Court in the 1940 case of *Minersville School District v. Gobitis*. Both cases involved compulsory flag-salute laws, objected to by Jehovah's Witnesses on grounds of freedom of expression, freedom of opinion, and freedom of conscience. In *Gobitis*, the Court, in an opinion penned by Frankfurter, ruled against the claim of freedom, and in *Barnette*, Frankfurter reacted in an extraordinarily churlish way when the Court, realizing its mistake, reversed itself (and thereby reversed Frankfurter). In 1940, Black had joined Frankfurter's *Gobitis* opinion, but unlike Frankfurter, he had no problem in *Barnette* candidly admitting his earlier error. For more on the Court's *Barnette* opinion, now considered one of the jewels of American constitutional law, see infra Chapter 3, p. 57, and p. 320n.2, for even more on this episode, and on Frankfurter's thin skin, see, generally, James F. Simon, *The Antagonists: Hugo Black, Felix Frankfurter and Civil Liberties in Modern America* (1989), 106–129; Feldman, *Scorpions*, 177–186, 226–234.

21. I am indebted to many conversations with Professor Charles Reich, and to his penetrating essay on Justice Black, for highlighting the importance of *Bridges* and several other cases in Black's early oeuvre. See Charles A. Reich, "Mr Justice Black and the Living Constitution," *Harvard LR* 76 (1963): 673. Reich had clerked for Black, and one of the last books the justice read before his death in 1971 was Reich's 1970 blockbuster book, *The Greening of America*. A copy of this book filled with the justice's marginalia may be found in the justice's home study, now replicated in the University of Alabama Law School library.

22. For the 1950s and early 1960s, see, e.g., *Feiner v. New York*, 340 U.S. 315 (1951); *Dennis v. United States*, 341 U.S. 494 (1951); *Scales v. United States*, 367 U.S. 203 (1961).

23. See, generally, Reich, "Mr Justice Black and the Living Constitution," 695–697. For an example of this absolutist rhetoric, see, e.g., *Smith v. California*, 361 U.S. 147, 157 (1959) (Black, J., dissenting) ("The First Amendment, which is the supreme law of the land, has thus fixed its own value on freedom of speech and press by putting these freedoms wholly 'beyond the reach' of federal power to abridge.").

24. See, generally, Alexander Meiklejohn, *Political Freedom: The Constitutional Powers of the People* (1960). Note that the text of the Constitution's speech-or-debate clause protects "Speech or Debate," not the "*freedom of* Speech or Debate." But various English and American precursors to the Article I speech-or-debate clause—the English Bill of Rights of 1689, the Articles of Confederation, and several early state constitutions—explicitly used the phrase "freedom of speech" to define the key principle of parliamentary free expression. See Amar, *ACAB*, 24–26, 321; Amar, *AUC*, 101–104, 540. See also infra Chapter 4, pp. 82–83. There is no reason to think that Article I's shorthand articulation of this venerable idea was intended to be any less expansive, even though it omitted the word "freedom."

25. See, generally, Alexander Meiklejohn, "The First Amendment Is an Absolute," *Supreme Court Review* 1961: 245; Meiklejohn, *Political Freedom*, 29–50. See also Jed Rubenfeld, "The First Amendment's Purpose," *Stanford LR* 53 (2000): 767. Note also that Meiklejohn appeared to discover part of the textual basis for incorporation—the linguistic link between the First Amendment language prohibiting "abridg[ments]" and the similar language of the First Amendment—at the very historical moment that Justice Black was

emphasizing this as the key clause of the Fourteenth Amendment. See Meiklejohn, *Political Freedom*, 53. For more discussion of this linguistic linkage, see Amar, *Bill of Rights*, 165–166, 191.

26. On Ely and *Brown*, cf. "Note, The Bounds of Legislative Specification: A Suggested Approach to the Bill of Attainder Clause," *Yale LJ* 72 (1962): 330 (authored by John Hart Ely). For more analysis of the deep structure underlying the attainder clauses, see Amar, *ACAB*, 124–125; Akhil Reed Amar, "Attainder and Amendment 2: *Romer's* Rightness," *Michigan LR* 95 (1996): 203; and see also infra Chapter 4, pp. 93–94, and Chapter 5, pp. 113–114.

27. On incorporation and juries, see, e.g., *Adamson v. California*, 332 U.S. 46, 68–123 (1947) (Black, J., dissenting); *Duncan v. Louisiana*. 391 U.S. 145, 162–171 (1968) (Black, J., concurring). On the petty crime issue, see, e.g., *United States v. Green*, 356 U.S. 165, 201, and n. 11 (1958) (Black, J., dissenting); *Cheff v. Schnackenberg*, 384 U.S. 373, 386–393 (1966) (Douglas, J., dissenting, joined by Black, J.); *Dyke v. Taylor Implement Mfg. Co.*, 391 U.S. 216, 223 (1968) (Black, J., dissenting); *Baldwin v. New York*, 399 U.S. 66, 74–76 (1970). Compare Felix Frankfurter and Thomas G. Corcoran, "Petty Offenses and the Constitutional Guaranty of Trial by Jury," *Harvard LR* 39 (1926): 917. On contempt, see, e.g., *Sacher v. United States*, 343 U.S. 1, 14–23 (1952) (Black, J., dissenting); *Green v. United States*, 356 U.S. 165, 193–219 (1958) (Black, J., dissenting); *United States v. Barnett*, 376 U.S. 681, 724–728 (1963) (Black, J., dissenting); *Bloom v. Illinois*, 391 U.S. 194 (1968). On implicit acquittal, see *Green v. United States*, 355 U.S. 184, 190–191 (1957) (Black, J.).

28. On the five outlier states in 1963, see Amar, *AUC*, 112, 538n.21, and sources cited therein.

29. In the 1963 term, out of a total of 77 dissenting opinions, Brennan wrote only 2; and out of a total of 320 dissenting votes, Brennan cast only 3. (Black wrote 14 dissents and cast 42 dissenting votes; Warren wrote 1 dissent and cast 10 dissenting votes.) "The Supreme Court, 1963 Term," *Harvard LR* 78 (1964): 177, 182. In the 1964 term, out of a total of 71 dissenting opinions, Brennan wrote only 1; and out of a total of 173 dissenting votes, Brennan cast only 2. (Black wrote 14 dissents and cast 39 dissenting votes; Warren wrote no dissents and cast 5 dissenting votes.) "The Supreme Court, 1964 Term," *Harvard LR* 79 (1965): 103, 108.

30. On the importance of incorporation, see William J. Brennan, Jr., "The Bill of Rights and the States: The Revival of State Constitutions as Guardian of Individual Rights," *New York U. LR* 61 (1977): 535, 535–536. Professor Van Alstyne has written that "it is difficult to imagine a more consequential subject," and Harvard Dean and Solicitor General Erwin Griswold declared that he could "think of nothing in the history of constitutional law which has gone so far since John Marshall and the Supreme Court decided *Marbury v. Madison* in 1803." William W. Van Alstyne, Foreword to Michael Kent Curtis, *No State Shall Abridge: The Fourteenth Amendment and the Bill of Rights* (1986), ix; Erwin N. Griswold, "Due Process Problems Today in the United States," in Bernard Schwartz, ed., *The Fourteenth Amendment* (1970), 161, 164.

31. For sharp criticism of these and similar cases, including criticism of Black's theories, see Amar, *CCP*; Amar, *AUC*, 114–116, 172–183, 222–223.

32. For more on *Brown* and *Bolling*, see infra Chapter 3, pp. 69–70; and see, generally, Chapter 5.

33. As for the geographic distribution of the *Brown* Court justices, we should note that Justice Stanley Forman Reed hailed from the Upper South state of Kentucky, which

of course had remained loyal to the Union in the Civil War; and Justice Tom C. Clark came from Texas, which, as we shall see in Chapter 9, only sometimes sees itself as southern. On occasion the state defines itself as western, but much of the time it sees itself and is seen by others as unique and singular: the Lone Star State.

34. On the importance of the ratification process of the Fourteenth Amendment itself and the implications of this birth logic for constitutional interpretation, see Amar, "Foreword," 49–51, 67. Viewing the Founding through the lens of Reconstruction also blunts much of the second Justice John Marshall Harlan's *Wesberry* dissent, which stressed that slavery and the three-fifths ratio complicated intrastate apportionment at the Founding—a point rendered moot by the Reconstruction Amendments. In emphasizing the need to read this particular Founding text through a Reconstruction prism, I follow the lead of my great teacher and colleague Bruce Ackerman. See Bruce A. Ackerman, "The Common Law Constitution of John Marshall Harlan," *New York Law School Review* 36 (1991): 5, 12–18; Bruce A. Ackerman, "Taxation and the Constitution," *Columbia LR* 99 (1999): 1.

35. See *Baker v. Carr*, 369 U.S. 186, 226 (1962) (suggesting a judicial standard invalidating only "arbitrary and capricious" apportionments); ibid., 244 (Douglas, J., concurring) ("Universal equality is not the test; there is room for weighting" of votes.); ibid., 260 (Clark, J., concurring) ("[T]here is no requirement that any plan have mathematical exactness in its application.").

36. Cf. *Gray v. Sanders*, 372 U.S. 368 (1963) (striking down Georgia's rather unusual unit-system for electing single statewide officers, and distinguishing the narrow issue at hand from the much more wide-ranging and general issues of apportionment in multi-member legislatures).

37. See also *McCollum v. Board of Education*, 333 U.S. 203 (1948) (Black, J.); *Zorach v. Clauson*, 343 U.S. 306, 315–320 (1952) (Black, J., dissenting). In both cases, involving public school systems of "release time," Black objected to governmental schemes that in his view aided religion as such, deployed coercion of mandatory school attendance laws to promote attendance at religious events, and openly separated students in public schools along religious lines.

38. For a troubling dissenting opinion by Black, late in life, that moved away from the best aspects of *Everson* and foreshadowed some of the mistakes of the Burger Court—which at times tended to emphasize the idea of "separation" of church and state as distinct from, and at odds with, the proper touchstone of religious equality and neutrality—see *Board of Education v. Allen*, 392 U.S. 236, 250–254 (1968) (Black, J., dissenting). For more on all this, see Amar, *AUC*, 170–172, 218–222.

39. On Harvard men's skewed rankings, see, e.g., supra p. 44, n.* (summarizing Harvard-product Cass Sunstein's Harvard-skewed Hall of Fame nominees); infra Chapter 3, p. 77, n.* (summarizing similar Harvard-product John Roberts's similar Harvard-skewed Hall of Fame nominees). On the Black-Frankfurter rivalry, see, generally, Simon, *The Antagonists*; Feldman, *Scorpions*. The late Yale law professor Robert Cover shared my view that Frankfurter is, in general, overrated. See Cover, "Your Law-Baseball Quiz."

40. At least one leading commentator (who studied law at Harvard and later became a professor at Yale) glimpsed the truth of Black's intellectual leadership, but found both Black and the Warren Court in general less than admirable. See Alexander M. Bickel, *The Morality of Consent* (1975), 9 ("The Warren Court in its heyday was Hugo Black writ large."). More recent commentators often miss Black's leadership altogether and misconstrue his vision

and its implications. See, e.g., Morton J. Horwitz, *The Warren Court and the Pursuit of Justice* (1998). According to Horwitz (who studied law and now teaches law at Harvard)—and contrary to the ideas that I have presented in this chapter—Black in general had "extremely doctrinaire" and "dogmatic" views about constitutional interpretation that "enmeshed him in contradiction" (ibid., 5, 110); Black in particular "rejected any use of a 'balancing test' to decide First Amendment questions," and adhered to a "dogmatic" First Amendment "absolutism," a position beset with "intellectual difficulties" (ibid., 67–68, 105); Brennan was "the most important intellectual influence on the Warren Court" (ibid., 8); and the key voting cases were *Baker v. Carr*, featuring a "great scholarly opinion" by Brennan, and Warren's *Reynolds v. Sims*, with Black and *Wesberry* unworthy of mention (ibid., 82–85). Horwitz also claims that neither *Brown* nor the one-person, one-vote principle could be supported by constitutional text, history, and structure and could only be defended by appeal to a "living Constitution" approach (ibid., 110). I respectfully disagree. On voting equality, see Amar, *AUC*, 183–194, 223–230; and on *Brown*, see infra Chapter 5.

41. See, e.g., *Eisenstadt v. Baird*, 405 U.S. 438 (1972) (unmarried heterosexual contraception); *Roe v. Wade*, 410 U.S. 113 (1973) (abortion).

42. For my own effort to defend *Griswold*'s result—based on deep privacy principles underlying the Third and Fourth Amendments, the broad references to unenumerated rights in the Ninth Amendment and the Fourteenth Amendment's privileges-or-immunities clause, and the customary rights lived out and celebrated daily by ordinary citizens in ways that connect up with the Constitution's text even as these practices exist outside the text, see Amar, *AUC*, 117–130.

43. See, e.g., *Korematsu v. United States*, 323 U.S. 214 (1944) (opinion of the Court, per Black, J.) (upholding forced evacuation of Japanese Americans during World War II); *South Carolina v. Katzenbach*, 383 U.S. 301, 355–362 (1966) (Black, J., concurring and dissenting) (voting to invalidate the preclearance regime established by the Voting Rights Act of 1965). See also supra pp. 49, 54; infra Chapter 6, p.136n*. For more on how to properly tally up good and bad days, see infra Chapter 3, n. 2; infra Chapter 4, p.96.

CHAPTER 3: NEW YORK
ROBERT JACKSON AND THE JUDICIALIZATION OF THE JUDICIARY

1. See, e.g., Cass R. Sunstein, "Home-Run Hitters of the Supreme Court," *Bloomberg View*, Apr. 1, 2014. Jackson is the only person to make Professor Sunstein's list of history's eight greatest members of the Court who was neither a chief justice nor a Harvard man. Note that although Jackson was formally a justice for thirteen years, he did not sit on the bench during his yearlong leave of absence as a special prosecutor at Nuremberg. Special thanks to John Barrett for this specific reminder and for his broader assistance in helping me to think straight about Jackson in general.

2. Many consider Justice Oliver Wendell Holmes a great stylist, and a great constitutional jurist, to boot, but not I. Style must ultimately subserve substance, and I do not find in Holmes's body of work on the Court an edifying substantive vision of American constitutional law. Many of Holmes's most notable one-liners are lazy, incomplete, cruel, or clueless. For example, in his dissent in the 1905 case of *Lochner v. New York*, involving a constitutional challenge to a state law limiting the maximum number of hours an employer could require bakers to work, Holmes famously quipped that the Fourteenth Amendment

"does not enact Mr. Herbert Spencer's Social Statics." So far, so good—and this snappy line does feature a lovely use of iambic meter. But Holmes failed to tell us clearly what the Fourteenth Amendment *does* enact. Over the course of a long career, he did a poor job of explaining and defending the Reconstruction Amendments' core commitments—antislavery, free expression, racial equality, and the like. Why does a justice who is willing to allow state judges, on their own say-so, to punish a newspaper simply for lampooning those very same judges in a cartoon (see *Patterson v. Colorado* [1907]); willing to uphold years of imprisonment for a major political figure who merely voiced sharp opposition to federal war policies (see *Debs v. United States* [1919]); and also willing to uphold peonage for southern blacks, forced sterilization of powerless women, and massive disfranchisement of African Americans (see *Bailey v. Alabama* [1911], *Buck v. Bell* [1927], and *Giles v. Harris* [1903])—and who never clearly recanted these and many, many similarly misguided votes; and who failed to offset these large lapses with a comparably large set of truly impressive affirmative constitutional ideas, à la Hugo Black—deserve to be ranked among our nation's greatest constitutional figures? Long before Holmes came along, the constitutional principles he garbled had been made clear by other, far better constitutional thinkers and doers, including James Madison and John Bingham, who helped birth the First and Fourteenth Amendments, respectively.

In contrast to Holmes's style and substance, consider Robert Jackson's stirring words, writing for the Court in the 1943 compulsory flag-salute case *West Virginia State Board of Education v. Barnette*: "If there is any fixed star in our constitutional constellation, it is that no official, high or petty, can prescribe what shall be orthodox in politics, nationalism, religion, or other matters of opinion or force citizens to confess by word or act their faith therein. If there are any circumstances which permit an exception, they do not now occur to us." Hearken, too, to the following passage from the same pen in the same case: "The very purpose of a Bill of Rights was to withdraw certain subjects from the vicissitudes of political controversy, to place them beyond the reach of majorities and officials and to establish them as legal principles to be applied by the courts. One's right to life, liberty, and property, to free speech, a free press, freedom of worship and assembly, and other fundamental rights may not be submitted to vote; they depend on the outcome of no elections." Though perhaps overstated, these words begin to help us see what the First and the Fourteenth Amendments *did* enact, and why.

3. For more on *Youngstown*, see infra pp. 72–74. For more on *Barnette*, see the preceding endnote; see also supra Chapter 2, n. 20; infra Chapter 4, n. 2; infra Chapter 6, p. 136, n.*.

4. Jackson was born in Pennsylvania and raised in upstate New York; Felix Frankfurter was born in Austria and came to New York at the age of twelve. The current Court boasts four native New Yorkers—John Roberts, Ruth Bader Ginsburg, Sonia Sotomayor, and Elena Kagan—three of whom spent all their early years in New York. Roberts moved to Indiana as a fourth grader. Antonin Scalia was born in Trenton, New Jersey, and moved to the New York City area (Queens, to be precise) at the age of six.

5. I do not mean to suggest that Rehnquist's relationship with Jackson was entirely friendly, filial, and loyal. For one view of some of the complexity here, see Noah Feldman, *Scorpions: The Battles and Triumphs of FDR's Great Supreme Court Justices* (2010), 392–395, 406, 412–414. For Rehnquist's own account, which paints a rosier picture, see William Rehnquist, *The Supreme Court* (1987), 3–20, 169–192. For a recent proposed synthesis of the general relationship, see Brad Snyder and John Q. Barrett, "Rehnquist's Missing

Letter: A Former Law Clerk's 1955 Thoughts on Justice Jackson and *Brown*," *Boston College LR* 53 (2012): 631.

6. For a magisterial account of these and closely related developments, see A. E. Dick Howard's forthcoming article, "The Changing Face of the Supreme Court," *Virginia LR* 101 (2015).

7. On Jackson's rivalry with Black, see James F. Simon, *The Antagonists: Hugo Black, Felix Frankfurter and Civil Liberties in Modern America* (1989), 157–170; Feldman, *Scorpions*.

8. In order of official seniority: John Roberts (Harvard College, Harvard Law), Antonin Scalia (Georgetown, Fribourg, Harvard Law), Anthony Kennedy (Stanford, London School of Economics, Harvard Law), Clarence Thomas (Holy Cross, Yale Law), Ruth Bader Ginsburg (Cornell, Harvard Law, and Columbia Law), Stephen Breyer (Stanford, Oxford, Harvard Law), Samuel Alito (Princeton, Yale Law), Sonia Sotomayor (Princeton, Yale Law), and Elena Kagan (Princeton, Oxford, Harvard Law). Note that Roberts completed his four-year college experience in three years by taking an extra-heavy and demanding course load.

9. Justice Breyer clerked on the Supreme Court; Justices Ginsburg and Alito clerked for lower-federal court judges; and Chief Justice Roberts and Justice Kagan clerked at both levels.

10. Consider, for example, the following overlapping or abutting members of the Court, from 1789 to 2005, each of whom came to the Court without notable judicial experience: James Wilson, Bushrod Washington, John Marshall, Roger Taney, Salmon P. Chase, Morrison Waite, Melville Fuller, Charles Evans Hughes, James McReynolds, Hugo Black, and William Rehnquist.

11. In order of official seniority, the nine in 2006 were Chief Justice John Roberts and Associate Justices John Paul Stevens, Antonin Scalia, Anthony Kennedy, David Souter, Clarence Thomas, Ruth Bader Ginsburg, Stephen Breyer, and Samuel Alito.

12. Prior to Alito, Justice Horace Lurton, named to the Court in 1909, also brought sixteen years of federal circuit-court experience with him; and a handful of other justices in history had even more years on state courts under their belts before joining the US Supreme Court.

13. See, generally, Lincoln Caplan, *The Tenth Justice: The Solicitor General and the Rule of Law* (1987).

14. Although much of the work product of the OLC is not designed for direct use in Article III litigation, the OLC does function in a rather judicialized manner, with various judicial-like protocols and procedures. It is a kind of judicature for internal disputes and legal questions that arise within the executive branch.

15. Stanley Reed was another former solicitor general to reach the Court in the mid-twentieth century. Though he left the Court after Jackson's death, he had been appointed by FDR before Jackson.

16. Consider, for example, the following chain of overlapping or abutting justices from 1789 to 2006, each of whom brought considerable political experience to the Court: James Wilson, William Paterson, John Marshall, Roger Taney, Nathan Clifford, John Marshall Harlan I, Charles Evans Hughes, Mahlon Pitney, George Sutherland, Hugo Black, Potter Stewart, and Sandra Day O'Connor. Note that although Stewart joined the Court directly from a federal circuit, he had early in his career been twice elected to the Cincinnati city council, and had served one term as the vice mayor of that city (where his father had once been mayor). Note also that even after O'Connor's departure, David Souter sat until 2009

and brought to the Court his experience as a former appointed attorney general of New Hampshire.

17. On Marshall's presidential dreams and schemes, see Bruce Ackerman, *The Failure of the Founding Fathers* (2005), 36–54.

18. For more discussion, see the paperback edition of Amar, *AUC*, and my November 21, 2013, posting in Slate.com, "The Nuclear-Option Genie Is Out of the Bottle."

19. On the different tools and techniques of constitutional analysis and argumentation, see, generally, Philip Bobbitt, *Constitutional Fate* (1982); Amar, *AUC*.

20. "Rightly" and "really" are of course doing all the work here. These words encapsulate an implicit argument that in the particular situation at issue, the Court's precedent is inconsistent with constitutional text and/or original intent, or the document's overall structure, or the relevant traditions and institutional settlements, or what have you—and that precedent in this situation should yield to the greater force of these other constitutional considerations.

21. At pp. 640–641 of his concurrence, Jackson came close to rejecting the notion that the opening clause of Article II, vesting the president with "the executive power," contained within itself any residual authority above and beyond the individual executive powers itemized elsewhere in Article II, such as the president's power to pardon and his power to serve as commander in chief. Elsewhere I have explained why Jackson erred. In a nutshell, his reading rendered him "unable to explain, *textually*, where the president gets various powers that [the president] has always exercised and that even [Jackson himself, along with most sensible scholars of the subject] generally concede [the president] should exercise. To read out the vesting clause is thus to do one of three things: (1) Reject much of actual executive practice going back to George Washington, practice that made good constitutional sense at the time and continues to make good sense. (2) Uphold various actions of Washington and Lincoln—and most other well respected presidents—by stretching the enumerated list of executive powers beyond recognition. But what is gained by this? (3) Uphold actual practice by creating wholly nontextual doctrines. Again, what is gained thereby?" Amar, *ACAB*, 559–560n.22. For much more discussion of how the Article II vesting clause may be treated as a source of residual power without creating a presidential Frankenstein, see ibid., Chapters 4 and 5; Amar, *AUC*, Chapters 1, 8–9.

22. *Duncan v. Louisiana*, 391 U.S. 145, 165 (1968) (Black, J., concurring) (emphasis added).

23. See, generally, Akhil Reed Amar, "The Lawfulness of Health-Care Reform," posted on SSRN, June 2011 (prepared for the *Yale Law Journal* online).

24. Long before the Obamacare decision was announced, I told all who cared to listen, in both public and private settings, that I hoped and believed that John Roberts would provide the key fifth vote to uphold the Obamacare law and would do so on the tax theory. In other words, both publicly and privately I correctly forecast both the basic theory and the core lineup of the final decision. (I never had any doubt that the four Democrat-appointees would rule in favor of the law as both a proper regulation of interstate commerce and a proper exercise of taxing power; and I was unsure, to varying degrees, about how the other members of the Court would rule, though I hoped they would see the light—which, alas, they did not.) For an account of my private communications with the then–acting solicitor general of the United States (my friend and protégé Neal Katyal) long before the case reached the Court—an account based on Katyal's recollections—see Marcia Coyle,

The Roberts Court: The Struggle for the Constitution (2013), 319–322, 368, Chapter 14, n. 6. For my public statements to similar effect the day before the Supreme Court conference on the case, see the closing paragraphs of my March 29, 2012. Slate.com essay, "How to Defend Obamacare."

I admit that I cannot prove conclusively that John Roberts was inclined to rule as he did *because of* his executive-branch experience. He has not himself offered the kind of openly autobiographical statements that both Jackson and Black did; and human motivation is often complex and difficult to determine. My views about how John Roberts thinks about law have been informed by confidential interviews and conversations with several individuals who have worked very closely with Roberts at different points in his illustrious career.

CHAPTER 4: CALIFORNIA
Anthony Kennedy and the Ideal of Equality

1. See, generally, Joseph Goldstein, *The Intelligible Constitution* (1992) (discussing the Supreme Court's obligation to maintain the Constitution as something "We the People" can understand).

2. On Brennan's opinion, see Lackland H. Bloom, Jr., "*Barnette* and *Johnson*: A Tale of Two Opinions," *Iowa LR* 75 (1990): 417, 426–432 (describing *Johnson* as tinny and tone-deaf); Christopher L. Eisgruber, "Is the Supreme Court an Educative Institution?," *New York U. LR* 67 (1992): 961, 977–985 (similar). On Rehnquist's lapses, see Akhil Reed Amar, "Comment: The Case of the Missing Amendments: *R.A.V. v. City of St. Paul*," *Harvard LR* 106 (1992): 124, 132–146. In style (though not in substance), Brennan's opinion differs markedly from the far more impressive opinion by Justice Jackson in the 1943 flag-salute case of *West Virginia State Board of Education v. Barnette*, a case cited repeatedly (and correctly) by Brennan as providing strong support for his bottom-line result. Given that, under *Barnette*, there is a free-expression right to decline to salute the flag, it logically follows that there is also a free-expression right to express contempt for the flag. In other words, *Barnette* confirms that flags, flag ceremonies, and other sorts of symbolic expression are emphatically covered by the Constitution's free-expression principles. For a brief discussion of *Barnette*, and of Justice Jackson's stylish opinion in that case, see the preceding chapter, pp. 56–57, and accompanying n. 2, p. 319.

3. For more analysis, see Amar, "Comment," 133–139.

4. See, generally, Alexander Meiklejohn, *Political Freedom: The Constitutional Powers of the People* (1960), 26–27, 34–36.

5. On the connection between these two speech clauses, see Amar, *Bill of Rights*, 24–26; Amar, *ACAB*, 101–104; Amar, *AUC*, 32–38, 167–169. True, the Article I "speech" clause does not explicitly use the word "freedom"—but this clause was plainly bottomed on deeply rooted English and American ideas of "freedom of speech and debate" within legislative assemblies. See supra Chapter 2, n. 24, and sources cited therein.

6. *United States v. Kokinda*, 497 U.S. 720, 737 (1990) (Kennedy, J., concurring).

7. See, generally, Lawrence Lessig, "Fidelity in Translation," *Texas LR* 71 (1993): 1165 (describing model of applying old principles to new contexts).

8. Meiklejohn, *Political Freedom*, 19–20.

9. See, generally, Akhil Reed Amar, "The Central Meaning of Republican Government: Popular Sovereignty, Majority Rule, and the Denominator Problem," *U. of Colorado LR* 65 (1994): 749.

10. For a similar vision of the jury, published contemporaneously with *Powers*, see Amar, "The Bill of Rights as a Constitution," *Yale LJ* 100 (1991): 1131, 1182–1199. For a later version of this material, see Amar, *Bill of Rights*, 81–118.

11. For much more on the linkage between jury service and voting, see Vikram David Amar, "Jury Service as Political Participation Akin to Voting," *Cornell LR* 80 (1995): 203; Amar, *CCP*, 161–178; Amar, *Bill of Rights*, 272–274; Amar, *ACAB*, 399–401, 426–427, 612–613n.106, 619–621nn.51–52; Amar, *AUC*, 286–289, 563n.9.

12. See *Edmonson v. Leesville Concrete Co.*, 500 U.S. 614, 625–626 (1991) (discussing *Terry v. Adams*, 345 U.S. 461 [1953], and *Smith v. Allwright*, 321 U.S. 649 [1944]).

13. See, generally, Amar, *CCP*, 166–172.

14. On formulaic constitutionalism more generally, see Robert F. Nagel, "The Formulaic Constitution," *Michigan LR* 84 (1985): 165.

15. *Rosenberger v. Rector & Visitors of Univ.*, 515 U.S. 819 (1995).

16. For more on *Romer*, see, generally, Akhil Reed Amar, "Attainder and Amendment 2: *Romer*'s Rightness," *Michigan LR* 95 (1996): 203.

17. *Romer*'s most pointed allusion to attainder occurs in a passage citing and elaborating upon a case not cited by the parties or by the courts below—*United States v. Brown*, 381 U.S. 437 (1965), a landmark attainder case. For more discussion of this aspect of *Romer*, see, generally, Amar, "Attainder and Amendment 2."

18. While sitting on the Ninth Circuit, Judge Kennedy—who would later assume Justice Powell's seat on the Supreme Court—invalidated the efforts of the House of Representatives to single out "Jagdish Chadha" by name for disfavored treatment. Kennedy based his decision on general separation-of-powers grounds and noted that the treatment Chadha received also raised "serious bill of attainder and equal protection problems." See *Immigration & Naturalization Serv. v. Chadha*, 634 F.2d 408, 435n.42 (9th Cir. 1980), aff'd, 462 U.S. 919 (1983). The Supreme Court upheld Judge Kennedy's decision in an opinion that likewise focused on separation of powers. Justice Powell wrote separately to emphasize the attainder angle, among other things. See *Immigration & Naturalization Serv. v. Chadha*, 462 U.S. 919, 962 (1983) (Powell, J., concurring in the judgment).

19. On the Reconstruction Congress, see, generally, Eric Schnapper, "Affirmative Action and the Legislative History of the Fourteenth Amendment," *Virginia LR* 71 (1985): 753. On judicial race-conscious integration decrees, involving at least some individuals who were not themselves identifiable victims of illegal racial discrimination, see, e.g., *North Carolina State Bd. of Educ. v. Swann*, 402 U.S. 43, 45–46 (1971); Amar, *AUC*, 268–269.

20. In particular, Justice Powell endorsed a diversity theory of affirmative action that paradigmatically applied to education after rejecting other theories of affirmative action that would have swept more broadly outside the educational sphere. For more elaboration of Powell's vision, see Akhil Reed Amar and Neal Katyal, "Bakke's Fate," *UCLA LR* 43 (1996): 1745.

21. In *Noel Canning*, the four justices who did not join the Court's majority opinion concurred in the result, though for quite different reasons.

22. See *Parents Involved in Community Schools v. Seattle School Dist. No. 1*, 551 U.S. 701, 782–798 (2007) (Kennedy, J., concurring in part and concurring in the judgment).

23. Brennan was born and raised in Newark, New Jersey; Marshall in Baltimore, Maryland; and Scalia was born in Trenton, New Jersey, and grew up in the New York City area; see supra Chapter 3, n. 4.

24. For details and more discussion, see this book's Conclusion, p. 270.

25. My imagined conversation with Justice Kennedy here draws heavily from another Northern California lecture that I recently delivered, not far from the Kennedy family homestead. See Akhil Reed Amar, "The First Amendment's Firstness," *UC Davis LR* 47 (2014): 1015.

26. For more discussion and analysis of Justice Kennedy's historic *Lawrence* decision, see Amar, *AUC*, 121–122, 127, 130, 540n.35, 541n.42.

CHAPTER 5: KANSAS

LIVING IN THE SHADOW OF *BROWN V. BOARD*

1. See Alexander M. Bickel, "The Original Understanding and the Segregation Decision," *Harvard LR* 69 (1955): 1; Michael W. McConnell, "Originalism and the Desegregation Decisions," *Virginia LR* 81 (1995): 947; Michael W. McConnell, "The Originalist Case for *Brown v. Board of Education*," *Harvard Journal of Law & Public Policy* 19 (1996): 457; Bruce Ackerman, *We the People: Foundations* (1991), 142–150; Bruce Ackerman, "Opinion in *Brown v. Board of Education*," in J. M. Balkin, ed., *What Brown Should Have Said* (2001), 100; John Hart Ely, *Democracy and Distrust: A Theory of Judicial Review* (1980), 145–170; Michael J. Klarman, "The Puzzling Resistance to Political Process Theory," *Virginia LR* 77 (1991): 747, 788–814; Michael J. Klarman, "*Brown*, Racial Change, and the Civil Rights Movement," *Virginia LR* 80 (1994): 7; Michael J. Klarman, "*Brown v. Board of Education*: Facts and Political Correctness," ibid., 185. In more recent work, Professor Ackerman has offered yet another account of *Brown*. It, too, is distinctively Ackermanian, confirming my basic claim that different theories of *Brown* abound, and that each scholar tends to read *Brown* in light of that scholar's preferred constitutional framework. As Ackerman's general framework has evolved, so has his reading of *Brown*. For his more recent ideas, see, generally, Bruce Ackerman, *We the People: The Civil Rights Revolution* (2014). And for another notable recent defense of *Brown*, see Steven G. Calabresi and Andrea Matthews, "Originalism and *Loving v. Virginia*," *BYU LR* 2012: 1393.

2. See David A. Strauss, "Common Law Constitutional Interpretation," *U. of Chicago LR* 63 (1996): 877, 906; Cass R. Sunstein, "Foreword: Leaving Things Undecided," *Harvard LR* 110 (1996): 4, 31, 50–51; Edward P. Lazarus, *Closed Chambers* (1998), 10, 89–90, 110, 323; Gerald N. Rosenberg, *The Hollow Hope: Can Courts Bring About Social Change?* (1991); Derrick A. Bell, Jr., "*Brown v. Board of Education* and the Interest-Convergence Dilemma," *Harvard LR* 93 (1980): 518; Mary L. Dudziak, "Desegregation as a Cold War Imperative," *Stanford LR* 41 (1988): 61; Mary L. Dudziak, "The Little Rock Crisis and Foreign Affairs: Race, Resistance, and the Image of American Democracy," *Southern California LR* 70 (1977): 1641.

3. For this important insight about the Greeks, as for so many other things, I am indebted to the pioneering work of my colleague Jed Rubenfeld. See Jed Rubenfeld, "Reading the Constitution as Spoken," *Yale LJ* 104 (1995): 1119, 1143. For lots more on the democratic nature of the Preamble and the founding acts of 1787–1788, see Amar, *ACAB*, 3–21, 308–312.

4. For more elaboration, see Akhil Reed Amar, "The Central Meaning of Republican Government: Popular Sovereignty, Majority Rule, and the Denominator Problem," *U. of Colorado LR* 65 (1994): 749.

5. On the attainder clauses as a paired set, see Akhil Reed Amar, "Intratextualism," *Harvard LR* 112 (1999): 747, 769–770.

6. For more elaboration, see, generally, Akhil Reed Amar, "Attainder and Amendment 2: *Romer's* Rightness," *Michigan LR* 95 (1996): 203. See also U.S. Const. art. III, sec. 3, cl. 2. Note that the Philadelphia Framers initially put the federal attainder clause and the corruption-of-blood clause side by side. See *The Records of the Federal Convention of 1787*, Max Farrand rev. ed. (1937), 2:571.

7. Lincoln's main criticism of *Dred Scott* focused on the Court's claim that federal free-soil laws violated the Constitution—a claim that truly is astonishing; see supra Chapter 2, p. 31. For more on Lincoln on *Dred Scott*, and on *Dred Scott* generally, see Amar, *ACAB*, 252–254; Amar, *AUC*, 270–273.

8. For more on the equality mandate of the citizenship clause, see Act of Apr. 9, 1866, 14 Stat. 27; Amar, *Bill of Rights*, 171–174, 196 n.*, 281–283; Amar, *ACAB*, 383–384; Amar, *AUC*, 109–110, 150–151; Amar, "Intratextualism," 767–773.

9. For more on the relationship between equal protection and due process, see Akhil Reed Amar, "Constitutional Rights in a Federal System: Rethinking Incorporation and Reverse Incorporation," in Terry Eastland, ed., *Benchmarks: Great Constitutional Controversies in the Supreme Court* (1995), 71, 82–84; Amar, "Intratextualism," 771–773; Amar, *AUC*, 543–544n.5. For more on the Fifteenth Amendment and political rights, see sources supra Chapter 4, n. 11.

10. A similar one-paragraph summary of the basic Reconstruction argument for *Brown* and *Bolling* appears in Amar, *AUC*, 145–146.

11. For more elaboration of "paradigm cases" and their significance, see Jed Rubenfeld, *Freedom and Time* (2001), 178–195; Jed Rubenfeld, "The Paradigm-Case Method," *Yale LJ* 115 (2006): 1977.

12. See Amar, *Bill of Rights*, 216–218, 271.

13. On the jury-voting linkage and for abundant evidence that the Fifteenth Amendment was designed to protect all political rights and not just voting, see sources supra Chapter 4, n. 11.

14. See Paul Gewirtz, "Choice in the Transition: School Desegregation and the Corrective Ideal," *Columbia LR* 86 (1986): 728, 789.

15. See Ely, *Democracy and Distrust*, 11–41 ("The Impossibility of a Clause-Bound Interpretivism").

16. The need for holism is one of many lessons about law and life taught to me by my great friend, teacher, and role model Charles Black. See Charles L. Black, Jr., *Structure and Relationship in Constitutional Law* (1969). Professor Black was part of the legal team that helped Thurgood Marshall prevail in the *Brown* litigation. For Black's canonical short and sweet defense of *Brown*, which has profoundly influenced my own thinking about the case, see Charles L. Black, Jr., "The Lawfulness of the Segregation Decisions," *Yale LJ* 69 (1960): 421. Also highly relevant is Black's autobiographical companion essay—equally short and sweet—"My World with Louis Armstrong," *Yale LJ* 95 (1986): 1595.

17. For some of the reasons underlying *Brown's* lapses in this regard, see Amar, *AUC*, 213–215. For examples of candid confessions of error, see supra Chapter 2, pp. 40–41, and n. 20.

18. See, generally, Jack Balkin, *Constitutional Redemption: Political Faith in an Unjust World* (2011).

CHAPTER 6: IOWA
REREADING *TINKER V. DES MOINES*

1. Recall the discussion of this point in Chapter 1, pp. 16–17; for further discussion, see infra Chapter 11, pp. 245–246.

2. For additional background on the original Bill of Rights, recall the discussion in Chapter 2, pp. 31–32.

3. For more on *Barron*, see supra Chapter 2; Amar, *Bill of Rights*, 140–162.

4. Note that the Virginia legislature changed its name, but not its basic structure, during the American Revolution. See supra Chapter 1, p. 16.

5. Amar, *Bill of Rights*, 33.

6. See Lois J. Schwoerer, *The Declaration of Rights* (1981), 297. Recall the discussion of this point in Chapter 4, pp. 82–83.

7. Act of July 14, 1798, 1 Stat. 596.

8. Jefferson's electoral college victory was also aided by the three-fifths clause. See Amar, *ACAB*, 344–347. On the baseline issue raised by this clause, see infra Chapter 9, n. 1, and sources cited therein.

9. Trial of John Peter Zenger, 9 Geo. 2 (1735), reprinted in 17 Howell's State Trials 675 (1816).

10. For more on Founding-era criminal juries and their powers to "nullify" law by acquitting criminal defendants who are in fact guilty under the law as written, see Amar, *Bill of Rights*, 81–118; Amar, *AUC*, 117–448.

11. See Amar, *Bill of Rights*, 157–158, 277–278.

12. Recall the discussion of Hugo Black and the incorporation doctrine in Chapter 2, pp. 36–38, and Chapter 3, pp. 75–76.

13. See Amar, *Bill of Rights*, 32–42.

14. See Nadine Strossen, "Keeping the Constitution Inside the Schoolhouse Gate: Student Rights Thirty Years After *Tinker v. Des Moines Independent Community School District*," *Drake LR* 48 (2000): 445, 453–454.

15. See, generally, Amar, *Bill of Rights*, 231–257.

16. Emphasis added.

17. Special thanks to my mentor Owen Fiss for this reminder.

CHAPTER 7: FLORIDA
GETTING TO THE BOTTOM OF *BUSH V. GORE*

1. "554 Law Professors Say," *NY Times*, Jan. 13, 2001, A7.

2. Margaret Jane Radin, "Can the Rule of Law Survive *Bush v. Gore*?," in Bruce Ackerman, ed., *Bush v. Gore: The Question of Legitimacy* (2002), 14–15, 117, 122.

3. Jed Rubenfeld, "Not as Bad as *Plessy*. Worse," in *Legitimacy*, 20–21, 26; Jack M. Balkin, "Legitimacy and the 2000 Election," in *Legitimacy*, 210 (emphasis added).

4. Bruce Ackerman, "Off Balance," in *Legitimacy*, 195–196.

5. Richard A. Epstein, "'In Such Manner as the Legislature Thereof May Direct': The Outcome of *Bush v Gore* Defended," in Cass R. Sunstein and Richard A. Epstein, eds., *The Vote: Bush, Gore and the Supreme Court* (2001), 13, 36; Michael W. McConnell, "Two-and-a-Half Cheers for *Bush v Gore*," in *The Vote*, 98, 101, 108–109.

6. Charles Fried, "An Unreasonable Reaction to a Reasonable Decision," in *Legitimacy*, 3 (emphasis altered).

7. Ibid., 8–10.

8. Ibid., 19 (claiming that the "mirror image" of the actual *Bush v. Gore* would have been a case in which "a state court had been caught trying to steal the election for George Bush," thus implying that in *Bush v. Gore* itself, the Florida Supreme Court was caught trying to steal the election for Al Gore).

9. David Strauss, "*Bush v Gore:* What Were They Thinking?," in *The Vote*, 184.

10. *Palm Beach County Canvassing Board v. Harris*, 772 So. 2d 1220, 1227–1228 (Fla. Nov. 21, 2000—corrected Nov. 28, 2000) ("Twenty-five years ago, this Court commented that the will of the people, not a hyper-technical reliance upon statutory provisions, should be our guiding principle in election cases. . . . 'By refusing to recognize an otherwise valid exercise of the right of a citizen to vote for the sake of sacred, unyielding adherence to statutory scripture, we would in effect nullify that right'—a right guaranteed by '[o]ur federal and state constitutions.'") (quoting *Boardman v. Esteva*, 323 So. 2d 259, 263 [Fla. 1975]); ibid., 1227–1227 (quoting *Treiman v. Malmquist*, 342 So. 2d 972, 975 [Fla. 1977]); ibid., 1237.

11. For one promising passage that began to lay the foundations of such an explanation, but failed to drive home the source and the breadth of the state judiciary's authority to forcefully deploy the state constitution in presidential elections, see *Gore v. Harris*, 772 So. 2d 1243, 1253–1254, and n. 11 (Fla. Dec. 8, 2000).

12. *Gore*, 1262, 1270 (Wells, C.J., dissenting).

13. *Palm Beach County Canvassing Board v. Harris*, 772 So. 2d 1273 (Fla. Dec. 11, 2000). Chief Justice Wells dissented (ibid., 1292).

14. *Bush v. Gore*, 531 U.S. 1046 (Dec. 9, 2000).

15. Epstein, "In Such Manner," 19–37; McConnell, "Two-and-a-Half Cheers," 103–105, 108–109.

16. See *Palm Beach County Canvassing Board v. Harris*, 772 So. 2d 1273, 1279n.2 (Fla. Dec. 11, 2000) (explaining the time crunch).

17. Ibid., 1282, 1291. In general, subsequent scholarly commentary has tended to slide past three crucial Article II points, as I see them: First, whether or not the Florida Constitution applied of its own automatic self-executing force to the presidential election in Florida, it surely applied because the Florida legislature implicitly incorporated its principles into the basic structure of the unitary Florida election statute. Second, the Florida Supreme Court failed to make this first point crystal clear in its initial expositions. Third, had the Florida Supreme Court made the first point clear before the Rehnquist Court issued its fateful December 9 stay, the basic error of the Rehnquist concurrence would have been glaringly obvious; Rehnquist's Article II argument boomerangs once we see that the Florida legislature itself gave the Florida judiciary the authority to deploy the Florida

Constitution to interpret and implement the entire statutory election code and to adjust or even abandon provisions of the code that violated basic state constitutional principles as construed by the state judiciary. For a particularly thoughtful, albeit less emphatic, exposition of the first point, see Robert A. Schapiro, "Conceptions and Misconceptions of State Constitutional Law in *Bush v. Gore*," *Florida State U. LR* 29 (2001): 661, 683–688.

18. Although the notion that a state court can cabin, modify, disregard, and even supplement—in effect, "rewrite"—various parts of a state statute in order to bring the statute into conformity with the state constitution might initially raise an eyebrow, the judicial power to "rewrite" a statute in certain remedial situations is simply one aspect of American-style judicial review. For a prominent recent example of a federal court in effect "rewriting" a federal statute so as to render that statute compliant with the federal Constitution, as construed by the Court, see, e.g., *United States v. Booker*, 543 U.S. 220, 244–268 (2005) (opinion of the Court in part, per Breyer, J.) (effectively rewriting the federal sentencing-guidelines statute so as to bring the statute into compliance with the Supreme Court's interpretation of the Sixth Amendment). For an even more recent case in which the US Supreme Court sharply bent the seemingly plain meaning of a statute in order to minimize the statute's arguable unconstitutionality, see *Northwest Austin Mun. Util. Dist. No. One v. Holder*, 557 U.S. 193 (2009).

19. *Palm Beach County Canvassing Board v. Harris*, 772 So. 2d 1220, 1236–1237 (Fla. Nov. 21, 2000—corrected Nov. 28, 2000); *State ex rel. Carpenter v. Barber*, 144 Fla. 159 (Fla. 1940); *Boardman v. Esteva*, 323 So. 2d 259, 269–270 (Fla. 1975); *Treiman v. Malmquist*, 342 So. 2d 972, 975 (Fla. 1977). See, generally, Richard L. Hasen, "The Democracy Canon," *Stanford LR* 62 (2009): 69.

20. See Michael J. Klarman, "*Bush v. Gore* Through the Lens of Constitutional History," *California LR* 89 (2001): 1721, 1743, and n. 113.

21. Steven G. Calabresi, "A Political Question," in *Legitimacy*, 129, 132.

22. Op. Att'y Gen. Fla 2000–65 (Nov. 14, 2000).

23. See Fla. Const. art. III, sec. 2 ("Each house shall be the sole judge of the qualifications, elections, and returns of its members.").

24. See Laurence H. Tribe, "*eroG .v hsuB:* Through the Looking Glass," in *Legitimacy*, 39, 59 (federal statute "empowers the legislature to direct the choice of a new set of electors only when the state 'has held an election and has *failed to make a choice* on the day prescribed by law,' not when it has *made* a choice but the choice has yet to be ascertained"); but see Calabresi, "A Political Question," 134 (suggesting, albeit with a notable hedge, that "[b]ecause Florida had *arguably* failed to make a choice on November 7," the Florida legislature could properly jump back in under the terms of 3 USC section 2) (emphasis added).

25. Bruce Ackerman, "As Florida Goes," *NY Times*, Dec. 12, 2000, A33.

26. See, generally, Amar, *ACAB*, 208–209, 210–211.

27. Tribe, "*eroG v. hsuB*," 50.

28. *Bush v. Gore*, 531 U.S. 98, 109 (Dec. 12, 2000) (per curiam) ("The recount process, in its features here described, is inconsistent with the minimum procedures necessary to protect the fundamental right of each voter in the special instance of a statewide recount under the authority of a single state judicial officer. Our consideration is limited to the present circumstances, for the problem of equal protection in election processes generally presents many complexities.").

29. See, e.g., *Delahunt v. Johnston*, 671 N.E. 2d 1241 (Mass. 1996).

30. See Tribe, "*eroG v. hsuB*," 45–46.

31. For a fascinating analysis of earlier Rehnquist Court election-law cases with very different facts, but similar voting line-ups, see Richard H. Pildes, "Democracy and Disorder," in *The Vote*, 140.

32. See supra n. 27.

33. See *Bush v. Gore*, 531 U.S. 98, 147 (Dec. 12, 2000) (Breyer, J., dissenting).

34. For a similar analysis of the justices' behavior in *Youngstown Sheet & Tube v. Sawyer*, 343 U.S. 579 (1952), see Paul Brest, Sanford Levinson, Jack M. Balkin, Akhil Reed Amar, and Riva B. Siegel, eds., *Processes of Constitutional Decisionmaking: Cases and Materials*, 5th ed. (2006), 836. For a wide-ranging discussion of possible strategic voting in *Bush v. Gore*, see Michael Abramowicz and Maxwell Stearns, "Beyond Counting Votes: The Political Economy of *Bush v. Gore*," *Vanderbilt LR* 54 (2001): 1849.

35. On the opposing rationales of these two dissents, compare *Bush v. Gore*, 531 U.S. 98, 123 (Dec. 12, 2000) (Stevens, J., dissenting) ("The federal questions that ultimately emerged in this case are not substantial."), with ibid., 133–134 (Souter, J., dissenting) ("It is only on the [equal-protection] issue before us that there is a meritorious argument for relief, as this Court's *Per Curiam* opinion recognizes. . . . I can conceive of no legitimate state interest served by these differing treatments of the expressions of voters' fundamental rights. The differences appear wholly arbitrary."). Yet somehow Justice Breyer was willing to join both opinions in their entirety. See ibid., 123 (Stevens, J., dissenting, joined [entirely] by Justices Ginsburg and Breyer), 129 (Souter, J., dissenting, joined [entirely] by Justice Breyer and joined in part [but note: only in part] by Justices Stevens and Ginsburg).

36. Ibid., 145–146 (Breyer, J., dissenting) ("[S]ince the use of different standards could favor one or the other of the candidates, since time was, and is, too short to permit the lower courts to iron out significant differences through ordinary judicial review, and since the relevant distinction was embodied in the order of the State's highest court, I agree that, in these very special circumstances, basic principles of fairness may well have counseled the adoption of a uniform standard to address the problem. In light of the majority's disposition, I need not decide whether, or the extent to which, as a remedial matter, the Constitution would place limits upon the content of the uniform standard.").

37. See, e.g., U.S. Commission on Civil Rights, "Voting Irregularities in Florida During the 2000 Election," June 2001, www.usccr.gov/pubs/vote2000/report/main.htm.

CHAPTER 8: OHIO

A BUCKEYE-STATE VIEW OF PRESIDENTS WITHOUT MANDATES

1. See Akhil Reed Amar and Vikram David Amar, "Is the Presidential Succession Act Unconstitutional?," *Stanford LR* 48 (1995): 118, 133, 138n.144.

2. See Act of Mar. 1, 1792, 1 Stat. 239 (repealed 1886).

3. On issues of rank and title in early America, see, generally, Gordon Wood, *The Radicalism of the American Revolution* (1991). In the Constitution itself, see art I, sec. 9, cl. 8 (barring federal titles of nobility); ibid., sec. 10, cl. 1 (barring state titles of nobility). Article VI of the Articles of Confederation had imposed similar restrictions on both Congress

and the states—a striking fact when we recall how few limits that document generally imposed on then-sovereign states.

4. For a superb general discussion, see John D. Feerick, *From Failing Hands: The Story of Presidential Succession* (1965), 117–139.

5. Ibid., 118–119.

6. See Amar and Amar, "Presidential Succession," 139.

7. See Akhil Reed Amar and Vik Amar, "President Quayle?," *Virginia LR* 78 (1992): 913. Professor Richard Friedman made this suggestion even earlier. See Richard D. Friedman, "Some Modest Proposals on the Vice-Presidency," *Michigan LR* 86 (1988): 1703, 1726–1729.

8. See Robert A. Rutland, Thomas A. Mason, Robert J. Brugger, Jeanne K. Sisson, and Frederika J. Teute, eds., *Papers of James Madison* 14 (1983): 235 (Letter to Edmund Pendleton, Feb. 21, 1792). On the correctness of Madison's original objections, see Amar and Amar, "Presidential Succession"; Amar, *ACAB*, 170–173; Amar, *AUC*, 403–405.

9. On the Wade-Johnson issue, see John D. Feerick, *The Twenty-Fifth Amendment*, 2nd ed. (1992), 214; Amar, *AUC*, 3–5, 14–21.

10. See Act of Jan. 19, 1886, ch. 4, 1, 24 Stat. 1 (repealed 1947). The soundness of certain details of the 1792 act's timetable might well be questioned—exactly when and how a special election should be held, and the term of office that should follow upon victory in this special election. In saying the act got the "how long" question right, I thus mean to endorse only the act's big idea that statutory succession should generally trigger a special election to replace a caretaker officer.

11. See 3 U.S.C. 19 (1994).

12. See Akhil Reed Amar, "Presidents, Vice Presidents, and Death: Closing the Constitution's Succession Gap," *Arkansas LR* 48 (1995): 215 (based on testimony before the Senate Judiciary Subcommittee on the Constitution, Feb. 2, 1994).

13. For additional explanations, see Carl N. Degler, *The Age of the Economic Revolution, 1876–1900*, 2nd ed. (1977), 89–93.

14. For some thoughts about how America could achieve direct popular election of the president without a formal constitutional amendment, see Amar, *AUC*, 456–463.

15. An alphabetical list of the fifty states and the most recent presidential election in which each state was on the losing side (and for the asterisked twelve most populous states per the 2010 census, the two most recent elections in which the state was on the losing side): Alabama (2012), Alaska (2012), Arizona (2012), Arkansas (2012), *California (2004, 2000), Colorado (1996), Connecticut (2004), Delaware (2004), *Florida (1992, 1960), *Georgia (2012, 2008), Hawaii (2004), Idaho (2012), *Illinois (2004, 2000), Indiana (2012), Iowa (2000), Kansas (2012), Kentucky (2012), Louisiana (2012), Maine (2004), Maryland (2004), Massachusetts (2004), *Michigan (2004, 2000), Minnesota (2004), Mississippi (2012), Missouri (2012), Montana (2012), Nebraska (2012), Nevada (1976), New Hampshire (2004), *New Jersey (2004, 2000), New Mexico (2000), *New York (2004, 2000), *North Carolina (2012, 1996), North Dakota (2012), *Ohio (1960, 1944), Oklahoma (2012), Oregon (2004), *Pennsylvania (2004, 2000), Rhode Island (2004), South Carolina (2012), South Dakota (2012), Tennessee (2012), *Texas (2012, 2008), Utah

(2012), Vermont (2004), *Virginia (1996, 1992), Washington (2004), West Virginia (2012), Wisconsin (2004), Wyoming (2012).

CHAPTER 9: TEXAS
A LONE-STAR VIEW OF
PRESIDENTIAL SELECTION AND SUCCESSION

1. My claim that the three-fifths clause gave slave states *extra* seats and was thus a proslavery provision that *tilted* apportionment in slave states' favor obviously presupposes an analytic baseline. For elaboration and defense of the baseline I have chosen—in which a truly neutral policy on slavery would have counted slaves at zero-fifths, thereby making any counting of slaves a genuine proslavery bonus—see Amar, *ACAB*, 87–98.

2. Although Woodrow Wilson was a southerner deep down, having been born in Staunton, Virginia, and raised during the Civil War in Confederate Georgia, he ran for the presidency as a northerner with distinctly northern political credentials as the sitting governor of New Jersey and the former president of Princeton University.

3. Ike's hometown of Abilene, Kansas, is just a hair east of Fort Worth. More to the point, Ike formally sought the White House from New York, where he was president of Columbia University; and by the time he was chosen as America's president, he had made Gettysburg, Pennsylvania, his permanent family home.

4. A small wrinkle: In 1988, the Democrats ran Texan Lloyd Bentsen as their vice presidential candidate—but he was outvoted and out-Texaned by Bush 41 running at the top of the Republican ticket. On his way to national victory, Bush won Texas that year.

5. Query: May a president unilaterally and temporarily fill a vice presidential vacancy, under the Constitution's Article II Recess Appointments Clause, if the vacancy arises when the Senate is not in session?

6. John D. Feerick, *The Twenty-Fifth Amendment: Its Complete History and Applications*, 2nd ed. (1992), 33.

7. For the context of the Lincoln quote, see supra Chapter 1, p. 7.

8. According to Article I, section 6, "no Person holding any Office under the United States, shall be a Member of either House during his Continuance in Office." The presidency is an "Office under the United States," and thus no sitting House or Senate member may serve as president. In order to serve as president, the House or Senate member must thus resign from Congress—just as Senator Hillary Clinton had to resign from the Senate in order to serve as secretary of state, which is also an "Office under the United States" within the meaning of this clause. In keeping with this clause, the 1947 Presidential Succession Act does require a Speaker of the House who becomes acting president to resign from the House first. See 3 USC 19 (a) (1) ("If, by reason of death, resignation, removal from office, inability, or failure to qualify, there is neither a President nor Vice President to discharge the powers and duties of the office of President, then the Speaker of the House of Representatives shall, *upon his resignation as Speaker and as Representative in Congress*, act as President."). (Emphasis added.)

9. See Sanford Levinson and Ernest A. Young, "Who's Afraid of the Twelfth Amendment?," *Florida State U. LR* 29 (2001): 925.

10. See, generally, Amar, *AUC*, 403.

11. For more on the implications of this broad, not-entirely-medical, understanding of presidential disability, see infra pp. 202, and infra nn. 12, 15.

12. True, the Constitution entitles a president to serve four complete years, but it nowhere obliges him to do so. It expressly permits presidential resignations—see Article II, sec. 1, para. 6. And nowhere does the text say that resignations for reasons of political honor or political disgrace are somehow improper. Nor would it be sensible to think this. Consider, finally, the key precedential fact that Richard Nixon resigned before the end of his term and expressly invoked his *political* unviability as his reason for resignation. As we have seen, this resignation occurred within the framework of the Twenty-fifth Amendment.

13. Readers interested in more ways in which transfers of power—congressional as well as executive—could occur more quickly after Election Day may wish to consult my May 14, 2010, posting on Slate.com, "Insta-Gov."

14. For an earlier flight of fancy, in 2008, involving the theoretical possibility that Barack Obama and Hillary Clinton could run as a presidential tag team through creative use of the JFK-LBJ Amendment, see my March 21, 2008, Slate.com posting, "Obama-Clinton, Clinton-Obama: How They Could Run Together and Take Turns Being President."

15. For a more general analysis, see Adam R. F. Gustafson, "Presidential Inability and Subjective Meaning," *Yale Law and Policy Review* 27 (2009): 459.

CHAPTER 10: WYOMING
A ROCKY-MOUNTAIN VIEW OF THE SECOND AMENDMENT

1. Conversation with criminologist Gary Kleck, August 2, 2001 (summarizing data that, in the Rocky Mountain West, about 28.6 percent of households have handguns, compared to a national rate of 22.7 percent; overall gun possession rates are estimated at 43.7 percent in the Rocky Mountain West and 41.8 percent nationally).

2. The material over the next several pages closely overlaps with my presentation and analysis in Amar, *ACAB*, 322–325.

3. See Neil H. Cogan, ed., *The Complete Bill of Rights* (1997), 169–173, 183–185. For more discussion and documentation, see Amar, *Bill of Rights*, 60–61, 332n.33.

4. Cogan, ed., *Complete Bill of Rights*, 170–173. Cf. *Elliot's Debates* 3:425 (remarks of George Mason at Virginia ratifying convention) ("Who are the militia? They consist now of the whole people . . ."); ibid., 112 (remarks of Francis Corbin at Virginia ratifying convention) ("Who are the militia? Are we not militia?"); "Letters from the Federal Farmer (XVIII)," reprinted in Herbert J. Storing, ed., *The Complete Antifederalist* (1981), 2:341 ("A militia, when properly formed, are in fact the people themselves . . . and include . . . all men capable of bearing arms . . .").

5. On the apparent ability of a few women to vote early on in New Jersey, see Amar, *ACAB*, 19, 513n.36.

6. For more support for my reading of the core assembly right, see Amar, *Bill of Rights*, 26–32; for more support for my populist reading of the Ninth and Tenth Amendments, see ibid., 119–122.

7. We shall return to the role of Fourth Amendment juries in the next chapter.

8. See sources cited supra n. 3; 1 W. & M., ch. 2, secs. 6–7 (1689).

9. See, e.g., David C. Williams, "Civic Republicanism and the Citizen Militia: The Terrifying Second Amendment," *Yale LJ* 101 (1991): 551.

10. The reference here is to Robert D. Putnam, *Bowling Alone: The Collapse and Revival of American Community* (2000).

11. See Kenneth L. Karst, "The Pursuit of Manhood and the Desegregation of the Armed Forces," *UCLA LR* 38 (1991): 499.

12. See Don B. Kates, Jr., "The Second Amendment and the Ideology of Self-Protection," *Constitutional Commentary* 9 (1992): 87; Don B. Kates, Jr., "Handgun Prohibition and the Original Meaning of the Second Amendment," *Michigan LR* 82 (1983): 204.

13. The amendment explicitly limited state governments, but its authors made clear that no government, state or federal, had authority to violate fundamental rights of citizens. See Amar, *Bill of Rights*, 196n.*, 281–283; infra text accompanying n. 32.

14. See Stephen Halbrook, *That Every Man Be Armed* (1984); Stephen Halbrook, *Freedmen, The Fourteenth Amendment, and the Right to Bear Arms, 1866–1876* (1998); Michael Kent Curtis, *No State Shall Abridge* (1986); Robert J. Cottrol and Raymond T. Diamond, "The Second Amendment: Toward an Afro-Americanist Reconsideration," *Georgetown LJ* 80 (1991): 309; Lucas A. Powe, "Guns, Words, and Constitutional Interpretation," *William & Mary LR* 38 (1997): 1311; Amar, *Bill of Rights*, 257–268. I am taking poetic license here, using the word "Klansmen" generically to refer to all sorts of white terrorists and thugs who emerged in the aftermath of the Civil War.

15. 14 Stat. 173, 176 (1866) (emphasis added). Amar, *Bill of Rights*, 261–262. Although the linguistic connection between Blackstone's chapter on personal self-defense and the Freedman's Bureau Bill of 1866 is evident on the face of the bill and confirmed by abundant historical evidence, it is doubtful that there was any comparably strong link between this Blackstone chapter and the language of the Second Amendment at the time of its drafting and ratification. See infra pp. 217–218.

16. *Dred Scott v. Sandford*, 60 U.S. (19 How.) 393, 416–417 (1857).

17. See National Rifle Association of America, *Americans and Their Guns*, James B. Trefethen, compiler, and James E. Serven, ed. (1967), 31–35.

18. See, generally, Chapter 2, pp. 31–41; see also supra n. 14. In the case law, see *McDonald v. Chicago*, 561 U.S. 742 (2010).

19. See, e.g., Amar, *Bill of Rights*, 47, 262 (quoting amendment proposed by some Pennsylvania Anti-Federalists affirming a right of the people to "bear arms for the defence of themselves and their own State, or the United States, or for the purpose of killing game").

20. For a recent catalog of state constitutional provisions, see David B. Kopel, Clayton E. Cramer, and Scott G. Hattrup, "A Tale of Three Cities: The Right to Bear Arms in State Supreme Courts," *Temple LR* 68 (1995): 1177, 1180–1183n.13. See also Wisc. Const., art. I, sec. 25 (adopted in 1998, three years after the *Temple Law Review* catalog). For a reminder that many state constitutions circa 1866 also affirmed an individual right of gun ownership, see Steven G. Calabresi and Sarah Agudo, "Individual Rights Under State Constitutions When the Fourteenth Amendment Was Ratified in 1868: What Rights Are Deeply Rooted in American History and Tradition?," *Texas LR* 87 (2008): 7.

21. On the importance of the historical "paradigm case," see Jed Rubenfeld, *Freedom and Time* (2001), 178–195.

22. See, e.g., Robert J. Cottrol and Raymond T. Diamond, "The Fifth Auxiliary Right," *Yale LJ* 104 (1994): 995 (book review).

23. See Amar, *Bill of Rights*, at 226n.*, 261–266. On the evident linguistic link between the Freedman's Bureau Bill language and Blackstone's section on self-defense, see supra p. 214.

24. Cf. *McCulloch v. Maryland*, 17 U.S. (4 Wheat.) 316, 419 (1819); *Martin v. Hunter's Lessee*, 14 U.S. (1 Wheat.) 304, 328–329, 332–334 (1816).

25. Akhil Reed Amar, "Intratextualism," *Harvard LR* 112 (1999): 747.

26. Senate rules circa 1866 apparently did not allow foreigners to petition that body, on the theory that petition was a right of "the people." See Amar, *Bill of Rights*, 174, 364n.41.

27. See, generally, Williams, "Civic Republicanism."

28. See Amar, *Bill of Rights*, 50–59. See also Amar, *AUC*, 88–94.

29. For more detailed analysis of the interactions and implications of these provisions for nonspecified rights, see Amar, *CCP*, 94–96, 132; Akhil Reed Amar, "Constitutional Redundancies and Clarifying Clauses," *Valparaiso LR* 33 (1998): 1, 18–20; Amar, *AUC*, 99–102.

30. 1 W. & M., ch. 2, sec. 9 (1689). See also supra Chapter 2, n. 24 and sources cited therein, and Chapter 4, n. 5. For state constitutions, see Amar, *Bill of Rights*, 24–25, and accompanying endnotes.

31. See Amar, *Bill of Rights*, 241–246.

32. See, generally, Amar, *Bill of Rights*, 137–294, and sources cited therein; Amar, *AUC*, 151–167; see also supra Chapter 2.

33. See, generally, Amar, *Bill of Rights*, 281–283.

34. This brand of constitutional traditionalism has been ably expounded by others. See, e.g., Michael W. McConnell, "The Right to Die and the Jurisprudence of Tradition," *Utah LR* (1997): 665, 681–701. See also Amar, *AUC*, 95–138 (defending the view that "we must take account of—and take a count of—how ordinary Americans have lived their lives in ordinary ways and thereby embodied fundamental rights"). On gun rights in state courts, see David B. Kopel, Clayton E. Cramer, and Scott G. Hattrup, "A Tale of Three Cities: The Right to Bear Arms in State Supreme Courts," *Temple LR* 68 (1995): 1177; Seven H. Gunn, "A Lawyer's Guide to the Second Amendment," *BYU LR* (1998): 35. For an outstanding general treatment, see Adam Winkler, *Gunfight: The Battle over the Right to Bear Arms in America* (2011).

35. Cf. Lawrence Lessig, "Fidelity in Translation," *Texas LR* 71 (1993): 1165 (discussing the need to translate old texts to meet new contexts).

36. Act of March 2, 1867, ch. 153, 14 Stat. 428. For general discussions of this act, sometimes referred to as the Military Reconstruction Act, see Michael Les Benedict, *A Compromise of Principle* (1974), 223–243; Eric Foner, *Reconstruction* (1988), 271–277, 307–308, 438; Kenneth Stampp, *The Era of Reconstruction, 1865–1877* (1965), 144–147. Note also that in the months following the first Reconstruction act, Congress adopted additional Reconstruction legislation that sharpened the role of the federal military in the Union effort to rebuild the South on a sound constitutional footing.

37. For more elaboration, see Amar, *AUC*, 88–94. The ideas presented in this paragraph may profitably be compared and contrasted with the fascinating work of my colleague Bruce Ackerman. See, generally, Bruce Ackerman, *We the People: Foundations* (1991); Bruce Ackerman, *We the People: Transformations* (1998).

38. See Aileen S. Kraditor, *The Ideas of the Woman Suffrage Movement, 1890–1920* (1965), 3.

39. Ibid., 192, 204n.20.

CHAPTER 11: MASSACHUSETTS
A BAY-STATE VIEW OF THE FOURTH AMENDMENT

1. On the claimed linkage between the writs and the amendment, see, e.g., *Riley v. California* (2014) (slip opinion 27–28). For earlier examples in case law, see, e.g., *Stanford v. Texas*, 379 U.S. 476, 481–482 (1965); *Monroe v. Pape*, 365 U.S. 167, 208–209 (1961) (Frankfurter, J., dissenting); *Frank v. Maryland*, 359 U.S 360, 364 (1959) (Frankfurter, J.); *United States v. Rabinowitz*, 339 U.S. 56, 69–71 (1947) (Frankfurter, J., dissenting); *Harris v. United States*, 331 U.S. 145, 157–158 (1947) (Frankfurter, J., dissenting); *Davis v. United States*, 328 U.S. 582, 604 (1946) (Frankfurter, J., dissenting); *Olmstead v. United States*, 277 U.S. 438, 474–475 (1928) (Brandeis, J., dissenting); *Boyd v. United States*, 116 U.S. 616, 624–625 (1886). Note that the *Boyd* Court included Justice Horace Gray, a Harvard-trained Bostonian whose scholarship on Otis and the writs of assistance was pointedly mentioned by the Court (ibid., 625n.*). Among scholars, see, e.g., Tracey Maclin, "The Central Meaning of the Fourth Amendment," *William & Mary LR* 35 (1993): 197, 218–228. Maclin teaches in Boston. For more on *Boyd*, see Amar, *AUC*, 177–179, 548n.47; Amar, *CCP*, 22–25.

2. See Del. Const. of 1776 (Declaration of Rights), sec. 17); Md. Const. of 1776 (Declaration of Rights), art. XXIII; Mass. Const. of 1780, pt. I, art. XIV; N.H. Const. of 1784, pt. I, art. XIX; N.C. Const. of 1776 (Declaration of Rights), art. XI; Pa. Const. of 1776 (Declaration of Rights), art. X; Va. Const. of 1776 (Declaration of Rights), sec. 10; Vt. Const. of 1786, ch. I, sec. XII; Vt. Const. of 1777, ch. I, sec. XI. See also Amar, "Fourth Amendment First Principles," *Harvard LR* 107 (1994): 757, 763nn.11–12 (citing many early cases).

3. William Blackstone, *Commentaries on the Laws of England* 4:*292 (emphasis added). The clause "committed in his view" was first added by Blackstone in his fifth edition, published in 1773.

Professor Thomas Y. Davies has argued that these warrantless arrests and intrusions incident to arrest do not squarely rebut an implicit warrant requirement. Professor Davies's argument, it seems, is that these arrests and intrusions did not really count as state action, because they were no greater than a private person's power to make a "citizen's arrest." Statement of Professor Thomas Y. Davies, Hearing Before the Senate Judiciary Committee on Bill to Abolish Fourth Amendment Exclusion of Unconstitutionally Seized Evidence and to Create a Tort Remedy, March 7, 1995, 6–8, 11 (Davies Testimony hereafter) (an incomplete version of the testimony is available in 1995 WL 231846). But to the extent that the government authorizes "citizen's arrests," such arrests are indeed a form of state action. The government is in effect deputizing its citizens, just as it does when it uses the militia or the posse to enforce its laws, or when it commissions privateers through letters of marque and reprisal. Even if mere governmental permission to effect a "private" arrest is not state action, surely a government requirement to arrest is state action; and at common law, constables were often required to arrest in situations where truly private persons were, at most, permitted to do so. See *Davis v. Russell*, 5 Bing. 354, 365, 80 Eng.

Rep. 1098, 1102 (C.P. 1829), 7 L.J.M.C. (O.S.) 52, 59; *Cowles v. Dunbar*, 2 Car. & P. 565, 567–568, 172 Eng. Rep. 257, 258 (K.B. 1827); *Samuel v. Payne*, 1 Dougl. 359, 360, 99 Eng. Rep. 230, 231 (K.B. 1780); Matthew Hale, *The History of the Pleas of the Crown* (1736) (Professional Books Ltd., 1971), 2:*82, *84–85, *91–92.

4. Blackstone, *Commentaries*, 4:*289; see also Hale, *Pleas*, 2:*72 (similarly distinguishing between the arrest powers of private persons and those of officers by virtue of their office, "virtute officii").

5. Blackstone, *Commentaries*, 4:*293 ("Upon probable suspicion also a private person may arrest the felon or other person so suspected. But he cannot justify breaking open doors to do it."); see also Hale, *Pleas*, 2:*92 (discussing "the difference between private persons arresting upon suspicion and constables": "the constable may break open the door, tho he have no warrant," but "private persons . . . cannot break open doors" upon suspicion); ibid., *82 (similar). But see ibid., 1:*588 (muddying the waters on this point). As the more modern and more consistent commentator on this issue, Blackstone (who had many years to revise his treatise, once published) is a more reliable compiler of common law circa 1780 than Hale, whose notes from the 1670s were published many years after his death.

6. Blackstone, *Commentaries*, 4:*292–293; see also ibid., *142, *146–153 (making clear that many breaches of the peace are not felonies). Here, too, Hale's analysis closely tracks Blackstone's. See Hale, *Pleas*, 2:*88–89 (describing "the original and inherent power in the constable" to "imprison a person" for "breach of the peace and some misdemeanors, less than felony" and to "arrest suspicious night-walkers" and "men[ ] that ride armed" though no felony be committed or proved); see also ibid., 1:*587 (offering other examples of constable's power to make "arrests ex officio without any warrant").

Consider also the following Blackstone passage, explicitly distinguishing the search-and-seizure powers of ordinary citizens from those of constables: "Affrays [which are mere misdemeanors, not felonies] may be suppressed by any private person present, who is justifiable in endeavouring to part the combatants, whatever consequence may ensue. But more especially the constable, or other similar officer, however denominated, is bound to keep the peace, and to that purpose may break open doors to suppress an affray, or apprehend the affrayers, and may either carry them before a justice, or imprison them by his own authority for a convenient space till the heat is over." Blackstone, *Commentaries*, 4:*146; see also William Hawkins, *A Treatise of the Pleas of the Crown* (1721) (Arno Press, 1972), 2:81 (the "Constable hath Authority not only to arrest those whom he shall see actually engaged in an Affray, but also to detain them till they find Sureties of the Peace . . . whereas a private Person seems to have no other Power in a bare Affray, not attended with the Danger of Life, but only to stay the Affrayers till the Heat be over, and then deliver them to the Constable") (footnotes omitted).

7. 1 Dougl. 359, 99 Eng. Rep. 230 (K.B. 1780) (footnote omitted).

8. Ibid., 360, 99 Eng. Rep. at 231; see, generally, Hale, *Pleas*, 1:*587; ibid., 2:*85, *88–98; see also ibid., 2:*83 (noting that an innocent arrestee is not bound to submit to a citizen's arrest, but is obliged to submit to "a constable arresting in the king's name"). Blackstone offers a similar account in *Commentaries*, 4:*292–293.

9. 4 Dougl. 338, 343, 99 Eng. Rep. 911, 913 (K.B. 1785). See also *Lawrence v. Hedger*, 3 Taunt. 14, 14, 128 Eng. Rep. 6, 6 (C.P. 1810) ("Watchmen and beadles have authority at common law to arrest and detain in prison for examination, persons walking in the streets at night, whom there is reasonable ground to suspect of felony, although there is no proof of a felony having been committed") (reporter's case summary). For similar discussions of

the special ex officio arrest and detention powers of watchmen, see Blackstone, *Commentaries*, 4:*292; 2 Hale, *Pleas*, 2:*98.

10. *Holley v. Mix*, 3 Wend. 350, 353–355 (N.Y. Sup. Ct. 1829).

11. Telford Taylor, *Two Studies in Constitutional Interpretation* (1969), 28–29; Amar, "Fourth Amendment," 767 & nn.30–33.

12. For ships, see Act of July 31, 1789, ch. 5, sec. 24, 1 Stat. 29, 43 (repealed 1790). Similar provisions were passed in 1790, 1793, and 1799. Amar, "Fourth Amendment," 766. For liquor, see Act of Mar. 3, 1791, ch. 15, secs. 25, 29, 1 Stat. 199, 205–206.

13. On the importance of public trials to monitor possible abuse and corruption, see Amar, *CCP*, 116–124.

14. 6 B. & C. 635, 638–639, 108 Eng. Rep. 585, 586; 5 L.J.M.C. (O.S.) 132, 9 D. & R. 487. In holding that reasonable suspicion alone would uphold a constable's arrest, Lord Tenterden went one step beyond *Samuel* and *Cooper*, which spoke of a "charge" of felony. The court drew support on this point from *Lawrence v. Hedger*. Ibid., 637, 108 Eng. Rep. at 586, 9 D. & R. at 491; see also supra n. 9 (discussing *Lawrence* holding).

15. 6 B. & C. at 638, 108 Eng. Rep. at 586 (emphasis added). Lord Tenterden's analysis here is strikingly similar to the one I earlier attributed to Lord Mansfield in *Money v. Leach*, 19 Howell's State Trials 1001, 1026 (K.B. 1765), 97 Eng. Rep. 1075, 1087. See Amar, "Fourth Amendment," 776 & n.69. Professor Davies has sharply criticized me for perverting this passage. See Davies Testimony, 12n.12 (describing me as "flat-out wrong"). But a parallel report of this case, authored by Blackstone, strongly confirms my initial reading, as do later opinions, such as Lord Tenterden's. See *Money v. Leach*, 1 Black. W. 555, 560, 96 Eng. Rep. 320, 323 (K.B. 1765) ("Lord Mansfield, C.J.—What is a probable cause of suspicion, and what is a reasonable time of detainer, are matters of fact to be determined by a jury.") In other cases, as I have noted elsewhere, Lord Mansfield was not always a champion of the jury. For a case remarkably similar to *Beckwith*, where Abbott, C.J. (soon-to-become Lord Tenterden), made a very similar point, see *Cowles v. Dunbar*, 2 Car. & P. 565, 567, 172 Eng. Rep. 257, 258 (K.B. 1827) ("A constable is obliged to act if there is a reasonable charge of felony: whether there was such here, is for the jury to say."). Elsewhere in *Cowles*, the chief justice sharply distinguished between constables' and private persons' arrest powers. Ibid., 568, 172 Eng. Rep. at 258.

16. For more on the jury in the Founding era, see supra Chapter 6, pp. 129, 133; supra Chapter 10, pp. 209–210.

17. See *Bostock v. Saunders*, 3 Wils. K.B. 434, 440–442, 95 Eng. Rep. 1141, 1145 (C.P. 1773); 2 Black. W. 912, 914–916, 96 Eng. Rep. 539, 540 (C.P. 1773) (recording remarks of De Grey, C.J.). See also William J. Stuntz, "Warrants and Fourth Amendment Remedies," *Virginia LR* 77 (1991): 881, 883, 907, 917 (portraying warrant as a "safe harbor" insulating police from liability). Stuntz's imagery was beautifully foreshadowed by Lord Mansfield: "The statute has chalked out a way by which [the government searcher] may be safe." *Cooper v. Boot*, 4 Dougl. 339, 349, 99 Eng. Rep. 911, 916 (K.B. 1785).

18. For a general discussion of this "upside-down effect," see Amar, *CCP*, 155–156.

19. *Wilkes v. Wood*, 19 Howell's State Trials, 1153 (C.P. 1763), 98 Eng. Rep. 489; *Entick v. Carrington*, 19 Howell's State Trials, 1029 (C.P. 1765), 95 Eng. Rep. 807.

20. Technically, Chief Justice Charles Pratt did not become Lord Camden until after *Wilkes*. For more discussion of these two landmark cases, and much more discussion of Pratt/Camden himself and the implications of his vision for modern American constitutionalism, see this book's Chapter 12, pp. 250–254.

21. Maclin, "Central Meaning," 208–210; Davies Testimony, 11–16. For especially vivid examples of a stand-alone reasonableness requirement for all searches and seizures, omitting all mention of warrants, see John P. Kaminski and Gaspare J. Saladino, eds., *The Documentary History of the Ratification of the Constitution* 13 (1981): 239 (recording Richard Henry Lee's proposed amendments, Sept. 27, 1787) ("That the Citizens shall not be exposed to unreasonable searches, seizures of their papers, houses, persons, or property"); "Letters from the Federal Farmer (VI)," reprinted in Herbert J. Storing, ed., *The Complete Anti-Federalist* 2 (1981): 256, 262 (stating a man should be "subject to no unreasonable searches or seizures of his person, papers or effects"); *Debates and Proceedings in the Convention of the Commonwealth of Massachusetts Held in the Year 1788* (1856), 86–87 (February 6, 1788, amendment proposing that the people should be protected against "unreasonable searches and seizures of their persons, papers or possessions").

Professor Maclin tries to downplay the status of the reasonableness clause of the Fourth Amendment by arguing that "undisputed history" shows that the amendment's final wording was due to "a single congressman" who rewrote the amendment in a last-minute style committee and slipped his rewrite past an unwary House. See Maclin, "Central Meaning," 208–209. In fact, however, House records contradict Maclin's account: the amendment contained an independent reasonableness clause before the style committee was even created. See Linda Grant DePauw, ed., *Documentary History of the First Federal Congress, 1789–91: House of Representatives Journal* 3 (1977): 159 (recording independent reasonableness clause, as in the amendment's final version, in place as of Aug. 21, 1789); ibid., 165 (appointing style committee on Aug. 22, 1789).

22. Edward Dumbauld, *The Bill of Rights and What It Means Today* (1957), 184, 191, 200–201, 207.

23. Professor Thomas Y. Davies has argued that "ships" were simply not "effects" under the Fourth Amendment. Davies Testimony, 5 & n.2. His motivation, it seems, is to explain how the amendment could indeed require warrants in all situations covered by the Fourth Amendment, despite the clear early history of warrantless searches of ships. But the "all possessions" language of Article XIV clearly suggests a broad scope for the principle banning unreasonable searches and seizures—as does the analogous sweeping catchall "property" language of the Virginia, New York, and North Carolina ratifying conventions, and of Madison's first draft. The "effects" gambit tries to save a warrant requirement, but ends up dismembering the Fourth Amendment. Taken to its logical conclusion, the refusal to give effect to the broad intended sweep of "effects" would leave us with an amendment that applies only to persons, houses, and papers. The Supreme Court has never thought so, thank goodness; nor has any notable state or lower federal court. Shall we say that office buildings are not protected by the Fourth Amendment because they are not "houses"? Or that computers and hard drives are wholly outside the scope of the amendment because they are not "papers"? Or that cars are wholly unprotected because they are like ships? Surely true friends of the amendment should reject such an outlandish and crabbed approach. See *Black's Law Dictionary*, 4th ed. (1968), 605 (offering one quote that the word "effects" is a term "more comprehensive than the word 'goods,'" and another definition of "effects" as "every kind of property, real and personal"). Even if we accepted the "effects" gambit, we would not be left with a warrant requirement for all remaining searches and seizures of "persons," "houses," and "papers," as Davies appears to desire. Such a requirement would still lack affirmative textual, historical, and practical support. If the amendment really always requires warrants, why does it not say so; why did no Framer or early commentator

say so; and how are we to deal with metal detectors of persons, building-code inspections of houses, and regulatory oversight of business papers? Even if "ships" somehow weren't "effects," "persons" on ships surely were "persons"; and they, too, were detained—seized, temporarily—without warrants under early ship statutes. (And in arrests, and in border searches, and so on.) So, too, early statutes authorized warrantless searches of "houses" storing liquor, as we have seen. Rather than claiming that all of these searches and seizures were simply beyond the Fourth Amendment's scope, à la Davies, surely it makes more sense to say that the amendment applies broadly, but does not always require warrants. Though mistaken, the Davies gambit is nevertheless illuminating, because it illustrates that the over-reading of some clauses often leads to the under-protection of others: a rigorous warrant requirement creates perverse hydraulic pressure to deny that certain intrusions are Fourth Amendment searches and seizures.

24. Personal and political papers were not really at issue in the Boston writs-of-assistance case; the main focus of concern seems to have been searches of buildings rather than of persons. Note also that both constitutions speak of "warrants" and not "writs"—yet again highlighting the English general warrant cases more than the Boston writ case.

25. 59 Mass. (5 Cush.) 281–286 (1850) (emphasis added) (citing *Davis v. Russell*, 5 Bing. 354, 365, 130 Eng. Rep. 1098, 1102 [C.P. 1829]). Elsewhere, the *Davis* court chief justice had this to say: "For though a private individual cannot arrest upon bare suspicion, a constable may. This has been decided in so many cases, that it is unnecessary to refer to them; and unless the law were so, there would be no security for person or property." 5 Bing. at 363–364, 130 Eng. Rep. at 1101. See also *Holley v. Mix*, 3 Wend. 350, 353 (N.Y. Sup. Ct. 1829) (affirming power of warrantless arrest "whether there is time to obtain [a warrant] or not").

26. 72 Mass. (6 Gray) 435, 436, 439 (1856) (emphasis added).

27. Here is what the court said:

It cannot be doubted that by adoption of the 14th article of the Declaration of Rights it was intended strictly and carefully to limit, restrain and regulate the granting and issuing of warrants . . . to the general class of cases, in and to the furtherance of the objects of which they had before been recognized and allowed . . . , and certainly not so to vary, extend and enlarge the purposes for and occasions on which they might be used. . . . Certainly no person ought to be compelled to disclose any facts or information to be given as evidence . . . until he has at least had an opportunity of urging his objections . . . before some competent judicial tribunal.

Robinson v. Richardson, 79 Mass. (13 Gray) 454, 457, 458 (1859).

28. *United States v. La Jeune Eugenie*, 26 F. Cas. 832, 843, 844 (C.C.D. Mass. 1822) (No. 15,551).

29. *Commonwealth v. Dana*, 43 Mass. (2 Met.) 329, 334–337 (1841). Elsewhere in the opinion, the court quoted extensively from *Entick v. Carrington* and paid tribute to "the able opinion of Lord Camden." The Court also passingly mentioned the writs of assistance, but not Massachusetts attorney James Otis by name.

30. See Simon Greenleaf, ed., *A Treatise on the Law of Evidence*, 14th rev. ed. (1883), 1:325–326, sec. 254a; John Henry Wigmore, *A Treatise on the Anglo-American System of Evidence in Trials at Common Law*, 3rd ed. (1940).

31. See O. M. Dickerson, "Writs of Assistance as a Cause of the Revolution," in Richard B. Morris, ed., *The Era of the American Revolution* (1939), 45n.6. See "Paxton's Case of the Writ of Assistance," in Josiah Quincy, Jr., *Reports of Cases Argued and Adjudged in the Superior Court of Judicature of the Province of Massachusetts Bay Between 1761 and 1772* (1865), 51 (Quincy's Reports hereafter); ibid., app. I, 395–540 (recording Horace Gray's notes) (Gray's Notes hereafter); *Davis v. United States*, 328 U.S. 582, 604 (1946) (Frankfurter, J., dissenting) (alluding to *Paxton's Case*). On the slight imprecision of label here, see M. H. Smith, *The Writs of Assistance Case* (1978), 147n.35, 397.

32. For details, see Amar, *Bill of Rights*, 66n.*

33. For sources quoting Adams, see supra n. 1.

34. For a somewhat similar suggestion, see Smith, *Writs*, 250–254, 380, 384, 466, 508, 518.

35. See Dickerson, "Writs," 40, 43.

36. See ibid., 49–75; Smith, *Writs*, 6, 462, 476, 497.

37. Joseph Story, *Commentaries on the Constitution of the United States* (1833) (Fred B. Rothman and Co., 1991), 3:748–750, sec. 1895.

38. See Smith, *Writs*, 29–30, 33, 101–102, 122, 277n.8, app. M at 563; Dickerson, "Writs," 45n.6 (writ commanding assistance of "all others"); Silas J. Wasserstrom, "The Incredible Shrinking Fourth Amendment," *American Criminal LR* 21 (1984): 257, 284n.148; cf. Jon C. Blue, "High Noon Revisited: Commands of Assistance by Peace Officers in the Age of the Fourth Amendment," *Yale LJ* 101 (1992): 1475.

39. See William J. Stuntz, "The Substantive Origins of Criminal Procedure," *Yale LJ* 105 (1995): 393, 404–409.

40. On Parliament's condemnation of certain warrants in 1766, see Taylor, *Two Studies*, 34–35. On Parliament's reaffirmation of writs of assistance in 1767, see Smith, *Writs*, 438–464.

41. See, generally, Eric Schnapper, "Unreasonable Searches and Seizures of Papers," *Virginia LR* 71 (1985): 869. On the Parliamentary response to *Wilkes* and *Entick*, see ibid., 909–910.

42. *Redshaw v. Brook*, 2 Wils. K.B. 405, 405, 95 Eng. Rep. 887, 888 (C.P. 1769).

43. 3 Wils. K.B. 61, 61–64, 95 Eng. Rep. 934, 934–935 (C.P. 1770).

44. 4 Dougl. 339, 348–349, 99 Eng. Rep. 911, 916 (K.B. 1785) (emphasis added); cf. *Cooper v. Booth*, 3 Esp. 135, 145–146, 170 Eng. Rep. 564, 568 (K.B. 1785) (same case) (reporting similar language of Lord Mansfield).

45. *Cooper v. Boot*, 4 Dougl. at 343, 99 Eng. Rep. at 913 (emphasis added); see also *Cooper v. Booth*, 3 Esp. at 138, 170 Eng. Rep. at 565 (Lord Mansfield) ("[T]he distinction I have always taken is this, that to justify under a writ of assistance, the officer must find the goods he searches for; but a warrant will justify without."). *Cooper v. Boot's* holding—that a proper warrant immunized the officer for a search that turned up nothing—was applied to seizures under warrant, where the officer seized goods that ultimately turned out to be innocent, in the 1800 Court of Common Pleas case *Price v. Messenger*, 3 Bos. & Pul. 158, 158 n.(a), 126 Eng. Rep. 1213, 1213 n.(a) (C.P. 1800).

46. See Gray's Notes, app. I at 471 and n.(9). For discussion, see Smith, *Writs*, 13n.9, 310. Otis made a similar suggestion in an anonymous essay. See ibid., 424, app. M at 563; see also ibid., 333n.3, app. G at 538 (noting similar suggestion in an influential 1760 *London* magazine article).

47. Gray's Notes, app. I at 533n.41; see also Smith, *Writs*, 128n.5.

48. *Cooper v. Boot*, 4 Dougl. at 347, 99 Eng. Rep. at 915 (recording argument of Plumer).

49. 2 Black W. 912, 914–916, 96 Eng. Rep. 539, 540 (C.P. 1773).

50. See ibid., 915–916, 96 Eng. Rep. at 540 (opinion of Blackstone, J.) (instrument at hand "is improperly called a warrant" and thus it does not immunize at all events).

51. Blackstone, *Commentaries* (1765), 4:288. Later editions of Blackstone refined and expanded this language to make clear that under English statutes even certain defective warrants could immunize. American law, it seems, tracked the narrower first-edition formulation. See Amar, "Fourth Amendment," 779–781, and nn. 86, 89, 91–92.

CHAPTER 12: NEW JERSEY
Lord Camden Meets Federalism

1. *Wilkes v. Wood*, 19 Howell's State Trials 1153 (C.P. 1763), 98 Eng. Rep. 489; *Entick v. Carrington*, 19 Howell's State Trials 1029 (C.P. 1765), 95 Eng. Rep. 807. For more on these cases, see Telford Taylor, *Two Studies in Constitutional Interpretation* (1969), 19–44; Eric Schnapper, "Unreasonable Searches and Seizures of Papers," *Virginia LR* 71 (1985): 869, 875–915. See also supra Chapter 11, pp. 240–242.

2. *Wilkes*, 19 Howell's State Trials at 1168, 98 Eng. Rep. at 499 (1000 pounds); *Entick*, 19 Howell's State Trials at 1036, 95 Eng. Rep. at 811 (300 pounds).

3. Reuel Robinson, *History of Camden and Rockport Maine* (1907), 85–86.

4. See, generally, Akhil Reed Amar, "Using State Law to Protect Federal Constitutional Rights: Some Questions and Answers About Converse-1983," *U. of Colorado LR* 64 (1993): 159, 163–172; Akhil Reed Amar, "Of Sovereignty and Federalism," *Yale LJ* 96 (1987): 1425, 1492–1519.

5. See *McCulloch v. Maryland*, 17 U.S. (4 Wheat.) 316, 425–430 (1819) (speaking of "*constitutional* laws of the Union," "laws made *in pursuance* of the constitution," "*legitimate* operations of a supreme government," and a federal "*right* . . . to preserve" the bank) (emphasis added). See also ibid., 427 ("The power of congress to create, and of course, to continue, the bank, was the subject of the preceding part of this opinion; and is no longer to be considered as questionable.").

6. See Antonin Scalia, "The Rule of Law as a Law of Rules," *U. of Chicago LR* 56 (1989): 1175, 1180–86; Amar, "Fourth Amendment," 817–819; Alan H. Scheiner, "Note, Judicial Assessment of Punitive Damages, the Seventh Amendment, and the Politics of Jury Power," *Columbia LR* 91 (1991): 142.

7. *Elliot's Debates* 2:550. For more documentation of the Fourth Amendment–Seventh Amendment linkage, see Amar, "Fourth Amendment," 775–778.

8. We should also note that prior to 1938, federal procedure often borrowed from state law, and even today some federal procedural issues are governed by state law; see, e.g., Fed. R. Civ. P. 4(k)(1)(A).

9. See Amar, *Bill of Rights*, 88–93.

10. See *Dice v. Akron, Canton & Youngstown R.R.*, 342 U.S. 359 (1952).

11. On the special interpretive importance of historical paradigm cases underlying certain patches of constitutional text or components of constitutional structure, recall the discussion in Chapter 10, p. 217. See, generally, Jed Rubenfeld, *Freedom and Time* (2001), 178–195.

12. Paul M. Bator, Daniel J. Meltzer, Paul J. Mishkin, and David L. Shapiro, eds., *Hart and Wechsler's The Federal Courts and the Federal System*, 3rd ed. (1988), 533.

13. See, e.g., ibid., 564–567; *De Sylva v. Ballentine*, 351 U.S. 570 (1956). See, generally, Paul J. Mishkin, "The Variousness of 'Federal Law': Competence and Discretion in the Choice of National and State Rules for Decision," *U. of Pennsylvania LR* 105 (1957): 797.

14. See, generally, Amar, "State Law"; Amar, "Of Sovereignty."

15. See, generally, William J. Brennan, Jr., "State Constitutions and the Protection of Individual Rights," *Harvard LR* 90 (1977): 489. For a discussion and critique, see Amar, "State Law," 176–178; Akhil Reed Amar, "Five Views of Federalism: 'Converse-1983' in Context," *Vanderbilt LR* 47 (1994): 1229, 1243–1246.

16. See also *New York v. United States*, 505 U.S. 144, 156 (1992). For a discussion of *Gregory's* vision, see Amar, "Five Views."

17. See, e.g., *Harlow v. Fitzgerald*, 457 U.S. 800 (1982).

18. For more discussion of the points highlighted in this paragraph, see Amar, "State Law," 172–176.

19. See *State v. Alston*, 88 N.J. 211, 440 A.2d 1311 (1981) (rejecting *Rakas* and recognizing standing of car passenger to challenge unreasonable search based on New Jersey state constitutional provision echoing, but construed more broadly than, the federal Fourth Amendment). *Alston*, however, involved state officers, and New Jersey judges have, unfortunately, hesitated to apply its logic against federal officers. See, e.g., *State v. Mollica*, 114 N.J. 329, 352, 554 A.2d 1315, 1327 (1989) (search and seizure case declining to apply state constitutional provision to limit federal agents: "Stated simply, state constitutions do not control federal action.").

20. See Amar, "Of Sovereignty," 1506, 1511n.337 (state law can often create legal interests whose violation creates legal injury and thus confers Article III standing).

21. In fact, a post-*Greenwood* state court case, construing a state constitutional provision, does exist in New Jersey. See *State v. Hempele*, 120 N.J. 182, 576 A.2d 793 (1990) (holding that, under the New Jersey Constitution, a person does enjoy a reasonable expectation of privacy in his curbside trash bag). Alas, the *Hempele* court acted as if this state law ruling had no bearing on the federal Fourth Amendment. See *ibid.* at 191–195, 798–799.

22. *California v. Greenwood*, 486 U.S. 35, 40, 43–44 (1988). Unlike our city of Camden hypothetical, California apparently did not purport to vest trash-owners with property and privacy rights vis-à-vis the world. For a more recent exclusionary-rule case once again dismissing, too quickly and confidently, the Fourth Amendment significance of the privacy-protective law of the state in which a search and seizure took place, see *Virginia v. Moore*, 553 U.S. 164 (2008).

23. See, e.g., *Stanford v. Kentucky*, 492 U.S. 361, 369–372 (1989). See, generally, Amar, *AUC*, 95–138. Note that in *Greenwood* itself, the Supreme Court canvassed state appellate court rulings, implying that such rulings were indeed probative of societal understandings and expectations of privacy. *Greenwood*, 486 U.S. at 41–43, and n.5.

24. For details on Camden's remedial creativity, see Amar, "Fourth Amendment," 814–815.

CONCLUSION

1. Our most recent nineteen presidents, in chronological order, including the years they were on the presidential ballot and the major colleges and graduate schools they

attended: Theodore Roosevelt (1904, 1912) (Harvard College, Columbia Law); William Howard Taft (1908, 1912) (Yale College, Univ. of Cincinnati Law); Woodrow Wilson (1912, 1916) (Davidson, Princeton, Univ. of Virginia Law, Johns Hopkins Grad.); Warren Harding (1920) (Ohio Central); Calvin Coolidge (1924) (Amherst); Herbert Hoover (1928, 1932) (Stanford); Franklin D. Roosevelt (1932, 1936, 1940, 1944) (Harvard, Columbia Law); Harry Truman (1948); Dwight Eisenhower (1952, 1956) (West Point); John F. Kennedy (1960) (Harvard); Lyndon B. Johnson (1964) (Southwest Texas State); Richard Nixon (1968, 1972) (Whittier, Duke Law); Gerald Ford (1976) (Univ. of Michigan, Yale Law); Jimmy Carter (1976, 1980) (Naval Academy); Ronald Reagan (1980, 1984) (Eureka); George H. W. Bush (1988, 1992) (Yale); Bill Clinton (1992, 1996) (Georgetown, Yale Law); George W. Bush (2000, 2004) (Yale, Harvard Grad.); Barack Obama (2008, 2012) (Occidental, Columbia, Harvard Law). Non-incumbent presidential runners-up who attended Harvard, Yale, Princeton, or Columbia: Charles Evans Hughes (1912) (Columbia Law); Thomas E. Dewey (1944, 1948) (Columbia Law); Adlai Stevenson II (1952, 1956) (Princeton, brief attendance at Harvard Law); Michael Dukakis (1988) (Harvard Law); Al Gore (2000) (Harvard); John Kerry (2004) (Yale); Mitt Romney (2012) (Harvard Law, Harvard Business School). The only eight modern elections without a graduate of these four schools topping the ticket of a major party thus occurred in 1920, 1924, 1928, 1964, 1968, 1972, 1980, and 1984.

2. In 1972, Democratic vice presidential nominee Sargent Shriver was a graduate of both Yale College and Yale Law; in 1976, incumbent Ford was also a Yale Law grad; in 1980 through 1992, Yale grad George H. W. Bush was on the ballot, twice for the vice presidency and then twice for the presidency; in 1988, Bush bested Michael Dukakis, a Harvard Law graduate; Bill Clinton, a Yale Law grad, was on the presidential ballot opposite Bush in 1992, and again in 1996; his running mate both times, Al Gore, was a Harvard grad; in 2000, Gore ran for the presidency in his own right against George W. Bush, a graduate of Yale College and Harvard Business School; in 2004, Bush 43 ran again, this time against another Yale College grad, John Kerry; and in both 2008 and 2012, Harvard Law grad Barack Obama was on the presidential ballot, most recently against Mitt Romney, a graduate of both Harvard Law and Harvard Business School.

INDEX

Abolitionists, 13, 33, 55, 130–131,
134
Absolutism, 44–45
Ackerman, Bruce, 110, 143, 153
Adams, Abigail, 208
Adams, John, 11, 31, 128, 245
Adams, John Quincy, 165
Adamson v. California, 36, 38–39, 41, 42,
48, 49
Affirmative action, 94–95, 97–99,
117
Agnew, Spiro T., 187, 189
Airports, 83, 84
Alabama, 30, 33, 38, 39, 42, 43, 48, 278
Albert, Carl, 189–190, 196
Alito, Samuel, 63, 64–65, 66, 77, 96, 98,
223(n), 268
American Enterprise Institute, 192(n)
America's Constitution: A Biography (Amar),
280
*America's Unwritten Constitution: The
Precedents and Principles We Live By*
(Amar), 73, 280
Ammunition, 206, 215
Amsterdam, Anthony, 110
Anarchy, 7, 14
Antebellum era, 31, 32, 41, 114
free blacks in, 131
Apportionment issues, 12, 29, 50–51, 52,
157, 276
Aristocracy/nobility, 112–113, 168
Arrests, 232–233, 236, 243
Assassinations, 168, 169, 171, 172, 180,
183, 186(n), 189(n), 192, 195
Arthur, Chester A., 169–170, 172
Articles of Confederation, 17, 20, 22, 111,
125, 271
Attorney generals, 57, 65, 66, 71, 74, 76,
122, 150

Baker v. Carr, 50, 51
Barron v. Baltimore, 32, 33, 35, 126,
222
Bathrooms, 116–117, 119, 213
Beckwith v. Philby, 236, 243
Bell, Derrick, 111
Bentsen, Lloyd, 273
Betts v. Brady, 47–48, 49
Bickel, Alexander, 110
Biden, Joe, 173, 199
Bill of Rights, 29, 42–43, 125–126, 230,
244, 277, 279
applied only to federal government,
126 (*see also Barron v. Baltimore*;
States: and Bill of Rights)
declaratory interpretation of, 33
and Fourteenth Amendment, 36–37,
75–76, 131, 133, 139, 221
and Fourth Amendment, 236
Framers' vs. Incorporated, 40
and incorporation process, 38
and juries, 47
and Second Amendment, 205, 208
and states, 31–41 (*see also* States: and
Bill of Rights)
*Bill of Rights, The: Creation and
Reconstruction* (Amar), 34(n)
Bills of attainder, 46, 93
Bingham, John A., 34, 75, 78, 181, 279
Bipartisanship, 68
*Bivens v. Six Unknown Named Agents of
Federal Bureau of Narcotics*, 260, 261,
263
Black, Hugo La Fayette, 30–31, 35, 62, 65,
68, 69, 70, 71, 251, 276–277, 278,
279
academic credentials of, 54
Adamson dissent of, 36, 38–39, 40, 41,
48, 49, 75–76

Black, Hugo La Fayette (*continued*)
  as dominant justice of twentieth
    century, 30
  early years on the bench, 41–43
  and First Amendment absolutism,
    44–45
  humility of, 40–41
  and juries, 46–47
  as most valuable player on Warren
    Court, 48–55
  and racial justice, 50, 50(n)
  and Robert Jackson, 58–59, 74, 75
  scholars who celebrated/disparaged
    Black, 54(n)
  as southern liberal/nationalist, 40
  textualism of, 72–73, 75
  theory of total incorporation, 36–37,
    40, 41
  and *Tinker*, 136(n)
Black, Hugo, Jr., 30
Black Codes, 117
Blackman, Harry, 69, 99–100
Blacks, 69, 110, 116, 117, 131, 138, 157,
    161, 197, 214, 221, 222, 225,
    227
Blackstone, William, 18, 58, 214,
    217–218, 232–233, 248
Blair, Tony, 201
Bobbitt, Philip, 192(n)
Bolling v. Sharpe, 50, 109, 112,
    114
Bork, Robert, 68
Bostock v. Saunders, 248
Boston, 229–230, 241–249, 268, 270
Boyd v. United States, 230
Brandeis, Louis, 53, 77(n), 229–230
Brandenburg v. Ohio, 53
Brennan, William, 37, 41, 43, 48, 49, 50,
    51, 52, 53, 54, 80, 99, 259, 279
Breyer, Stephen, 59, 64, 96, 141(n),
    160–161, 223(n)
Bridges v. California, 42–45, 46
Britain, 10, 21–22, 124, 201, 245, 254
  Act of Union with Scotland, 18
  British Commonwealth, 16
  British Empire, 211, 240
  Court of Common Pleas, 247, 250

English Bill of Rights (1689/1789),
    103, 128, 205, 209, 217
English common law, 42, 232, 234,
    236(n), 237
Parliament, 82, 102–103, 125, 126, 128,
    129, 131, 133, 176, 220, 229, 244,
    247, 252, 253
unwritten British Constitution, 251
Brookings Institution, 192(n)
Brown, Gordon, 201
Brown v. Board of Education, 50, 63, 65, 66,
    68, 69, 109–122, 161, 251, 278
  and Constitution, 111–119
  and legal academy, 110–111
  and meaning of life, 120–122
  unanimity of *Brown* court, 111
Bruce v. Rawlins, 247, 248
Buchanan, James 4, 13, 14
  Address to Congress in December
    1860, 19
Buchanan, Pat, 155(n), 159
Buckley v. Valeo, 56–57
Burger Court, 54, 89
Burton, Harold, 65, 68, 69
Bush, George W., 180, 193–197, 199, 201.
    See also Bush v. Gore
Bush, H. W., 190–191
Bush, Jeb, 197, 200, 274
Bush v. Gore, 96, 140–162, 272
  law professors' joint statement
    concerning, 141–142
  and voter intent, 149, 150, 156,
    158–161 (*see also* Butterfly ballots;
    Chads)
Bush v. Gore: The Question of Legitimacy
    (Radin), 142
*Bush v. Palm Beach County Canvassing
    Board*, 143–144, 145–146, 147
Butterfly ballots, 155, 155(n), 159

Cabinet posts, 31, 57, 58, 65, 66, 175, 187,
    191–192, 194
Calabresi, Guido, 31
Calabresi, Steven, 150
Calhoun, John C., 31, 68
California, 44, 69, 78, 104, 122(n), 123,
    182, 263, 268, 272, 275, 279

University of California at Davis
Medical School, 95
See also San Francisco
California v. Greenwood, 263–264
Camden (Lord), 240, 248, 250–251, 252,
256
cities named after, 252, 265
Campaign finance reforms, 101
Canada, 10, 22
Cantwell v. Connecticut, 36
Cardozo, Benjamin, 36, 41
Career tracks, political vs. judicial, 57–58
Carter, Jimmy, 190, 273
Cellphones, 229, 230
Censorship, 42, 44, 45, 123, 127, 137–138
Chadha, Jagdish, 93
Chads, 155, 155(n), 156, 157, 158, 197
Chambers v. Florida, 49
Chase, Salmon P., 66, 175, 181
Cheney, Dick, 193–197, 198, 199, 204,
273
Chicago, University of, 61
Chicago Burlington case, 35
Children, 52, 53(n), 114, 136(n), 138,
218
Christie, Chris, 274
Citizenship, 33, 34, 115, 116, 139, 168,
194, 214, 215, 222
Citizens United v. FEC, 56, 100–101
Civil Rights Act of 1866, 115, 214
Civil Rights Act of 1964, 69, 110, 182,
273
Civil War, 32, 34, 39, 124, 130–134, 181,
182, 211, 213, 255, 268
Clark, Tom, 66
Cleveland, Grover, 179, 198
Clinton, Bill, 182, 198, 275
Clinton, Hilary, 200, 275
Cold War, 44, 111
Colegrove v. Green, 51, 52, 276
Colorado (Amendment 2), 92–94, 104
Colorblindness, 94, 95
Columbia Law School, 58, 59, 61, 62(n),
275
Columbine High School, 206
Commentaries (Blackstone), 18, 58, 214,
217–218, 232–233, 248

Common law, 254, 258. *See also* Britain:
English common law
Common sense, 234, 237, 238, 239
Communism, 53, 131
Computers, 84
Confederate States of America, 4, 9, 10,
122, 182, *See also* Secession
Conflicts of interest, 175, 177
Congress, 4, 20, 29, 41, 72, 94, 126, 131,
152, 255, 258
and alternation of president and vice
president, 201–202
and *Brown v. Board of Education*, 69
confirmation hearings in, 67, 68
First Congress, 31, 32, 168, 234, 239
House of Representatives, 51, 113, 126,
173, 175, 177, 181, 188, 208, 269,
271, 276 (*see also* Congress: Speaker
of the House)
and presidential power, 73–74
and presidential/vice presidential
succession, 167, 171, 174–177, 184,
185
Reconstruction Congress, 110, 115(n),
214, 215
Senate, 6, 68, 126, 169, 173, 175, 269
Senators becoming Supreme Court
justices, 65–69, 71
Speaker of the House, 189, 191, 192
tax power of, 76–77
Thirty-ninth Congress, 34
Constables, 233, 234, 236, 243
Constitution, 4, 15, 39, 81, 101, 125,
153–154, 168, 173, 267
as act as well as text, 224
amendments to, 6, 8 (*see also*
Constitutional Amendments)
Article I, 23, 34, 45, 46, 51, 93, 112,
113, 127, 208, 218–219, 258, 276
Article II, 73–74, 145, 146, 147–148,
150, 151–152, 160, 166, 172, 272
Article IV, 9, 10, 86, 112, 114, 118,
159(n)
Article V, 6, 8, 9, 18
Article VI, 17, 23, 254–255
Article VII, 6, 17–18
conflicting with state constitutions, 17

Constitution (*continued*)
  constitutional gradualism,
    110
  interpreting, 216–219, 223, 226,
    280
  original intent, 71, 110
  "persons" in, 138–139
  Preamble, 18, 111, 114, 208, 218
  and presidential electors, 177
  ratification of, 6, 17, 18–19, 111,
    242, 244
  and slavery, 26–27, 113–116
  three-fifths clause in, 13, 181
  the Union as older than, 21
  as varying, 277
  See also Bill of Rights; Constitutional
    Amendments; Rights:
    unenumerated rights
Constitutional Amendments, 94
  Third Amendment, 23, 32, 205,
    207, 218, 229
  Fifth Amendment, 31, 32, 33, 34(n),
    35, 36, 115(n), 133, 205, 209, 216,
    236, 258, 259, 277
  Sixth Amendment, 32, 47, 133, 205,
    209, 236, 258
  Seventh Amendment, 32, 133, 205,
    209, 237, 256–257, 257–258
  Eighth Amendment, 47, 264
  Ninth Amendment, 54, 208, 218,
    219
  Tenth Amendment, 32, 127, 205,
    208, 218, 254(n), 256
  Twelfth Amendment, 173, 193, 194,
    195–196, 201
  Thirteenth Amendment, 26–27, 115,
    116
  Fifteenth Amendment, 88, 115–116,
    118, 119, 157, 159(n), 225, 227
  Seventeenth Amendment, 9
  Nineteenth Amendment, 205, 212,
    225, 227, 228, 275, 279
  Twenty-second Amendment, 201
  Twenty-fifth Amendment (JFK-
    LBJ Amendment), 171, 174, 180,
    183–190, 189(n), 192, 194–195,
    198, 200, 201
  Twenty-sixth Amendment, 227
  See also First Amendment; Second
    Amendment; Fourth Amendment;
    Fourteenth Amendment
Constitutional law, 60–61, 71, 78
Continental Congress, 16
Continuity of Government Commission,
    192(n)
Cooper v. Boot, 233–234, 248
Copyright law, 258
Cornyn, John, 192(n)
Corporations, 56, 101, 102
Criminal trials, 29, 38, 46, 47–48, 49–50,
    219. *See also* Exclusionary rule;
    Juries: peremptory challenges
    concerning
Crittenden, John J., 8
Cruz, Ted, 200, 202, 274
Customs officers, 244, 246, 247
Cynicism, 175, 177

Davis, Jefferson, 14
Death penalty, 110, 264
Debs, Eugene, 42
Declaration of Independence, 111, 230,
    246
Deep South, 30, 48, 50, 51, 78, 131, 278.
    See also States: southern states
De Gray, William, 248
Delaware, 109
Democracy, 5, 7, 45, 46, 83, 86, 88, 94–95,
    125, 131, 201, 211, 221
  and the military, 207
  and militias, 212
  and presidents relinquishing power,
    11–12
  and secessionists' claim to minority
    veto, 8
Democratic Party, 13, 69–70, 74, 190
Dewey, Thomas, 66
Dissent (political), 46, 129, 130, 133–134,
    137, 247
Dole, Elizabeth and Bob, 174
Double jeopardy, 237
Douglas, Stephen A., 9, 12–13
Douglas, William O., 37, 63, 65, 66
Douglass, Frederick, 134

Dred Scott v. Sanford, 31, 33, 114, 120, 214, 215
Dudziak, Mary, 111
Due process, 31, 34(n), 35, 36, 114, 115, 115(n), 237
Dukakis, Michael, 273

Eckhardt, Christopher, 135
Economy, 199
Edmonson v. Leesville Concrete Co., 88, 94, 97, 97(n), 98–99
Education, public, 52, 117
    classroom flag salute, 53(n), 57, 136(n)
    graduation prayers, 89–91
    integration of schools, 94, 98 (*see also Brown v. Board of Education*)
Eisenhower, Dwight D., 275
Elections, 39, 101, 126, 185, 195
    of 1858, 9, 12–13
    of 1860, 4, 12, 13, 14, 48, 131, 181
    of 1864, 11–12, 168
    of 1888/1892, 179
    of 1948/1964, 273
    of 1968, 276
    of 1972, 189
    of 1976, 190
    of 1980, 190, 191
    of 1901, 276
    of 2000, 193, 197–200, 271
    of 2008, 173–174, 199
    of 2012, 272
    of 2016, 200–202, 274–275
    of 2020, 201
    contested ballots in, 155
    counting protocols used in, 156, 157
    failed elections, 152
    minority voters, 154
    off-year/special elections, 167, 176
    overvotes and undervotes in, 159, 160
    postponing, 178
    primary elections, 88–89
    reforms concerning, 161
    strategic voting in, 158, 159, 160
    and ticket balancing, 167, 169, 170, 172, 173
    voting machines used in, 158, 197

    See also Bush v. Gore; Electoral college; Voting rights
Electoral college, 12, 113, 140, 150, 151, 177–179, 181, 182, 190, 193, 195–196, 271
    and popular vote, 178–179, 195
    and slavery, 270(n)
Ely, John Hart, 46, 110, 120
Emancipation Proclamation, 26
Emerson, Ralph Waldo, 134
Engel v. Vitale, 52–53
Entick, John, 251, 252
Entick v. Carrington, 240, 242, 245–246, 251, 253, 256
Enumerated power, 255
Epstein, Richard, 143, 145, 146
Equality, 79, 82, 83, 86, 101, 102, 103, 115, 116, 124, 154, 156, 158, 161, 230
    equal-protection clause, 94, 116, 118, 157, 159(n), 159–160
    and free expression, 100
    separate but equal doctrine, 72, 120
Erie Railroad v. Tompkins, 254
Establishment clause, 89, 91
Everson v. Board of Education, 36, 52, 53(n)
Exclusionary rule, 49, 239–240, 243–244, 253, 261, 263, 264

Fairman, Charles, 41
Fairness, 37, 91, 115(n), 219
Federal bank, 255
Federalism, 250, 252, 254, 259–260, 264, 267, 271
    Federalists/Anti-Federalists, 5, 19, 31, 32, 125, 126, 127, 128, 250, 257
Federalist, The, 18
    No. 10, 21
    No. 11, 279
    No. 28 and No. 51, 260
    No. 37, 216
    No. 83, 257
Fehrenbacher, Don E., 14
Felons/felonies, 210, 233, 234
Field, Stephen, 34–35
Filibusters, 68, 69, 70
Fillmore, Millard, 165, 168

First Amendment, 29, 34, 36, 42, 43, 47,
    52, 80, 82, 89, 91, 102, 137, 138,
    211, 221
  and felons, 210
  models for, 128
  and Revolutionary War, 124–130
  and Second Amendment, 205, 208,
    210, 218, 221
"First Amendment is an Absolute, The"
    (Meiklejohn), 45
Fisher v. University of Texas, 99
Flag burning, 80–82, 85, 99–100
Florida, 48, 140–162, 271, 272, 273, 279
  black precincts in, 157–158, 197
  Florida Constitution, 145, 146–147,
    148
  Florida legislature, 145, 146, 148,
    150–154, 272
  Florida Supreme Court, 141, 142, 143,
    144, 145, 146, 147, 148–149, 154,
    156
Foley, Tom, 192(n)
Ford, Gerald, 171, 187–188, 189, 189(n)
Formalism, 81, 84, 90, 93, 95
Fortas, Abe, 135
Fourteenth Amendment, 32, 33, 34, 35,
    43, 52, 54, 78, 80, 88, 93, 102, 110,
    115(n), 118, 119, 194, 221, 279
  and Civil War, 130–134
  equal-protection clause, 94, 116, 118,
    157, 159(n), 159–160
  and gun ownership, 214, 222, 223–224,
    226
  and outsiders, 138
  and Second Amendment, 205, 224
  as second Bill of Rights, 131
  See also under Bill of Rights
Fourth Amendment, 32, 33, 47, 84,
    208–209, 218, 229–249, 254, 255,
    260–261, 262, 263, 264, 277
  first draft of, 242
  and Seventh Amendment, 256
  three questions concerning, 231–232
France, 10, 23, 124, 130, 137
Frankfurter, Felix, 37, 41, 43, 44, 46, 47,
    48, 53, 53(n), 63, 77(n), 136(n),
    229–230

Freedman's Bureau Bill of 1866, 214, 215,
    221
Freedom of assembly, 36, 42, 84, 86, 102,
    208
Freedom of speech, 13–14, 33, 35, 36,
    41–42, 44–45, 56, 82–83, 84–85, 86,
    123, 132, 135, 219–220
  political expression, 30, 45, 46, 81, 82,
    102–103, 128, 134, 136
Freedom of the press, 35, 36, 41, 44,
    84–85, 103, 132, 219–220, 238
Free Enterprise Fund v. Public Company
    Accounting Oversight Board, 96
Fried, Charles, 143–144, 145, 146
Friendly, Henry, 77(n)
Fuller, Melville, 63
Fundamental fairness, 37. See also Fairness
Fundamentalism, constitutional/biblical,
    39–40

Garfield, James, 169–170, 172
Garner, John Nance, 273
Gay rights/same-sex marriage, 92, 97(n),
    104–105, 105(n), 121–122, 122(n),
    225, 274, 278
Geography, 4, 5, 16, 18, 19(n), 21–25,
    39, 57, 59, 71, 100, 121, 125, 190,
    267–271
  bond of people and land, 25–26
  Founders' view of geography and
    Union, 21
  interior region of United States, 24–25
  replaced by demography, 269
  and worldviews, 30
  See also Presidency: home states of
    presidents
George III (King), 240, 251
Georgia, 51, 124
Gerrymandering, 12
Gibson v. Mississippi, 115
Gideon v. Wainwright, 38, 48, 50, 251
Gingrich, Newt, 192(n)
Ginsburg, Ruth Bader, 59, 96, 141(n),
    223(n), 268
Gitlow v. New York, 36
Gore, Al, 197. See also Bush v. Gore
Gould, Henry, 247–248

Grant, Ulysses S., 25, 166, 177, 181, 213
Gray, Horace, Jr., Esq., 248
Greeley, Horace, 177–178
Greenleaf, Simon, 244
Gregory v. Ashcroft, 259–260
Griswold v. Connecticut, 38, 54
Grutter v Bollinger and *Gratz v. Bollinger*,
    97, 99
Guiteau, Charles, 169, 170
Gun control, 206, 210
Gun ownership, 204. *See also* Gun control;
    Second Amendment

Habeas corpus, 133
Hale, Sir Matthew, 233, 234
Hamilton, Alexander, 18, 257, 259, 260,
    279
Hand, James, 123
Harding, Warren G., 166
Harlan, John Marshall, 35, 39, 93, 94, 115,
    136(n)
Harris, Katherine, 150, 161
Harrison, Benjamin, 179, 198
Harrison, William Henry, 165, 166, 172
Hart, Henry, 258
Harvard University/Law School, 30, 41,
    44(n), 53–54, 54(n), 59, 60–61,
    77(n), 218, 274, 275–276
Hawaii, 183(n), 280
Hayes, Rutherford B., 179
Heller v. United States, 223(n)
Hinckley, John, 190
History of the Pleas of the Crown, The
    (Hale), 233
Holism, 120, 205
Holmes, Oliver Wendell, Jr., 35, 36, 42,
    45–46, 53
Holy Roman Empire, 128
Hoover, Herbert, 182
Hoppe, Art, 123
Houston Space Center, 202, 203
Hughes, Charles Evans, 42, 63, 66

Illinois, 3–4, 14, 20, 27–28, 132, 183(n),
    279
    election of 1858 in, 9, 12–13
Indiana, 20, 132

Individuals, 134, 208, 209, 210, 214. *See
    also* Second Amendment: and
    individual right to own guns
In re Oliver, 49–50
*International Society for Krishna
    Consciousness v. Lee*, 83–86, 87, 95
Iowa, 130, 132, 135–139, 278–279
Israel, 201

Jackson, Robert, 53(n), 63, 69, 70, 71,
    77(n)
    effect of geography on, 57
    and Hugo Black, 58–59, 74, 75
    key decision of, 72–75
    legal education of, 58–59, 60
    as solicitor general, 64
    writing style of, 56
Jefferson, Thomas, 12, 23, 128, 129, 165
JFK-LBJ Amendment. *See* Constitutional
    Amendments: Twenty-fifth
    Amendment
Jim Crow, 29, 50, 92, 109, 113, 116, 120,
    121
Jindal, Bobby, 274
Johnson, Andrew, 168–169, 172, 175
Johnson, Gregory Lee, 80–81
Johnson, Lyndon B., 69, 137, 171, 180,
    182, 185, 199, 202, 203, 273
Johnson v. Zerbst, 47, 49
Jones v. Root, 243
Judiciary, 42, 43, 46, 58
    circuit judges/courts, 68–69, 71,
        269–270
    European, 61
    judicial Hall of Fame, 77(n)
    judicialization of, 58, 64, 65, 71
    judicial review, 238, 255
    state courts, 272
Judiciary Act of 1789, 255, 256
Juries, 32, 35, 46–47, 60, 95, 116, 129–130,
    133, 137, 208, 209, 218, 226, 227,
    236–237, 240, 251, 256, 257, 258
    jury service and voting, 87–89, 97(n)
    and militias, 209, 210, 212
    peremptory challenges concerning,
        86–87, 89, 94, 97, 97(n), 98
    protecting free expression, 130

Kagan, Elena, 56, 59, 61, 62, 65, 96, 268
Kalven, Harry, 44, 86
Kansas, 278–279
    Kansas-Nebraska Act (1854), 121, 268
Kennedy, Anthony, 56, 77, 141(n), 268(n),
        272–273, 279
    centrality of, 95–96
    early portrait, circa 1996, 78–95
    and equality, 79, 100–101
    and freedom of speech, 82–83, 84–85
    and *McCutcheon v. Federal Election
        Commission*, 102–103
    as swing vote, 80, 89, 98, 104
    as teacher, 79
    updated portrait, circa 2015, 95–105,
        105(n)
Kennedy, John F., 171, 180, 183, 185, 202,
        203, 273
Kentucky, 20, 129, 181, 278
King, Martin Luther, Jr., 44
Klansmen, 214
Klarman, Michael, 110

Lawrence v. Texas, 104
Law schools, 53, 57, 58–62, 270–271. *See
    also individual schools*
Lazarus, Edward, 110–111
Lee, Richard, 20
Lee, Robert E., 15, 20
Lee v. Weisman, 89–91, 103–104
Legitimacy, 142, 177, 178, 179, 200
Lemon v. Kurtzman, 89
Levinson, Sanford, 193–194, 196, 210
Libel laws, 38, 43, 129
Libertarianism, 206, 207, 209, 210, 219,
        221, 222, 234
Lieberman, Joe, 193, 195, 196, 197
Lincoln, Abraham, 3–4, 40, 42, 48, 54, 61,
        121, 131, 165, 181, 191, 267, 279
    and American Revolution, 15
    assassination of, 168, 172
    and compact theory of the Union, 5–6
    education of, 58, 60
    First Inaugural Address, 4–5, 6, 8, 11,
        12, 14–15, 19, 23
    forebears' state origins, 20
    funeral of, 3
    and geography and Union, 21, 23–25
    at Gettysburg, 25–26
    Lincoln-Douglas debates, 12
    Lincoln-Douglas Senate race of 1858,
        9, 12–13
    and multiracial society, 27–28
    and perpetuity of the Union, 5
    Second Annual Message to Congress
        (1862), 23
    Second Inaugural Address, 26
    Special Session Address to Congress
        (1861), 7, 9, 11, 12, 15
Localism, 32, 34, 125, 126, 211
Louisiana/Louisiana Territory, 10, 23, 130

McCain, John, 173–174, 183, 199
McConnell, Michael, 110, 143, 145, 146
McCulloch v. Maryland, 254, 255
McCutcheon v. Federal Election Commission,
        101–103
McDonald v. City of Chicago, 223(n)
McKinley, William, 172
Madison, James, 18, 21–22, 31, 32, 91,
        129, 137, 165, 175, 176, 216, 242,
        259, 260, 264, 277
Madmen, 211
Maine, 10
Majority rule, 6–8, 14, 21, 126, 134
Mansfield (Lord), 233–234, 248
Mapp v. Ohio, 38, 49
Marshall, John, 32, 55, 63, 66, 70, 126,
        218, 255
Marshall, Thomas, 170
Marshall, Thurgood, 65, 99
Maryland, 47
Massachusetts, 229–249, 277
    Constitution (Article IV), 241–242,
        243, 246
Massiah v. United States, 49
Meiklejohn, Alexander, 45–46, 82, 86
Mexico, 10
Michigan, University of, 97
Military, 207–208, 209, 212, 213, 219,
        223–224, 225
    gender issues in, 227
    military technology, 211
    See also Standing armies

Militias, 125, 211, 212, 223, 224, 237. *See also under* Second Amendment
Mill, John Stuart, 134
Minersville School District v. Gobitis, 136(n)
Minor v. Happersett, 118
Minton, Sherman, 63, 65, 68
Miranda v. Arizona, 38
Mississippi, 48
Mississippi River, 25
Missouri Compromise (1820), 31, 130
Monroe, James, 31, 165–166
Monroe Doctrine, 23
Montesquieu, 18
Moon landing, 202
Moore, Sara Jane, 189(n)
"More perfect Union," 18, 19, 21
"Most Overrated Supreme Court Justice, The" (Sunstein), 44(n)
Murphy, Frank, 37
Muskets, 210–211

Nader, Ralph, 158
National Guard, 206, 207, 210
Nationalism, 34
National Labor Relations Board v. Noel Canning, 96
National referenda, 8–9
National Rifle Association (NRA), 205, 206, 212, 215, 219
Navies, 21–22
Negro and the First Amendment, The (Kalven), 44
New Deal, 69, 110, 273
New Hampshire, 267
     Constitution of 1784, 241–242
New Jersey, 250, 259, 261–262, 262(n), 263, 264–265
     New Jersey Plan at the Philadelphia Convention, 264
New Orleans, 25
New York ratifying convention, 18–19
New York State, 57, 59, 62, 77(n), 124, 242, 268
     New York Supreme Court, 234
New York Times, 141–142, 153, 193
New York Times Co. v. United States, 57

New York Times v. Sullivan, 38, 43–44, 45, 53
NFIB v. Sebelius, 76
Nixon, Richard, 123, 187–188, 189, 276
North Carolina, 17, 48, 242, 252, 272
Northwest Ordinance, 31, 181
NRA. *See* National Rifle Association

Obama, Barack, 61, 173, 182–183, 199, 274
     Obamacare, 70, 76–77, 96
O'Connor, Sandra Day, 63, 66, 83, 91, 95–96, 97, 99, 100, 141(n)
Office of Legal Counsel (OLC), 64, 65
Ohio, 78, 162(n), 175, 272, 273, 274, 279
     presidents from, 165, 166, 177, 179, 181
Old Northwest Territory, 20, 21
O'Neill, Tip, 191, 192
One-person, one-vote principle, 50–51, 101, 102
Ordered liberty, 37, 39
Otis, James, 229, 244–245, 246

Paine, Thomas, 85
Palin, Sarah, 173, 183, 199, 274
Palko v. Connecticut, 36, 39, 41
Parents Involved v. Seattle School District, 98, 99
Parliamentarianism, 176
Patronage, 13, 14
Patterson v. Colorado, 35–36, 42, 43
Paul, Rand, 274
Paxton's Case, 244, 246, 248
Pence, Mike, 274
Pennsylvania, 267. *See also* Philadelphia
Peres, Shimon, 201
Perot, Ross, 182
Perry, Rick, 274
Philadelphia, 245, 250, 270
     Philadelphia Convention of 1787, 31, 125, 208, 264
Pierce, Franklin, 13
Plessy v. Ferguson, 72, 93, 94, 115, 120
Police, 225, 229. *See also* Searches/seizures
Port cities, 268, 270
Portman, Rob, 174, 274

Post office, 13, 14
Powell, Lewis, 93, 95, 117
Powell v. Alabama, 47
Powers v. Ohio, 87–89, 94, 95, 97, 97(n),
    98
Prayer in public schools, 52, 53, 89–91
Prayer in town council meetings, 104
Precedents, 71, 72, 74, 99, 168, 169, 170,
    223(n)
Presidency, 11, 12, 13, 66, 165–179
    acting presidents, 166, 167, 169, 171,
        184, 186, 188, 189, 198, 202, 198
    alternation of power with vice
        president, 200, 201
    home states of presidents, 165, 166,
        177, 179, 181, 182
    impeachments, 169, 176
    mandate concerning, 166, 167, 168,
        175–176, 178–179
    presidential disability, 169–170, 174,
        186–187, 192, 194, 198
    presidential power, 73–74, 179
    Presidential Succession Acts (1792,
        1886, 1947), 167, 174–175,
        176–177, 184, 189(n), 191, 192
    president's relationship with vice
        president, 194, 197
    salary for, 167–168, 184
    succession issues concerning, 167,
        171, 174–177, 180–203, 273
    and ticket-flipping, 200–201
    See also Assassinations; *Bush v.
        Gore*; Cabinet posts; Vetoes; Vice
        presidents
Press, 100–101, 128, 129. *See also* Freedom
    of the press
Princeton University, 59, 61, 274, 275
Prior restraint, 129–130, 133
Privacy, 38, 54, 208, 213, 230, 252
    expectation of, 261, 262, 263, 264,
        277
Probable cause, 231, 234, 237, 238–244,
    247, 251
Property rights, 102, 259, 262, 263,
    277. *See also* Searches/seizures
Protests, 43, 80
Public forum doctrine, 84–85, 86, 94

Quartering Act (1774), 229

Race-labeling, 98
Racial discrimination/segregation, 88–89,
    109, 110, 111, 112, 116, 117, 119,
    121, 157, 225
    racial discrimination in the military,
        213
Radin, Margaret Jean, 142
Railroads, 268
Rakas v. Illinois, 261, 262, 264
Reagan, Ronald, 80, 190, 202, 273, 274
Reasonableness, 237, 238, 241, 243, 246,
    247, 252, 253, 256, 264
Recess appointments, 96
Reconstruction, 33, 39, 51, 94, 114–115,
    120, 158, 159(n), 213, 218, 222
    Reconstruction Act of 1867, 223–224
    See also Congress: Reconstruction
        Congress
Redshaw, 247, 248
Referenda, 8–9. *See also* Colorado
    (Amendment 2)
*Regents of the University of California v.
    Bakke*, 95, 99, 117
Rehnquist, William, 57, 63, 64, 77(n), 80,
    96, 100, 141(n), 145, 159–160
Reich, Charles, 45
Religion, 30, 33, 34, 42, 45, 52, 53, 89, 90,
    91, 97(n), 102, 122, 127–128, 132,
    138, 208, 221
    religious speech, 134
    and slavery, 130
Republican Party, 13, 30, 42, 115, 115(n),
    131, 134, 142, 168, 170, 181, 189,
    200, 213, 222, 273
    liberal/moderate Republicans, 69–70
Restraining orders, 237
Revolutionary War, 32, 124–130, 213, 217,
    218, 237
Reynolds v. Sims, 50, 51, 276
Rhode Island, 17
Rights, 139
    free expression rights, 43, 53, 100,
        123, 130, 137. (*see also* Freedom of
        speech)
    political/social rights, 118–119, 221

right of counsel, 29, 38, 47–48, 49
unenumerated rights, 54, 219–221, 224
See also Bill of Rights; Civil Rights Act
   of 1866; Civil Rights Act of 1964;
   States: states' rights; Voting rights
Roberts, John, 56, 57, 62, 63, 65, 76–77,
   100, 102, 229, 244, 270
Rockefeller, Nelson, 171, 188, 189, 190
Rocky Mountain West region, 204, 206,
   227, 278
Rohan v. Sawin, 242–243
Romer v. Evans, 92–94, 104
Romney, Mitt, 174, 275
Roosevelt, Franklin D., 57, 69, 273
Roosevelt, Theodore, 170, 172, 275
Rosenberg, Gerald, 111
Rosenberger v. Rector, 91
Ross, Nellie Tayloe, 228
Rubenfeld, Jed, 142
Rubio, Marco, 274
Rule of law, 85, 142, 143, 151, 152
Rutledge, Wiley, 37
Ryan, Paul, 274

Samuel v. Payne, 233, 234, 236, 243
Sanford, Edward, 36
San Francisco, 268, 268(n), 270, 271
Savage, John, 234
Scalia, Antonin, 40, 56, 59, 64, 65, 77,
   91, 96, 100, 105(n), 141(n), 145,
   159–160, 268
Searches/seizures, 32, 33, 49, 133, 209,
   238, 243, 246, 251, 253, 277. *See also*
   Fourth Amendment
Secession, 4–10, 17–18, 48, 131, 182, 191,
   267, 278
   as anarchy, 7, 14
Second Amendment, 23, 204–228
   and background checks and licensing,
      206, 215
   "bear Arms" phrase in, 205, 206, 207,
      212, 213, 214, 215, 216–217, 219,
      221, 224
   broad reading of, 206, 207, 210, 212,
      219, 221
   and companion amendments, 205, 210,
      218

   and individual right to own guns,
      205, 206, 213–215
   and militias, 32, 133, 205, 206–207,
      208, 210, 218–219
   republican reading of, 208, 209
   and state/local governments, 215
Secretaries of State, 192
Sedition Act of 1798, 31, 41, 43,
   128–129, 137
Segregation. *See* Racial discrimination/
   segregation
Selective service, 213
Self-defense/-protection, 213, 215, 217,
   219, 221, 222
Separation-of-powers, 56, 57, 72, 96,
   176
Seven Years War, 124
Sexuality, 54. *See also* Gay rights/same-sex
   marriage
Shamir, Yitzhak, 201
Shaw, Lemuel, 243
Sherman, William Tecumseh, 181,
   213
Slaughterhouse Cases, 34–35
Slavery, 13–14, 28, 33, 113–114, 121,
   181, 269, 270(n)
   as America's original sin, 26
   antislavery forces, 32–33, 41 (*see also*
      Abolitionists)
   as sin, 130
   Slave Power, 13, 131
Solicitor generals (SGs), 64, 67, 76
Sotomayor, Sonia, 61, 63–64, 96,
   223(n), 268
Souter, David, 70, 141(n), 160–161
South. *See* Deep South; States: southern
   states
South Carolina, 9, 14, 48, 109, 124,
   252
Sovereignty
   of the people, 9, 103, 111–112, 128,
      207, 226
   of states, 14, 15, 16, 17, 18
Standing armies, 22–23, 32, 125, 207, 209,
   212, 213, 217
Starr, Kenneth, 76
State-action doctrine, 119

States, 4, 46, 49, 112, 118, 171, 206, 209, 222
  and Bill of Rights, 31–41, 126, 221 (*see also Barron v. Baltimore*)
  as building blocks, 271–277
  constitutions of, 16, 17, 111, 145, 205, 207, 209, 217, 222–223, 232, 240, 241–242, 252, 257, 259, 263, 264, 277
  death-penalty laws of, 264
  and Fourteenth Amendment, 36, 80, 132, 133
  legislatures of, 9, 12, 21, 29, 52, 126, 128–129, 132, 154, 160, 172, 173, 272, 276 (*see also* Florida: Florida legislature)
  and Second Amendment, 215
  southern states, 33, 39, 40, 41–42, 44, 109, 114, 138, 157, 181, 182, 225, 269 (*see also* Confederate States of America; Deep South)
  state-law jury rules, 257
  state remedies for federal wrongs, 252–262, 263, 264
  states' rights, 19, 32, 34, 127, 130
  as territories, 132
  as threatening liberty, 132, 133, 161
  unanimity of, 6, 7
  the Union as older than, 21
  See also under Sovereignty; *individual states*
Stevens, John Paul, 70, 100, 141(n), 160–161, 223(n)
Stone, Harlan Fiske, 63, 66
Story, Joseph, 218, 243–244, 246
Stowe, Harriet Beecher, 134
Strauss, David, 110, 144
Strikes, 72
Succession issues, 162. *See also* Presidency: Presidential Succession Acts
Sunstein, Cass R., 44(n), 110
Supreme Court, 13, 30, 31, 154
  appointments/confirmations of justices, 67–69
  chief justices, 63
  clerkships, 62, 65, 77(n)
  as correcting past mistakes, 72

  geographical apportionment of, 268, 269, 270(n)
  judicial experience of justices, 62–65, 67
  legal background of justices on current Court, 59
  non-judicial experience of justices, 65–66, 70–77
  per curiam opinion, 140, 141(n), 145, 154, 157, 159–160
  replenishment process of, 58, 62

Taft, William Howard, 66, 170
Taney, Roger, 66, 114, 115, 214
Taxation, 76–77, 125, 126, 246, 251, 255
Taylor, Zachary, 168
Television, 67, 202
Tenterden (Lord), 236, 243
Texas, 10, 15, 17, 20, 162(n), 180–203, 204, 272, 273, 278, 279
Texas v. Johnson, 80–82, 85, 87, 99–100
Textualism/intratextualism, 72–73, 75, 118, 216, 218–219
Thacher, Oxenbridge, 248
The Vote: Bush, Gore and the Supreme Court (Epstein), 143
Thomas, Clarence, 40, 61, 96, 100, 141(n), 145, 159–160, 223(n), 270
Thoreau, Henry David, 134
3 USC federal statute, 152
Tilden, Samuel J., 179
Tinker v. Des Moines Independent Community School District, 123, 130, 135–139, 161, 278, 279
Tocqueville, Alexis de, 87
Topeka, Kansas, 109–110, 121. *See also Brown v. Board of Education*
Torts, 234, 236, 239, 240, 251–252, 253, 254, 256
Totalitarianism, 138
Town of Greece v. Galloway, 104
Treaties, 10, 17, 23
Trespass, 84, 234, 236, 239, 240, 244, 247, 248, 251, 254, 255, 256, 257, 260
Tribe, Laurence, 154
Truman, Harry, 72, 73

Twelve Score: America's Constitutional Conversation, 1761–2000 (Amar), 280

Tyler, John, 166–169, 172

United States v. Brown, 46
United States v. Dennis, 53
United States v. Lovett, 46
United States v. Nixon, 56
Universities, 94–95. *See also* Affirmative action

Vetoes, 166, 168
Vice presidents, 165–174, 178, 273
    disability of, 171, 174
    mandate for, 186(n), 194, 196, 197
    See also Constitutional Amendments: Twenty-fifth Amendment (JFK-LBJ Amendment)
Vietnam War, 124, 135–139, 227
Viewpoint discrimination, 81, 86
Virginia, 13, 16, 21, 40, 109, 113–114, 122, 122(n) 126, 129, 272, 278
    convention of 1788, 242
    as preceding America, 20
    presidents from, 165–166, 181
Volokh, Eugene, 210
Voting rights, 27, 110, 111, 116, 118, 145, 147, 148, 150, 157, 159(n), 161, 208, 211, 212, 226, 227, 227–228, 278
    and jury service, 87–89
    Voting Rights Act of 1965, 69, 70, 273

Wade, Ben, 172, 175
Walker, Scott, 274
Warrants, 231, 232–238, 246, 247, 248–249, 251–252
    issued *ex parte,* 236, 237, 238–239
    overbroad, 240, 241, 242
Warren, Earl, 46, 50, 52, 63, 66, 69, 251, 273, 274, 279. *See also* Warren Court
Warren, Mary Otis, 244

Warren Court, 37, 40, 44, 46, 47, 48–55, 279
    important achievements of, 49–53
Washington, George, 3, 11, 17, 31, 165
    Farewell Address, 23
Watergate scandal, 188
Wechsler, Herbert, 258
Weisman, Deborah, 89
Wesberry v. Sanders, 51–52, 276
West Virginia State Board of Education v. Barnette, 53(n), 57, 136(n)
Whig Party, 167
White, Byron, 100
White, Ruth Ann, 123, 124
White Primary Cases, 88–89
Wigmore, John Henry, 244
Wilkes, John, 251, 252
Wilkes v. Wood, 240, 242, 245–246, 251, 253, 256
Wilson, James, 18
Wilson, Woodrow, 170, 227, 275
Wiretaps, 84
Women, 138, 206, 209, 218, 221, 222, 225, 227
    in combat, 212–213
    free women in 1787, 208
    woman suffrage, 227–228, 278 (*see also* Constitutional Amendments: Nineteenth Amendment)
World War I, 227
Writs-of-assistance, 229–230, 244–249
Wyoming, 193, 204, 205, 208, 227–228, 278, 279
    "Equal Rights" motto of, 228

Yale University/Law School, 30–31, 54(n), 59, 60–61, 62, 62(n), 270–271, 274, 275–276
Youngstown Steel Seizure Case (1952), 57, 72–75

Zenger, John Peter, 129